T0244200

TABLETS
SHATTERED

TABLETS SHATTERED

THE END OF AN AMERICAN JEWISH CENTURY AND THE FUTURE OF JEWISH LIFE

JOSHUA LEIFER

DUTTON

DUTTON

An imprint of Penguin Random House LLC
penguinrandomhouse.com

LIBRARY OF CONGRESS CATALOGING-IN-PUBLICATION DATA

Names: Leifer, Joshua, author.
Title: Tablets shattered: the end of an American Jewish century and the future of Jewish life / Joshua Leifer.
Other titles: End of an American Jewish century and the future of Jewish life
Description: [New York]: Dutton, [2024] | Includes index.
Identifiers: LCCN 2024000346 (print) | LCCN 2024000347 (ebook) |
   ISBN 9780593187180 (hardcover) | ISBN 9780593187197 (ebook)
Subjects: LCSH: Jews—United States—Identity. | Jews—United States—Politics and government. | Jews—Attitudes toward Israel. |
   United States—Race relations. | Leifer, Joshua.
Classification: LCC E184.355 .L45 2024 (print) | LCC E184.355 (ebook) |
   DDC 305.892/4073—dc23/eng/20240418
LC record available at https://lccn.loc.gov/2024000346
LC ebook record available at https://lccn.loc.gov/2024000347

Printed in the United States of America
1st Printing

Book design by Silverglass Studio

To my parents and sister

NOTHING JEWISH IS ALIEN TO ME.
—*Franz Rosenzweig*

CONTENTS

AUTHOR'S NOTE

I began this book during the COVID-19 pandemic, and I completed it just before the Hamas attacks on October 7, 2023, and the subsequent devastating war in Gaza. While I have tried to update the text in places to reflect the terrible effects of the war—the death toll in Israel/Palestine, the further curdling of public discourse in the United States—there are still parts that would surely read differently had I started this project on October 8, 2023. Nevertheless, I believe that the analysis holds up, that the fissures in American Jewish life I document remain. In fact, they may have only deepened. The world of this book is still our world, even if things have grown darker.

TABLETS
SHATTERED

INTRODUCTION

What I remember most is the sound the tear gas canister made as it left the barrel of the gun. The low thunk, then the harsh crack as the canister broke the air. The echoes: off the flat stones of the protesters' barricade, the barred windshield of the soldiers' armored car, the coarse walls of the squat homes in the village. The vicious whoosh as it flew over the panicked crowd. The hiss of the gas as it spread. Coughing, retching, moaning. In the distance, the weak scream of a battered ambulance. The frantic slapping of rubber soles on concrete. The fearful shouts of people running away.

It was a cloudless January afternoon in the occupied West Bank village of Nabi Saleh, and I was standing on the wrong side of an Israeli soldier's gun. I had graduated college the previous summer. I had just turned twenty-four.

I was there to cover a protest—to bear witness, or so I thought at the time. One month earlier, the Israeli army had arrested Ahed Tamimi, a Palestinian teenager, for having slapped an armed soldier who approached the threshold of their home. The army had also arrested Ahed's mother, Nariman, for filming the encounter. The video transformed Ahed almost overnight into a tragic symbol: of courageous defiance in the face of power, and of the crushed dreams of successive Palestinian generations that have come of age under military rule.

In the late 2000s and early 2010s, Nabi Saleh was the epicenter of an unarmed popular resistance movement. Every week for nearly a decade, the village's residents, accompanied by dozens and sometimes hundreds of international and Israeli solidarity activists, would attempt to march to a spring that Jewish settlers, backed by the Israeli army, had confiscated. But by 2018, when I was there, the weekly protests had largely ebbed. The toll—psychic, physical, human—had grown too high. This was the first big demo in a long time, a rally to demand Ahed's release and the release of other imprisoned Palestinians.

Nabi Saleh is a village disfigured by the violence of the occupation, marked by indescribable suffering and unthinkable sacrifice. The Israeli army has fired so much tear gas over the years that some villagers have hung the empty canisters from carob trees like macabre Christmas ornaments, mangled black rubber orbs swaying in the wind. Midnight raids at gunpoint pull fathers and mothers away from their screaming children, who awake suddenly from nightmares for years after. Nearly every journalist I know who has been to Nabi Saleh left the village in some way changed by what they saw.

I should not have been there in Nabi Saleh on that bright winter day. Everything in my life should have led me in the exact opposite direction, to the other side of the barricades. Like many American Jews, I was raised in a traditional Jewish community where Israel was the spiritual and geographic center of the universe. Every morning in religious day school, we sang the Israeli and American national anthems, then davened Shacharit, the morning prayer service.

We were an outpost of Israel in New Jersey's northwest Bergen County. Identification with the state of Israel was total, even if it was an Israel frozen in time, roughly the 1970s, the years of our Israeli teachers' childhoods. We observed Israeli civil holidays with an ardor we never showed for their American equivalents. On Israel's Independence Day, we marched in the town's quiet, tree-lined streets. On Israel's Memorial Day, the entire school assembled to sing maudlin songs mourning the handsome young soldiers who had given their lives for Israel—for us. We rehearsed for days to give them a proper honor.

We learned we needed Israel because only a Jewish state could protect the Jews after the Holocaust. Our teachers, many of them survivors or their children, imparted to us the inhumanity of the camps, regaled us with stories of escape under impossible conditions, and stressed the importance of resistance—the doomed rebellion in the Warsaw Ghetto, the partisans camped in the Lithuanian forest. We learned that Israel not only constituted the Jewish people's rebirth out of literal ashes but also exemplified the only reasonable response to the Holocaust's most fundamental lesson: that the Jewish people must be prepared to fight if we are to survive. On Holocaust Remembrance Day, which we observed on the Israeli date, we wore all black, affixed stickers to our shirts that said "Remember" in Hebrew, and meditated on this terrible necessity.

At home as in school, Judaism and Zionism were synonymous. I had no sense of where one ended and the other began. At lunchtime, we belted out the lines from the blessing after meals—"May Jerusalem the holy city be rebuilt speedily in our days"—and imagined not the celestial Jerusalem but the real, physical place. At home for Shabbat dinner on Friday night, my sister and I would recite the blessings over the bread and wine in our best approximation of Israeli-accented Hebrew. For her bat mitzvah, we traveled to Israel so that she could read Torah at the Western Wall and prayed with our hands pressed against the ancient stone blocks, which glowed pink in the early morning sun. A few days later a guide took us to a firing range where we learned to shoot Uzis and emerged awed by the display of Jewish power.

An overly serious and earnest kid, I took this mix of religion and nationalism to heart. I relished spending much of the day speaking Hebrew, and when I got home, I fell asleep listening to long-unfashionable Israeli folk songs on cassette tapes. I proudly sported an olive-green Israeli army T-shirt until holes formed in the armpits.

The martial aesthetic was not coincidental. By the time I entered grade school in 2000, the cautious optimism that followed the Berlin Wall's fall in 1989 and the signing of the Oslo Accords in 1993 had largely evaporated. War seemed omnipresent. September 11 soon exploded any illusions about a better, more peaceful century. America invaded Afghanistan and then Iraq. I came to awareness of the broader world, and of America, only after the skies had darkened.

In Israel/Palestine, the second intifada was in its bloodiest stage. Fear and grief contorted my small community and hardened it against the outside world. Everyone seemed to know someone who had been killed or wounded or nearly wounded in a terrorist attack. There were stark black-and-red posters with the faces of the "victims of terror" plastered on the walls of the school gym. I would stop on the way to the water fountain and look at their pictures and their names, so much like those of the people around me, so much like my own.

The Land of Israel, we were taught, was ours, and that meant we needed to defend it. To reinforce our sense of ownership, we learned to draw its outlines, including the West Bank and the Gaza Strip, almost with our eyes closed. On the chalkboard we practiced tracing the small nook where the city of Haifa sits, then the slope down the Mediterranean coast; the sharp V of the border with Egypt, separating the Negev from the Sinai; the small circle of the Sea of Galilee, and the longer, oblong loop of the Dead Sea on the southeastern border.

Ours was a *kishkes* Zionism. Blunt, passionate, reactionary: a religious nationalism but with history in the place of providence. It was not a liberal Zionism. Two states, negotiations, compromise—these were not part of the lexicon, let alone words like "occupation," "siege," or "military rule." I can hardly recall hearing the word "Palestinian" unaccompanied by the word "terrorist."

It was the bellicose nationalism of people who, bound together by the trauma of the Holocaust, having only understood themselves as history's ultimate victims, could not recognize that they now possessed power, who could neither acknowledge the means by which they had

attained such power nor contemplate the ethical responsibilities that
its possession required.

———————

Such rigidity and simplicity also made this ideology vulnerable to challenge. In 2008, Israel launched Operation Cast Lead, a massive aerial
bombardment and ground assault on the Gaza Strip. TV news broadcast the brutal offensive for hours all day: images of maimed children,
collapsed houses, entire families wiped out. I had no ability to understand how the country that I had been taught to love, that formed a
part of my own self-understanding, could have done something like
this. Worse, no one around me seemed particularly disturbed. If anything, my community's attitude seemed to be the reverse. Level the
Gaza Strip, a friend's father said. Turn it into a parking lot.

But these were also the golden years of the internet: forums, Wiki-
pedia, the blogosphere. I searched on Google for whatever I did not
recognize or understand about Israel/Palestine: the Geneva Conven-
tions, the Sabra and Shatila massacre, the civil administration in the
occupied territories. Gradually, I started to encounter a very different
Israel than the one I had thought I knew.

Late in my teenage years, I broke with the Zionist dogmatism of
my upbringing. I became enraged by my community's open support
for the occupation of the West Bank and siege of Gaza and its justifi-
cations for the brutality that this entailed. At first I tried to suppress
my fury, but eventually, as a volatile adolescent, I ignited. I threatened
to run away. I was forcefully asked to leave a Passover seder for calling
Israel an apartheid state in a heated argument with close family friends.
More than once I announced that I would burn my personal belong-
ings on the front lawn in an act of protest. (Fortunately, I never did.)

My parents suffered through all this. They wanted quiet normalcy.
I gave them ceaseless friction. They are not ideologues, but they are
conservative in disposition, and in a particularly Jewish way. Too
young to remember the counterculture of the sixties, they came of age

in the Reagan years. They had little patience for protest politics. They had little acquaintance with protest at all. To them, a radical was simply an undesirable thing for a person, and certainly for a Jew, to be. I felt they wished that the arguments, the fighting, the shouting, would go away.

Eventually, my anger, confusion, and grief did lead me far from home. I went back to Israel and lived there, on and off, for a few years. Although I had rejected the ultra-hawkish ideology that said Israel could do no wrong, I had not given up on the place. I thought I could contribute to making it better. It was too fundamental to my Jewishness. It *was* my Jewishness.

Besides, it didn't make sense to spend so much time arguing about a faraway place when I could go there and figure things out for myself. I sought out new forms of religious expression in alternative communities where I would not have to conceal my politics or forgo the rituals I still treasured. In the Jerusalem neighborhood of Nachlaot, where mysticism permeates the streets, I dreamed of finding a charismatic rebbe who might teach me how to reconcile commitment to justice for the oppressed with the texts of the tradition, only to run up repeatedly against the hard walls of Jewish parochialism. In the hamlets south of Hebron, in the occupied West Bank, I joined Palestinian farmers and shepherds trying to reclaim their land, hoeing the rocky soil with my soft, unworked hands while Israeli soldiers brandished M16s on the hills above.

I'm not sure what my mother worried about more: that I'd come back to the States wearing the black hat of ultra-Orthodoxy, or that I'd end up in jail. The one night I did spend in the Manhattan Detention Complex, after protesting Israel's 2014 war in Gaza, nearly broke our relationship for good.

———————

Over the last decade, I have moved between Jewish communities in the United States and Israel, initially as a young activist, then, and ever since, as a journalist. During this time I have met many other young American Jews. Some grew up like me, within what one might call mainline affiliated Judaism, and were on similar paths out of it. Others endured far more dramatic breaks. They had lost their faith in God or Zionism or both. Many had lost much more than that.

I began to wonder if perhaps their stories amounted to something more than isolated cases of adolescent rebellion. Of course, the break with one's home is a foundational Jewish motif, ever since Abraham wrecked his father Terah's idols and set out for the Land of Canaan. But to me, the distinct contours of a broader phenomenon seemed to emerge: a widespread and profound disillusionment with the shape of American Jewish life and an intense yet unrealized desire for a Judaism awake to the injustices of the world, including, or perhaps especially, to those for which we, as Jews, were directly responsible.

It made sense to me why. Those of us in our twenties or thirties came of age in a world defined by the experience of turmoil and catastrophe. The September 11 attacks, the 2008 financial crisis, Occupy Wall Street, Black Lives Matter, #MeToo, the election of Donald Trump, the COVID-19 pandemic, and the ever-worsening climate disaster—these upheavals have given rise to a shared sensibility, mainly but not exclusively among young people, that our society and our communities require dramatic, fundamental transformation.

During this time Israel became the enduring source of the most intense intracommunal conflict. The emergence of new, youth-led protest against Jewish communal institutions' support of Israel's occupation of the West Bank and siege of Gaza reconfigured American Jewish politics.

But Israel is far from the only fault line in contemporary American Jewish life. In the last quarter century, American society has undergone profound changes when it comes to norms of gender and sexuality and notions of race and whiteness, and fights over these, too, have both divided and remade American Jewish communities. Once a source of unity among American Jews, the idea of America and its history has become the source of often bitter contention. The binding trauma of the Holocaust is receding as those who lived through World War II pass away. At the same time, the broader cultural habits that once sustained the central institutions of mainline affiliated Jewish life—synagogues, federations, community centers, day schools—have shifted so dramatically that the future of these institutions increasingly appears to be in jeopardy.

These processes began many years ago. Now the full force of their effects has begun to be felt. American Jewish life is perhaps more contentious, more incoherent, and more disorganized than at any point in the last seventy-five years.

———

American Jews have never agreed about everything. There is not and has never been unanimity on any issue, and especially not on religious matters: not about the strictures of Jewish law, marriage between Jews and non-Jews, or the place of women in ritual life. Unlike in most other countries, there is no chief rabbi of the United States, nor is there any organizational body designated as the official, government-recognized representative of the country's Jews. Though this decentralization has often frustrated U.S. politicians and Jewish communal leaders alike, it is arguably one of the reasons for American Judaism's persistent diversity.

Yet there *was* for a time a consensus about the core pillars of mainstream American Jewish identity. It began to emerge at the turn of the twentieth century. By mid-century, with the end of World War II and Israel's founding shortly thereafter, it had solidified.

The consensus was a product of the period that *Life* magazine founder Henry R. Luce famously deemed "the American century"— an era of national prosperity and optimism, of American stewardship of a new international order, and, for most American Jews, of upward mobility and integration. It was a time, in other words, very different from our own.

The first pillar of this consensus was Americanism. Most Jews today are the descendants of immigrants who arrived in the United States between 1880, when a wave of pogroms began in eastern Europe, and 1924, when the United States effectively closed its doors to Jews. They came to this place because they believed in America's promise: that even if they would need to work hard until the day they died, they, and certainly their children, would have a greater chance at a better life than in the old country.

America delivered on this promise. It provided the Jews who fled eastern Europe in the first decades of the century with a level of material and physical security that they had never known before. Although America was not free from antisemitism, and forms of anti-Jewish discrimination would remain legal until after World War II, the country's commercial and meritocratic culture offered Jews the opportunity to ascend through the echelons of the class structure. In the postwar period, the elimination of limits on Jewish civil rights in America made possible a once unthinkable level of prosperity and integration. At the same time, America's cold war against Soviet totalitarianism and support for Israel seemed to confirm America's role as guardian of the Jewish people on the world stage.

Such conditions produced a belief in the inherent and exceptional goodness of America, at home and abroad. It was, this Americanism, a kind of faith. Even as early as 1911, the German-born Kaufmann Kohler, a leading Reform rabbi, proclaimed "the concordance of Judaism and Americanism" and celebrated America as "the land of promise for all the persecuted." Throughout the first half of the twentieth century, prominent American Jewish intellectuals continued to formulate arguments about how the American spirit and the Jewish ethos were providentially matched. For much of the last one hundred years, and especially the last fifty, this faith in the unique benevolence of America as demonstrated by the singularity of the American Jewish experience has been shared across the American Jewish political and religious spectrum: liberals and conservatives, Ruth Bader Ginsburg and Irving Kristol, Reform and Modern Orthodox Jews.

But while Americanization gave much to American Jews, it also exacted a significant and ultimately devastating cost. The theorists of cultural pluralism might have hoped otherwise, but, in practice, fully joining the American project entailed the suppression and surrender of what had been the dominant forms of eastern European Jewishness: traditionalist Orthodoxy and left-wing Yiddish radicalism. These were the roots of eastern European Jewry; making it in America required that they be severed.

They did not disappear without resistance, and Orthodoxy would later be revived and reinvented. Their eclipse by the belief in Americanism was, however, as much the product of a consensual relinquishment as it was of cultural and state repression. With remarkable rapidity, American Jewish integration and upward mobility accomplished the wholesale destruction of older forms of life, organizations, languages, and cultural memory. The second half of the twentieth century witnessed a collective act of willful self-denial fueled by the hope of a materially better and physically more secure life. That this hope was realized made the price seem reasonable for a long time, when it was perceived at all.

———————

The second pillar was Zionism. It emerged later and only became a dominant fact of American Jewish life in the years after Israel's founding in 1948. Zionism rescued American Judaism at the very moment, marked by mid-century embourgeoisement and suburban anomie, when a cultural and religious crisis appeared imminent. In the words of the socialist literary critic Irving Howe, Zionism enabled American Jews "to postpone that inner reconsideration of 'Jewishness' which the American condition required." Difficult questions about theology or the adaptability of halacha (Jewish law) to postwar realities diminished in significance or could be sidestepped with the material fact of a sovereign state at the center of Jewish life. If meaning could not be found in liturgy or in synagogue, it could now be found in fundraising for the United Jewish Appeal, the American Jewish Committee, and the American Israel Public Affairs Committee (AIPAC). American Jews imagined Israel as a moral beacon and Zionism as the secular fulfillment of the religious faith in which they could no longer really believe.

Zionism was not unconnected to Americanism. The two reinforced each other, particularly after the 1967 Six-Day War. Since the places where most American Jews' families came from no longer existed, Israel provided American Jews with a stretch of territory with which they could identify and with an existential insurance policy for Jewish life in the Holocaust's shadow. American Jews would no longer be uniquely homeless among the other "hyphenated Americans," who could all point back with pride to some ancestral homeland. With the first wave of identity politics in the 1960s, the image of the Israeli sabra—assertive, militant, masculine—gave American Jews a new and inspiring archetype of Jewishness radically opposed to the weak and neurotic figure of the nebbish. And Israel offered not only psychological compensation; it also offered a pathway, aliyah, for the Jews of the diaspora to become like their Israeli counterparts, although it was an option that very few American Jews chose. At the level of politics, Zionism provided a unifying framework for American Jewish organizations to lobby, like other ethnic groups, for what they took to be their group interest. And as the Cold War brought Israel into the Western camp, opposed to the Soviet Union and its proxies in the Third World, American Jews came to see the United States not simply as Israel's most important guarantor but as an exemplar of the values Israel embodied in miniature.

Yet, if the adoption of Americanism required self-amputation, the enthusiastic embrace of Zionism has engendered a moral myopia. American Zionism, which imagined the Jewish state as the telos of Jewish history and the culmination of its religious development, substituted an ancient ethical tradition of divine commandment with the profane imperatives of a modern nation-state. And whereas Americanism demanded the abandonment of older forms of Jewish being, Zionism degraded these older forms of diasporic Jewishness as inferior. In its classical political version, Zionism sought "the negation of the diaspora," to reinvent a "new Jew" who was the photographic negative of his older counterpart.

Worse, it did not take long for the violence that Israel's founding entailed to inflect Jewish life across the Atlantic. Today, Israeli nationalism threatens to transform Jewish ritual into something hard and violent: into a weapon. It has buoyed chauvinist, selfish, even racist forms of Jewish expression. From the late 1950s onward, Israel's reliance on U.S. military backing has imbricated Jewish flourishing with the exercise of American power as oppressed people around the world began to throw off empires' chains.

———

The third pillar was liberalism. When the great masses of European Jewry arrived in the United States at the turn of the twentieth century, America's liberalism enabled their flourishing. The old ecclesiastical barriers to Jewish political participation—exclusionary oaths and religious tests for public officeholders—had long since fallen away. With no established church or state religion, the modern liberal constitution did not make citizenship contingent on confession or creed. With its emphasis on the rights of the individual, liberalism claimed to diminish the significance of ethnic or religious background and group belonging. (Race, of course, was an entirely different matter.) And with religious observance considered, for the most part, a private matter of personal choice—in no small part due to advocacy efforts of American Jewish organizations—American Jews could fully realize the emancipationist goal, as the Russian Jewish poet Yehuda Leib Gordon famously put it, of being Jews in the home and men on the street.

Beneficiaries of the country's pluralism, individualism, and voluntarism, American Jews quickly adopted these liberal values as the basis for Jewish life. By the early postwar years, sociologists began to observe that most American Jews had relinquished whatever vestiges of traditionalist Judaism they had inherited from earlier generations. They no longer heeded divine authority as the arbiter of Jewish practice. Instead, as historian Stephen Whitfield put it, they surveyed their "vast sacramental heritage" and selected the practices that they found "subjectively possible to accept." They fit Judaism into the mold of their suburban, middle-class lives, and whatever could not fit they cast aside. American Judaism's most fundamental axiom was not sacred obligation; it was now reduced to personal choice.

But it soon turned out that what worked for liberal America could not work for Judaism. The idea of obligation—the meaning of mitzvah, the core of Jewish life—fell out of fashion in a liberal capitalist culture that sacralizes individual self-expression and self-gratification. The logic of the market reduced all aspects of life to fungible value, and religious practice became, like Pilates or yoga, just another consumer good. In a world of infinite choice and limitless growth, the kind of commitment and restraint required to sustain community increasingly appeared as an unjustifiable and unpalatable anachronism. By the late twentieth century, American Jews had become such good liberals that they could no longer give themselves compelling reasons for why they should live Jewish lives in terms other than those American liberalism furnished for them.

In the political realm, American Jewish liberalism also reached its apex during the postwar years. Liberalism both absorbed and outlived the energies of the immigrant radicalism that Jews brought with them from the Pale of Settlement. With the start of the Cold War, Jewish intellectuals began to articulate a more conservative liberalism that saw in almost all forms of mass politics the threat of totalitarianism or the risk of another Auschwitz. Many American Jews, now newly middle-class, arrayed themselves fully behind anti-communism, which would remain a dominant tendency in Jewish life until the Soviet

Union's fall. In the late 1950s and early 1960s, most Jews supported
the civil rights struggle in its heroic period, when its goals remained
the full realization of procedural egalitarianism and the elimination of
discrimination. But by the early 1970s, the rise of Black Power and the
demands for reparative and redistributive measures such as affirmative
action and busing met resistance from many American Jews. For some,
like the neoconservatives, the appearance of a more assertive Black
politics precipitated a break with the postwar liberal consensus entirely.

Now, in the third decade of the twenty-first century, the pillars that
once defined American Jewish life have ceased to be viable. The re-
emergence of antisemitism in U.S. politics, crystallized so brutally
with the 2018 massacre at the Tree of Life synagogue—the deadliest
antisemitic attack in U.S. history—has ended any last illusions about
America's exceptional goodness. So, too, has the eruption of antisemitic sentiment against the backdrop of the 2023–2024 Gaza war. At
the same time, the so-called national reckoning on race has prompted
a reconsideration of once overlooked parts of American history, cast-
ing new light on past injustices that continue to shape the present,
blemishes now thought to be irrevocably woven into the national design. At home, a divided, polarized polity has begotten new species of
collective delusions and violent extremisms; each attempt to reform a
broken system is met with a more ferocious backlash. Abroad, two
decades of a disastrous war on terror revealed the projection of U.S.
power to be not a heroic and liberatory force but a deadly and destruc-
tive one. The world that gave rise to Americanism in the twentieth
century is gone.

Zionism, likewise, is cracking. For an older generation of American
Jews, a mythologized vision of a progressive, social democratic Israel
served as a source of moral inspiration. That view is much less preva-

lent today. While there are still young Jews—mainly those who grew up in mainline affiliated communities like mine—who continue to view Israel as a spiritual beacon, increasing numbers of young American Jews have only known Israel as an authoritarian state and regional military power hurtling down a path of ever more extreme ethnonationalism. At the same time, Palestinians have found new platforms for describing their ongoing dispossession and oppression after having long been denied what Edward Said called the "permission to narrate" their own experiences. Among the non-Jewish public, too, the Zionist narrative is weaker than at any time since the 1960s.

The imagined perfect compatibility of Judaism and American liberal capitalist culture is also unraveling. Unadulterated liberalism has begun to erode the Jewish communities whose flourishing it once enabled. Jewish organizational leaders lament endlessly about rising rates of disaffiliation and intermarriage, seemingly unaware that the decline of religious participation is not a unique Jewish phenomenon but a feature of life in most postindustrial Western democracies. Desperate to reverse these sociological trends, they propose futile and shallow outreach efforts—singles events, Birthright Israel—that reduce Judaism to a frivolous ornament. They plow vast sums of money into superficial programming in the hope that pro-Israel hedonism can restore the mid-century status quo.

What these Jewish establishment leaders fail to realize is that their institutions are declining, not because Judaism has been insufficiently liberalized, commodified, or sanitized, but because individual fulfillment, gratification of the sovereign self, has replaced communal and familial obligation as the basis for the good life. A live-and-let-live relativism has made it impossible to justify commitment to one form of life over another. The cultivation and pursuit of endless options have become obstacles that fatally impede the long-term work of creating and sustaining community. Most establishment Jewish leaders still believe that Judaism ought to be in harmony with America's individualistic and liberal capitalist culture, rather than an alternative to it. They do so, I believe, at their institutions' peril.

Finally, two of the most fundamental anchors of mainstream American Jewish life are also falling away. More than seventy-five years after the liberation of Auschwitz, the memory of the Holocaust grows ever more attenuated. Soon there will no longer be any living survivors.

In the American Jewish collective consciousness, the Holocaust has functioned as the historical glue of the postwar synthesis. The Holocaust illuminated America's exceptional goodness by contrast to European barbarism and by virtue of America's defeat of the Nazis. It confirmed the absolute necessity of Israel as existential insurance policy. It reinforced the necessity of the open, liberal society for Jewish flourishing. Holocaust memory concretized a shared sense of victimhood, a sensitivity to the historically precarious nature of Jewish survival, and a filial duty that, for many American Jews, is often the primary reason they give for their continued Jewish identification. But this is a role the Holocaust can fulfill for only so long. While creative opportunists continue feverishly to mine the event for content, this is just another indication that the Holocaust is leaving the realm of present memory, transforming, like the Spanish Inquisition, into a matter of the distant Jewish past.

An equally seismic shift will have been completed within the next two decades. Contemporary American Jewish identity took shape during the half century when the United States boasted the world's largest and most affluent Jewish population in the world. Today, not only has Israel already overtaken the United States as the largest single locus of global Jewish life; by 2050, demographers predict, the *majority* of the world's Jews will live in Israel, an estimated 8.1 million, compared to the estimated 5.4 million who will remain in the United States.

For the first time in two millennia, diaspora will not define the condition of Jewish life. Instead, most Jews will live in a sovereign nation-state, led by Jews, where the language of the Bible is spoken as the vernacular, where Jewish holidays set the calendar, where an Orthodox rabbinate rules on all matters between birth and death, and where Jews constitute the privileged class within a regime that denies equal rights to all who live under it. The Israeli Jew, raised to live by the sword, his Jewishness taken for granted, will become the norm. The diaspora Jew, the American Jew, defined by a certain double consciousness, by the ambivalences of past exclusion and tentative inclusion, has begun his slouch off of Jewish history's center stage.

It is, therefore, no surprise that the prevailing emotions of contemporary American Jewish life are anxiety and division. American Jewish life is more conflictual than at any point since the first half of the twentieth century because the foundations of American Jewish life that were built in the last century have begun to crumble.

But, perhaps counterintuitively, this is also a reason for optimism. "Destruction," the great scholar of Judaism Gershom Scholem once said, "is both liberation and risk." There may be opportunity in the collapse of an ossified and fatally obsolete consensus.

Traditional Jewish sources teach us about the necessity of destruction for the sake of preserving the sacred community. In Tractate Shabbat of the Babylonian Talmud, the compendium of Jewish law completed in the fifth century CE, a well-known passage comments on Moses's destruction of the first pair of stone tablets when he discovered that the people of Israel had begun to worship the golden calf. "Moses did three things of his own accord that God agreed with," the sages write. "He added one day ahead to the preparations for receiving the Torah, he instructed the Israelites to separate men from women before it, and he broke the tablets." How do we know that God agreed with Moses's breaking the tablets? the sages ask. "Because it says the tablets *that you broke*"—in Hebrew, *asher shibarta*. To which the sage Reish Lakish replies, punning on the line *"Yasher koach she'shibarta"*: "Congratulations that you broke them." The rabbis of the Talmud took the implicit rhyme to show that Moses's actions and God's intentions were in sync.

For Rabbi Yitzchak Hutner, a powerful and enigmatic Orthodox thinker, this was a remarkable text. It testified to the recognition, deep within the tradition, that received wisdom sometimes requires a radical challenge: that "sometimes," he wrote, what appears to be "the nullification of the Torah may in fact be its upholding." In the same way, if the pillars that once sustained Jewish life have lost their power, if they have become pernicious idols like the golden calf, then letting them fall—or, better yet, bringing them down—is not a betrayal of Judaism but the first step to its renewal. If today the old assumptions of American Jewish life are shattered like the first pair of tablets broken by Moses in the shadow of Mount Sinai, that may not be a bad thing at all.

———

This book is about the fracturing of American Jewish life in the twenty-first century. It is also about attempts to reconstitute Jewish life amid the ruins. It traces how the pillars of the postwar Jewish consensus were built and why they began to crumble. It seeks to provide a tour of the contemporary Jewish landscape and illuminate the diverse and sometimes contradictory attempts by American Jews to find new foundations for their religious identities and communal lives. It surveys the shifting center of global Jewish gravity—from the United States to Israel—and assesses the conflicts that are already arising between the two countries' vastly divergent forms of Judaism and Jewish identity. Lastly, it charts four paths for the future of American Jewish life.

Over the two years of working on this book, I interviewed more than one hundred people. They are communal leaders, Jewish educators, and Torah scholars; anti-occupation and Palestine-solidarity activists, advocates for racial equality, and defenders of immigrants' rights; pathbreaking gay and lesbian rabbis, innovators of queer Talmud study, and Jewish ritual entrepreneurs; Haredi community leaders, Orthodox education reformers, and whistleblowers; and Israeli journalists, politicians, and former peace negotiators.

Naturally, this book is also personal. I am a product and symptom of nearly all the historical and sociological processes that I cover here. I am implicated in the collectivities that I analyze. Born within a mainline affiliated community, I married into a Haredi family. My children will have Israeli citizenship. I live "al hakav"—on the line, as Israelis say—between New York and Tel Aviv.

The history of the last century of American Jewish life is the history of my family, which I chart here, beginning with my great-grandmother Bessie's arrival to New York. The construction and collapse of the postwar consensus has conditioned the course of my life. I, too, have been guided by my individual conscience and have tried on different modes of life in search of one that fits.

Tablets Shattered is the result of my past and present grappling with Jewishness, America, and Israel, and it is informed by, and indebted to, the many people I have met, debated, and befriended in the process. I have felt this wrestling with Jewish politics and identity to be an urgent task, not only because of the sense of crisis that has pervaded my entire early adulthood, but also because the future of Jewish life, in the United States and in Israel, is of the utmost significance to me.

How to reconstitute Jewish life amid the unraveling of American society and the moral bankruptcy of contemporary Zionism. How to build community in an age of widespread alienation and atomization. How to live justly in a culture that often prioritizes selfishness over compassion. These are the questions that motivate this book. They keep me up at night. As this book shows, they sit at the center of many people's lives too.

Although my adolescent break with the community in which I grew up first turned me into an activist—and this is largely how I spent my early twenties—I ceased to view myself as an activist long ago.

Instead, I am by trade a journalist. While I have made no secret of my political and religious commitments here, I have endeavored to be fair to those with whom I disagree. It is not possible to write from the perspective of "no place" or with the voice from "nowhere."

It is my hope that the story of modern American Jewish life, the disintegration of the consensus that once defined it, and the efforts by American Jews to reconstitute communal life anew appear here in a new light. While parts of this story have been told before, the act of retelling and reinterpreting is at the core of Jewish practice. The perennial return to and reimagining of common narratives, which renders them at once strange and familiar, is perhaps the essence of what it means to belong to a particular tradition.

So we begin at the beginning, with the dawn of the American Jewish century.

PART ONE

1

UP FROM RIVINGTON STREET

I.

In the small town of Lyuban, which was itself an appendage to the larger town of Slutsk, in what is today the country of Belarus, Europe's last dictatorship, a young woman named Bessie Levine awoke one morning, in or around 1912, knowing that when she left her home that day, she would never come back. That day, for one last time, she would have gazed up at the dark fir and spruce trees in the old forest that extended far into the distance and looked out across the shallow green bogs that surrounded the town. As she alighted the wagon that would take her and her sister very far away from Lyuban, she would have glanced down at the hard black dirt on which the fragile town stood. Lyuban's life was nearing its end. It would barely survive another two decades. But Bessie's was just beginning.

Perhaps she packed the night before. Maybe a siddur, or a book of psalms; almost certainly, clothes for the journey, which would lead her across the borders of the crumbling czarist empire, through the fragmented territories of Poland, and into imperial Germany. What I know for sure is that she packed a set of copper pots, a pair of bronze Shabbat candlesticks, and a mortar and pestle stamped with the year 1909 on the bottom. I know this because Bessie was my great-grandmother, and for much of my childhood the mortar and pestle sat on a shelf above my bed. It was given to me by her daughter, my grandmother Charlotte, not long before she died.

Most American Jews have a story like this. It is the opening act of the American Jewish century. The narrative of flight from the shtetl and successful settlement in the United States recalls our historical victimhood and celebrates our subsequent prosperity. The tale of exile and arrival allows us to revel at once in our former foreignness and contemporary at-homeness. Most of all, the Jewish immigrant story as it developed has cast America in the role of savior. Through this idealization of our country of refuge, the Americanism of American Jews—the belief in America's exceptional goodness as confirmed by its treatment of its Jews—was born.

Out of Lyuban

Lyuban in the early twentieth century was a village suspended in time, sunken deep in the grooves of tradition. It was "a forgotten corner on the edge of Slutsk," the Lyuban native and writer Rachel Feigenberg remembered years later. Into the twentieth century, Lyuban had no train station; it was connected to Slutsk only by a dirt road. To the extent that there was industry, aside from the reproduction of pious Jews, there were timber mills that drew from the surrounding woods and a carpentry workshop, allegedly famous for its chairs. There was also a primitive factory that made candlesticks for the Jewish Sabbath.

Lyuban's main export was people. For the most part it sent its young working-age people, specifically its young women, to serve as maids in the homes of the wealthier Jewish families in nearby cities like Babruysk, one of the oldest in present-day Belarus.

Yet by the 1890s, Slutsk and its better-off environs ceased to be the primary destination for the young and in search of work. Now it was America. "The town began to move, torn from its place," Feigenberg recalled. "Every worker and artisan instantly became raw materials for export. The American sweatshops ate the village whole." The sweatshops would eat Bessie and her sisters, Ida and Nesha, too.

The Levine family was devout. Most Jews from this part of the world during this time tended to be. Bessie's father, Akiva, had no trade. He was a rabbi, a teacher, in a culture where the study of Torah was the most exalted activity a man could do. In some parts of the Jewish world, it still is. Growing up, my ultra-Orthodox aunt would often speak with pride about the man who she said was Bessie's uncle, a great rabbi named Yeruchom Levovitz, who served as the *mashgiach ruchani*, the chief moral instructor, of the Mir Yeshiva, one of the few of the storied eastern European yeshivas whose members would mostly survive World War II as refugees in Shanghai, among them some of Bessie's cousins.

It was important to my aunt that we were related, however distantly, to this man because it was our only claim to *yichus*, a term which literally means "relation," but which in the Orthodox world refers more specifically to the connection via blood to a figure or family with a claim to great learning, deep wisdom, and spiritual grandeur. It formed a tie between her and the traditional Orthodoxy that she had rediscovered. It also reflected a much more widespread American Jewish form of wishful thinking, the desire to imagine one's origins as more noble than they were; or, as rabbi and historian Arthur Hertzberg put it, "to describe grandfather or great-grandfather not as a tailor whose greatest achievement was to read the daily paper in Yiddish but as a man who learned Hebrew texts."

Bessie's uncle, Rav Yeruchom, as he is still known, owed his reputation for great learning, deep wisdom, and spiritual grandeur to his role as a leading figure of the mussar movement, an exacting form of moral education that emerged in the world of Lithuanian yeshivas during the late nineteenth and early twentieth centuries. A response to the crisis of the traditional way of life, which was cracking under the pressure of modern secular ideologies and the political chaos of the czarist empire's waning days, mussar—its closest English cognate is "instruction"—sought to recommit young Jewish men to the theory and practice of spiritual and ethical perfectionism. It combined both the study of texts and acts of self-cultivation that would enhance one's *midos*, or virtues. One particularly radical school of mussar teaching associated with the Novardok Yeshiva, a rival to Rav Yeruchom's, would have its students enter a hardware store to ask for bread, to eradicate pridefulness and inculcate humility.

In the best-known picture of Rav Yeruchom, he looks very much like my father, and even more like my grandmother's brother, my great-uncle Ken. They have the same proud nose, the same strong brow, the same big, soft, dark eyes. At the risk of indulging in the fantasy against which Hertzberg warned, I find not only the physical resemblance to have been passed down through the generations but also some vestigial form of the sensibility and culture of the larger world of mussar, even after several generations of secularization.

There is, for instance, a well-known story about Rav Yeruchom. One year he rebuked a student who thanked him for lending him money to visit his parents because this diminished the kindness of the charitable act. The next year, when the student again borrowed money, Rav Yeruchom rebuked him again, this time because the student failed to offer his thanks. To the confused student, he explained that while it was technically forbidden to express verbal gratitude, "the feeling of gratitude inside you should have been so strong that it would have been hard for you to remain silent." It's the familiar, humorous Jewish double bind: *Don't thank me; thank me.* I have had similar conversations with my father many times.

Personally, I connect just as much to the Rav Yeruchom, who once said in a sermon that God razed the cities of Sodom and Gomorrah because they had failed to welcome the stranger from foreign lands. As fascism began to engulf Europe, and America closed its doors to the desperate, Rav Yeruchom likened the new world of militarized borders and draconian restrictions, where "without a passport or visa it's impossible to go anywhere," to those cities infamous for their sin. His death in 1936 meant that he did not live to see the extent to which this world would be destroyed.

The Great Migration

Like most Jews from their part of eastern Europe, the Levine family was also poor. Even worse, they were short on luck. When Bessie was still a child, her mother, Tchira, fell ill and died on the way to the doctor in Minsk. Her father, Akiva, died not long after. Bessie and her sisters, Ida and Nesha, now orphans, fell into the care of the network of relatives, which had just begun to extend beyond the shtetls of Greater Slutsk to the boroughs of New York City. The Levine family was being pulled apart by the same forces that had begun to shake the ground beneath the small towns and shtetls like Lyuban.

The turmoil that preceded the First World War produced a Jewish refugee crisis, which the war later exacerbated exponentially. The inhabitants of the shtetls fell under the brutal hands of advancing and retreating imperial armies and attempted to flee. They were the *Ostjuden*, whom right-wing nationalist and antisemitic political movements in Germany sought to keep out and expel.

It was, in other words, a time very much like our own: the vulnerable, the stateless, the poor, forsaken by empires, trapped by borders, forced into treacherous seas, hated for their wretchedness. In 1912, after arriving in Bremen, Germany, from the east, Bessie and Ida would board a ship named the SS *Neckar*—later, in 1917, commissioned by the U.S. Navy and renamed USS *Antigone*—which would take them to New York.

They were part of a great migration. Between 1880 and 1924, more than 2 million Jews left Europe, departing mainly from the cities and shtetls of the disintegrating Austro-Hungarian and Russian Empires. During the years between 1881 and 1918, the period when Bessie and her younger sister Ida left Lyuban, one-third of eastern European Jews left their homes behind, primarily for United States, the *goldene medine* (golden land). It was, wrote Irving Howe, "a migration comparable in modern Jewish history only to the flight from the Spanish Inquisition." Bessie and Ida were among the "numberless ordinary Jews, the folksmasn," whose path Howe chronicled in his classic *World of Our Fathers*, those who left behind everything they had known for the chance at a new life.

But not just any kind of new life. Even as the Zionist movement had begun to gather strength, these Jewish masses sought out neither pioneering toil in the nascent Jewish settlements of the Galilee nor pious devotion of Jerusalem's Old Yishuv. Instead, they sought the promise of physical security, political stability, and material comfort in the world's emerging capitalist superpower. They did not come to America "to create a base for a rebirth of their religion, or to become the other front for Israel," Arthur Hertzberg wrote. "They came to succeed." The overwhelming majority of American Jews today are the descendants of these Jews. We are their success.

Departure

My forebears left eastern Europe at an opportune time, a necessary time, more so than they could have known. In the wake of the 1905 revolution, political violence, pogroms, and police repression convulsed the czarist empire. The Russian imperial prime minister, a man named Pyotr Stolypin, first tried to quell peasant unrest through land reform, then brutally attempted to reimpose order by martial law. Stolypin was assassinated in 1911 by Dmitri Bogrov, a Jewish revolutionary (who was, vexingly, also a czarist secret police informant). During these years, as pogroms engulfed the territories of what are now Ukraine and Belarus, the Jews of Slutsk and its environs organized self-defense committees and prepared for the worst. In 1917 the Bolsheviks overthrew the Romanov monarchy. Within less than a year, the old czarist territory would be engulfed in a vicious, multi-front civil war.

The pogroms over the first decade of the century turned out to have been but a prelude to those of the second. In 1920, the ominously named anti-Bolshevik general Stanisław Bułak-Bałachowicz besieged Slutsk and the surrounding shtetls as part of a campaign to establish a counterrevolutionary "White Russian" state in the western periphery of the collapsing Russian Empire. The Bolsheviks had promised the Jews of the former czarist empire full political freedom. In the eyes of the White forces, this made all Jews obvious Bolshevik sympathizers.

As they saw it, Bułak-Bałachowicz's forces sought to put the Jews back in their place. The plan, the general announced, was "to murder the Jews, to take their property, and to erase them from the earth." In the early morning hours of May 26, 1921, according to an eyewitness account later published in the *Jewish Daily Forward*, Bułak-Bałachowicz's men entered Lyuban and raided the shtetl, shooting at the Jews who came across their path. Those who failed to flee in time, roughly two hundred Lyuban Jews, were herded into the synagogue by the attackers. "Then they picked out the prettier and younger girls, 17- and 18-year-olds, dragged them to the women's section in the balcony of the synagogue, and in the most vicious manner raped them." Bułak-Bałachowicz's troops demanded an exorbitant ransom for the girls, which the Jews of Lyuban obviously could not pay, and it was only with the intervention of a nearby village priest that the prisoners in the synagogue were spared. Twenty-eight people were left dead. The town was pillaged: homes, synagogues, and businesses destroyed. Many who fled would never return.

It was likely not long after Bułak-Bałachowicz's attack that Nesha, Bessie's youngest sister, left Lyuban and made her own journey through the newly independent country of Poland into Germany, and then onto a transatlantic ship. In the years since her sisters' departure, Nesha—Tante Nesha, as my father would call her as a child—had married

Leyzer Kustanowitz, himself a member of a large, well-respected, and pious family.

I have often wondered why they left so late into the catastrophic events that followed the end of the Great War. Perhaps they could not see the dangers posed to them by the collapse of empires, revolution, and reaction. Perhaps they did, but stayed put because they believed that God would keep watch over his people. Perhaps they feared, as the rabbis of Slutsk and Lyuban and countless shtetls across the Pale of Settlement preached, that even if life in Europe was one of arduous survival and certain suffering, America guaranteed spiritual death.

Even up until the Nazi invasion of what historian Timothy Snyder has called Europe's "bloodlands," many of the leading eastern European Orthodox rabbis trumpeted the dangers of moving to America and stridently denounced those who left. Rabbi Jacob David Wilovsky, the chief rabbi of Slutsk, known as the "Ridbaz," declaimed that "anyone who emigrated to America was a sinner, since, in America, the Oral law is trodden under foot." Bessie and Ida, Nesha and Leyer, surely heard such lines. But their affliction in this world was too great to worry about what it might be in the next. Wilovsky himself would eventually leave, first to New York, then to Palestine.

In 1922 the family reunited. Nesha and Leyzer arrived in New York barely two years before America shut its golden doors. A decade later, when the Jews of Europe faced annihilation and sought a place of refuge during the century's darkest hours, America would keep its doors shut.

The End of Slutsk

In the fall of 1944, the journalist Maurice Hindus was among the first Americans embedded with the Red Army to enter the eastern European cities and towns reoccupied after Nazi Germany's retreat. Hindus himself was Jewish and born, not unlike my great-grandparents, in an impoverished Russian town in 1891 to a family that emigrated to

America in 1905. It was a fortuitous decision that made the difference between Hindus riding into what is now Belarus with triumphant Soviet troops and dying in a mass grave dug in its black soil.

When Hindus first tried to find the town of Slutsk, to which Bessie's Lyuban was a minor appendage, he drove right over its ruins. Hindus described passing on the road to Slutsk "clusters of blackened chimney stacks, all that was left of once thriving villages and towns." The devastation must have seemed overwhelming, interminable, for Hindus wrote of how he and his companions "drove for hours" without finding the town. "Only when we inquired of an old peasant woman bent under a load of firewood how far we were from Slutsk, did we learn that we had driven about ten kilometers beyond it," he wrote. "I am mentioning this incident," Hindus reflected, "because driving along the chaussee we could not identify the town, and the reason we could not, was because Slutsk was one of the bleakest, flattest ruins I had seen in war-torn Russia, and I had seen Stalingrad."

The Jewish community in Slutsk and its environs dated its origins to the sixteenth century, when the Radziwiłł family, an old clan of Polish-Lithuanian nobility, invited the Jews to settle on its estates. Before the twentieth century was middle-aged, it was gone.

The Task of Memory

Bessie's story is not unique. It has been told many times before, in many different variations. It has been told so often that it has lapsed into cliché, been reduced to kitsch. Yet this American Jewish obsession with memory in fact masks an epidemic of forgetting; that an entire industry of Jewish genealogical research has arisen indicates its scale. The people who lived this story, and those to whom they told it, have almost all passed away. Their deaths marked the closing of the century that shaped American Jewish life into what it is today.

The making of American Judaism contained within it the seeds of its own unmaking. "Americanization," Irving Howe once wrote, "that destruction of memories." Preoccupied with becoming Americans, the eastern European Jews thought little about whether their old world, their old lives, would be worth remembering. "Or if they did," Howe wrote, "it was with the shrug of resignation their fathers had taught." In the late 1970s, it was, in part, an anxiety about the onset of memory's destruction that drove Howe, a founding editor of the socialist magazine *Dissent*, to write *World of Our Fathers*, which revisited his own family's journey out of eastern Europe. "History," he said not long after the book's publication, "is pulling down the curtain on my Jewish tradition."

Now, nearly fifty years later, the process of forgetting has advanced much further than even in Howe's day. It has reached the point where we can no longer even remember that we forgot.

"Inheritance is never a *given*, it is always a task," the French Jewish philosopher Jacques Derrida writes in his book *Specters of Marx*. "That we *are* heirs does not mean that we *have* or we *receive* this or that . . . but the *being* of what we are is first of all inheritance, whether we like to know it or not." I owe my being, my existence, to Bessie, to her decision to leave her home, cross the Atlantic, and make her life anew. Over the years of my young adulthood, I have returned repeatedly to her past so that I might learn what form the task of my own life would take. To discover who I was to be and to discover the obligations that this being entailed, I felt I needed to know how she, and her children, had lived.

The problem, however, was that they had not prepared me at all to succeed in this specific task.

I did not learn the story of my forebears from its subjects. They died before I was born. Nor did I learn it, really, from their immediate descendants. These relatives were, as my father would say, "concrete people." They did not leave behind florid journals or formal recollections. They could not have imagined that what they experienced might be significant in any way. When they began to speak about their past, it was, for the most part, too late, and only once the generation that had been born and steeped in American culture had begun its search for its roots.

What little I gleaned from my grandmother and her generation was, by the time I met them, inflected by myth, embellishment, and distortion, burnished by the mediatized culture of pseudo-memory that developed in postwar America. They spoke as if they had outsourced the recollection of their own parents to Broadway: *You know, Fiddler on the Roof, it was like that.* If it were not for the initiative of a great-aunt who had the foresight to ask Bessie and Ida questions before they died, the answers to which she narrativized in a photocopied pamphlet that she sent around to the grandchildren and great-grandchildren, I would know not even the most skeletal outline of my ancestors' lives.

Which is to say that they were ordinary people, like most of us, whose lives blink into forgottenness. But if oblivion is the ultimate end of all mortal beings, the innovation of tradition is to resist this inexorable fate, to imbue meaning in transient existence, by tying the life of an individual to a great chain of being stretching infinitely backward into the past and forward into the present.

The Jewish tradition orients the individual in time through repetition and cycle. Each year Jews celebrate on Simchat Torah the completion of reading the Torah, and that same week we begin to read it again. Each year, when Jews observe the holiday of Passover, we fulfill the commandment that demands of every successive generation "to see themselves as if they had left Egypt."

Bessie's story, then, is an exodus.

II.

In America, life was different, or so it seemed. There was no risk of pogroms by enraged and frenzied Cossacks. There was no danger posed by invading counterrevolutionary armies. From the moment

Jewish immigrants like Bessie and her sisters landed on the country's shores, they became full citizens-in-waiting.

But contrary to the myth that would crystallize later, it was not, in fact, the promised land either. In the first decades of the twentieth century, Jews in America faced pervasive violations of their civil rights. They encountered discrimination in housing, employment, and higher education; stores, country clubs, medical schools, lawyers' offices, and even entire neighborhoods barred Jews from entry. If eastern European Jews who arrived in the United States enjoyed roughly the same political rights as other white Americans, theirs was, as historian Matthew Frye Jacobson writes, "a whiteness of a different color"— provisional, subject to negotiation, even occasionally threatened with revocation.

Still, compared to life in Russia, where they had been subjects not citizens, their movement restricted, their lives threatened by periodic upsurges of violence, it was better. And this palpable difference gave rise to new feelings of freedom and lightness and, eventually, to what historian Eric L. Goldstein calls "the exhilaration of acceptance" into non-Jewish society. Subsequent generations would not look back and recall America as it had felt in daily life during those years of arrival: America the sweatshop, America the slum, America the devourer of its poor and working classes. Instead, they would construct the myth of America's exceptionality, of its unparalleled goodness and its providential meaning in the American Jewish imagination.

Rivington Street

Like many of the young women and girls who arrived in the United States without their parents, Bessie and Ida lived with an uncle before they found a place of their own on Rivington Street, in New York's Lower East Side. New York during these decades had become the new Jerusalem, and the Lower East Side was its pulsating, squalid center.

"More Jews lived there than anywhere else in America," historian Hasia Diner writes. "Indeed, more Jews lived there than in any other city in all of Jewish history."

The Lower East Side's poverty, its foreignness, its simultaneous backwardness and modernity, provoked the horror of urban reformers and fueled anti-immigrant sentiment. On East Broadway, young news-boys just barely into their teens hawked copies of the socialist Yiddish papers *Forverts* and *Morgen Freiheit* in the shadow of garment union offices. Just down the street, in basement shuls and bigger yeshivas, religious men pored over the Talmud and rabbinic texts. A few blocks north, on Allen Street, sex workers took in customers under the vexed gazes of children living in the tenements above. The pious and the sin-ful walked through the same muck.

At the center of Lower East Side life was work. Bessie and Ida labored with other young immigrants, many still children, in the crowded sweatshops and factories. They endured "twelve-to-fourteen-hour days in the harshest of atmospheres," writes historian Annelise Orleck. "Their bodies and minds reeled from the shock of the shops: the deafening noise, the brutal pace, and the rebukes of the foremen." In the winter, they suffered in the city cold with barely any heat. In the summer, they gasped for breath in air made thick by toxins. Was this still better than what they had left behind?

The answer was not always clear. As much as America was "the golden land," Arthur Hertzberg wrote, it was also "'America, the thief,' in which the dreams of many came to naught." In the darkness of a late-night shift, the promise of America could appear as "nothing but a shadow—an echo—a chimera of lunatics and crazy immigrants," the novelist Anzia Yezierska, born in the Pale of Settlement, wrote in 1923. The prosperity of American life proved more elusive than some had expected. "The long desert of wasting days of drudgery stared me in the face," Yezierska remembered. "The drudgery that I had lived through, and the endless drudgery still ahead of me rose over me like a withering wilderness of sand." The impoverished, oppressed Jews of eastern Europe had come to America in search of safety, freedom, and plenty. What they found instead was capitalism.

And American capitalism was an especially brutal master. Karl Marx once likened capital to a vampire that "lives only by sucking labor, and lives the more, the more labor it sucks." But even that may have been too subtle, too gentle a description.

After Triangle

Perhaps no event illustrated the sheer quotidian brutality and rapacity of capitalism in this period more than the Triangle Factory fire. On March 25, 1911, in the Asch Building at the northeast corner of Washington Square, flames broke out and quickly engulfed the top three floors of the ten-story building. It was nearing the end of the day, and many of the workers were preparing to leave. Within minutes, hundreds of factory employees found themselves trapped by the inferno, which blocked the building's single fire escape. Facing all-but-certain death by suffocation or incineration, the stranded workers, most of them teenage girls, began to jump.

"They crashed through broken glass, they crushed themselves to death on the sidewalk," the *New York Times* reported. Some leapt from windows with their hair and clothes on fire. "A heap of corpses lay on the sidewalk for more than an hour" as firefighters tried to put out the blaze. Meanwhile, the pavement of Greene Street became "a mass" of blood and ashes. When the flames subsided enough for police and firemen to enter the building, they found the charred remains of workers inside. In total, 146 workers, 123 of them young eastern European and Italian women, were dead.

The response was an outpouring of anger and mourning. "For days after the fire, hundreds of workers came to the site of the Triangle Factory on their way home from work and silently prayed," the historian Richard Greenwald wrote. "Some vowed to avenge the deaths of their loved ones." Workers debated the best path for vengeance: union struggle or armed struggle. More than half a million people took to the streets for a memorial demonstration held to mark one month since the fire. It was a display of mass working-class—and mass Jewish—politics, the likes of which have long since vanished.

It was also part of a wider labor uprising that had already begun to shake the city's industries. Even before the fire, New York's immigrant workers had been in revolt. In 1909, more than 20,000 garment workers had gone on strike to protest low wages and the same deadly conditions that led to the Triangle disaster. In 1910, the city's cloak makers staged a general strike. (According to family lore, Bessie's sister Ida, a regular on the picket lines, was beaten and even arrested in demonstrations.) Soon the uprising would spread to other parts of the country, working-class power rippling out from Manhattan to Chicago and beyond. "Between the fall of 1909 and the spring of 1914, a round of paralyzing strikes hit one trade after another," the Jewish labor historian Melech Epstein wrote. "One by one, the sweatshops were assaulted and demolished."

From within this crucible of organizing and protest, a distinct working-class Jewish culture emerged. It was a culture anchored in the garment unions, which represented the multitude of Jewish workers in those years. It was inflected by the eastern European radicalism that many Jewish workers had encountered in the old country. But it was also a thoroughly American phenomenon. It provided to the first- and second-generation Jewish immigrants an elemental safety net, a social services network—a community. It spoke of universal concepts—class struggle, the emancipation of the worker, the liberation of mankind— in the language of Yiddish secularism.

At the heart of this Jewish working-class culture there was also a constitutive tension. Its success would mean its extinction. The institutions of the Jewish working class were engines of Americanization: through making America into a place where working people could live a decent life, they made themselves into Americans. But this also meant that as they paved the way for Jewish upward mobility into the middle class, they simultaneously abolished the working-class base on which they depended. To the extent that this Jewish labor politics was a self-conscious ideology, its aim was not the perpetuation of the culture it produced but its eventual transcendence. And that happened far sooner than many had ever expected.

A Once Mighty Oak

In the early spring of 1892, two cloak makers named Sam Greenberg and Harry Lasker stood together overlooking the East River. It was a time of ideological ferment and strife. The anarchists sparred with the communists who sparred with the socialists who sparred with them both. The city's Jewish working class had not yet achieved the organizational strength it later would, and that meant that ordinary immigrant Jewish workers lacked even the most basic social safety net.

Greenberg and Lasker proposed a new kind of organization. Not a party or a union but a mutual aid society that could attend to the immigrant workers' needs—to provide care when they fell ill, insurance for when they got injured, and a dignified burial for when they died. At the first meeting in April 1892 of this new organization, which they called in Yiddish the Arbeiter Ring (Workmen's Circle), its initial members, though few, planted what its official historian Maximilian Hurwitz called the unlikely "acorn" that, in a short period of time, would grow "into a mighty oak with hundreds of branches and myriads of leaves."

The Workmen's Circle indeed expanded rapidly. In 1901, it had just 872 members. By 1915, it had more than 49,000. At its peak, in 1925, it boasted 87,000 dues-paying members and several hundred branches across the country. The new immigrants streaming in from eastern Europe found the organization ready to aid them. Some, especially those marked by the waves of revolution that washed over that region, saw in the Workmen's Circle a new political home, shaped by the spirit of the Bund, the great Yiddish socialist movement of the czarist Pale of Settlement. Others, perhaps those who arrived alone, ill, or even more impoverished than the ordinary masses of poor, found in the Workmen's Circle a support to lean on before getting to the work of building a new life.

Solidarity, mutuality, obligation: these values, modern in their articulation but rooted deep in Jewish folkways and tradition, gave the Workmen's Circle its shape. It is not a coincidence that remains of Triangle Factory martyrs are buried together in a common Workmen's Circle plot in Queens.

Yet the organization was also emblematic of another tension at the heart of that left-wing, working-class Jewish culture: the tension between the radical hope for the liberation of all humanity and the prosaic desire for upward mobility. The Workmen's Circle's first general secretary was the idiosyncratic Marxist intellectual Benjamin Feigenbaum, who urged the Jewish masses toward rationalism, education, and uplift *as well as* toward militant social action. The Workmen's Circle declaration of principles defined the organization as an expressly transformative project aimed at "the complete emancipation [of the worker] from exploitation and oppression." It positioned itself as "the third partner in the alliance and joins the two wings of the Army of Labor—the trade unions and the social labor movement." Its specific role would be to provide the ordinary kinds of care and support those Jewish workers required. For this reason, the Workmen's Circle became known as the labor movement's "Red Cross."

The day-to-day focus of its activities, the direct provision of services, gave the organization a pragmatic orientation. The Workmen's Circle ran schools where children learned English, math, and Yiddish. It operated summer camps for children who otherwise would have been left in the slums. It offered life insurance to workers to give their families security and provided cemetery plots at rates the working Jewish masses, and later their children, could afford.

Like a great many American Jews, my own family owes much of

the stability that it came to enjoy to the Workmen's Circle. The Workmen's Circle schools educated my grandmother Charlotte, Bessie's daughter. Its Camp Kinder Ring was where Charlotte and my grandfather Leonard met and where my father and his siblings spent their summers. Its cemetery plot in Queens is where Charlotte and Leonard are buried, alongside their close friends and family. Their graves are the last vestige not only of a world now passed but of a spirit, of a kind of Jewishness, that is disappearing.

Over time, the pragmatism of the Workmen's Circle would supplant its earlier radicalism. External pressures forced the organization to shift its tone. State repression and rising American anti-communism made the cost of anything that smelled of revolutionism prohibitively high. The immigration restrictions of the 1920s meant that the influx of new members who might have brought with them the fire of eastern European radicalism stopped entirely. There were also tactical considerations. Conscious of their difference, sensitive to the tentativeness of their acceptance, American Jews increasingly sought to articulate an American Jewish politics that would not appear threatening to American norms.

The change was largely the product of the organization's success. Increasingly its members were not only immigrants but their American-born children, and their Americanism was just as strong, if not stronger, than the earlier generation's socialism. The socialist millennium proved no match for the American dream. In his official history of the organization, Hurwitz described the new, more moderate, and aspirational middle-class sensibility it gradually embraced. "Though no less an idealist than the intellectual," he wrote, "the laboring man knows that an acre in Long Island is worth a million acres in utopia."

The Workmen's Circle was just one part of the dense network of organizations that Jewish immigrants built in the American cities that they now called home; to enumerate them all would require several books. They founded Landsmanshaften, fraternal orders based on towns and cities of origin in the old country, which also provided mutual aid and death benefits to their members. They catalyzed the creation of new unions, like the International Ladies' Garment Workers' Union (ILGWU), which in the span of the two decades after its founding in 1900 became one of the largest and most powerful in the American Federation of Labor (AFL).

Newspapers like the social democratic *Forverts* and the conservative, Orthodox *Morgen Zhurnal* knitted together a vibrant, disputatious Yiddish public sphere. Political parties and myriad socialist and communist sects gave political content to the snatches of life beyond the workplace—education, scouting and youth movements, summer camps, and night school—that the working masses managed to carve out for themselves. Later, in the 1920s and into the 1930s, the organizations of the Jewish working class would even establish housing projects, like the Coops in the Bronx and the Amalgamated Clothing Workers' Housing Cooperative's towers, in whose shadows my maternal grandmother and her sister grew up.

A century later, only traces of this culture remain—in faded inscriptions on buildings in the Lower East Side and the Bronx, in the accents and expressions of a generation now dying out, in organizations now reduced to little more than letterhead. For the most part, the descendants of the great migration have neither seen this culture as worth perpetuating nor built anything, no institution or organization, that endeavored to embody the same synthesis: that expressed the universal through the particular and worked for the betterment of all mankind, all while grounded simultaneously in the lifeworld of eastern European Jewry.

The Last Days of the Jewish Working Class

In the span of barely half a century, working-class Jewish culture peaked, then began its irrevocable decline. In 1969, Melech Epstein, author of a multivolume history of the Jewish labor movement, reflected on the looming oblivion of the American Jewish working class from

Florida, where he was living out his days along with much of the former Jewish proletariat. "The gradual disappearance of the Jewish
working class," he wrote in the preface to his opus, "should not be
considered a calamity."

Epstein had lived through the American Jewish working class's
entire trajectory. In the years between his arrival in the United
States in 1913—from a town in today's Belarus, much like my great-
grandmother—and his retirement in Miami Beach, he had witnessed
the rise of the Jewish working class out of the sweatshops into middle-
class prosperity in America. A former socialist militant who had once
been imprisoned by the czarist regime, he had also watched from afar
as the Bolshevik revolution devolved into despotism. The class to
which he had belonged, and whose struggle he had devoted his life to
chronicling, had not achieved its world historical task. For Epstein this
was a source of disillusionment. "The classical Marxist doctrine that
the proletariat is destined to change the world is outdated," he wrote
in the last years of his life.

But Epstein also found consolation in the Jewish working class's
contribution to the betterment of American society. "The Jewish labor
movement, in its peak years, sparking with that elusive attribute, the
spirit, was a vital force not merely to its own people," he wrote. "Its
voice, bringing new ideas, was heard in every corner of the American
labor movement, thus contributing to American society as a whole."
Through self-organization and institution building, through its values
of mutuality and solidarity, the Jewish working class buoyed the American labor movement. It was, in no small part, through the pressure of
the Jewish-led garment unions that some of the most important workplace regulations were passed. The institutions of the Jewish labor
movement fought not merely for their own members but for the American working class as a whole. This was its greatest achievement.

In the process, however, the same Jewish working class abolished
itself through prosperity. It was a slow but simple transition: the abandonment of left-laborite commitment for embourgeoisement and con-

formity. It *was* the product of intention—no Jewish worker hoped that his son would take his place on the sweatshop floor—even if the effects were unintended. For the resulting transformation was so successful that it eventually obscured its own origins. The later disavowal of immigrant radicalism, born of mid-century middle-class Jewishness—of the crystallization of Americanism, Zionism, and liberalism as the pillars of American Jewish life—required the forgetting of the institutions and values that structured working-class Jewish existence. Already by the 1940s a Jewish version of Horatio Algerism had begun to eclipse the Jewish socialism that made its existence possible. The myth of Jewish meritocratic accomplishment began to supplant the fact of Jewish working-class mutual aid and self-organization.

III.

On the Lower East Side they were immigrants. In the Bronx they became Americans. When Bessie and her husband, Louis, made the move uptown, they embarked on what Hasia Diner called the "main event" of American Jewish history: between the years of 1920 and 1948, the Jews of the great migration and their children began and largely completed the "lengthy and complicated process of middle-class Americanization."

In theory, the ideological orientation of the Jewish communal structures remained intact. The old immigrant institutions continued to shape Jewish life. The Jewish neighborhood still formed an entire world unto itself. "The Jewish community enclosed one not through choice as much as through instinct, and not often very gently or with the most refined manners," remembered Irving Howe, himself a son of the East Bronx.

In practice, the old pattern of Jewish life faced challenges everywhere, in what was always a losing competition. The American-born generation did not see it as their goal to maintain the immigrant ghetto or to perpetuate that way of life. Instead, they wanted to transcend its particularity and join American society. Their romance with American culture—synonymous with modernity, universalism, youth, prosperity—made escaping the old neighborhood an urgent task of self-creation. Like Howe, my grandmother Charlotte and her brother Ken grew up in the immigrant enclave. Their aim, too, was to leave it behind.

They succeeded. But that they did so was much less the result of some intangible, beneficent American spirit than it was the product of America's, and especially New York's, fleeting social democratic moment. American Jews did not rise from the sweatshop to the suburb solely through individual mettle and sweat. Rather, they did so in large part because an array of public institutions facilitated their education and thus their "middle-class Americanization." If the institutions of the Jewish labor movement accounted for one half of the real American Jewish success story, the emerging social safety net of the New Deal accounted for the other.

New York Jews

In the Bronx, the Jews practiced an improvisational pluralism. As early as the 1930s, this ad hoc arrangement survived less by virtue of sincere commitment than by a mixture of custom and nostalgia. "Almost everyone retained some strands of religious feeling, almost everyone regarded himself as something of a socialist," Howe wrote. "Almost everyone hoped soon to improve the conditions of his existence." The old immigrant father—and my great-grandfather—prayed at the Orthodox synagogue during the High Holidays, paid his union dues to the socialist-run ILGWU, and sent his children to the best schools he could find. The geography of the East Bronx reflected the immigrant-Jewish-socialist mélange.

But it was not a balanced mixture. The socialist, radical, and secularist organizations promised progress, which meant modernity, which meant prosperity. The Orthodox shuls and yeshivas seemed to point backward to the Old World, tradition, and darkness. It was for this reason that "on Washington Avenue, the activities of the Yiddish schools, Workmen's Circle Clubs, union locals, and socialist meeting halls overshadowed those of the *landsmanshaft chevras* and the Yeshiva Rabbi Israel Salanter, the Bronx's only Jewish day school in the 1920s," historian Deborah Dash Moore wrote. "The few synagogues and talmud torahs hugged the middle-class blocks or clustered near Hunts Point."

If America was the future, what could the tradition offer but the misery of the past? How could the demands of Torah study compare to the thrill of the city? Or as Alfred Kazin put it, describing his childhood in the parallel immigrant neighborhood of Brownsville, Brooklyn: "That poor worn synagogue could never in my affections compete with that movie house."

Tradition faced another challenge in the form of capitalism. Like Bessie's father, her husband, Louis, was a religious man. But he confronted the dilemma that every observant immigrant faced—the reason why the Orthodox authorities of the *alte heym* (old country) had warned of America as the *treyfene medine*, the unholy state. To escape not just the experience of poverty but its social markers required working on the Sabbath. It was the only way to keep his wife from needing to work outside the house. Louis and Bessie had significant household responsibilities. Louis had been married once before to a woman named Yehudit, a friend of Bessie's who died young. Together they had two children, whom Bessie raised as her own.

Capitalism's coercive power forced Louis to compromise his faith. On early Saturday mornings my great-grandfather would take the IRT El downtown to the Garment District for the weekend shift instead of heading to the synagogue. Viewed this way, the warnings of the old country's rabbis were not unfounded. Capitalist modernity dissolved the old bonds of tradition. In Judaism, the Sabbath requires abstention from work and a temporary retreat from market relations. Capitalism demands ceaseless production; it makes no such allowance.

My grandmother's family, in other words, was typical of the twentieth-century Jewish immigrant experience in almost every regard. But for one. While most first- and second-generation immigrants attended public schools, those factories of Americanization, my great-uncle Ken would walk in the mornings across Crotona Park to the Salanter Yeshiva, named after Rabbi Yisrael Salanter, one of the founding spirits of the mussar movement. It was where the few neighborhood families who would not trust the secular authorities sent their children to learn, out of a combination of religious conviction and suspicion of the quality of public education.

Orthodoxy, however, offered much less for women. And my grandmother knew at an early age that she would not be a homemaker. Her way out of the life that appeared all but destined for her at birth went through the Workmen's Circle Yiddish *schule*, or secondary school, where she learned the secular subjects, math and history, and English and Yiddish under the wings of earlier generations of Jewish socialists. She was, in this sense, like many a daughter of shtetl people, convinced that knowledge would give her control over her own fate.

More than in God or in socialism, the Jewish immigrants and their children believed in the transformative, propulsive power of education. It was education that would guarantee an escape from the drudgery and danger of the sweatshop, the airlessness of the immigrant neighborhood, and the indignities of poverty—and it was the immigrant parents' responsibility to impress upon their children this value. "It was not for myself alone that I was expected to shine, but for them—to redeem the constant anxiety of their existence," Alfred Kazin wrote of his own immigrant parents. "I was their first American child, their offering to the strange new God; I was to be the monument of their liberation from the shame of being—what they were." No Jewish immigrant parent wanted their son or daughter to follow them into the trade in which they had toiled. No immigrant parent hoped their child would return to live in the flat they'd scraped to secure. That was not the point of the journey they had made—not for this had they sacrificed.

My grandmother Charlotte and her brother Ken both graduated from college in the 1940s: Charlotte from Hunter; Ken from City College of New York. They and the other children of immigrants no doubt worked hard. They no doubt possessed a certain zeal to succeed. But their striving required more than that to bear fruit. It also required luck.

The American-born generation came of age in a New York City where the public institutions, from the local public schools to the great CCNY system, still functioned as engines of social mobility. By providing an affordable education of reasonable quality, CCNY took working-class kids and fast-tracked their ascent to the middle class. Of course, those who became the leading intellectuals of the next half century, the famous denizens of City College's Alcoves One and Two, represented only a fraction of the students at City. But nearly all who passed through CCNY's campuses saw their life trajectories dramatically modified. New York City in its fleeting social democratic heyday, in no small part, made Jewish immigrant uplift possible.

At the same time, the experience of higher education also catalyzed a break with the old ways of immigrant life and thought. In her memoir *Fierce Attachments*, Vivian Gornick, a daughter of the Jewish Bronx, describes how City College, "benign in intent, only a passport to the promised land," in effect rent her permanently from the fabric of her Pale of Settlement–born mother's world. "I lived among my people, but I was no longer of them," Gornick writes:

I think this was true for most of us at City College. We still used the subways, still walked the familiar streets between classes, still returned to the neighborhood each night, talked to our high-school friends, and went to sleep in our own beds. But secretly we had begun to live in a world inside

our heads where we read talked thought in a way that
separated us from our parents, the life of the house and that
of the street.

For my grandmother Charlotte and her brother Ken, the experience was similar. They moved out and eventually far away from the
old family home. The distance, physical as much as it was emotional,
left its mark in the shape of the loneliness felt by their immigrant parents. Every Sunday my great-grandparents would religiously tune in to
a Yiddish radio show called *Tsuris bay Laytn* (*People's Troubles*),
which ran on WEVD, the *Forward*'s radio station, named after the
great socialist leader Eugene V. Debs. It was, my great-uncle explained,
a "Dear Abby" variant. "The theme that most often came up," he remembered, "was 'My children are ashamed of me. Because I'm an
immigrant, and I don't have an education. They're trying to hide me.'"

"Only in America"

If the real conditions that enabled American Jewish success now appear obscure, it is in large part because a cohort of the much-celebrated
New York Intellectuals, who had themselves risen from Brooklyn and
the Bronx to the peaks of American culture and literature, would rewrite their own story, just as the first- and second-generation sons and
daughters began to enjoy lives of affluence and influence in postwar
America. By the 1970s, this new story had become American Jewish
canon.

Propounding from their new positions of bourgeois security, the
neoconservatives—self-described former radicals "mugged by reality,"
in Irving Kristol's turn of phrase—took aim at the social democratic
ideals to which, in some sense, they owed their own lives. Although
educated in New York City's public institutions, they articulated a
story of Jewish meritocratic achievement in which one individual with
wit and grit could climb the rungs of class hierarchy. They elided the

way state and federal programs—good public schools and state universities and, later, the G.I. Bill—enabled American Jews to thrive. They denied the determining power of socioeconomic conditions and state structures on the fate of the individual. In the neoconservative imagination, Jewish experience confirmed the viability of the *schmatte*-to-success story. And if the Jews could do it, so, too, in theory, could anyone else.

During the years of civil rights struggle and after, this argument would take on a distinctly racial, even racist cast. In the view of neoconservatives like Nathan Glazer, if other minorities, by which he generally meant African Americans, failed to achieve what American Jews had managed, that was because they lacked the same innate cultural proclivities and inherited traits; because they did not value hard work and learning the way Jews did; because they lacked the familial stability that Jews possessed. They remained enmeshed in "a culture of poverty," unlike the culture of achievement that, the neoconservatives argued, upwardly mobile Jews had created. The neoconservatives further developed the theory of the Jews as the American model minority, which explained their remarkable ascent to middle-class affluence.

And it was a narrative that many American Jews in the postwar decades were happy to hear. It flattered their sense of exceptionality at the same time as it mitigated the ambivalence that accompanied middle-class Americanization.

The transformation, in the late sixties and after, of the neoconservative narrative into the new hegemonic framing of Jewish identity was only possible because the old Jewish ideologies had fallen away or terminally weakened. Mid-century prosperity eroded the immigrant socialist values of solidarity, mutuality, and obligation. The liberal capitalist ideals of individual striving and meritocratic achievement replaced them. Americanism and liberalism fused in this new form of Jewish self-understanding: what was felt to be the exceptional success of American Jews confirmed America's exceptional goodness. By the last quarter of the twentieth century, this mythological thinking had become so dominant that it was shared and expressed even by those taken to be progressive paragons.

There is a one-liner that the late Supreme Court justice Ruth Bader Ginsburg liked to tell: "What is the difference between a bookkeeper in the Garment District and a Supreme Court Justice?" The answer: "One generation." In her July 1993 Senate confirmation hearing, Ginsburg articulated the American meritocratic myth in its most distilled form. "I am a first-generation American on my father's side," she said, "barely second-generation on my mother's. Neither of my parents had the means to attend college, but both taught me to love learning, to care about people, and to work hard for whatever I wanted or believed in."

She continued, "Their parents had the foresight to leave the old country when Jewish ancestry and faith meant exposure to pogroms and denigration of one's human worth." She concluded: "What has become of me could happen only in America."

More than the socialism of the new immigrant or the Orthodoxy of the old country, more than any other ethical or religious precept, this—the narrative of Jewish uplift made possible by the combination of individual hustle and America's unique benevolence—became, for most American Jews, a central article of faith.

IV.

In 1987, Saul Bellow sent a letter to Cynthia Ozick. Then in his seventies, Bellow looked back on the years of World War II, the Holocaust, and its aftermath, and found his generation lacking. They had not properly recognized the gravity of the time, he lamented. "It's perfectly true that 'Jewish Writers in America' (a repulsive category) missed what should have been for them the central event of their time, the destruction of European Jewry," he wrote. "We (I speak of Jews now and not merely of writers) should have reckoned more fully, more deeply with it."

Why *was* it, Bellow asked, that American Jews had so failed in the task of grappling with what their European relatives had endured? Perhaps it was the terrible nature of the events, so horrifying that they eluded understanding: "There were," Bellow observed, "no minds *fit* to comprehend." Perhaps it was nevertheless the case that, even if American Jews had failed, "the Jews as a people reacted justly to it," he added. "So we have Israel." But, in a blunt admission, Bellow concluded that, much to his regret, he and his generation had been "too busy becoming" to have given the destruction of European Jewry much thought or time. "I was involved with 'literature' and given over to preoccupations with art, with language, with my struggle on the American scene, with claims for recognition of my talent," Bellow wrote. "With anything except the terrible events in Poland."

"Too Busy Becoming"

In the 1940s, most American Jews were not novelists on the make. They were not nearly as self-absorbed as Bellow and his generation of Jewish, and mostly male, authors. But their preoccupations were, even if in miniature, not so different from Bellow's. They, too, were "busy becoming"—becoming Americans, becoming middle-class, becoming fathers and mothers, husbands and wives. They, too, were struggling for their place "on the American scene" and for recognition—not simply of their work but of their value as citizens irrespective of their Judaism.

Most American Jews were, by this time, no longer foreign-born. By 1950, three-quarters of American Jews were U.S.-born. They were at least one generation out of the factory, the sweatshop, the ethnic neighborhood. Many were on their way into the professions. Their project, *their* art, was not Bellow's literature but the hard work of assembling their new Americanness. Europe was what their parents, like my great-grandparents, had left behind.

Of course, many American Jews knew about the cataclysm unfolding on the continent, even if they were not aware of the magnitude. That terrible realization would only be possible later, after the liberation of the camps. American Jews, especially older people—those with living ties to Europe, who still spoke its languages—read the reports and testimonies that filtered out in the newspapers. Jewish communal representatives lobbied U.S. government officials and mobilized to save those they could. The Orthodox-run Vaad Ha-Hatzalah rescued eastern Europe's rabbinical leadership from certain extermination. Universities and foundations gave lifesaving positions and posts to Jewish émigré luminaries, many of whom would bring their tragic consciousness to bear on the problems of American politics, reshaping American intellectual life in the process. But any form of mass rescue of the Jews trapped in Nazi-dominated lands remained beyond reach.

What to do about the fate of European Jewry in the 1930s and '40s—the term "Holocaust" had not yet come into public use—presented a serious dilemma to American Jews. Conscious of their own recent arrival in the United States, they wanted to appear as good Americans. They felt themselves to be so already. But to others they were far from secure in their status. Jewish visibility in the fight against antisemitic violence abroad still risked stoking antisemitism at home. Jewish communal leaders feared providing ammunition to the antisemitic figures who denigrated U.S. involvement in World War II and denounced it as a Jewish war. They worried that publicly criticizing the Roosevelt administration—for not acting swiftly enough, for not taking enough refugees, and later for not bombing the tracks to Auschwitz—would cast doubt on Jewish loyalty to the country. It was one thing to be your brother's keeper; it was another entirely to doubt your ability to keep yourself.

Such fears were not unfounded. Political antisemitism in America had reached its peak in the years before the U.S. entrance into the war.

The famed aviator Charles Lindbergh and his America First Committee trafficked in antisemitic rhetoric while opposing U.S. involvement
in the war. From his pulpit in Detroit, Father Charles Coughlin
preached antisemitic conspiracy theories to millions of listeners over
the radio. In 1939, the German American Bund, a pro-Nazi organization, held a mass rally of 20,000 people in New York's Madison
Square Garden. It turned out that there were many Americans who
defined their country not in terms of the civic nationalism that had
facilitated Jewish integration but as a white Christian nation. Only
the U.S. declaration of war against the Nazi threat would make the
fascist kind of exclusionary ethnonationalism unmentionable in public
life—an old norm that, like so many, frighteningly seems to have been
broken.

The Early Postwar Era

In the years after the Allies' victory in World War II, America claimed
responsibility not only for defeating Nazi fascism but also for liberating the camps—never mind that it was the Soviet Union that reached
Auschwitz first. Indeed, as the historian Peter Novick observes, while
the "liberation of the camps" later became "emblematic of Americans'
face-to-face encounter with the Holocaust" in the 1970s and after,
American troops in 1945 encountered not the death camps of Auschwitz and Treblinka but the concentration camps of Buchenwald and
Dachau, where Jews accounted for only a portion of the imprisoned.
In fact, Novick points out, the words "Jews" and "Jewish" do not
appear in the journalist Edward R. Murrow's broadcast from Buchenwald or in President Eisenhower's description of the camps upon his
visit to Europe that year. "None of this," Novick writes, "was an encounter with 'the Holocaust' as we understand the term today."

Still, for many American Jews, their country's wartime performance abroad confirmed what they already thought to be true at
home: that America was uniquely beneficent to Jews compared to all

previous sites of diasporic life and that this reflected America's exceptionality in an almost cosmic sense. "Much of the exuberance with which I and others of my generation of Jewish children seized our opportunities after the war—that wonderful feeling that one was entitled to no less than anyone else, that one could do anything and could be excluded from nothing—came from our belief in the boundlessness of the democracy in which we lived and to which we belonged," Philip Roth wrote in his autobiography, *The Facts*. "It's hard to imagine," he continued, "that anyone of intelligence growing up in America since the Vietnam War can have our unambiguous sense, as young adolescents immediately after the victory over Nazi fascism and Japanese militarism, of belonging to the greatest nation on earth."

The American exceptionalism of Roth and his generation was possible in large part because the defeat of Nazi Germany hastened the banishment of antisemitism from public life. Limitations on Jews' civil rights began to diminish. In the late 1940s, U.S. states and municipalities began to bar discriminatory hiring practices. In the 1950s, restrictive covenants that barred Jews from gentile neighborhoods started to fall to legal challenges. By the 1960s, Jewish quotas at prestigious universities were gradually being abandoned. These gains were spectacular in the eyes of those who experienced them. In his book *The Masks Jews Wear*, Eugene Borowitz, the son of Yiddish-speaking immigrants, described "American Jews of the 1960s" as "the first free generation of Diaspora Jews."

More fully accepted by American society than ever before, American Jews thus embraced Americanism even tighter. And in the new political climate, the shedding of their Jewish difference proved almost effortless. They began their out-migration from the city to the suburbs—in my grandparents' case, from the Bronx to New Rochelle—where they molded their houses, their synagogues, their lives, on the prevailing style and form of the Protestant Modern. In their homes, they abandoned the restrictions of kashruth and the observance of Shabbat that they had maintained as children. My own grandmother

Charlotte—Bessie's daughter Charlotte—now with three kids of her own, marked Saturday by cooking bacon in an electric frying pan.

Of course, the new suburbanites had not forgotten that they were Jews. They were reminded of this inexorable fact of their being with each visit to immigrant grandparents in the old city neighborhood, by the folkways of humor and food. "About being Jewish there was nothing more to say than having two arms and two legs," Roth wrote of his own childhood in an almost entirely Jewish neighborhood in 1940s Newark. "It would have seemed to us strange *not* to be Jewish—stranger still, to hear someone announce that he wished he weren't a Jew or that he intended not to be in the future."

But they no longer believed, with a few exceptions, that this Jewishness demanded anything beyond what their Americanness already entailed. "The truth is that for most Jews the American way has become the real faith, the effective Torah, by which they have lived," Borowitz wrote. By the 1960s, Jewish writers and communal leaders alike had begun to fret publicly about whether this all-encompassing Americanness threatened the future of American Jewish life. "There will be no death camps in the United States that we live in," the novelist Herman Wouk wrote in *This Is My God*. "The threat of Jewish oblivion is different. It is the threat of pleasantly vanishing down a broad highway at the wheel of a high-powered station wagon, with the golf clubs in the back."

American Unease

Against this backdrop—religious dissolution, embourgeoisement, and integration—Israel and Zionism became, as Irving Howe observed, a substitute for Judaism. In the postwar years, Zionism served as the new glue for a Jewish identity that could no longer rest on faith in God or adherence to halacha. Israel provided American Jews with a real, concrete nation-state with which they could identify. And such identification required little religious knowledge or ritual familiarity.

It did not require observance. Instead, Israel enabled Jews to imagine themselves like other ethnic minorities—or "hyphenated Americans," in the phrase made famous by the singer Paul Robeson. By restoring the Jews to world history, Israel normalized them; it made their difference intelligible within the familiar Western nation-state schema.

Yet, beneath the surface of suburban comfort, there lurked another source of unease. The destruction of European Jewry lingered in the mind but could not be easily processed. The simultaneous remoteness and intensity of the Holocaust made it hard to know precisely how to mourn. Most American Jews were not, and are not today, the direct descendants of Holocaust survivors; in 1990, survivors and their children constituted only an estimated 8 percent of American Jewry. But many a Jewish family of European descent could count a family member who perished in the catastrophe. Had they done enough in the 1940s to help their suffering relatives? Or had they acted selfishly, cowardly, callously, and failed to respond, as Bellow wrote to Ozick, with the requisite gravity and intensity?

In the 1960s and '70s, when American Jews, and the World War II generation more broadly, began to reexamine the past, the response to these questions was erratic, uncertain, sometimes even uncontrolled. Bellow himself wrote a belated, manic attempt at making sense of the Holocaust in the form of *Mr. Sammler's Planet*, in which an urbane, professorial survivor, Arthur Sammler, recoils from the decadent, libertine society of post-'60s New York and fears that it presages a new disaster that might unfold on America's shores. Nearly everyone seemed to agree that even if there could be no agreement on how to remember the Holocaust, the act of remembering would need to be pursued vigorously. If American Jews had failed to respond adequately to the suffering of their brethren, they would never fail to do so again.

The hyperactive production of Holocaust literature, film, and even kitsch that has characterized American Jewish life over the last quarter century is the result of this anxiety about how precisely to remember. It is not just a fear that the terrible events might be forgotten, or that the ignorant and the antisemitic cease to believe the Holocaust happened. It is, instead, a deep, abiding, almost definitional uncertainty about how American Jewry should relate to a tragedy that did not befall it but could have. As Peter Novick observed, perhaps the last commonality shared by the vast majority of American Jews is "the knowledge that but for their parents' or (more often) grandparents' or great-grandparents' immigration, they would have shared the fate of European Jewry." I once asked my great-uncle if Bessie and Louis regretted the hardships they found in America. "It was clear that they felt it was not a mistake to come," he said. "They and their children probably would have been wiped out."

For the foreseeable future, this spectral quality of the Holocaust as it appears in the American mind will persist, a lingering, invisible pain, like a phantom limb. As the Holocaust becomes more distant in time, that phantom quality will only become greater. For the last three-quarters of a century, the Holocaust has fulfilled the role of the binding trauma of American Jewish identity. It has been the mortar keeping intact the postwar American Jewish consensus. If the surveys are to be believed, remembering the Holocaust is, for many American Jews, one of the only reasons they can give for continuing to be Jewish. The maintenance of the edifice of memory—donations to Holocaust museums and groups like the Anti-Defamation League—constitutes their sole form of Jewish practice.

But the centrality of the Holocaust has also enabled the indefinite deferral of articulating reasons for continued Jewish identification on more positive grounds, leading to a crisis of meaning. "A community cannot survive on what it remembers," the sociologist Will Herberg wrote. "It will persist only because of what it affirms."

2

COMPLETE ZIONIZATION

I.

As a child I would often wander into my father's home office to look at his books. The shelves could have belonged to a small synagogue library. On the double-stacked, dark-wood built-ins, rival editions of the Tanakh, the Hebrew Bible, sat next to commentaries on the weekly Torah portion, interpretations by figures like Israeli rabbi Pinchas Peli and American rabbis Joseph Telushkin and Harold Kushner, English translations of Aggadah and midrash, sourcebooks on Jewish ethics, and books with foreboding titles like *Marital Relations, Birth Control, and Abortion in Jewish Law*. Beneath them lounged books dealing with more contemporary matters: autobiographies of towering Israeli figures (Abba Eban, Moshe Dayan, Golda Meir), accounts of Israel's wars (the doorstoppers *O Jerusalem!* and *From Beirut to Jerusalem*), and confessional meditations on Jewish identity and faith (Ari Goldman's *The Search for God at Harvard*, Alan Dershowitz's *Chutzpah*, Wouk's *This Is My God*). More numerous, however, were the volumes on Jewish history, especially Jewish antiquity: academic monographs, obscure and classic (Israeli historian Gedaliah Alon's *Jews in Their Land in the Talmudic Age*, Jacob Neusner's *Method and Meaning in Ancient Judaism*). Most appealing to me as a young child were the popular oversized hardcovers (Moshe Dayan's *Living with the Bible*, Yigael Yadin's *Bar-Kokhba*), which for a time I insisted on reading with my father before I went to sleep.

On slow weekend afternoons I would pull the books down from the shelves and peruse them. Sometimes I would take them back to my room for a more extended exploration. Other times I would plant myself on the window seat and absorb the spirit of a time—the late 1970s and '80s—that was not my own. The books seemed to me relics from an almost unrecognizable past: the thick, worn paperbacks, the simple serif font covers, the back flaps with black-and-white pictures of their authors, invariably sporting the largest, thickest pairs of eyeglasses I had ever seen.

But it was also the cumulative impression of the world that these books conveyed that seemed at once exhilarating and inaccessible to me. They spoke of an Israel whose military prowess could still seem shocking, even miraculous, and whose warrant for existence and armed self-defense extended back millennia. They described an America in which the political difficulties of being a traditionally practicing Jew required that we wear our Jewishness more proudly and insist on its visibility. They invoked a God who was not an interventionist supreme being but a higher power that bound the Jewish people in a covenant of fate.

When I got older and would return home from college to make my regular pilgrimage to the shelves, the books began to vex me. It was not only that I had come to view the hawkishly Zionist, religiously traditionalist, occasionally maudlin Weltanschauung that they represented with suspicion. It was also that I could not quite understand where they had come from. For the most part they had not been inherited. I knew my father's parents had met at a Yiddish socialist sleepaway camp and that they had been ardent secularists, barely willing to enter the suburban synagogue to which they belonged. They were Jewish nationalists of a certain, nearly extinct variety. They were not religious Zionists. Which meant the books were, for the most part, products of my parents' lives, the milieu in which they had ensconced themselves as young adults, and, above all, the moment in American Jewish life when the culture of the communal mainstream swung to the right.

To understand this shift, I began to read the books again, and more carefully. I started to research. I rifled through boxes of old family documents and pictures in my parents' basement: slides of trips to Israel, sleepaway camp songbooks, membership dues to Jewish organizations. The great transformation of late-twentieth-century American Jewish life, I discovered, had taken place at the very moment when the old arguments about the place of Jews in American society and the forms of faith and observance appeared to have been settled. In the uneasy tranquility of postwar America, especially after the Six-Day War in 1967, the pillars of the American Jewish consensus—Americanism, Zionism, liberalism—consolidated into their current shape. In the 1970s, what the late historian Judith Stein called for very different reasons "the pivotal decade," American Jewish identity as we know it was made.

"Complete Zionization"

In the comfort of suburbia, American Judaism seemed like it would soon disappear. Or so some began to worry. The sociologist Marshall Sklare looked out on what he called "the suburban frontier" of the 1960s—where ritual practice, synagogue attendance, and holiday observance appeared in terminal decline—and pondered morosely "whether the present generation of American Jews will not be the last to maintain any semblance of religion in its homes." In 1964, the glossy magazine *Look* ran a cover story titled "The Vanishing American Jew"—it charged that low Jewish birthrates, born of newfound affluence, had set American Jewry on the path to extinction. In the pages of Jewish magazines like *Commentary* and the now-forgotten *Midstream*, Sklare and other Jewish intellectuals such as Milton Himmelfarb fulminated about growing rates of intermarriage between

Jews and non-Jews. They predicted that within the next century there would hardly be any American Jews left. Needless to say, they were wrong.

But these were halcyon, white-picket times. Things were good: too good, the demographers worried. The old Yiddish line "*Shver tsu zayn a yid*" ("It's hard to be a Jew") no longer seemed to ring true in America. Before the 1960s, American Jewish communal organizations had been substantially concerned with eliminating the remaining restrictions on Jewish civil rights: quotas at universities and medical schools, discriminatory hiring practices at elite law schools, redlining, restrictive covenants, and other forms of housing discrimination. As soon as these barriers to integration fell, Jewish leaders began to fear that there was nothing left to stop Jews from getting lost in America's melting pot. For the first half of the century, America's relative freedom had been a balm to Jewish anxieties; in the immediate postwar years, it appeared as a threat. Jacob Neusner, a popular and prolific writer as well as an academic, asked, "Can Judaism survive in freedom?"

Most American Jews, however, expressed ambivalence more than alarmism. After all, they were, like my grandparents, not merely satisfied and grateful for America's gifts; they embraced the myth of the American dream fully. They were among its biggest exponents. They viewed their experiences, the rise from shtetl to suburb in the span of one lifetime, as proof of its reality. That this prosperity might threaten Jewish survival was a thought they relegated to the rumination of a sleepless night. Yes, they understood the risk that much of the Old World culture of Yiddishkeit might disappear, but on balance the trade-off almost always seemed worth it. Besides, as the awareness of what had not yet been named the Holocaust germinated through the collective mind suggested, it was not as if there had been another option.

My parents breathed as children this air of tentative comfort. Life for them was summer camp. It was Little League. It was the Boy Scouts. They pursued these activities surrounded, in large part, by other Jews, but this Jewishness was almost purely incidental, a mere fact of life. As children, they thought little of it. The world outside the suburb was still in turmoil; it never ceased to be. But for a moment the churn and violence could hardly be seen or felt from the manicured lawns of Short Hills or Scarsdale, Edison (my mother's childhood home) or New Rochelle (my father's), and the distance between the suburban idyll and the working-class Bronx of their parents' childhoods seemed to indicate that all was, basically if torpidly, well.

But everything about American Jewish identity changed in the flash of an Israeli Mirage fighter jet scraping over the Sinai Desert. In the span of six days in the summer of 1967, Israeli warplanes destroyed the Egyptian air force while it was still on the ground. Israeli tanks barreled into the Sinai. Israeli ground troops and armored divisions captured the Golan Heights from Syria and East Jerusalem and the West Bank from Jordan. To many Israelis and American Jews, the lightning victory was nothing short of miraculous, even messianic.

In the United States, Jewish pride in Israel—tough Israel, victorious Israel, strong Israel—swelled into expressions of ecstasy and euphoria. There was dancing in the street and special prayers of thanksgiving in synagogues. Israel had not previously been such a widespread source of Jewish identification. While there had long been Zionist groups in Israel, they had never claimed the sympathies of affiliation of anything close to the majority of American Jews, many of whom were not Zionists at all. In a matter of days, however, the meaning of American Jewish identity was redefined. Israel now stood at its center.

The Six-Day War, to be sure, did not convert all American Jews into militant Zionists overnight. But from then on Jewishness was no longer confined within the staid suburban synagogue. Its expression was no longer epitomized by the perfunctory bar mitzvah service. If Zionism refashioned American Judaism so rapidly, that is because many Americans, whether consciously or not, felt it needed revitalizing. And the form this revivification most often took was a militant and militarist, tribalist, and particularistic kind of Zionism. Rooted in an old sense of Jewish vulnerability, it gradually fueled a belief in Jewish exceptionalism, sometimes verging even on Jewish supremacy.

Just as important, this new American Zionism was an undemanding faith. As a mode of Jewish identification, it required little daily activity or commitment. In the place of the Torah, of the commandments, all it asked of American Jews was that they feel a sense of closeness to Israel and, when they felt so inclined, donate money to Zionist philanthropies. Unlike the obligated life prescribed by traditional observance, this Zionism conformed fully to the liberal voluntarist patterns of American life. A Jew might attend the local Hadassah chapter meetings the way a non-Jew would attend meetings of the Rotary; in some places, American Jews did both. Zionism as American Jews interpreted it did not force them to choose between their Americanness and their Jewishness: instead, it enabled them to fully embrace the former without relinquishing the latter. To observe the Sabbath entailed a certain separation from the American mainstream. Zionism entailed no such sacrifice.

If the Six-Day War marked the dawning of a new, triumphal phase in American Jewish life, the Yom Kippur War soon after in 1973 imbued the new American Zionism with a feeling of desperate urgency. The war in 1967 was the good war, the heroic war. It rallied American Jews enthusiastically to the Israeli cause. By contrast, the Yom Kippur War was the war that Israel would have lost if not for American emergency aid. Nearly every American Jew of my parents' generation can recall hearing of the war's outbreak while in synagogue. Many bear with them still the memory of Judaism's most sacred day shattered by the threat of Israel's destruction.

Unlike the 1967 war, the war in 1973 alerted American Jews acutely to the precariousness of their new source of pride. And it was the fear that Israel—the new essence of their Judaism—might disappear that ultimately caused what Norman Podhoretz called "the complete Zionization" of American Jewish life and made criticism of Zionism tantamount to betrayal. "So long as it goes hanging on in the ominous political air," Podhoretz wrote of Israel, "there will be no defections from the Zionism" to which American Jews "have all by now been so thoroughly and passionately and unequivocally converted."

Other once repressed fears also began to reemerge against the backdrop of the wars. During this time, the Holocaust received its name and became a central theme not just of Jewish life but of American culture. The publication of Hannah Arendt's *Eichmann in Jerusalem* exploded into a controversy over the extent of Jewish resistance to the Nazi Final Solution. The subsequent flood of Holocaust films and TV specials reminded American Jews of the existential dangers from which the Jewish people had only recently escaped. Although separated by decades, the Holocaust and Israel's wars now appeared within the same continuous history of the Jewish people's imperiled survival. In unstable and uncertain times, Israel rooted the Jewishness of American Jews firmly in its newly conquered territory and committed to the defense of Jewish existence through force of arms. While Jewish theologians debated the meaning of the Holocaust for religious life, ordinary American Jews understood the lesson of the catastrophe in unequivocal terms: the necessity of the Israeli state.

No corner of American Jewish life was left untouched by this change. But it was the communal institutions that translated it into politics and policy. In the 1950s and '60s, some of the most important Jewish establishment organizations had been active, even central participants in the broad struggle for civil rights and against discrimination. Their rhetoric had been universalist, their outlook cosmopolitan. After 1967, they increasingly shifted their mandate to Israel advocacy and Zionist programming. Their outlook became more unapologetically particularist, their rhetoric blunter in its defense of Jewish self-interest. Once primarily concerned with shaping Jewish life at home in America, the new foci of their activities became "fundamentally vicarious," in the words of the eminent historian David Sorkin. The global center of Jewish activity had begun to shift toward Israel.

Of course, decades and even centuries are imprecise metrics for historical change; history does not heed round numbers. But they can be useful for taking stock of broad shifts over time. The historian Bruce J. Schulman calls the period between the late 1960s and the early 1980s "the long 1970s," and it was within this span that American Jewish life reconstituted itself with Israel and Zionism at its center. These were also years of tremendous upheaval in the United States—urban riots, assassinations, the oil embargo, and the end of the Vietnam War—and American Jewish life was not insulated from these events. As American politics turned rightward and inward, so, too, did American Jewish life. As religious revivalism reemerged with the eclipse of the 1960s counterculture, traditional practice and even messianism returned to American Jewish communities in which the flame of piety had long since diminished to embers.

In the long 1970s, the pillars of postwar American Jewish life took on the appearance that held up until, in our day, they began to falter.

Jews with Power

In 1971, my grandparents Charlotte and Leonard took my father and his two siblings on a trip to Israel, organized by the American Jewish Congress (AJCongress), to celebrate his sister's bat mitzvah. One of the three central Jewish "self-defense" organizations, the AJCongress had devoted the bulk of its efforts in the preceding half century to fighting racism, discrimination, and antisemitism. It had been founded as a more progressive, even populist alternative to the conservative, bourgeois American Jewish Committee and Anti-Defamation League. Its former president, the German-born rabbi Joachim Prinz, had helped organize the 1963 March on Washington with Martin Luther King Jr. But by the time my father embarked on the plane to join the group's trip, it was in the process of metamorphosing, reorienting its focus toward Israel advocacy, subordinating its residual progressive civil rights liberalism to an increasingly muscular Zionism.

My father and his family landed in an ecstatic and bellicose Israel. "The mood that had engulfed the country immediately after the military victory" in 1967 was, in the words of Israeli writer Amos Oz, "a mood of nationalist intoxication, of infatuation with the tools of statehood, with the rituals of militarism and the cult of generals, an orgy of victory." It was also an Israel coarsened toward the several million Palestinians who, after the war, found themselves living under its control. In 1971, although Israel had conquered the West Bank and the Gaza Strip, it had not yet established the legal and military architecture that would later define its occupation of the Palestinians. The oppression, therefore, was not as direct as it would later become.

The AJCongress tour took my father and his family into the West Bank. There, in the city of Hebron, he and a group of sunscreen-slathered, hat-wearing Jewish tourists took in the sights and sounds of occupied Palestine. On one of the main streets of the city, my father remembered, he encountered a young boy, not far from his age, who tried to sell him a drum. A depressing if too-common scene of misunderstanding and unbalanced power ensued. The boy tried to cajole my father into buying the drum, but they lacked any common language in which to communicate. The boy tried, my father recalled, to force the drum into his hands, but he refused. In the commotion, the drum fell and broke. As my father rejoined the tour bus, he saw behind him an older Palestinian man. The man was running after him, yelling, demanding that he pay for the broken drum. Frightened, my father scampered back onto the bus, but the Palestinian man was close on his heels. When the old man reached the threshold of the bus, the Israeli driver met him by landing a firm kick square at his chest, then closed the doors as the man staggered on the road below.

As American Jews with an inborn sense of vulnerability, they feared the "Other," the Palestinian, and his presumed violence; they still saw themselves as history's ultimate victims. They could not see the poverty of the West Bank or the brutality of military occupation. But it was also the case that American Jewish boys—timid, rule-abiding—did not, could not, act like that. Israeli men could. If Zionism had promised to "straighten the back" of the hunched diaspora Jew, Israel's occupation revealed that, with his back straightened, he had no less of a capacity for cruelty than the Boer.

The experience of Jewish power in the form of a sovereign state would remake American Jewish identity. While American Jews would continue to see themselves as weak, even marginalized, Israel's existence and military prowess made Jews appear much different from those other peoples, especially those without a state, who could only dream of such power. The dissonance between Jewish and non-Jewish perceptions of Jewish might in the wake of 1967 would become a central tension of American Jewish life as the long 1970s wore on.

The Crisis of Jewish Liberalism

It was not only suburban synagogue members and their teenage Jewish sons who were overwhelmed by militarist fervor and Zionist ardor after 1967. Even those least inclined, at least in theory, to be swayed by it found it irresistible. Some Jewish anti-war activists and members of the New Left, who until the day before had protested adamantly against the Vietnam War, now fell in behind Israel in the after-war mania. In pamphlets and essays circulated through the Jewish student counterculture, they proclaimed their conversions to Zionism in frenzied, absolutist tones. "Israel is the ultimate reality in the life of every living Jew today," declared erstwhile '60s radical M. J. Rosenberg in an essay titled "Israel Without Apology." "I believe that Israel surpasses in importance Jewish ritual," he wrote. "It is more than the Jewish tradition; and, in fact, it is more than Mosaic Law itself."

Rosenberg simply articulated with unusual bluntness the view that many American Jews now held: Judaism *was* Israel, far more than it was anything else.

Such dramatic conversions as Rosenberg's were also part of a much larger reconfiguration of American liberal politics and, as a consequence, of American Jewish politics. At roughly the same time as Israel's victory in the 1967 war, the Black freedom struggle in the United States shifted from its integrationist phase to its Black Power phase. Having been overrepresented among white freedom riders in the early 1960s, American Jewish activists now found themselves asked to step aside, and sometimes even to leave, Black activist spaces. "In the past," charged Student Nonviolent Coordinating Committee (SNCC) leader Stokely Carmichael in a 1966 *New York Review of Books* essay, "white allies have furthered white supremacy without the whites involved realizing it—or wanting it." It was time, he argued, for Black people to organize in the Black community. "Only black people," Carmichael wrote, "can convey the revolutionary idea that black people are able to do things themselves."

The Black freedom struggle's turn to Black Power shocked American Jewish liberals. They found not only that Black radicals counted them as white people, seemingly no different than white Christian Americans, but also that they seemed to face special opprobrium from their erstwhile comrades for this fact. "The Jew is a white man," James Baldwin wrote in his now-famous 1967 *New York Times* essay, "Negroes Are Anti-Semitic Because They're Anti-White." True, Baldwin acknowledged, Jewish historical suffering made Jews different, in a way, from other white people in America, yet for Baldwin that fact also only made matters worse. "The Jew," Baldwin wrote, "is singled out by Negroes not because he acts differently from other white men, but because he doesn't." Baldwin continued sharply: "One does not wish, in short, to be told by an American Jew that his suffering is as great as the American Negro's suffering. It isn't, and one knows it isn't from the very tone in which he assures you that it is."

Nor was it only in domestic American affairs where Jews found themselves refigured not on the side of historical victims but instead on the side of oppressors. Israel's victory in the Six-Day War brought Israel more firmly into the Western, U.S.-led camp, opposed to the Soviet Union and the liberationist movements of the Third World that stood in solidarity with the Palestinian cause. Within the American New Left and Black radical movements, Israel appeared as an imperialist power, Zionism an ideology of colonization. At the New Politics conference held in Chicago in September 1967—ostensibly an attempt to unify the broad U.S. left, but which dissolved into infighting and acrimony—Black activists denounced Israel's "imperialistic Zionist war." For many Jewish antiwar activists, the extraordinarily fractious conference—denounced by the writer Renata Adler in the *New Yorker* as "an incendiary spectacle, sterile, mindless, violence-enamored form of play"—marked a definitive break, after which participation as Jews in U.S. radical politics would not be possible.

The much vaunted "Black-Jewish alliance" of the heroic stage of the civil rights movement was often more myth than reality, more the product of overlapping interests than a coalition of true friends. Still, the eruption of enmity between Black and Jewish activists remains a painful rupture, certainly for many of the Jewish veterans of the New Left who lived through it. American Jewish activists mourned their rejection by groups like Carmichael's SNCC. They found their assignment to the "oppressors" side of the equation, in domestic and world politics, to be at odds with their own self-understanding.

Out of their grief, some spun a new narrative of what had happened. According to this historical revisioning, it was not the newly "Zionized" Jews of the New Left who had changed but the movement that had betrayed them. If, in the new militant Zionist faith, Judaism *was* Israel, then to criticize Israel was to attack Jews, and Black activists' expressions of solidarity with the Palestinians a form of veiled antisemitism. In some cases—but not all—it was.

Yet Black Power was not only an antagonist for the new American Zionists. It was also a model for what a self-confident politics of ethnic pride could look like. "The legitimation of the assertion of the validity of distinctive group interests, which was one result of the Black revolution, made it easier for Jews, too, to directly support the interests of

Israel," wrote the sociologist Nathan Glazer. "The black example," he continued, "should not be underestimated in explaining why young Jews turned inward and became active supporters of what they now conceived of as Jewish interests." Previous generations of Jewish activists had sought to cloak their work in support of Jewish interests in universalistic language, in appeals to the betterment of the broader society. But the emergence of a Black politics of identity—and soon identity politics more broadly—meant that such strategic articulation was no longer necessary.

The Movement to Free Soviet Jewry that emerged in the late 1960s exemplified, perhaps as much as the Zionist revival with which it dovetailed, this rediscovery of Jewish self-interest. The most committed members of the movement, aimed at enabling the roughly 2 million Jews in the Soviet Union to leave freely, came from a different part of American Jewish society than the civil rights movement. The Jewish activists who joined the Black freedom struggle tended to hail from liberal, less observant, and highly acculturated Jewish homes. They were often the children of red diaper babies or red diaper babies themselves: their parents or grandparents were members or fellow travelers of the Communist Party and other small left-wing groups.

The Soviet Jewry movement, by contrast, drew its activists from more observant Jewish homes, the Orthodox, and children of Holocaust survivors. In this sense, they reflected an important if overlooked fact of American Jewish reality. "For most Jews, and Orthodox ones in particular, active involvement in the civil rights movement was 'past nicht' [unfitting]," Glenn Richter, one of the leaders of the Student Struggle for Soviet Jewry, told the historian Adam Ferziger. "In those days, Jews simply didn't do those things, the very act of protest was a big *hiddush* [novelty]."

The Soviet Jewry movement broke old taboos in more ways than one. Its blunt, assertive style was unlike any other form of Jewish politics in the postwar period. So, too, were some of its tactics: disruptive civil disobedience, rowdy protest, and, on the fringes, even terrorism. Although Meir Kahane, the extremist rabbi and founder of the Jewish Defense League (JDL), did not represent the mainstream of the Soviet Jewry movement, he was among its most visible advocates, and his group provided the shock troops for what was, in the main, a peaceful protest movement. In 1972, for instance, Kahane's followers staged a bomb attack at the office of Sol Hurok, a dance impresario who brought Russian performers to the United States, killing a twenty-seven-year-old Jewish secretary named Iris Kones. The long 1970s were, of course, a decade of political terrorism, and not only in the United States. But what Kahane and the movement he headed illustrated was that American Jewish politics was not immune to the pathologies that afflicted the American polity—far from it.

Before the 1960s, American Jews had generally seen a commitment to a civic-minded liberalism as synonymous with the pursuit of Jewish interests in America, which made the explicit articulation of the latter often unnecessary when clothed in the language of the former. With the events of the late sixties, this long-held assumption began to unravel.

———————

When my grandmother Charlotte died, among the few knickknacks she left behind were several faux bronze medallions engraved with the names of "Prisoners of Zion," Jews jailed in the Soviet Union for trying to practice their Judaism openly. She must have received them as part of fundraising efforts, although, without any accompanying paperwork, I could never know for sure. Looking at the medallions, I remembered how, at one Passover seder when I was a child, she introduced me to several guests, people whom I had never seen before, as distant cousins of hers who had been lost behind the Iron Curtain and who had now been found.

My grandmother was not an activist, nor were her children, nor, really, was anyone they knew. Like most ordinary American Jews, and counter to popular progressive mythology, they related to the Black freedom struggle primarily as observers. They expressed their new-found Jewish pride, their fiercely held Zionism, more often in silent yet powerful ways—donations to Zionist and Jewish nationalist organizations—than in brash and public demonstrations.

Nevertheless, the new style of Jewish politics constituted a shift of remarkable magnitude and speed. Within a generation, Zionism moved from a marginal movement to the essence of American Jewish life. The articulation of Jewish interest took the place vacated by more ideologically expansive forms of Jewish politics, in particular Yiddish socialism and secularism, which had begun to pass from the scene. And if Black politics now centered on pride and cultural affirmation, American Jewish politics would do the same, without apology.

In a 1979 report, the political scientist Charles Liebman surveyed the metamorphosis that the AJCongress—the same group that brought my father and his family to Israel—and American Jewish life more broadly had undergone in the span of less than a decade. In practical terms, the defense of Jewish interests had come to conflict with the pursuit of liberal politics, Liebman observed. The group's "Israeli policy is one of unequivocal support for Israel, a policy that puts it out of touch with its non-Jewish allies on domestic issues," he wrote, by which he meant Black and civil rights organizations.

This reflected a much larger dynamic, what Liebman referred to as a "survivalist" dialectic. The more American Jewish leaders cared about Israel, the more they feared for its future, the more they deepened their "survivalist orientation," which translated into a greater concern for Israel. The survivalist dialectic entailed significant consequences for foreign policy as well. Whatever skepticism toward the projection of U.S. military power American Jews had expressed during the Vietnam War appeared to have ebbed. "A strong America and strengthening America's global position is now viewed by many as essential for Israel," Liebman continued. At the conferences where American Jewish leaders met to set the communal agenda, Liebman noted, "the positions reflected in *Commentary* magazine" were increasingly "well received."

The Rise of the Neoconservatives

If there was any single group that embodied the seismic shift in American Jewish politics over the long 1970s and articulated its meaning to the broader world, it was the neoconservatives. Clustered around magazines like *Commentary* and the *Public Interest*, these intellectuals, many of them formerly of the left (or at least sympathetic to it), synthesized the new enthusiasm for Zionism, the anti-communism of the Soviet Jewry movement, and the growing consciousness of the Holocaust into a potent new ideological amalgam. They described the tumult of post-1960s America—post–civil rights, post-Vietnam—as a moment of unique, even existential threats to Jews: imperiled by Black nationalist antisemitism and left-wing anti-Zionism at home; menaced abroad by Arab nationalism and its underwriter, Soviet communism.

Against this alarmist backdrop, the neoconservatives called on Jews to put their own interests first. "I think that Jews must once again begin to look at proposals and policies from the point of view of the Jewish interest, and must once again begin to ask what the consequences, if any, of any proposal are likely to be, so far as the Jewish position is concerned," Podhoretz wrote in 1972. The question "Is it good for the Jews?" had been seen during the first postwar decades by most American Jewish intellectuals and leaders as an obsolete, narrow-minded, even crass way to think about the place of Jews in American politics. Now the neoconservatives demanded that it serve as "a litmus test to all political judgments." And the leaders of American Jewish institutions would very quickly accede to their demands.

The neoconservatives were not themselves Jewish communal leaders. Yet they redefined the content of the Jewish communal consensus from the 1970s onward. They reformulated the dominant expressions of Americanism, Zionism, and liberalism in line with their swing to the right. These ideological pillars gained an agonistic edge. The Jewish experience in America and America's role in World War II continued to affirm America's exceptional goodness in the world—but now Americanism, too, was imperiled by enemies internal (left-wing radicals) and external (the Soviet Union) whose hostility to America betrayed a simultaneous and mutually reinforcing hostility to Jews.

Anti-Americanism appeared in the neoconservative mind as a surrogate for antisemitism; indeed, this was perhaps the neoconservatives' most enduring political innovation. According to this view, anti-imperialist militants, whether fighting wars of liberation in the Third World or protesting on the streets of Western metropoles, were, in effect, antisemites because they linked their critique of American global power to U.S. support for Israel against the Arab nationalist regimes. Likewise, attacks on the putatively meritocratic, individualist spirit of American capitalism also smacked of antisemitism because it was precisely that spirit that had enabled American Jews to achieve their remarkable prosperity in the United States. The neoconservatives thus formed an iron semantic chain linking Americanism, Zionism, and liberalism (in the classical, capitalist sense). To criticize one was to criticize all.

Within American Jewish life, neoconservative hegemony would peak in the 1980s. (In terms of political power, the neoconservatives themselves would reach their apex during the George W. Bush presidency.) When, in 1980, roughly 40 percent of American Jews voted for Ronald Reagan—the highest share of the Jewish vote that a Republican has won in the last half century—neoconservatives like Podhoretz believed that a new, right-wing electoral Jewish politics was set to become dominant. "Those Jews who had voted for [Reagan] did so because, like most other Americans (myself emphatically among them), they, too, wanted to see the country becoming great again," he mused uncannily in 2009.

Much to the perpetual dismay of Podhoretz and his acolytes, there was no mass conversion to right-wing politics by American Jews. The neoconservatives never constituted a majority among American Jews; only briefly did their beliefs appear to represent a large plurality. But more significant and of long-lasting impact, they claimed the mantle of intellectual leadership in mainstream Jewish life for several generations. They conflated Jewishness with hard-line Zionism and unquestioning support for Israel. They defined political seriousness as ruthlessness. They identified the defense of Jewish interests with the extension of American military power. To be a real, *thinking* Jew was to hold such views.

II.

The nationalist fervor of the late 1960s fueled a religious revival in the 1970s and into the 1980s. In the decade after the Six-Day War, American Jews not only turned to the right; they also returned to tradition, or at least a reimagined version of it. Thousands of Jews—perhaps more; no one knows for sure—from almost entirely secularized families, with little or no formal religious education, embraced ritual observance with a new zeal. People who'd never once balked at a bacon, egg, and cheese sandwich began to keep kosher. As children, they had spent Saturday mornings in front of the television. Now, they observed Shabbat, or tried to—if not strictly according to halacha, then in their own way.

Yet this resurgence of religious practice was not motivated primarily by theology, at least not at first. It was not the ancient God of Israel but the modern state of Israel that catalyzed many American Jews to return to Jewish practice. The Jewish religion, centered on the 613 commandments, long preceded the advent of the modern nation-state. But in the last quarter of the twentieth century, Zionism increasingly subsumed Judaism: the state of Israel now appeared as the telos, the preordained culmination, of Jewish history and religious yearnings. The majority of American Jews who recommitted themselves to Jewishness during this period did so from a groundswell of ethnic pride and nationalist enthusiasm. Theirs was an expression of what the scholar of religion Shaul Magid has called "identity spirituality." The Torah, Jewish law—these were ancillary. Israel was the center.

Those Who Return

Some people, of course, did become Orthodox. They merged their new sense of tribal belonging with commitment to living under the Torah's yoke. This was a phenomenon with no precedent in modern Jewish history. It was a reversal of the centuries-long process of ever-increasing Jewish integration into Western society. These mainly young American Jews attempted a movement of dissimilation. And many returned not simply to the faith of their fathers but to a faith more devout, a religiosity more stringent than perhaps anyone in their families had practiced. The sociologist Marshall Sklare had once called Orthodoxy in America "a case study in institutional decay." In the long 1970s, American Orthodoxy underwent a curious resurrection.

The newly Orthodox were, and still are, known as *ba'alei teshuva*—those who return. But they did not simply become more religious. Many broke with their nonreligious, nonpracticing families and flocked to yeshivas and seminaries newly built in Israel for young people, fleeing the moral laxity and vacuous secularism of mainstream American life. In America, old Orthodox institutions experienced a renaissance thanks to these recommitted Jews, who had been born again through enthusiasm for Israel as much as through the encounter with the divine. Groups like the Hasidic Chabad-Lubavitch sect began to devote substantial resources for outreach to potential returners.

At its most extreme, the *ba'al teshuva* movement took on many of the trappings of an antimodern revolt, accompanied by a retreat from conventional rationality and deference to charismatic spiritual leaders. (In this sense, it sometimes had more in common with the trend of new age experimentation and alternative communities that characterized 1970s America more broadly.) Yet, as historian Matthew Frye Jacobson writes, "if antimodernism has been one of modernity's most potent legacies, a certain tribalism has been antimodernism's chosen idiom." A strong undercurrent of ethnic tribalism defined the *ba'al teshuva* movement, the charge of Zionist fervor just below the surface. It was, on the one hand, a messianic fundamentalism, on the other, an intensified Jewish nationalism—an amalgam that had never before appeared in the history of Jewish life.

Ba'alei teshuva, to be sure, have only ever constituted a very small portion of American Jews. But in post-1960s America they represented the most visible edge of what was a much more widely felt trend. Even those who did not become Orthodox felt the renewed tug of Jewishness on their hearts. In his 1982 memoir, *An Orphan in History*, Paul Cowan, a *Village Voice* journalist raised in a highly assimilated Jewish home, described his process of rediscovering Jewish tradition and religion—his "way home," and "search for [his] patrimony"—which began after reporting a 1972 piece on old immigrant Jews trapped in decaying housing on the pre-gentrification Lower East Side.

Cowan saw correctly that his own journey represented a much broader generational phenomenon. "Many people who might have once explored the nation's physical or economic frontiers are journeying inward," he wrote. "Some adopt creeds that are new to them— Eastern religions, or an all-embracing born-again Christianity. But many, like me, seek to synthesize their Old World heritage with the America that has shaped their consciousness." As the countercultural energies of the 1960s burned out, people, especially young people, looked for new ways to make meaning of their lives. Protests faded to mantras, to experimentation in cults and eccentric forms of Hinduism and Buddhism, to the search for roots—to the enthusiastic embrace of ethnic pride and, for many Jews, the revaluation of their identities.

Two mutually reinforcing processes thus conjoined to produce the phenomenon that contemporary observers and scholars have called the "inward turn" in late twentieth-century American Jewish life: First, the state of Israel and Zionism came to occupy the center of Jewish life; second, and as a consequence, American Jews began to emphasize their ethno-religious roots, revalorizing traditional religious practice even when they did not return to strict observance. The inward turn expressed itself across the Jewish denominations; it was not exclusively, or even primarily, experienced by the Orthodox "returners." Reform Judaism—the once arch-assimilationist denomination, whose members in the early twentieth century *removed* their hats upon entering the sanctuary—reemphasized the Hebrew liturgy that the movement had left behind for its Anglicized hymns and recommitted the once doctrinally non-Zionist movement to Zionism.

———

The inward turn in large part determined the trajectory of my own life. My parents did not become Orthodox—although my father's sister did—but their young adult lives unfolded within a Jewish world remade in the aftermath of the Six-Day and Yom Kippur Wars, in the throes of the post–civil rights Jewish renaissance. They floated through the newly Zionist and neo-traditionalist mainstream: summers in Israel, Shabbat meals in college at the nascent Hillels and kosher dining halls. When they moved to New York City as a young couple, they found themselves with many other traditionally inclined yuppies, like Cowan himself, on the Upper West Side, the epicenter of the American Jewish revival. And when they retreated to the New Jersey suburbs to raise children, they sent my sister and me to an intensely Zionist religious day school. It was this period, I realized, that explained the books on my parents' shelves.

On the Upper West Side

In the late 1970s and through the 1980s, on the Upper West Side, that stretch of concrete between Fifty-Ninth Street and 110th, the new dominant Jewish sensibility was taking shape. It was bourgeois but skeptical of crass materialism. It was essentially parochial—this was a life among almost exclusively practicing Jews—but with a veneer of cosmopolitanism born of affluence and upward mobility. It was un-selfconsciously American, generally unalienated from American culture. But it was even more ardently Jewish. It was Zionist without apology.

Perhaps no place on the Upper West Side exemplified the synthesis of Zionist neo-traditionalism and post-sixties conservatized liberalism more than the Lincoln Square Synagogue, and perhaps no figure embodied its trajectory more than its spiritual leader, Rabbi Shlomo Riskin. Beginning in the late 1960s, Riskin transformed what had been a sleepy, moribund Conservative synagogue into a booming experiment in Orthodox outreach. In the 1970s, the synagogue became a social center for newly recommitted Jews and a meeting place for Jewish singles, which earned it its nickname, "Wink and Stare." Then, in the early 1980s, Riskin moved, along with a core of synagogue families, to the newly founded Jewish settlement of Efrat in the occupied West Bank.

The synagogue would continue to operate; it still does today. But Riskin's failure to turn his celebrity into a movement for mass American Aliyah to Israeli settlements revealed some truths about the quality of the Jewish revivalists' religion and politics. Their ritual observance was more socially than theologically informed. Their Zionism was, ultimately, a vicarious, long-distance nationalism.

Riskin was something of a *ba'al teshuva* himself. He grew up in the Bedford-Stuyvesant neighborhood of Brooklyn, raised by relatively nonobservant parents. But he was close to a devout and learned grandmother from whom he gained a love for Orthodox Judaism. As he would often recall, he chose Yeshiva University over Harvard because of the value he placed on his faith. Yet his relatively unreligious home life meant that, unlike many Orthodox rabbis raised within traditionalist enclaves, he could bridge the observant and nonobservant worlds. He understood American culture and the changes it was undergoing: the gradual movement toward gender equality, the liberalization of sexual mores. He did not compromise on matters of religious law, but he embraced certain elements of post-sixties liberalism, giving lectures on Jewish approaches to sexuality. Later, in the 2000s, he would break with Orthodox precedent and support ordaining women as rabbis.

With Israel's victory in the Six-Day War, the same messianic passion that gripped much of the organized Jewish world took hold of Riskin and his synagogue. The war, he told his congregants, marked the beginning of a new spiritual-historical epoch. The world was now in the time of *ikveta de-meshicha*, the footsteps of the messiah. "Within the walls of Lincoln Square Synagogue," one congregant recalled, "redemption had seemed near." Even, or perhaps especially, those who did not believe in divine providence of this kind still saw the appearance of Jews as fierce, triumphal warriors—the same Jews who only two decades before had been incinerated in the gas chambers—as a reversal explicable only in religious, even mystical terms.

It turned out that Riskin's take on the postwar Jewish synthesis had many buyers. "Rabbi Riskin was the Pied Piper," his former colleague Rabbi Ephraim Buchwald told me. "They used to call him Stevie Wonder." Buchwald, in his eighties when we spoke over Zoom in 2021, is an ebullient, fast talker. In the 1970s, he took over Lincoln Square's educational programming as the demand exceeded what Riskin himself could provide. In those years "Lincoln Square was exploding," Buchwald reminisced. On Friday nights and Saturday mornings, the main sanctuary, which could fit several hundred, was at capacity; late arrivals had to sit in the aisles. For those unfamiliar with the traditional liturgy, Buchwald led a beginner's service in a class-room from 1975 onward that became a phenomenon in its own right. "It was a happening," he said, borrowing, symptomatically, a term of the now obsolete '60s counterculture. "It took off. In 1981, the *New York Times* got wind of it." After that, he said, the fifty-person-capacity room "was standing room only."

Cultural trendspotters took notice of Lincoln Square. In November 1986, *New York Magazine* ran a cover story by the journalist Cathryn Jakobson titled "The New Orthodox: A Jewish Revival on the Upper West Side." The cover image depicted a young heterosexual couple standing against a dramatic sunset over the Hudson River, shot from an apartment in Lincoln Towers. The man, David Eisner, is an investment banker. His suit is crisp and dark, his blue striped tie tucked beneath his jacket. His wife, Karen, is a filmmaker. She wears a wide gray blazer; its padded shoulders extend almost halfway across the frame. Two strings of pearls drape easily across her red blouse. David looks slightly apprehensive, while Karen's gaze is more skeptical, almost defiant. Together, their image conveys power. Their clothes are bold, they are young, the implication is clear. The future—of American Judaism, and perhaps, in a sense, the country—belongs to people like them.

Jakobson's article suggested that the yuppies were finding God, embracing Gordon Gekko aspirations while flirting with Modern Orthodoxy. People like the Eisners, affluent and educated, who had recommitted to Jewish tradition, seemed to have found a way to have it all. Investment bankers informed their firm's senior partners that they had begun to observe Shabbat and therefore could no longer work on Friday nights and Saturdays. Some professional women eschewed their pantsuits for long skirts and spoke earnestly of keeping a Jewish home. But they did not give up the good life. They continued to live in spacious Manhattan apartments, which they furnished with fine modern and Israeli art. They ate at upscale kosher restaurants, which opened to feed those who maintained their dietary strictures outside the house. They sent their children to new and expensive private religious day schools. Conspicuous consumption could be reconciled with Jewish neo-traditionalism. It was not a matter of either/or.

Lincoln Square's affluence made it the epitome of an Americanized yet observant Judaism. And while this Judaism has never claimed anything close to a majority of American Jews, it was increasingly the kind of Judaism from which the leaders of American Jewish institutions, their donors, and their most active participants hailed. It was a worldview in which Americanism and Judaism fit together seamlessly, perfectly complementary. Zionism, especially as a politicized expression of Jewish pride, occupied the center of its ideological edifice. But liberalism, in a sense, remained the communal lingua franca. Its affluent, educated adherents—doctors, lawyers, investment bankers— dissented neither from the voluntarist logic of American religious life nor from the dictates of the capitalist market. Religious commitment did not impinge on the ambitions of the entrepreneurial self.

The rabbis of Lincoln Square helped to popularize a new style of Jewish worship, particularly for a traditionalist congregation. They broke with the somber mumbling of the conventional Orthodox service and the somnolescent decorum of the suburban liberal synagogue. Riskin and Buchwald's leadership was charismatic, even ecstatic. At times, Riskin would jump up and down on the pulpit as he exclaimed, almost like a Pentecostal preacher. It was a paradigm shift that a great many American rabbis, Orthodox and non-Orthodox, would attempt to follow.

Lincoln Square embodied a kind of Jewish evangelism. Its rabbis called Jews back to Judaism with the language of Jewish nationalism and ethnic pride. During Hanukkah, they assembled a massive menorah on Seventy-Second Street. They staged Passover seders outside on the sidewalk with music and loudspeakers. They acquired a van, Buchwald recalled, "outfitted with a little *aron kodesh* [holy ark] and

Torah in there." It became a fixture on the Upper West Side. "Basically," Buchwald said, "it was a vehicle to market Judaism."

To earlier generations of Jews, this behavior would have been unthinkable. For centuries, a diametrically opposed paradigm of Jewish conduct in public had prevailed. The traditional Jew, the observant Jew, the God-fearing Jew—he was supposed to keep his head down, walk humbly, avoid provocation and confrontation. The great rabbis of Europe abhorred pride and recoiled from displays of strength. The insistence of Jewish symbols on street corners would have seemed to many Jews a risky act that could draw the ire of unfriendly non-Jews.

The Zionist revolution that began in the late nineteenth century sought to banish this ideal. And it was a continuation of this same Zionist spirit that brought the Jews of the Upper West Side out to dance on Broadway and West End Avenue during Simchat Torah beginning in the 1970s, to make their presence felt by all those around them. The public display of Jewishness grew out of a renewed sense of pride, fueled by Israel's emergence as a heroic military power. Today, the celebration of Jewish ritual in public may seem unremarkable. But when it emerged in the post-sixties moment, it was like nothing that had been seen before.

Such public Jewishness also reflected, even if less than consciously, a new understanding of religion in late twentieth-century America. Religion increasingly was something that one chose. It was no longer inherited or taken for granted. And as many American Jews began to leave behind even residual practices of Jewish ritual—despite pockets of revivalism, like on the Upper West Side—leading rabbis and Jewish communal figures continued to worry that American Jewish life was in existential danger. Displays of Jewishness in public, then, were not just performances of pride but attempts to bring Jews back into the fold—proselytizing Judaism to other Jews. The greatest risk was no longer that the loud, public, unabashed celebration of Jewishness might provoke antisemitism; instead, the danger, as Buchwald saw it, was that even with dogged outreach efforts, American Judaism might still be lost to the ease and freedom of unaffiliated life. "Our parents prayed for a melting pot," Buchwald said, reprising his frequent lament. "What they've gotten is a meltdown."

What About the Messiah?

Since the nineteenth century, the strictest of Orthodox authorities have viewed Zionism as a heresy—an attempt to undo through human action the Jewish people's divinely sanctioned exile from the Land of Israel and a violation of the halachic precept that the Jewish people must accept their fate. They also saw it as a rival ideology that replaced God and his sacred commandments with secular nationalism. On the eve of World War II, Lithuanian rabbi Elchonon Wasserman described Zionism as a plot "to drive G-d out of the house of Israel, and from the hearts of the children of Israel." Rabbi Yoel Teitelbaum, the great Satmar Hasidic rebbe, described Zionism as a satanic test of the Jewish people's faith before their final, yet perpetually deferred, redemption. Even Rabbi Menachem Mendel Schneerson, the Lubavitcher Rebbe who would later wield significant influence in Israel politics, opposed the singing of "Hatikva," Israel's national anthem, because it failed to mention God.

But in the wake of the Six-Day War, even some of those who counted themselves among the stringently Orthodox began to embrace Jewish nationalism. At the very least, they sought to surf the upswell of Jewish pride.

In the case of Chabad, the shift to the embrace of public Jewishness, the emphasis on intra-Jewish evangelism, and the celebration of Jewishness through the rediscovery of tradition had begun earlier, roughly a decade after Israel's founding. In 1958, Rabbi Schneerson, then the newly minted young leader of the Chabad-Lubavitch movement, began to stress the imperative of bringing nonobservant Jews back to religious Judaism. "One must go to a place where nothing is known of Godliness, nothing is known of Judaism, nothing is even known of the Hebrew alphabet," he told an assembly of his faithful, "and ensure that the other calls out to God." This was the start of Chabad's outreach efforts for which the group would become widely known.

After the wars of 1967 and 1973, the ambient nationalist and messianic spirit fueled Chabad's intensified efforts. Rabbi Joseph Telushkin recalled how, in 1974, "parked Ryder trucks started to appear in Manhattan with their back doors rolled up, and young men with beards and hats stood inside and outside, asking passersby, 'Excuse me, are you Jewish?'" These were Chabad's "mitzvah tanks," which soon became ubiquitous in cities around the country. (There is a one-sided debate between Rabbi Buchwald and Chabad over who invented the mitzvah tank first.) Young Chabad emissaries cropped up on street corners offering to help Jewish men wrap tefillin and distributing Shabbat candles. They are still standing there today. More Americans may come in contact and participate in Chabad-led activities than they do with any other denomination or organization in contemporary American Jewish life.

The Lubavitcher Rebbe was never doctrinally Zionist. But he adamantly believed that all the Land of Israel belonged to the Jews and that the state of Israel should have expelled the Palestinians from the West Bank and into Jordan. A militarist sensibility lay just beneath the sunny efforts of his ardent followers. When they journeyed out to bring Jews back to the fold, Chabad evangelizers understood themselves as embarking on *mivzaim*, the Hebrew word for military operation. They referred to Shabbat candles by their Hebrew acronym, *neshek*, which stands for *neirot shabbos kodesh*, or holy Sabbath candles, but which is also the Hebrew word for weapon. The Lubavitcher Rebbe referred collectively to his *schluchim*, his emissaries, as *tzivos Hashem*, the army of God.

Well-established, conventional modern Orthodox authorities likewise proved utterly susceptible to the messianic fervor of the period. In the pages of *Tradition*, the journal published by the Rabbinical Council of America, Modern Orthodoxy's leading figures in the United States and Israel debated the "religious meaning of the Six-Day War." While some rabbis, like the late Norman Lamm, president of Yeshiva University, cautioned against viewing the war through a messianic lens, others, especially his Israeli counterparts, insisted otherwise. In the words of Rabbi Pinchas Hacohen Peli, Israel's victory reflected more than just the footsteps of the messianic age. "We are already on a very advanced stage of the Messianic era," he stressed, "not just on the verge of it." The Ashkenazi chief rabbi of Haifa, Rabbi Eliyahu Shear Yashuv Cohen, put an even greater emphasis on the eschatological quality of the events. "There is no doubt in my mind that we are now living in *yemot ha-mashiach* [the messianic era]," he wrote. ". . . I have no other explanation for the miracles of the Six-Day War but the belief that we are part of the final *geulah* [redemption]."

Not even the Haredi, or ultra-Orthodox, standard-bearer, the Agudath Israel organization, escaped the nationalist hysteria that gripped American Jewish life. In the summer of 1980, *Jewish Observer*, the magazine published by Agudath Israel, released a special issue focused on the growth of the *ba'al teshuva* movement. The issue contained a pseudonymous reflection by a newly Orthodox Jewish student that exemplified the combination of messianism, pride, and violence that had swept through institutional Jewish life over the course of the decade. "Singing the *Gemora* tune with redoubled vigor, in the drone of the jet planes, I felt elevated, way above them, and had a new exciting thought—'This is the core, the essence of the Holy Land!'" wrote the self-named Avraham ben Shmuel. He then switched into a hortatory mode, a hybrid of Zionist militarism and familiar American vernacular:

Praise the Lord and pass the ammunition! Bombard the
PLO—and the evil inclination within us! Bring *both* to

submission! And let us not forget to pray, and say *Tehilim* [psalms] and ask fervently for *hashem* to speedily bring about the unimaginably sweet reality of seeing all our brothers and sisters, the whole *mishpacha* [family], united, as once on Har Sinai [Mount Sinai], in love and fear of Him, and may we all, soon be able to say *Ze Keili* [this is my God].

Downstream from Eschatology

Most American Jews, to be sure, did not know of, and probably could not have participated in, the conversation about the Six-Day War's theological significance or the criteria for the dawn of the messianic age. Yet these debates nonetheless had far-reaching consequences for the texture of American Jewish life. Whether in the form of outright religious messianism or Zionist zeal at fever pitch, the belief that Jewish existence would never be the same after 1967 and 1973 was shared across denominations and levels of observance. The flexible (and paradoxically named) Conservative movement, whose siddur I grew up using, adopted a "Prayer for the State of Israel" that described the modern state of Israel as *reishit tzemichat geulateinu*—"the beginning of our redemption." But this represented, again, less a straightforward theological assertion than a nationalist statement and cultural commitment dressed in theological language. Israel had become the paramount matter of importance in Jewish life. It had come to supersede, in the words of former leftist M. J. Rosenberg, the Torah, the commandments, "the Mosaic law itself."

In this sense, Rabbi Lamm's learned resistance to the messianic disposition turned out to be more prescient than he could have imagined. In the 1967 *Tradition* symposium, Lamm had insisted that the messianic age was not something that one could simply declare. The Messiah could not be reduced to a shift in geopolitics. To do so was to begin walking down the path to Reform Judaism, even to secularism:

toward relinquishing the binding obligations of Jewish law and scripture that defined Orthodoxy.

He was right. But because he was still a religious Zionist, he did not go far enough. The elevation of the modern nation-state of Israel to the level of supreme religious significance did not pose a threat just to Orthodoxy; it posed a threat to Judaism itself.

When the Jewish ethnic revival fizzled out toward the end of the 1980s, it was, for the most part, not traditional religious practice that lingered on in mainstream affiliated Jewish life but militant nationalism. What appeared at first as the flowering of a new religiosity turned out—with the important exception of the small cohort who would go on to lead mainline affiliated Judaism—a passing product of a tumultuous time.

Still, the cumulative effect of the ethnic revival on American Jewish culture was transformational. From the totalizing embrace of Israel and Zionism flowed a new enthusiasm for Hebrew poetry and prayer. Israeli music became a central feature of Jewish religious and cultural life. A new Zionized liturgy crystallized.

These songs formed the backdrop of my childhood. The tunes of the *chalutzim*, of Israel's settling pioneers—songs like "Zum Gali Gali" and "Emek Sheli" as well as the hippie-Hasidic renditions of liturgy popularized by Rabbi Shlomo Carlebach—this was the music that I grew up on as a grade school student in the early 2000s. I enthusiastically chanted "Am Yisrael Chai," Carlebach's anthem written for the Soviet Jewry movement, during school celebrations of Israel's Independence Day. During assemblies to mark Israel's consequent conquest and occupation of East Jerusalem and the West Bank, my classmates and I tearfully sang Naomi Shemer's "Jerusalem of Gold" as if we ourselves could breathe "the mountain air, clear as wine," but which was, in reality, 6,000 miles away.

Beneath this surface of sweetness, there was, however, a hard and stubborn militarism. The gentle melodies I grew up singing often glorified violence and sanctified war. Shemer's iconic "Jerusalem of Gold" was, in practice, a paean to conquest and territorial expansion. We gave almost no thought to non-Jewish causalities of Israel's military struggles—the Palestinians.

III.

In the middle of the upheaval of the long 1970s, the sociologist Bernard Rosenberg and Irving Howe took stock of the already visible changes that the decade had wrought on American Jewish life. They saw the shift primarily in political terms. In a 1974 article published in *Dissent* magazine, they asked, "Are American Jews turning to the Right?" Even by then, it seemed undeniable that American Jewish life was in the process of restructuring itself along new ideological lines.

It had taken, they confirmed, "an inward turn." The narrow politics of Jewish self-interest as propounded by Norman Podhoretz and the neoconservatives was quickly gaining ground. Expressions of Jewish pride, often verging on chauvinism, were becoming more common. In the past, Jewish organizations like the Workmen's Circle had maintained democratic—and even social democratic—values as part of the mainstream of Jewish life. Groups like the American Jewish Congress and the American Jewish Committee had done the same for their moderate, civil rights liberalism. But now Zionism—expressed most often through support for Israel and the conviction that it represented the central commitment and telos of Jewish existence—had become the singular focus of Jewish communal life. It had supplanted nearly all other commitments once held by most American Jewish organizations.

The basic material conditions of Jewish life—class and demography— had also undergone a fundamental change. The postwar years saw the large-scale rise of American Jews into the middle and upper-middle classes. "There is no longer a proletarian majority, even among immigrant Jews," Rosenberg and Howe wrote. The once robust Jewish labor movement had withered. Jewish socialism as a mass politics was but a fading memory. In its place stood the pillars of the postwar consensus: a celebratory embrace of Americanism, an increasingly truculent pro-Israelism, and a liberalism now buttressed by the individualist spirit of 1968.

Unlike many of their upwardly mobile and affluent non-Jewish counterparts, however, most newly middle-class and upper-middle-class Jews did not become conservatives or Republicans as the long 1970s wore on. They never would. The right-wing Jewish intellectual Milton Himmelfarb famously (and frequently) lamented that Jews "earn like Episcopalians but vote like Puerto Ricans." For many Jewish liberals, as the writer Leonard Fein would later stress, this reflected an important, if vestigial, aspect of the old Jewish commitment to the underdog and the open society. Jewish intellectuals might wish that most American Jews saw more in their Judaism than voting for Democrats, but at least they had not fully switched sides.

Still, Rosenberg and Howe, like many other left-leaning Jews in the long 1970s, found reasons to worry that American Jewish life was sliding to the right. The aftermath of the 1960s had left a heavy mark on American Jewish politics. And it was not just Israel's rapid victory in 1967. Under the shadow of the riots that followed Martin Luther King Jr.'s assassination, American Jews with the means to do so completed their migration to suburban enclaves, which had begun years earlier. (In part, this is why my parents grew up in the suburbs of Westchester and New Jersey.) Those who could not leave the cities stayed behind and clashed with their African American neighbors over desegregation and busing in Forest Hills and the excesses of efforts to assert community control of schools in Ocean Hill–Brownsville, Brooklyn. (This is, in part, why my grandmother Charlotte, a public school teacher in the Bronx, joined the walkouts by New York City teachers in 1968.) Gradually, vocal institutional support for the civil rights movement began to give way to suspicion or even outright hostility to Black power as Jewish communal leaders emphasized the pursuit of Jewish self-interest and saw it threatened by the problem of "Black antisemitism."

Meanwhile, a less perceptible but no less significant change in the organizational structure of American Jewish life was underway. As Jewish communal institutions began to shift their focus from mutual aid and civil rights work to fundraising for Zionist causes, the relative power of wealthy donors increased. Organizations such as the American Jewish Committee and the Anti-Defamation League increasingly eschewed outward-facing work for Israel advocacy and other particularist concerns. From within the ranks of the Soviet Jewry movement and right-wing Zionist groups, a new generation of communal leaders took the reins from their predecessors, whose ideology reflected the changes of the long 1970s. "Certainly," Rosenberg and Howe wrote, "we are witnessing a regrouping of forces within the Jewish world, which will result in a conservatizing of its dominant liberalism."

The Bifurcation of American Jewish Life

Rosenberg and Howe were right, although in a very particular way. As historical processes go, the inward and rightward regrouping happened rapidly, within the span of the long 1970s. Yet its conservatizing effects were felt very unevenly.

American Jewish life was bifurcating. Among the broad American Jewish laity, unlike the communal leadership, there was no great lurch toward political conservatism, although there was certainly a reappreciation of Jewish particularism and a wholesale embrace of Zionism. No Republican presidential candidate ever exceeded Ronald Reagan's 40 percent of the Jewish vote in 1980. What Norman Podhoretz hoped would prove an inflection point turned out merely to be an outlier.

Yet it was not only that the Jewish communal leadership had begun to diverge politically from their putative constituents. They had literally begun to grow apart. Most American Jews *were* drifting away from institutional and religious life. Mainline affiliated Judaism claimed to represent most American Jews—but more and more American Jews had hardly anything to do with the organizations that spoke in their name.

Within the Jewish communal institutions and among their leaders and most devoted members was thus where the conservative shift was most acutely felt—where the inward turn became not simply a sociological trend but an ideological project. The demographic that Jewish sociologists call the "committed core," the Jews who engage daily in Jewish communal life—board members and synagogue presidents, part-time teachers, volunteer prayer leaders—these were the people who took the spirit of the 1970s inward turn and institutionalized it. They articulated the new communal consensus. While they have never constituted the majority of American Jews, they have set the terms and tone of American Jewish life ever since.

Even by the early 1980s, it was clear they had completed their project of transforming Jewish communal politics, largely along the lines that Rosenberg and Howe had predicted. It was the same transformation that had appeared in other studies, like Charles Liebman's 1979 examination of the American Jewish Congress. Or take the scholar Jonathan S. Woocher's 1981 survey of emerging local Jewish leaders. Their responses to his questions about their views on Jewish identity illustrated what Woocher called "the ascendancy of Jewish survivalism" as the "reigning ideology of Jewish communal life." The survey subjects named as their most serious concerns "the conflict between Israel and its neighbors," "the treatment of Jews in the Soviet Union," and "the high rate of intermarriage." Asked by Woocher to rank communal priorities, they listed "to provide financial support to Israel" first. They listed "to provide welfare services for anyone in need" second to last.

To call this an inward turn would be an understatement. Instead, it was a definitive abandonment of the values that had enabled American Jewish integration and prosperity during the first half of the century. It was a rejection of the idea that Jewish organizations had a substantial obligation to care for their non-Jewish neighbors. It was a final departure from the belief that there was a role for Jewish organizations to play in improving the overall conditions of American life. "Among communally active Jews today," Woocher wrote in 1981, "there is a substantial consensus that Jewish group survival and welfare, rather than integration within or modification of American society, are the primary collective tasks of the hour." That hour lasted into the present day.

In his 1986 book *Sacred Survival*, which expanded the research of his earlier survey, Woocher argued that survivalism had not simply become the dominant ideology of Jewish communal life. Survivalism had become the new Jewish "civil religion." Its focus was the securing of particular Jewish interests in the material realm: fundraising, lobbying, and organizing. And Israel was almost always the cause to which such efforts were dedicated. "Conspicuously missing from the picture of civil religion," Woocher wrote, was "reference to God or some form of transcendent deity." Survivalism replaced traditional Judaism with nationalist politics.

Yet at its core, survivalism was also a contradictory ideology. It saw the Jewish people as embattled: threatened geopolitically—vis-à-vis Israel's wars against its Arab neighbors and the plight of Soviet Jewry—and existentially, by insufficiently high levels of endogamy in the United States. There was something paradoxical about the simultaneous anxieties of physical safety, on the one hand, and assimilation on the other. The world according to the Jewish survivalist, Woocher observed, is "at once too hostile and too hospitable for them to feel secure about the Jewish future."

Survivalism furnished the vocabulary for Jewish communal life's turn to the right. As employed by Jewish communal leaders and prominent Jewish intellectuals, the rhetoric of survivalism stressed, as the scholar Michael Staub wrote, "the paramount moral importance of pursuing Jewish self-interest and worked to make those who called for

altruism or self-sacrifice not just ridiculous, and not even only obnox-
iously self-righteous, but also genuinely dangerous." Survivalism, Staub
wrote, enabled Jewish communal leaders to frame the retreat from
older civil rights and social democratic commitments as "not only appropriate but ethical in its own right."

The survivalist lens painted all matters as life or death. To dissent
from the Zionist consensus was thus to put Jewish lives at risk; to suggest that Jews ought not to focus exclusively on their own pain was to
make Jews vulnerable to marginalization at the hands of others. The
dilemmas of organized Jewish life—rising rates of disaffiliation and
intermarriage—took on the weight of a mortal threat to "Jewish
continuity"—in other words, to survival.

The Jewish institutional world has been defined by more than four
decades of survivalist ideological hegemony. The worldviews of the
men—and they have almost all been men—who led the Jewish communal establishment from the 1980s onward were forged in the rightward
retrenchment of the long 1970s: men like longtime Anti-Defamation
League CEO Abraham Foxman, former American Jewish Committee
chief executive David Harris, and former Conference of Presidents of
Major American Jewish Organizations leader Malcolm Hoenlein.
They were products of the period's Zionist fervor, ethnic revival, and
militant anti-communism. As the self-appointed leaders of American
Jewry, they enforced the postwar communal consensus with vigilance,
without hesitation, and with zero tolerance for opposition.

3

RABIN SQUARE

I.

In Tel Aviv, a small corner of the restless city sits still in perpetual mourning. The memorial to Yitzhak Rabin, the Israeli prime minister assassinated by a far-right ultranationalist in 1995, lies quietly tucked behind the city hall parking lot, set aside from the wide and bustling Ibn Gabirol Street. It is a simple shrine. An array of dark, uneven slabs of rock marks the place where Rabin stood the moment he was shot. It suggests, at once, split earth and an altar: the sacrifice of Isaac, *Yitzhak*, only this time God did not spare him. On the wall of an adjacent building, graffiti and wheat-pasted posters put up in the days after Rabin's death—exhortations to remember, calls for peace—are preserved behind a glass plate. Nearly three decades since, the city of Tel Aviv and Israel itself have changed dramatically. But this gash of concrete has remained the same.

The site became a monument even before the significance of Rabin's killing could fully be known. Thousands of mainly young and secular Israelis kept vigil there, from the night when Yigal Amir fired the fatal shots into Rabin's back and for many days after. Now the plaza across from the city hall, once known as Kings of Israel Square, bears Rabin's name. Since 1995 the Israeli peace camp has held an annual rally there to mark his death and to attest that some fragment of his vision of

territorial compromise still lives on. In recent years these rallies have
become anemic. People have begun to ask if, perhaps, it would not be
better to bury Rabin with finality, to give up on this melancholy ritual
and relinquish the hope that his vision will someday return in another
form.

There was a parallel memorial at the front of the religious day
school in New Jersey where I spent the first decade of my school-going
life. It was a small garden that greeted the students upon their entry.
Each morning I would walk past the bed of rumpled flowers, a wilting
tulip or two and a few sad peonies. A faux gilded plaque stood in their
midst bearing the words "Yitzhak Rabin, 1922–1995," almost as if he
were interred there. Rabin was killed a year after I was born, and I,
like all children born in the nineties and after, would never feel the
sense of possibility that he embodied for so many Israelis and American Jews. Instead, Rabin hovered above us like a long-deceased grandfather, peering down through his thick glasses from faded pictures
hung high on the school walls. We learned little about Rabin's politics,
only that he had advocated for some vaporous notion of peace. We
learned even less about the man who killed him. Rabin's death was a
natural disaster, an act of God.

The memorial garden in front of my school was more than a memorial to Rabin the man. It was a memorial to the concatenation of aspirations, commitments, and desires that Rabin incarnated while he was
alive, and which reflected the American Jewish communal consensus
at the apex of its strength.

For many American Jews, Rabin as the leader of a peace-seeking
Israel testified to the plausibility of a liberal Zionism, of reconciling
their commitment to liberal democracy with their support for a Jewish-
majority ethno-state. At the same time, the signing of the first Oslo
Accords between Rabin and Palestine Liberation Organization (PLO)
leader Yasser Arafat on the White House lawn, in a heavily stage-
managed ceremony presided over by President Bill Clinton, confirmed
for them America's providential role in Jewish history. In the early

1990s, Israel under Rabin seemed poised on the cusp of resolving its conflict with the Palestinians, headed toward becoming just another normal nation, all the while guided by America's steadying hand. The pillars of Americanism, Zionism, and liberalism never looked sturdier.

But just beneath this optimistic façade, the communal consensus had begun to crack. And it was the Jewish right, in Israel and America, that delivered the shattering blow. In Israel, radical West Bank settlers and messianic ultranationalists fomented the atmosphere of religious violence that encouraged Yigal Amir, a law student in his twenties, to kill the prime minister. In America, while most American Jews tacitly supported Rabin's peace plan, their views hardly found representation within Jewish communal organizations. Instead, Rabin's opponents, right-wing and religious Zionist Jews, spoke the loudest, and, like their Israeli counterparts, frequently in violent terms. As the eighties gave way to the nineties, the messianic fervor and nationalist revivalism that had increasingly defined observant Jewish communities during the previous decade hardened by the early nineties into vociferous hostility to any Israeli withdrawal from territory under its control.

To be sure, Israel had also faced intense criticism in the 1980s, including from some American Jews. In 1982, Israel's invasion of Lebanon provoked international outcry. The Sabra and Shatila massacre—in which the forces of the right-wing Lebanese Christian Phalange militia raped, killed, and dismembered at least eight hundred civilians under the glow of the Israeli army's flares—received widespread media coverage and prompted condemnation around the world. At the start of the war, some prominent American Jewish intellectuals, such as Saul Bellow, Alfred Kazin, Irving Howe, and Michael Walzer, published an op-ed in the *New York Times* denouncing Israel's invasion while asserting the fundamental justness of Zionism. After the Sabra and Shatila massacre several months later, even leading figures such as Rabbi Arthur Hertzberg denounced Israel's political leadership while affirming that Israel "is not a militaristic country."

But such criticism did not soften the American Jewish establishment's unequivocal backing for the Israeli government. In fact, the opposite happened. In the aftermath of Israel's invasion of Lebanon, American Jewish organizations began to devote increasingly substantial resources to rebutting criticism of Israel, discrediting journalists, and denouncing intellectuals who challenged Israeli policies. As a response to criticism of the 1982 war, the Jewish communal establishment developed the strategies it has used ever since to bolster Israel's image in the public sphere. "In its desperate effort to insist that the images and reports filtering out of Lebanon were to be doubted or even disbelieved," journalist Natasha Roth-Rowland writes, Jewish establishment organizations wrote the playbook "automatically deployed when Israeli aggression makes headlines. The dissembling; the accusations of bias and lying by omission or misrepresentation; the minimizing or dismissal of Palestinian and Arab suffering."

Right-wing antipathy to the Rabin government shattered fully the post-1967 taboo on criticizing Israel from within the Jewish communal mainstream. But the right did not do so alone. They had help from the leaders of establishment Jewish organizations who met right-wing incitement with muted rebukes and, just as often, with silence. The American Jewish establishment had long insisted that its policy was to support the Israeli government unconditionally. But when Rabin's government moved toward territorial compromise, that support did not simply become conditional; it morphed into opposition. Rabin's death would mark the breaking point, after which Israel would never again be a matter of uncomplicated consensus within the Jewish communal mainstream. The consensus on Israel in American Jewish life had begun to fracture, ruptured by the tensions it had once contained.

A Death Foretold

Yitzhak Rabin died a victim of the violence that he warned was threatening to overwhelm his country. On the evening of November 5, 1995, he appeared at a rally in Tel Aviv aimed at boosting support for the negotiations between Israel and the PLO. Before a crowd of roughly 100,000 supporters, he described Israel as besieged from within by far-right nationalists, messianic settlers, and religious extremists united in their opposition to his plan for peace. "Violence," he said, "is eroding the foundation of Israeli democracy." As the rally closed, he sang with the crowd "Shir L'Shalom," the anthem of the country's peace movement. Then, as Rabin descended the stairs from the stage, Yigal Amir—at the time twenty-five—fired three hollow-tipped bullets into Rabin's back. He was pronounced dead in the emergency room of Tel Aviv's Ichilov hospital that night. It would turn out to be, as journalist Dexter Filkins wrote, "one of history's most effective political murders."

The Israeli right never accepted Rabin's vision for territorial compromise with the Palestinians, even though Rabin had been elected with a mandate to pursue it. Rabin never said the words "Palestinian state," yet even the mere proposal to withdraw from parts of the occupied West Bank was unacceptable. Right-wing hawks accused Rabin of endangering Israeli lives. Messianic settlers denounced Rabin for betraying the Torah and violating God's promise to the Jewish people. Ensconced in hilltop yeshivas in the occupied West Bank, hard-line rabbis debated whether Rabin was a *rodef*, a person who acts with the intent to kill innocents, or a *moser*, a person who endangers the lives of Jews by placing them in the hands of the enemy. In both cases the penalty, according to Jewish law, is death.

Backed by a sense of divine justice, Amir appointed himself judge and executioner. But while he pulled the trigger, Rabin's murder was the culmination of a collective endeavor. By killing Rabin, Amir did not just kill a man. As the following years would demonstrate, Amir also killed a possibility, however faint it may have been: that of a negotiated resolution to the Israeli-Palestinian conflict.

Rabin's assassination was a death foretold. "There will be attempted assassinations," predicted Yehoshafat Harkabi, former director of Israel's military intelligence, toward the end of 1994. "Rabin will not die a natural death." In the months before his killing, Israeli security officials recommended that Rabin wear a bulletproof vest. He refused. He was not naïve or blind to threats posed by the right. But he did not, he could not, believe that he would be their victim. He had fought in the founding wars of the state. That he would be killed by his country-men was inconceivable.

The Israeli leaders who incited the violence that ultimately killed Rabin were never punished. Not only that, since his death, they have governed the country almost without interruption. Ariel Sharon and Benjamin Netanyahu presided over rallies where throngs of demon-strators brandished posters depicting Rabin in a Nazi SS uniform, with Yasser Arafat's kaffiyeh, with blood on his hands; where demon-strators held aloft coffins bearing Rabin's name; and where they chanted "with blood and fire we will expel Rabin" and "Rabin is a traitor." On the podium of the Knesset, Netanyahu denounced the Oslo Accords in the most severe terms: as "an attack on the basis of our existence and a real danger to our future in the Land of Israel." Little interpretation was required to divine what this implied. As a young far-right Kahanist militant, Itamar Ben-Gvir attacked Rabin's motorcade and tore the Cadillac symbol from its grille. In 2022, Net-anyahu appointed Ben-Gvir national security minister, responsible for overseeing the Israeli police.

The Revolt of the Right

In America, most Jews in the 1990s said they supported Rabin's pro-posed territorial compromise. But many of the most outspoken pro-Israel advocates and Jewish establishment leaders were less enthusiastic about Rabin's plan. They were products of the inward turn, shaped by the nationalist upsurge and religious revival of the preceding decade and a half. Often religiously observant, if not Modern Orthodox, and politically right leaning, they shared much more with Rabin's opponents than with the Israeli prime minister. When their side was in power, they clamped down on criticism of the Israeli government, which they construed as tantamount to betrayal of the Jewish people. When their side was out of power, different rules applied.

Leading pro-Israel figures in America mobilized to stop Rabin's agenda in tandem with their political allies in Israel. They "concluded that the Rabin government was on a suicidal course," journalist J. J. Goldberg wrote, "and they set out to derail it." They pushed for measures in Congress aimed at preventing the U.S. government from shepherding the Israelis and the Palestinians toward some kind of peace. "Others," Goldberg wrote, "threatened to withhold donations from Jewish organizations that supported Israel" unless they opposed Rabin's plan. And once the first Oslo Accord was signed, the powerful lobby AIPAC and other right-wing Jewish operatives pushed Congress to undermine the U.S. programs meant to enable its actualization and block crucial aid to the Palestinians.

Right-wing violence and terrorism also spread from Israel to the United States. In January 1994, two extremist Jewish groups called the Shield of David and the Maccabee Squad sent bombs to the Midtown Manhattan offices of Americans for Peace and the New Israel Fund, both liberal Zionist organizations that supported Rabin and the Oslo Accords. The far-right groups hoped that the bombs, which did not explode, would mark the opening of a "Jewish civil war." Right-wing activists shouted death threats at Colette Avital, Israel's consul general in New York, during her speaking events to explain Rabin's plan. They pelted Itamar Rabinovich, Israel's ambassador to the United States and a Rabin confidant, with eggs and tomatoes. These small acts of protest carried with them an undercurrent of greater menace. "I think," said Rabbi Avi Weiss, a staunch opponent of the Oslo Accords, in September 1995, "there is going to be a Jewish bloodbath."

Weiss was one to know. Alongside Lincoln Square's Shlomo Riskin, he had shepherded many young American Jews awakened by the nationalist and religious revival of the long 1970s into lives of greater Jewish practice and Zionist ardor. He had also become a celebrity of sorts for his prominent role in the Soviet Jewry movement and his affinity for attention-grabbing tactics. In 1989, for instance, Weiss staged a sit-in at a Carmelite convent near the site of Auschwitz, which he denounced as an affront to the Holocaust's victims. He was, therefore, plugged into roiling right-wing Zionist, anti-communist Jewish grassroots. While he distanced himself from the terroristic tactics of the extremist rabbi Meir Kahane (who was killed in 1990 by a Palestinian militant), Weiss respected Kahane and maintained a friendship with him. "Deep down, I loved Meir," Weiss wrote in his 2015 memoir, *Open Up the Iron Door.* "I believed in him and his sincerity." In Israel, the same Kahane's followers plotted and successfully carried out Rabin's assassination.

But Kahanist fellow travelers were far from the only ones who denounced Rabin as an enemy of the Jewish people and as violator of the Torah. American Jewish opposition was deeper than the Brooklyn vigilante fringe. American rabbis, many but not all of them religious Zionists, echoed and amplified in their sermons and public speeches the calls for Rabin's death. "He who gives away parts of the land, he who kills him first is rewarded," declared Rabbi Abraham Hecht, then president of the (Orthodox) Rabbinical Alliance of America. "Rabin qualifies as an enemy and therefore is subject to the rule, act swiftly to kill the person who comes to kill you," stated a prominent Chabad-Lubavitch rabbi in Florida. At Yeshiva University, the flagship institution of American Modern Orthodoxy, Rabbi Hershel Schachter accused Rabin of hating God and the Torah and described his policies as "national suicide." Rabbi Moshe Tendler, another Yeshiva University rabbi, declaimed that Rabin's supporters were complicit in murder.

At Congregation Bnai Yeshurun in Teaneck, a fifteen-minute drive from my childhood home, Rabbi Steven Pruzansky called the Rabin-led Israeli government the "Rabin Judenrat," a reference to the Nazi-created councils that oversaw the Jewish ghettos during the Holocaust.

Pruzansky also distributed to his congregants a prayer that called on God to "thwart the conspiracy of those destroyers and demolishers who desire to tear apart the land of our heritage." To his congregants, the allusion to Rabin's plan to withdraw Israeli presence from the occupied West Bank was no doubt clear.

The nationalist and messianic energies unleashed during the long 1970s had begun to overwhelm American Jewish life and destabilize it. The people who vituperated against Rabin, and those who nodded along silently in agreement, saw themselves as ultra-committed Zionists. They identified strongly with Israel. They imbued the state with religious, even messianic significance. But this also meant that their Zionism could not accommodate Israeli territorial compromise. Rabin appeared to them as a traitor for endangering the contiguity of the Land of Greater Israel, all of which they hoped would fall, one day, under Jewish sovereignty. Having adopted the blunt litmus test of "Is it good for the Jews?" as the defining criterion of their politics, they judged Rabin and found him lacking.

The magnitude of American Jewish opposition to his government exasperated Rabin. "We are ashamed that you are not partners," he told American Jewish communal leaders at a closed-door meeting in October 1995, which the most vociferous opponents of his peace plan boycotted. Rabin also recognized that this hostility constituted an unprecedented rupture in the diaspora-Israel relationship. "Never before have we witnessed attempts by Americans who live here to put pressure on Congress against the policies of the government of Israel," he said. "It cannot be tolerated."

And yet it was. Many of the leading Jewish establishment figures turned a blind eye to the incitement against Rabin for far too long because they agreed with his opponents on substance, even if they rejected their vitriolic style. They were part of the same nationalist milieu: the survivalist, "committed core" of American Jewish life whose Zionist pride had hardened into a near-fascistic militarism. Rabbi Pruzansky's remarks, for instance, only made national headlines when they prompted Anti-Defamation League CEO Abraham Foxman to renounce his membership to Pruzansky's synagogue in September 1995—just five weeks before Rabin's murder.

When Israeli officials sought help from establishment leaders in stopping the violent rhetoric emanating from American Jewish communities, their pleas fell on deaf ears. Israel's consul general in New York, Colette Avital, reached out to Malcolm Hoenlein, leader of the Conference of Presidents and one of the most powerful yet least-known American Jewish figures, but he reportedly "spurned repeated entreaties" from her to intervene and quell the incitement. That was no coincidence. Hoenlein himself was a right-wing, religious settlement advocate who had also emerged as a communal leader in the 1970s from within the ranks of the Soviet Jewry movement. Even while he claimed to occupy a communal role above partisan politics, he made it no secret that the Rabin-led Labor government was politically anathema to him.

The Characteristic Disjuncture

But if most American Jews said that they supported Rabin when polled, how was it that their views did not receive stronger representation?

The reason is that by the 1990s a disjuncture had emerged at the heart of American Jewish politics. The overwhelmingly liberal majority of American Jews simply were not involved, not even aware, of intra-Jewish communal politics. In his 1996 book *Jewish Power*, journalist J. J. Goldberg, former editor of the *Forward*, wrote of the "yawning chasm of ignorance and mutual incomprehension" that divided "the Jewish community's leaders from their presumed followers." And this chasm was an ideological and financial gulf as much as it was informational and organizational. It separated, Goldberg wrote, "the activists who conduct the Jewish community's business and represent its interests to the larger society, and the broader population of

American Jews who are almost entirely unaware of the work being done in their name." The chasm persists to this day.

The creation of the communal consensus had been possible in part because, in the immediate postwar years, the Jewish institutional leadership *did* generally reflect the views of most American Jews. It was not simply enforced from the top down. Americanism, Zionism, and liberalism were genuinely held dear across a wide swath of American Jewish life. Yet this consensus was also the product of the mid-century moment: a time defined by big institutions, mass-membership organizations, a dense civil society. The upheavals of the 1960s marked this moment's end.

The new cohort of communal leaders, fueled by the Zionist zeal and religious nationalism of the long 1970s, could not accept an Israeli government—moderate, secular, vaguely socially democratic—that did not share their views. They believed in the abstract, divine right of the Jewish people to the entire Land of Israel. Rabin believed that what was sacred was not land but Israeli security, the lives of Israeli people, above all else.

The most dogged of American Zionists thought that they were defending Zionism from the threat posed by Rabin's readiness for territorial compromise. In fact, their anti-Rabin vitriol fatally cracked the communal consensus on Zionism that for decades sustained the ideological edifice of American Jewish life.

The Inability to Mourn

After Rabin's murder, some communal leaders began the soul-searching and self-criticism that was long overdue. "When there were rabbinic colleagues in our midst that came forth with inflammatory rhetoric," acknowledged Rabbi Marc Schneier, "we did not respond to these very divisive remarks."

Yet the mood of introspection that crept over American Jewish life in the wake of Rabin's murder was not to last. Shortly after Rabin's death, liberal and Rabin-aligned American Jewish groups moved to organize a memorial event in conjunction with Israel's foreign ministry. When establishment Jewish groups like the Conference of Presidents sought to join in the organization, to give the event their imprimatur and to frame the event as an opportunity for communal unity, right-wing and Orthodox groups blocked them. They announced that they would participate in Rabin's memorial event only under strict conditions: that it would not entail any endorsement of the Oslo Accords and Rabin's plan for territorial compromise. They would, in other words, agree to pay lip service to the notion of a communal consensus, but they would not deign to respect Rabin's vision, even after his death.

There were fears that this opposition would prove insurmountable. Yet, in the end, the establishment organizations acquiesced to the right-wing and Orthodox groups' demands. In December 1995 an array of American Jewish organizations managed to put on a memorial gathering attended by 15,000 people at New York's Madison Square Garden. Its purpose was to reaffirm the communal consensus that was so evidently fraying. Accordingly, the organizers went to great lengths to stress that mourning for Rabin transcended politics, and to appease the right-wing and Orthodox dissenters. The result was that "all specific references to the peace process for which Rabin died were prohibited in promoting and publicizing" the event, observed journalist Lawrence Cohler-Esses. The event itself was "purged of references to the peace process that Yitzhak Rabin had died defending."

But even that was not enough to satisfy the staunchest anti-Rabin hard-liners. The National Council of Young Israel, a right-wing Modern Orthodox group, and the Zionist Organization of America (ZOA), an old Likud-aligned organization, boycotted the memorial event. (These groups would both play central roles in the creation of a right-wing Jewish counter-establishment during the Trump presidency.)

The Rabin memorial in New York event thus reflected, if not a turning point in American Jewish politics, then the crystallization of shift that had been years in the making. The decades of the broad consensus had ended. The investments and alliances of Jewish communal organizations would no longer reflect the broadly held views of American Jews. Instead, right-wing and Orthodox groups, representing statistically less than a quarter of the American Jewish population, would exert ultimate and uncontested veto power over the decisions of establishment Jewish organizations like the Conference of Presidents, the Jewish Federations, and of course the powerful lobby AIPAC.

American Jewish opposition to Rabin's peace plan gave the lie to the claim that wherever the Israeli government went, the organized American Jewish community would follow. After Rabin's assassination, the consolidation of right-wing dominance over Jewish establishment organizations would guarantee that American Jewish communal politics would never deviate from the Likud line, whether or not the Israeli right was in power. And lucky for them: since 1995 the Israeli right has enjoyed nearly uninterrupted political dominance, in power for all but two and a half years over the last three decades.

The shift in the dominant tone of American Jewish communal life was not confined to matters of Israeli policy. American Jewish politics, once dominated by arch-secularists and liberal assimilationists, also assumed a stronger tribalist and religious inflection. Its general outlook took on a more fearful and even more survivalist cast. Although Jews in America had never been more secure and prosperous, the conservative, post-1970s Jewish communal leadership described Jewish life as imperiled on all sides: by insufficient endogamy, which had produced the "continuity crisis"; by antisemitism, conceived of as an eternal transhistorical force; and by Palestinian nationalist militants and their anti-imperialist supporters in the West.

Beatification

Only once Rabin was buried, and with him his vision for territorial compromise, could he become a figure of communal consensus—the kind of figure that a religious day school might memorialize outside its front door. Rabin, the Israeli leader who spoke of peace, ceased to pose a threat to territorial maximalists and right-wing Zionists. In death he became useful.

After his assassination, Rabin became a stand-in for an imagined Israel that might have been, for a better and more attractive Israel, as the real country became a harsher and more intolerant place. Against critics of Israeli policies, professional Israel advocates found that they could now brandish his legacy. As the two-state solution that Rabin seemed to support began to appear increasingly infeasible, pro-Israel groups like AIPAC—the same AIPAC that had worked against Rabin—adopted the rhetoric of territorial compromise as a way to shield Israel from criticism. For them, Rabin offered proof that Israel really *did* want peace, and that it was the Palestinians who were to blame for the continuation of the conflict.

It helped that hagiographies sanded down Rabin's rougher edges, transforming him into a peacenik that he never was, construing his peace plan as more ambitious in retrospect than it was at the time. "It is wrong to remember and commemorate Rabin as a dovish leader," the former diplomat and Rabin confidant Itamar Rabinovich wrote in his biography of the late Israeli premier. Instead, "Rabin was a centrist leader preoccupied with Israel's security, and he came to the conclusion that the country should seek to moderate and eventually settle its conflict with its Arab neighbors." Yet the fantasy of Rabin as a starry-eyed dove proved too appealing for many to relinquish, especially after his death. American Jews wanted a comforting illusion.

In part but not only for these reasons, the image of Israel that Rabin embodied has retained its persistent totemic quality for many American Jews. The brief period of his tenure still carries a near-mythic significance. Rabin, after all, was an old warrior, a former defense minister who ordered Israeli soldiers to break the bones of Palestinian demonstrators during the first intifada, the popular Palestinian uprising that began in 1987. But in the 1990s, he claimed to have transformed himself, as he put it in a speech at the U.S. Congress, into "a soldier in the army of peace." When he signed the first of the Oslo Accords in 1993, Rabin seemed, to many American Jews, to incarnate in his person the overcoming of the self-evident tensions between egalitarian liberalism and Zionism, between universalism and particularism, the world and Jewishness. For many American Jews, he was living proof that Zionism could be just. Rabin's Israel appeared to them as mighty but gentle, willing to fight when necessary, but ready to make peace when the time was right.

"A Palestinian Versailles"

But what, actually, was Rabin's so-called peace plan? It was less than the mythic key to ending the conflict that his proponents imagined, and much less radical than his detractors feared. Rabin himself never uttered the words "two-state solution." In his final October 1995 speech in the Knesset one month before his assassination, Rabin vowed that Israel "will not return to the lines of June 4, 1967"—in other words, that Israel would not withdraw from all the territory it had conquered during the Six-Day War. Rabin declared that Israel's eastern border would remain the Jordan Valley "in the widest sense of this notion" and that Israel would eventually annex not only the settlement blocs near Jerusalem but additional settlements as well. He referred not to a Palestinian state but to a Palestinian "entity" that would be "less than a state." These were parameters that no Palestinian leader, even the most moderate and pragmatic, could ever accept. And if such a plan were implemented, it would all but guarantee perpetual Israeli domination over this Palestinian state-like "entity."

Some of those who worked with Rabin in negotiating the Oslo Accords maintain that this vision was wide enough and flexible enough to accommodate Palestinian demands. "I believe that, had he lived, the process would have continued," said Yossi Beilin, one of the Israeli architects of the Oslo process, when we spoke by phone in Israel.

"Rabin himself would not have stopped it." And while it is true that Rabin did not talk about a two-state solution, at that time "nobody talked about a Palestinian state," Beilin added. Rabin "was describing the Israeli opening position" in the negotiations, and "to take this as Rabin's own view is unfair to him." Perhaps, Beilin continued, the parameters Rabin laid would have proved a viable basis for a comprehensive final status solution.

But there were also those who identified the shortcomings of the Oslo Accords immediately—indeed, who predicted what they turned out to be. In a stunningly prescient 1993 essay in the *London Review of Books*, the Palestinian American intellectual Edward Said warned that the signing of the Oslo Accords was not the first step toward Palestinian statehood but rather "an instrument of Palestinian surrender, a Palestinian Versailles."

The terms of the agreement were profoundly unequal. "Israel has conceded nothing," Said wrote, except for recognizing the Palestine Liberation Organization as the official representative of the Palestinian people, while the Palestinians had ended the intifada and relinquished their right to resistance without ending the occupation of the West Bank and Gaza. Worse, when it came to territorial matters, by accepting that questions of land and sovereignty would be resolved only under a subsequent final status agreement, Said observed, "the Palestinians [had] in effect discounted their unilateral and internationally acknowledged claim to the West Bank." The plan that Rabin died for was, viewed from a different perspective, less a peace plan than a strategy of pacification.

The Oslo Accords turned out to be a blueprint for the permanent subjugation of the Palestinians, much as Said feared. "Rather than becoming stronger during the interim period, the Palestinians may grow weaker, come more under the Israeli thumb, and therefore less able to dispute the Israeli claim," he worried. Rather than becoming a state, the limited autonomy granted to the PLO, which would become the Palestinian Authority (PA), would transform the PLO into "Israel's enforcer," Said warned, enabling Israel to maintain control over the occupied territories indefinitely and indirectly. Rather than fostering a self-sustaining Palestinian economy, he wrote, "Israel will in effect incorporate the territories economically, keeping them in a state of permanent dependency."

Nearly every one of Said's predictions has come true in the last thirty years. The Oslo peace process, which sputtered after Rabin's death, did not end the occupation but gave Israel a convenient cover to maintain and deepen its control over the Palestinian territories. The PA indeed became Israel's subcontractor, carrying out the dirty work of surveillance and counterinsurgency in Palestinian cities and towns so that Israel does not have to. The economy of the Palestinian territories remains utterly dependent on Israel, with the shekel as the currency, a daily reminder of subjection. Israel also exercises ultimate control over what kinds of goods can move in and out of the West Bank and Gaza.

The Oslo Accords gave the Palestinians a small degree of political autonomy, a largely symbolic "state-like entity" in the Palestinian Authority, but little else. Said argued that this was not a bug but a feature of the negotiation process, that it was what Israel had intended from the start. Rabin's assassination meant that we could never truly know if things might have turned out otherwise.

II.

By the late 1990s, the Jewish communal consensus was unraveling. But two events slowed its collapse: the outbreak of the second intifada, this time an armed Palestinian uprising, and the attacks of September 11. The two events combined as a single phenomenon in the collective American Jewish mind. In each case the enemy was the same: Yasser Arafat and Osama bin Laden were two faces of an identical, fanatical Arab Other. And in each instance, the events could not be understood within the matrix of politics and history. The intifada was not an explosion of rage born of decades of oppression and occupation but simply a paroxysm of antisemitic violence, the latest expression of "the world's oldest hatred." The attacks of 9/11 were not fueled by the violence of military intervention abroad but by a baseless, "senseless" hatred of the American way of life.

The refusal to understand why these events had happened—to *think* about what they meant—closed down communal debate. Dissent disappeared as what seemed like all of American life moved to a war footing, just as Israel had only one year before. It was no longer acceptable to question or criticize Israeli government policies when buses were blowing up in Jerusalem and nightclubs were being incinerated in Tel Aviv, just as it was no longer acceptable to question or criticize U.S. government policies when terrorists had carried out the largest attack on American soil since Pearl Harbor.

Intifada

The second intifada began on September 28, 2000, when Ariel Sharon, Israel's parliamentary opposition leader at the time, ascended the Temple Mount/Haram al-Sharif in Jerusalem with a retinue of more than a thousand police officers, armed bodyguards, and fellow Likud politicians. They were met by a mass of Palestinian demonstrators, who began to throw stones, chairs, and garbage bins. Israeli forces responded with tear gas and rubber-coated bullets. Within twenty-four hours, one Israeli soldier and seven Palestinians were dead. A new Palestinian uprising had begun, which Israel would attempt to crush.

Only a few months before, in July, an attempt to revive the Oslo peace process through talks between Israel and the PLO at Camp David, in Maryland, had collapsed: Rabin's vision for territorial compromise died again—first as tragedy, then as farce. Israeli premier Ehud Barak returned to Israel after several weeks of negotiations and in a televised speech announced "there is no partner" for peace, blaming PLO leader Yasser Arafat for the failure to reach an agreement. In reality, the U.S.-led Camp David talks were ill-conceived and disorganized from the start. President Clinton genuflected too much to Barak, who demanded "general bases for negotiations," preliminary conditions that Arafat could never accept. "Strictly speaking, there never was an Israeli offer," Robert Malley and Hussein Agha wrote in a 2001 article in the *New York Review of Books.* Israeli demands were conveyed through the United States, with the hope that the Palestinians would provide a counteroffer. Instead, the Palestinians saw the proposals offered to them as proof that Israel was not serious about a just and equal peace, and that the United States was not a fair and honest mediator.

The Israeli government tried immediately to suppress the subsequent Palestinian uprising through overwhelming force. In the first few days after Sharon's ascent to the Temple Mount, Israeli forces in the occupied territories fired more than 1 million bullets at Palestinian protesters, most of them unarmed youths. But violence possesses its own escalatory logic. Beginning in October 2000, Palestinian militants began to carry out a wave of suicide bombings. Israel then besieged Palestinian cities like Ramallah and shelled others in the Gaza Strip. By the time the intifada ended in 2005, more than 3,000 Palestinians and roughly 1,000 Israelis had been killed.

The intifada was an early sign that the optimism with which the 1990s had begun would be short-lived. The return of this kind of violence was supposed to have been impossible in the new millennium. The Oslo peace process was supposed to have reflected the capacity of the United States to bring an end to once intractable conflicts in the new unipolar world. Instead, the collapse of the Israeli-Palestinian peace talks presaged the larger failure to cement a stable post–Cold War global order.

A Community of Fear

Among American Jews, the secondhand experience of the intifada coarsened attitudes toward the Palestinians and hardened collective opinion in opposition to any future territorial compromise. Around-the-clock news coverage inundated Jewish communities with images of mangled Israeli cafés and devasted buildings, scenes of gore and debris strewn across sidewalks. We saw much less of the Israeli army's brutal siege of Ramallah or its wholesale destruction of Jenin.

Communal rhetoric turned more belligerent and aggrieved. The problem, went a common riff on remarks made by Golda Meir, was that the Palestinians hated the Jews more than they loved their children, and until that changed there would never be peace. As a child, I cannot recall anyone ever blanching in response to the routine denial of Palestinian humanity.

The idea that the Palestinians were people who were also suffering was unthinkable. That several decades of ceaseless military occupation might have something to do with the intifada was unthinkable. That we did not have to "live forever by the sword," as Netanyahu insisted, was unthinkable.

To the extent that this pessimistic chauvinism was explicable, it was because the violence felt so intimate. Nearly everyone I grew up with had family living in Israel and at any given time knew someone visiting there. The threat of terrorism was not theoretical; it was visceral.

During the years of the intifada, the local Jewish paper was full of tragedies: the young couple blown up just weeks before their wedding, the day-school graduate killed in an attack on a bus. In the community paper, which arrived just before Shabbat, I would read about their funerals, the tributes from their friends, the pain of their bereaved parents. It was an atmosphere of such total fear and grief that the idea of empathy with the other side, with Palestinians, seemed unfathomable. Almost a decade later, when I lived in Israel, my mother asked me not to ride on public buses, which she feared still posed a lethal danger.

Naturally, this fear left its mark on communal politics. Since Jews were under attack, to criticize Israel's actions was to join the Jewish people's enemies. To "Stand with Israel"—as flyers in synagogues, banners in the day school vestibule, and kitschy rubber wrist bands all exhorted—became the most important act that a Jew could do. Amid the newfound unity, born of embattlement, the intracommunal acrimony of the mid-nineties and the Rabin years disappeared, sinking below the surface of communal life. It would be more than a decade before it resurfaced.

That Blue-Sky Morning

One year after the start of the second intifada, Al Qaeda operatives hijacked four commercial airlines and flew them into the World Trade Center, the Pentagon, and a field in Shanksville, Pennsylvania. Jihad had struck a bloody blow at the heart of McWorld. On that day, any hope that the post–Cold War period would usher in a new era of peace died. A week later, President George W. Bush signed the Authorization for the Use of Military Force. The U.S. War on Terror began. In November 2001, U.S. ground forces invaded Afghanistan. Less than two years later, in March 2003, the United States and coalition forces commenced their bombardment of Iraq. It was the start of more than two decades of U.S. occupation in the Middle East.

I am just old enough to remember 9/11 as flashes of anxiety, fear, and foreboding, but not the day in its fullness as it unfolded. This fragmentary recollection forms the foundation of my political memory. I can still see through the doorway of my second-grade classroom the assistant principal, heaving the heavy black TV cart into the cramped library so that the older students could watch the news. The loudspeaker announced that it was now a half day. At home the next morning, the newspaper's front page bore the headline "U.S. Attacked," beneath it a picture of the Twin Towers exploding against a cloudless, baby-blue sky.

All around the country, I would later learn, Jewish day schools closed early out of fear that they could be targets in what was imagined as a potentially expansive, coordinated string of attacks. The imagined total identity of Palestinian militants and Al Qaeda jihadists made this phantasm seems plausible. Parents arrived to pick up their children. But my mother, in the middle of her commute, was stuck on the George Washington Bridge, watching the pillar of fire and smoke as the towers collapsed. My father, a physician, was working at a hospital in New Jersey. I whiled away that bright fall day playing board games on the classroom's drab gray carpet. Or at least that's what I can recall.

In the weeks that followed, the extent of the losses emerged. In the communities of northern New Jersey like mine, it seemed, again, as if everyone knew someone whose loved one was missing or dead: banker fathers, accountant mothers, lost in the canyon of rubble that had opened up in Lower Manhattan. There were just as many stories of near misses: the friend's father who, but for a doctor's appointment, would have died in the steel inferno. Before 9/11, the front line of the war against Islamic terrorism had been far away, in places like Israel/Palestine. Now the war had come home.

In an instant, the hijacked planes tore through the fabric of life. When it was stitched back together, it appeared almost unrecognizable. American flags now adorned the doorposts of houses where they had never been before. "God Bless America" stickers were plastered on the bumpers of cars and SUVs. In my small Jewish community, we had never felt ourselves to be American in this way. Our Americanism had always presupposed a separation, however subtle, between Jews and America: America was good *to* us, which implied that we were, in some way, not quite fully American. Nor had our Americanism been defensive or frightened; it had been celebratory, an allegiance born of gratitude.

The post-9/11 sense of catastrophe brought down an internal barrier, even as it raised, for the first time in recent memory, the question of whether life in America was truly safe. The rituals of public mourning united us with our non-Jewish neighbors. With the invasion of Afghanistan came the signs of "We Support the Troops" pitched on well-groomed lawns. With the first U.S. casualties in Iraq came the yellow ribbons tied around the trunks of stout oak trees. Along Route 208, the massive message board of the Hawthorne Gospel Church affirmed "God Is on Our Side." Passing that church, I had often perceived its signage, proclamations of "Jesus Is King!" and similar sentiments, as a threat. It seemed less frightening now that we had a common enemy.

In response to the intifada and 9/11, American Jewish life plunged into a condition of hypervigilance, a state of siege, from which it has never really emerged. Heavily armed police began to guard Jewish day schools and were deployed outside synagogues. Lockdown and hostage drills with imagined Arab terrorists became the norm, years before the active-shooter drills meant to simulate school shootings started.

The communal vision narrowed to the small crack of a nearly closed door. All commitments were reduced to self-defense, security, and survival. We felt ourselves to be at war on two fronts. The threat was no longer only to Israel, where visiting Jerusalem had come to seem prohibitively dangerous. The threat was also to America: the place where we were supposed to be secure, the place that was supposed to have been a shelter from the vicissitudes of history.

III.

With so much fear and paranoia, it was often impossible to separate where Israel-related anxiety ended and where America-related anxiety began. In fact, they often appeared to Jewish writers and pundits as related. "America's war on terror merged with Israel's war against the Palestinians," the late historian Amy Kaplan observed. In *Commentary* magazine, the popular Jewish novelist Mark Helprin argued in November 2001 that the United States' failure to back Israel sufficiently in crushing the intifada had helped cause 9/11. "The price of this flaccid toleration of terrorism," Helprin wrote, "has been its appearance on American soil and its escalation beyond the proportions of a Pearl Harbor."

There emerged a substantial desire for revenge. In bellicose terms, Helprin called on America in the same November 2001 article "to pursue and obliterate the terrorist networks, to punish and deter the distant states that harbor them, and to liquidate in those states the nuclear, chemical, and biological weapons and their infrastructure." Already in the fall of 2001, the seeds of the next two decades of war were being planted.

Within American Jewish organizational life, there was also a grim sense of opportunity. There was even, Kaplan wrote, "a note of schadenfreude." Professional Israel advocates and Zionist organizations made the case that the U.S. experience with terrorism should increase American backing for Israel as it fought to crush the second intifada. They were not terribly subtle in doing so. On the morning after the September 11 attacks, one of the country's most prominent Jewish newspapers, the *New York Jewish Week*, carried the front-page headline "America: The New Israel." The subhead read, "As Fear and Vulnerability Grip U.S., Will Empathy with Jerusalem Increase?"

Today this seems like a shocking, narrow-minded, and insensitive statement. The paper's editor at the time, Gary Rosenblatt, later apologized in 2021 for the tone that his publication had struck two decades prior. But such blunt, myopic Israel-centrism also reflected the real sentiment of many of the most communally engaged American Jews, the kind of people who paid to subscribe to the *New York Jewish Week*. True, 3,000 Americans were dead, including more than a few members of New York's Jewish communities, but what the editor of the *New York Jewish Week* thought was most important and germane to his readership was that the experience of terrorism in America might mute U.S. criticism of Israeli policies.

The newspaper's framing of the relationship between 9/11 and the second intifada suggested that Americans had now gotten a taste of what it felt like to be Israeli. Americans had received a lesson, Rosenblatt wrote, in "what it is like to experience fear and vulnerability, to bear the brunt of blind hatred, to have innocent civilians targeted as victims of suicide bombings." As the United States moved to invade Afghanistan, Rosenblatt hoped that the American hunger for revenge would translate into U.S. support for giving Israel a freer hand. "Will the U.S. government, which pledged to strike back against those who committed these dastardly deeds, now see the folly in its calls to use restraint in the face of murderous terrorist acts?"

Such was the American Jewish mood, as expressed by those who saw themselves as its chief articulators. Vengeance was now a virtue. Restraint was foolhardy. Empathy was a luxury. Peace was naïve.

"It's Very Good"

Israeli leaders were even more explicit about how they hoped the American reaction to 9/11 would inform American views of Israel. The day after the attacks, James Bennet, the former *New York Times* Jerusalem bureau chief, asked Benjamin Netanyahu "what the attack meant for relations between the United States and Israel." Netanyahu's reply was striking in its honesty. "It's very good," he said, before correcting himself. "Well, not very good, but it will generate immediate sympathy."

Israel and its supporters would get their way. The U.S. War on Terror reaffirmed Israel as a crucial regional ally. The ranks of the Bush administration boasted many lifelong Israel advocates and neoconservatives. It was to be the apex of their political influence and power.

In the immediate aftermath of 9/11, the writer Susan Sontag warned against narrowing one's mind as Americans closed ranks. "Let's by all means grieve together. But let's not be stupid together," she wrote. Sontag lamented what she saw as "the self-righteous drivel and outright deceptions" that had come to dominate public discourse in the wake of the attacks. "Politics, the politics of a democracy—which entails disagreement, which promotes candor—has been replaced by psychotherapy," she wrote. Instead, Sontag argued, what was necessary was critical thought, clearheaded analysis, and patience. She was pilloried for this.

American public life, and American Jewish life with it, hurtled in the opposite direction. There was hardly a political left to speak up that could muster any measure of resistance. Critical voices were relegated to the late-night hours of Comedy Central, where Jon Stewart performed the double role of court jester and functional political opposition.

During these years, the Jewish communal consensus entered a period of deep freeze. Indeed, the post-9/11 moment had an almost cryogenic effect. The pillars of postwar Jewish life had increasingly been in poor health. But the War on Terror helped to prolong the consensus's life.

PART TWO

4

FALSE STABILITY

I.

When the Iraq War began, I had just turned nine. The day of the invasion, I came home from school excited. My teachers, or perhaps the older students, must have conveyed that something momentous was about to happen. In the peculiar way children can be when they fail to understand the real meaning of an event, when all they can sense is its bigness, I was giddy. I watched the electronic numbers on the clock above the old white stove tick toward evening, waiting to turn on the TV. As the U.S. bombardment began, the news showed images in night-vision green of explosions over the Baghdad skyline. It was not fear of what might follow or sadness at the impending loss of life that I felt, but a kind of satisfaction. I had come to learn that this war was good, that it was right, that it was just.

A fever gripped American society. The pro-war feeling filtered down through comments by rabbis and teachers and swirled through charged dinners with family and family friends. The same ideas washed over 1010 WINS radio in the car ride home from school and suffused the op-eds in the *Times*, which I would peruse in the mornings over cereal and milk. When the invasion began in mid-March of 2003, I was left with no doubt that I needed to root for *our* side.

After the fractiousness of the 1990s, Jewish liberals and conservatives now appeared united. They banged the war drums with equal fervor. *New York Times* columnist Thomas Friedman appeared on *Charlie Rose*, where he professed that the goal of the war was to send the message to America's ideological adversaries that "if you think we don't care about our open society . . . Well, Suck. On. This." Israel's Benjamin Netanyahu testified before Congress that "nothing less than dismantling [Saddam's] regime will do" to ensure Israel's security. Michael Walzer, the left-liberal Jewish philosopher, wrote in support of a "little war" in Iraq as an alternative to "the big war." Little wars, of course, almost never stay that way.

The Consensus Revived

What undergirded these bellicose expressions was the idea that America's interests and Israel's interests were identical. Among Jewish establishment leaders this was an article of faith and a kernel of dogma to be assiduously policed. "What's good for Israel is good for America," insisted the other David Harris, deputy director of the National Jewish Democratic Council, about the congruence of Israeli and U.S. interests in Iraq.

Most Jewish establishment leaders spoke in such bromides. The case for the Iraq War as articulated by prominent American Jewish figures reflected the hallucinatory belief in the perfect compatibility of Americanism and Zionism and the fundamental rightness of both. America needed to invade Iraq, as pundits like Friedman argued, to show that it would defend the open society from its enemies: the radical Islamists—or as Christopher Hitchens dubbed them, the "Islamofascists"—who also threatened Israel's existence, who shared with the Nazis their pathological hatred of Jews. To be Jewish politically in American public life became all but synonymous with support for the war on these grounds.

The equation, naturally, worked both ways. By securing the liberty of Americans—somehow, it was imagined, by bombing a country 6,000 miles away—the war would guarantee Israel's security. The invasion, as its proponents fantasized, would catalyze a democratic transformation of the Middle East more broadly, which would redound to both Israel and America's benefit. Here again was the presupposition of America's exceptional, even providential goodness, which would be tested and proved through its willingness to support the Jewish state. It was imagined, paradoxically, that only through this war would America and Israel alike know long-term peace. In the eyes of American Jewish leaders, the war, in other words, was "good for the Jews" in both global centers of Jewish life.

The American Jewish establishment found in George W. Bush's administration and its war an opportunity to reassert the communal-political creed: that America was a great nation, albeit bruised by September 11, and that America could restore its greatness through fighting the war in Iraq, which would spread the liberal-capitalist values that made America great to a region where they had not yet flowered and, in the process, eliminate one of Israel's better-armed adversaries. Bolstered by the conformity induced in the march to war, the pillars of the postwar Jewish consensus seemed stronger than they had in more than a decade.

Yet the triumphalist atmosphere of the war's first years was short-lived. After President Bush stood onboard the USS *Abraham Lincoln* aircraft carrier beneath the banner reading "Mission Accomplished," the Iraq War devolved into a grinding, brutal counterinsurgency operation. What the Bush administration had billed as a quick war of "regime change" became a protracted and increasingly deadly occupation. Worse, the Bush administration had deceived the public about the reasons for the war: no weapons of mass destruction ever materialized. Americans grew disillusioned with the mounting U.S. casualties fighting for a war that lacked a rationale, and many American Jews not only grew tired of the war but also began to fear the right-wing Christian and theocratic impulses the Bush administration had unleashed.

But rather than adjust to the disaster of the war and the Bush administration's deepening unpopularity, the American Jewish establishment doubled down in its support for an ultra-hawkish foreign policy. Nor would it tolerate even the slightest criticism of Israel, in the midst of a bloody counterterrorism campaign of its own to quash the second intifada, which drew international outcry over human rights abuses. The result: while the Jewish establishment and the consensus that it embodied had begun the Bush years more robust and less disputed than in many years, by the end of the decade both were poised on the precipice of a full-blown legitimacy crisis. The institutions that claimed to speak on behalf of American Jews came to represent a politics that most American Jews rejected, yet there were hardly any other expressions of Jewish politics in mainstream American life to be found.

The Establishment's Man

At the levels of both personnel and policy, George W. Bush's administration was the American Jewish establishment's dream. Bush surrounded himself with officials who boasted superlative pro-Israel credentials: people like Douglas Feith, who, before becoming Bush's undersecretary for defense and policy, had worked as a pro-Israel lobbyist at the law firm he cofounded with Marc Zell, a prominent advocate for building Jewish settlements in the occupied West Bank; like Elliott Abrams, a "fiercely pro-Israel" neoconservative figure convicted for his involvement in the Iran-Contra scandal, who became Bush's deputy national security advisor; and like Richard Perle, a veteran right-wing think tanker who had advised Benjamin Netanyahu before becoming chairman of the Pentagon's Defense Policy Board under Bush.

All were outspoken proponents and later architects of the U.S. policy during the Iraq War. All believed fervently that America's interests and Israel's interests were the same. All have continued to advocate stridently for U.S. military intervention abroad, against Israeli compromise with the Palestinians, and for Israeli territorial maximalism. Their ascent, or in some cases return, to political power in the 2000s showed that the Bush administration sought to deliver on the policy wish list of pro-Israel hawks.

And deliver it did—not only when it came to the Iraq War, but perhaps most spectacularly by supporting Ariel Sharon's 2006 unilateral withdrawal from the occupied Gaza Strip. The "disengagement," as it is known in Israel, was an attempt to forgo future Israeli concessions by relinquishing control of Gaza. Although adorned with the language of compromise, Sharon intended it as a permanent blow to a two-state solution. As Dov Weissglas, an aide to Sharon, admitted in 2004, "it [the disengagement] supplies the amount of formaldehyde that is necessary so there will not be a political process with the Palestinians."

In exchange for the feigned retreat of the disengagement, the Bush administration effectively green-lighted continued Israeli rule over the occupied West Bank. And by splitting Gaza from the West Bank politically—Israel never negotiated with the Palestinian Authority over assuming control of the territory after the disengagement—the move introduced an obstacle into the creation of a future Palestinian state that has since proved insurmountable.

To be sure, the Bush administration did not adopt such policies— war in Iraq, genuflection toward Ariel Sharon—because of the neoconservative, professional Israel advocates it placed within its ranks. Their presence was a symptom, not a cause. Rather, the Bush administration proved so hospitable to the neoconservatives and genial to the American Jewish establishment because Bush's American Christian imperialism rhymed with their own ideological orientation.

Like them, Bush espoused a vigorous American exceptionalism. A born-again evangelical, Bush believed that America's exceptional goodness, its providential character, would be ratified through its support for the Jewish state and by its role as armed agent of "the expansion of freedom in all the world." Like them, Bush also believed that true freedom meant free-market capitalism and American-style individualist consumerism, which would act as a salve to atavistic bigotries and militarized tribalism, often imagined as Arab or Islamic in character. Just when the hawkish, neoconservative articulation of the postwar Jewish synthesis attained hegemony in American Jewish life, the Bush administration marked the ascendancy of a parallel ideology in American politics.

In the lead-up to the invasion, the major American Jewish institutions almost uniformly threw themselves behind the Bush administration's war in Iraq. And not just the usual suspects—the pro-Israel lobbies like AIPAC and the Conference of Presidents—but also liberal groups, like Harris's National Jewish Democratic Council and the Union for Reform Judaism. In the fall of 2002, Rabbi David Saperstein, erstwhile leader of the Reform Movement's Religious Action Center, nominally one of the most liberal Jewish political groups in the United States, told the journalist Michelle Goldberg, "The Jewish community would want to see a forceful resolution to the threat that Saddam Hussein poses."

While there were, of course, many Jews who opposed the war, they had no representation in the mainstream political arena, and no representation *as Jews* against the war. That even prominent liberal Reform rabbis like Saperstein backed the invasion illustrated the extent to which the pro-war, pro-Israel position had subsumed other expressions of Jewish politics. Which meant that as more and more American Jews became outraged by the Bush administration and its mendacious war, they would have had to look outside the establishment organizations and mainstream denominations for anything approximating a political home.

The Real America

I grew up during these years of ideological enclosure. My germinal awareness of the world took its form and content from a community that treated the pillars of postwar Jewish identity as sacrosanct. Yet this also meant that, as the pillars began to fall, I internalized their fissures, their instabilities.

I might have become a Republican but for my parents' decision to transfer me to public school in sixth grade. The Jewish day school was, in their view, too small, too sheltered. Already, then, observant Conservative Judaism had become an unsustainable contradiction, caught between the more coherent ideology of Orthodoxy and the more lenient practice of Reform. Had I remained cocooned in religious day school, I might never have bristled against the community's narrow-mindedness or its chauvinism. I might have supported John McCain over Barack Obama, as many of my neighbors did, and later arrived in college prepared to defend Israel against its adversaries in the arena of campus debate.

None of this happened because life in public school during the Bush years made it impossible. I felt the switch to be a form of exile. For the first decade of my life, I had worn a kippah every day to school. I had prayed every morning. I had never sat next to a non-Jew in class. Now I was sometimes one of only two or three other Jews, and certainly the most religiously identifiable, in a classroom of all gentiles, the only Josh amid a sea of Johns, Nicks, and Anthonys.

Just as jarring, I went from never having more than three other boys as classmates to having many dozens. Their rituals of physical violence were strange to me; I was more accustomed to playing chess at recess than getting shoved on the asphalt. I suppose this was the sort of education my parents feared I was missing in the family-style school that I had left. I also gained an additional education: I learned about America in its unmediated, unmythologized form.

For the first time, I experienced antisemitism. Until I was twelve, this had mostly been a theoretical concept. In middle school, it became visceral. My new classmates pelted me with pennies and nickels in the hallways and jeered me to pick them up. They assailed me with epithets: Jew, Jewboy, Josh Jew. Only a few were brave enough, though, to call me a kike. They scrawled swastikas on my desk and papers and threw "Heil Hitler" salutes across the cafeteria. I dreaded the roughly two days in social studies class that were dedicated to learning about the Holocaust, when we read a novel or parts of Anne Frank's diary; instead of sensitizing my classmates, it only emboldened them. After all, these were boys who had never experienced marginalization in their lives, who had never felt themselves "other" or different in white Christian America. Naturally, they identified with power, and what conveyed a more terrible, violent sense of power than the iconography of Nazism?

My parents never grasped the nature of this antisemitic bullying. They did not know the extent to which they remained basically unaware of the non-Jews among whom we lived. Having grown up at a time when America was everything for Jews, when being American was everything, they were too invested in the ideal to grasp fully how their Americanization could at once be so comprehensive and yet so incomplete.

We *were* really very different from these non-Jews. For instance, they owned guns. And once my father discovered this fact, he insisted on calling the parents of any friend whose house I hoped to visit so that he could confirm that, if they indeed owned guns, which they inevitably did, their guns—usually handguns and hunting rifles—were unloaded and locked away. The parents mocked my father's neurosis, sometimes to my face, which guaranteed that among my classmates I remained, forever, the Jew whose physician father had called because he was worried about an old bolt-action rifle in the garage.

My non-Jewish classmates learned, in addition to their antisemitism, the right-wing politics of their parents and their evangelical or Catholic churches. In the second half of the 2000s, as the Iraq War turned bloodier, they turned more belligerently patriotic. With the backing of the middle school administration, a group of students, led by the most popular and athletic boys, began to hold their own Christian prayer circle around the massive U.S. flagpole in the parking lot. One teacher, whose son was rumored to be in a U.S. Special Forces unit, plastered behind her desk a picture of an American flag with a cross of light bleeding through its fibers. It was not a straightforwardly antisemitic image. Still, its implications menaced me. If this was America, I could not see my place in it.

Alienation, though, can be a gift. My feeling of out-of-placeness precipitated my burgeoning political consciousness. I resolved that everything these teachers and students supported, I would oppose. They loved Bush and identified with his simplistic faith; I would despise him. They worshipped the American flag and affixed it to their clothes, their backpacks, their cars; I would protest it and refuse to stand for the Pledge of Allegiance. If I was doomed to stand out, I would do so on my own terms.

As the papers filled with the portraits of dead young U.S. soldiers killed patrolling Mosul or Fallujah, I became, in my own absurd and inchoate way, an antiwar radical. I read everything I could about why the war was wrong. I clicked through links on liberal and left-wing blogs, eavesdropping on the netroots. I think, in retrospect, that I hoped to find other people beyond the world that I knew firsthand, people whom I could talk to, and with whom I could find common cause.

In the way that a child does when newly awakened to the violence and brutality of the real world, I felt that I was personally implicated in the deaths of millions of innocent Iraqis by virtue of my inaction, by having only just discovered for myself the injustice that was worsening with every passing moment. President Bush was destroying Iraq and I was obligated—we were *all* obligated—to stop him.

For the time being, my Zionism remained intact. Israel was still a source of strength for me. It was my own flag, which my adolescent antagonists could not share. In a way, it was beyond politics, protected within the realm of the sentimental. But I had also become more confused by it. The mass demonstrations that accompanied Israel's 2005 Gaza disengagement vexed me: in this internal fight between Israeli Jews, who was I supposed to support? The ensuing division within

Jewish life conveyed a sense of unease but I lacked the capacity to understand its stakes.

To solidify my own sense of self in my teenage mind, I tried to split Zionism from the Americanism that had been its twin and turn the former against the latter. I begged my parents to let me continue regular Hebrew lessons outside of school with a beloved Moroccan Israeli teacher, who also began to teach me French. Integration into public school did not dilute or mute my Jewishness; it strengthened it.

The encounter with real America, beyond Jewish day school and the synagogue, only confirmed for me how little I fit into this country, how little I belonged. It also imprinted on me an instinctual defense of the victim, the underdog, the marginalized. Having been educated by Holocaust survivors and their children, I saw this as the most natural outgrowth of Jewish experience in history.

––––––––––

The long War on Terror cast a dark shadow over life in the early 2000s. Torture, the Patriot Act, Abu Ghraib, Guantánamo Bay—the extraordinary measures of the state of exception became regular news items, then merely ordinary terms of daily speech. The effect of having a president who was as inept as he was malevolent was to shatter any illusions about the dignity of the office of the president, about the goodness or the intelligence of the people in power. America was an "idiocracy," as the title of a 2006 film suggested, doomed to a future of endless war, cultural decay, and social decline. Even if I could not quite articulate this sentiment, by the time of my bar mitzvah, in 2007, it was, to me, self-evident.

There was just one distant-seeming spark of hope during these years: Barack Obama. In eighth grade I brought Obama's memoir, *Dreams from My Father*, to class simply to antagonize the English teacher, whose cross of light glared down at me and who almost certainly doubted that Obama was really an American.

In the depths of the Bush years, Obama promised to redeem the country from war. The anticipation of what his election might do took on almost messianic proportions. Which meant that under almost any circumstances, reality would have fallen far short of the fantasy. The magnitude of disappointment that Obama's presidency entailed exceeded even the most jaded of political observers' expectations. By the end of his presidency, that disappointment had, for many young people, transmuted into rage.

II.

In the fall of 2008, the comedian Sarah Silverman appeared in an online video in which she declared, "If Barack Obama doesn't become the next president of the United States, I'm going to blame the Jews." I watched this clip countless times on the boxlike Dell desktop in what my family then called "the computer room" and sent it out excitedly from my new email address to a few friends and uncles.

Sitting beneath a printout of Shepard Fairey's radical-kitsch "Hope" poster, Silverman explained the problem. Old, right-leaning Jews in Florida viewed Obama with suspicion because of his race, his foreign-sounding name, and his rumored sympathy for the Palestinians, and they could very well tip the crucial swing state in favor of the Republican McCain-Palin ticket. "I know what you're saying, like, 'Oh my God, Sarah, I can't believe you're saying this: Jews are the most liberal, scrappy, civil-rights-y people there are,'" Silverman continued. "But you're forgetting a large group of Jews who are not that way, and they go by several aliases: Nana, Papa, Zeydie, Bubbie, Grandma, and Grandpa."

To bring these older, right-leaning Jews—many of them former Democrats, many of them devoted to mainstream Jewish organizations and synagogues—back into the party fold, Silverman called on young American Jews to join her in what she called "The Great Schlep": Visit your grandparents in Florida, convince them to vote for Obama.

Today, the video is almost unwatchable. Silverman's overgrown-child affect, her ironic-but-just-barely racism, the low-fi indie strumming in the background—all were symptoms of a complacent, naïve liberalism, a liberalism that imagined the stakes of politics as little more than image and representation, that evinced ignorance of the real suffering just below the surface of American life. It was a liberalism of innocence that Trump's election would puncture in 2016.

Still, the "Great Schlep" clip reflected a real phenomenon. Perhaps no event had so illuminated the deep and generationally inflected chasm in American Jewish life as Barack Obama's first presidential campaign. Young American Jews, like most young people, flocked to him. But older American Jews, especially those heavily involved in organized Jewish life—those who had, even if half-consciously, followed the neoconservatives in their journey to the right—viewed Obama with suspicion and even dislike.

The Establishment's War

Obama worried them in large part because many Jewish establishment leaders conveyed, in public statements and to private audiences, that they had reason to worry. Throughout the campaign, establishment groups scrutinized Obama's every word for evidence of his inadequate affinity for Israel. Right-wing and Republican Jewish groups intimated that he harbored animus toward Jews. Anodyne remarks were blown up into manufactured pseudo-scandals. In 2008, for instance, Obama told a group of Jewish leaders in Cleveland that "there is a strain within the pro-Israel community that says that unless you adopt an unwavering pro-Likud approach to Israel that you're anti-Israel, and that can't be the honest measure of our friendship with Israel." Anyone who has spent any time in the organized Jewish world could attest to the truth of that statement. And yet it became further proof of the paranoid lie that Obama harbored a secret anti-Israel agenda.

After the election many Jewish establishment leaders never reconciled themselves to the Obama presidency. They resented that the honeymoon they had enjoyed with the Bush administration was over. They barely concealed their antipathy toward his successor. For example, in 2009, after Obama's Cairo speech, which was intended to signal a new, post-Bush opening to the Muslim world, Jewish leaders attacked the president seemingly for the simple fact that he chose to address the concerns of Arabs and Muslims. "There's a lot of questioning going on about what [Obama] really believes and what does he really stand for," said Malcolm Hoenlein, leader of the Conference of Presidents, in response. "[Jews] are genuinely very concerned . . . about Obama."

Such comments typified the Jewish establishment's war against Obama. In the name of all American Jews, establishment leaders like Hoenlein attacked a president who, in fact, most American Jews supported. These attacks would peak after Obama's 2012 reelection, when his administration initiated its effort to reach a deal with Iran over its nuclear program. Jewish establishment groups like AIPAC launched all they could muster to scuttle the deal. In 2014 and 2015, AIPAC spent tens of millions of dollars in advertising and lobbying to block the administration's agenda. They framed the matter in stark terms: that Obama's plan to contain Iran threatened Israel and therefore endangered Jewish lives.

The Jewish establishment lost this war, and in more ways than one. Despite the resources that AIPAC marshaled, Obama secured enough support in the Senate to prevent the legislature from blocking the deal. But the significance of this defeat exceeded the matter of the deal itself.

The establishment's antipathy to Obama and his agenda triggered the gradual unraveling of the bipartisan pro-Israel consensus in U.S. politics that it had long worked to uphold. The ability to sway the members of both parties had been central to AIPAC's effectiveness.

Yet, by throwing all its weight against a Democratic president and working in close tandem with the Republicans, AIPAC cracked that bipartisan veneer. When the Republican House Speaker John Boehner, without informing the White House, invited Netanyahu to address Congress, where he denounced the Iran deal in fearmongering terms, it became impossible to deny that the pro-Israel lobby and the Republicans were aligned.

What of the majority of American Jews who supported Obama? The disjuncture at the heart of American Jewish politics deepened, and this meant that the strong pro-Obama sentiment among American Jews found little official expression in Jewish institutional life. Right-leaning communal elites worked to entrench U.S. support for Israeli government actions and shield Israel from consequences for its ceaseless settlement expansion. They did so with little input from the people in whose name they spoke—some of whom, repulsed or alienated by the expression of Jewishness represented by the establishment, had joined the ranks of the disaffiliated. But the intensity of the establishment's anti-Obama efforts also produced a countermovement that sought to offer a germinal alternative to the Jewish establishment. The passage of the Iran deal reflected the new weakness of groups like AIPAC as much as this countermovement's success.

J Street's Wager

Around the same time as Obama's 2008 election, a new organization called J Street appeared on the scene. Led by Jeremy Ben-Ami, a former Bill Clinton staffer, J Street promised to realign American Jewish politics. It aimed to echo and amplify the views of the majority of American Jews enthused by Barack Obama and who trusted his policymaking. J Street contended that, contrary to the claims of groups like AIPAC, the ADL, and the Conference of Presidents, most American Jews did not hold the hawkish, pro-Likud line when it came to Israel. Instead, J Street posited that most American Jews could be described, roughly, as liberal Zionists: supportive of the idea of Israel, willing to criticize its policies in the settlements in the occupied West Bank, and ready to pressure Israel to take more steps toward a lasting peace. The name "J Street" signaled to the missing street in the city of Washington's grid, "thus evoking," as journalist James Traub put it, "a voice missing from Washington's policy discussion"—and, just as significant, from the American Jewish discussion.

J Street was never radical. In nearly every public appearance, Ben-Ami made sure to boast of his impeccable Zionist and establishmentarian credentials: his father fought in the right-wing Irgun militia during the 1948 war; he was an unabashed D.C. insider. For years, Ben-Ami could barely bring himself to say the word "occupation" to describe Israel's military rule over the West Bank. He aimed to shift the American Jewish conversation, but only within clear limits.

That was the result of ideology as much as strategy. J Street sought to appear as the true standard-bearer of the American Jewish mainstream, a "pro-Israel, pro-peace" foil to the conservative-leaning, Israel-right-or-wrong AIPAC. If most Jewish establishment groups had come to support a two-state solution, to be achieved through a U.S.-mediated diplomatic process, the difference was that J Street would mean it. J Street did not challenge the pillars of the postwar Jewish consensus; it sought to salvage the synthesis of Americanism, Zionism, and liberalism as the pillars began to fall.

And yet, from the day J Street launched, the American Jewish establishment set out to crush the upstart group. Jewish leaders could not countenance any alternative to the form of Jewish politics that they enforced. They did not simply argue that J Street was wrong on policy grounds; they accused J Street and its supporters of lacking adequate love for Israel and their fellow Jews. They denounced J Street as a threat to Jewish flourishing. It is a measure of their smear campaign's success that, largely but not only within hawkish and traditionalist circles, J Street became, and remains, a dirty word.

When I arrived at Princeton in the fall of 2013, the first thing I learned when I stepped into the campus Hillel was that it was still reeling after a major donor withdrew a substantial funding commitment over the Hillel's decision to allow J Street to register as a Hillel affiliate group. There were similar fights on campuses across the country, and these fights were microcosms of the battle within American Jewish life writ large. In 2014, when J Street sought admission to Hoenlein's Conference of Presidents of Major American Jewish Organizations, it was denied. The rejection sent a clear message: no matter how in sync with the actual views of American Jews J Street might be, Jewish leaders found the group unacceptable, and that was enough to deny it the stamp of legitimacy. In the spring of 2016, when David Friedman, later Trump's ambassador to Israel, called J Street supporters "far worse than kapos—Jews who turned in their fellow Jews in Nazi death camps"—he was expressing in blunter terms a sentiment that was, and still is, widely shared among those who view themselves as Israel's most ardent American defenders.

J Street failed in supplanting the old pro-Israel hegemony with its sunnier liberal version. But by the early 2010s it began to cultivate the expression of a kind of Jewish identity that had long been suppressed in American Jewish life. It had created a new opening within the Jewish communal conversation. The existence of a national organization that offered criticism of Israeli government policies, however tepid at first, helped to erode the total taboo on challenging Israeli policy from the left that had prevailed in the early 2000s. In a way, J Street's opponents were right to see the group as a threat, but it was not the threat that they imagined. J Street in no way posed a danger to Israel's existence. It did, however, help to crack the façade of the pro-Israel consensus that groups like AIPAC enforced from above.

As a teenager, I sensed the thaw that J Street catalyzed. It became easier to argue with friends and relatives. Knowing that there were other people out there who had begun to ask questions about Israel and Israeli policies made me feel less like I had gone insane or that I was alone in rejecting the standard pro-Israel line. For me and many other young American Jews frustrated by the stultifying climate of organized Jewish life and politicized by the Iraq War, J Street offered a new political and Jewish home.

But not for long. Israel's ever-deepening military occupation of the West Bank and siege of Gaza meant that J Street could only ever be an ideological halfway house for many of the young people who were first drawn to it. The theory of change on which J Street operated dictated that by shifting the American Jewish discourse, the group's central policy goal, a two-state solution in Israel/Palestine, would become more feasible. On the ground in Israel/Palestine, however, the opposite happened. While J Street remained wedded to the two-state paradigm, the Israeli government shifted toward the de facto annexation of the West Bank, toward an inegalitarian, segregationist, one-state reality. J Street wagered that Israel could be rescued from the road to apartheid and pariah status on which it appeared to be hurtling. But what if this process could not be reversed?

Gradual Disillusionment

That, journalist Peter Beinart warned, was the conclusion at which many young American Jews seemed to be arriving. In "The Failure of the American Jewish Establishment," his 2010 essay for the *New York Review of Books*, Beinart warned that young Jews were abandoning Zionism—and, with it, organized Jewish life. They had grown tired of the American Jewish establishment's hypocrisy when it came to the two-state solution, endorsing it in theory while facilitating its dismantling in practice. They bristled at the establishment's intolerance of dissent. "For several decades the Jewish establishment has asked American Jews to check their liberalism at Zionism's door," Beinart wrote. "Now, to their horror, they are finding that many young Jews have checked their Zionism instead."

When he wrote the essay, Beinart still believed in the possibility of a two-state solution and saw himself as a defender of Zionism. "The Failure of the American Jewish Establishment" was diagnostic, but it also was a cri de coeur. As opposed to the "comfortable Zionism" of the establishment, which he denounced as a "moral abdication," Beinart called for an "uncomfortable Zionism, a Zionism angry at what Israel risks becoming, and in love with what it still could be." He articulated the stakes of J Street's work with much greater urgency and clarity than its leadership ever managed.

Beinart in 2010 was too optimistic. He hoped that a morally revitalized liberal Zionism would prove attractive to disillusioned young American Jews. The problem, though, was that young American Jews were not abandoning Zionism and mainstream Jewish life simply because the dominant *version* of Zionism was incompatible with their progressive politics. They were leaving because they rejected the entire ideological edifice represented by the Jewish establishment. They were leaving because the idea of American beneficence appeared laughable after Iraq and because Zionism as it actually existed on the ground in Israel/Palestine was becoming indefensible in progressive terms.

Liberal Zionism, as epitomized by support for a two-state solution, increasingly appeared to many as an oxymoron. In 2020, Beinart would come to this conclusion himself. "The painful truth," he wrote, "is that the project to which liberal Zionists like myself have devoted ourselves for decades—a state for Palestinians separated from a state for Jews—has failed."

I read Beinart's 2010 essay on a dusty Mac desktop during my tenth-grade "technology" class. Until then, I had only a fuzzy, half-formed awareness that my own gradual questioning of Israel and Zionism was part of a broader phenomenon in American Jewish life. Of course, I knew of the existence of Jews who criticized Israeli policies, who even dissented from Zionism. But they had always appeared to be marginal figures, like Noam Chomsky, whom rabbis and family members mentioned in passing as an exemplary apostate, his name spat like phlegm at the back of the throat. A religious teacher on a high school summer program in Israel once told me that it would be better if I had nothing to do with Judaism than to become like Chomsky, who had, she said, devoted himself to Israel's destruction. From Beinart, though, I learned that Chomsky was far less exceptional than I had been told.

In fact, the process of gradual disillusionment that Beinart identified in his 2010 essay had been underway for longer than many of his readers probably recognized. While in the second half of the 2010s, young American Jews who broke with the pro-Israel line often did so noisily and publicly, young Jews had been abandoning institutional Jewish life for years. They had just done so quietly. They tuned out. They folded away their Zionist sleepaway camp T-shirts, buried their olive-green IDF hoodies deep in a box in their parents' basements, and melted into the wider world.

For a long time I envied the people who were able to do this, who managed to close one chapter of their lives and move on to another. Throughout my teens and early twenties, I remained stuck, stewing in silent frustration at family events, smiling painfully when a relative told me how much they loved visiting the city of Hebron, one of the most violent sites of Israel's occupation, or how great a man Moshe Dayan was. A friend would later tell me that I was wasting my time arguing with a community whose politics were not worth taking seriously. I understood what he meant, but I have always thought it strategically wrong and morally wrong: strategically because, for anything to change, people need to be convinced; morally because, when the people we love support something immoral, we have the responsibility to help them right the injustice they have helped cause.

The American Jewish establishment's success was American Jewish life's tragedy. The establishment defeated all its rivals, dismissed every challenger to its claim to speak on behalf of all American Jews. In the process it made being Jewish in America appear, on the national level, synonymous with support for U.S. military adventurism abroad, and with unquestioning fealty to Israeli government policies. The establishment made no room for the expression of the values and commitments professed by many young American Jews who, alienated by the politics represented by Abe Foxman and the late right-wing megadonor Sheldon Adelson, gave up on institutional Jewish life. They left not just their Zionism but their Judaism behind.

Not all young American Jews, of course. There were those who never became alienated in the first place, who still identify with the myth of American goodness, and who have no qualms with a Zionism that rejects the possibility of freedom and equality for Palestinians. They are the next in line to succeed the Jurassic leaders who helm establishment institutions today. But there were also those young American Jews who set out to create new forms of Jewish identity unwedded to Americanism and Zionism, who endeavored to channel their disillusionment into building new kinds of community.

III.

Between 2008 and 2014, Israel waged three wars in Gaza. In the winter of 2008–2009, what the IDF dubbed Operation Cast Lead killed at least 1,385 Palestinians, most of them civilians, and 13 Israelis, of whom 3 were civilians. Operation Pillar of Cloud in 2012 was a smaller war: 167 Palestinians were killed, 87 of them civilians, and 2 Israeli soldiers and 4 Israeli civilians were killed. I was living in south Tel Aviv, close enough to an Iron Dome battery that the apartment shook each time it fired to intercept a rocket. Until the 2023–2024 Israel-Hamas war, the war in the summer of 2014 was the bloodiest: at least 2,104 Palestinians were killed, 1,460 of them civilians; 66 Israeli soldiers and 6 civilians were killed.

The half decade of stop-and-start fighting transformed the image of Israel in the American mind. Each additional war revealed the tremendous imbalance of power between the two sides. Increasingly, Israel appeared as the unambiguous aggressor, a nuclear-armed Goliath facing down a divided and enfeebled Palestinian adversary. Each additional war raised, for a small yet growing number of American Jews, and especially younger Jews, new and more intense doubts: about the morality of the pro-Israel consensus, the infallibility of Israel, and the justness of actually existing Zionism. The wars in Gaza rallied American Jewish institutions to Israel's defense. They also pushed any questioners out of the communal doors.

All wars are horrifying, but carnage of the 2014 Gaza war seemed exceptionally shocking at the time. The casualty numbers were massive, disturbing, but they conveyed only an abstract, dry impression of the scale of death. Images of grisly devastation, dead children pulled from collapsed houses, were live streamed on Twitter and broadcast on TV at all hours of the day. IDF shelling decimated entire neighborhoods; in Shejaiyah, one of Gaza's poorest, the Israeli army reduced homes, cars, and streets to rubble. The neighborhood became a massive charnel house. The bombardment killed at least sixty people in the span of twenty-four hours.

An American Jew who felt horrified by the violence or ashamed by Israel's seeming indifference to Palestinian suffering would have found no space within organized Jewish life to express such sentiments. It was not acceptable to criticize the obviously disproportionate nature of Israeli strikes. It was barely even acceptable to acknowledge the loss of innocent life on both sides.

Instead, an atmosphere of zealous belligerence prevailed. AIPAC issued its standard call on the U.S. government to back Israel's war without conditions. The Conference of Presidents minced no words and urged Israel's government "to take whatever steps necessary to defend its citizens." Even dovish groups fell in behind the establishment's line. J Street issued a statement of its own in support of Israel's actions during the war.

But that summer in 2014, the ground of American Jewish life began to shift. A new generation of young Jewish activists revolted against Jewish institutional support for Israel's wars on Gaza and its perpetual occupation of the West Bank. Disillusionment, even disgust, for the American Jewish establishment fueled the emergence of new movements like IfNotNow, and revitalized older, existing groups like Jewish Voice for Peace. Events abroad then conjoined in popular consciousness with events at home. That same August, Ferguson, Missouri, then the country, erupted after the police killing of Michael Brown. The first wave of Black Lives Matter demonstrations buoyed a new youth culture of protest and resistance. We did not know it then, but a cultural revolution had begun.

Slow Rupture

When the summer 2014 war started, I was working as an intern at *Dissent* magazine. I had just completed my first year of college. The one-room office, in a building at the southernmost edge of Wall Street, had enormous windows that overlooked the East River. From the balcony, Brooklyn and Queens spread out below, dark concrete and twinkling lights extending out to the horizon. The romance of the bygone age of the little magazine was preserved, almost like in a museum, in that small room. Irving Howe's old Rolodex sat on the coffee table where, in an idle minute, I could flip through to find an old calling card for John Rawls or Arthur Schlesinger Jr. Yet against the backdrop of the war, the work, mainly fact-checking and digitizing the archive, began to feel senseless, detached from reality.

I had spent the year before starting college under the auspices of a *mechina* in Tel Aviv. There are many such institutions in Israel, which enable Israeli eighteen-year-olds to defer their mandatory military service for a year of studying religious texts, ideological instruction, and physical and mental preparation for the army. While my views had moved leftward throughout high school, I remained in some sense a

Zionist. I wanted to immerse myself in Hebrew, I still loved the idea of Israel, and there seemed no better way to begin reconciling my growing criticism of Israel's government and my deep attachment to the place than to go live there. A rabbi who had become a mentor to me in my late teens encouraged me in his goading way: the experience might not cure me of my leftism, as if it were a disorder, but at least, when the year was up, I'd know what I was talking about.

So I dove in. I filled notebook after notebook, writing to absorb everything I could: the names of different army units and their roles, dates of significance in the development of Labor Zionism, passages about distributive justice in the Gemara, quotations by Hebrew poets like Shaul Tchernichovsky and the biblical prophets. A tenet of classical Zionism is *ahavat ha'aretz,* love for the land, and my new comrades and I embarked on days-long treks across the country's north and south. We would wake up in the mornings in our sleeping bags to the strange, sweaty scent of the carob trees and the rush of the burnt long grass. On long hikes we would practice carrying a stretcher laden with sandbags, as if a wounded soldier were splayed on it. At the time, it felt like the only real thing I had done in my life. Then, after a year, I left.

The news of the 2014 war wracked me with guilt. Many of my friends from the previous year were called up. I had grown very close to, had even begun to love, some of those friends. Now, here was proof that I had been an interloper, or worse, a parasite. I had popped into their reality for a short time only to retreat to the comfort of an expensive university in the United States. As the rockets fell in Israel, I sat in my dingy St. Marks Place sublet, glued to Facebook and WhatsApp late into the night, talking with whoever of my friends would still talk to me even though they knew I could not support the war. Connection, even of the perfunctory kind, still felt better than silence.

That year when I was eighteen had also altered my perspective of Israel. Frequent trips in and out of the occupied West Bank—conversations with both unrepentant settlers and Palestinian activists—began to cast doubt in my mind on the feasibility of a two-state solution. The settlements had been built to stay. Even if they could physically be dismantled, there was no real political will in Israel to do so. There might never be.

It also seemed to me that American Jewish institutions' ostensible commitment to an indefinitely deferred two-state solution masked the one-state reality of slow, ongoing Israeli annexation of the West Bank. While Hamas's rockets were frightening, and while they could be deadly, Israel's army was so much more technologically advanced, better trained, and more powerful that the Jewish establishment's framing of the war—as a symmetrical conflict between two equal sides—appeared to me as mendacious. Israel was an occupying power that held under its control millions of Palestinians who had no vote in the government that determined their fate. Certainly in the occupied West Bank, it looked like apartheid.

There was no singular moment of definitive rupture with the dogmatism of my Zionist upbringing. I did not wake up one morning and believe myself to have been brainwashed. Instead, there was a slow, yearslong process of wrestling. I do not feel it was something I chose or willed, but more like it was something that happened to me, that I even tried to resist at times. That was, I think, why I went to Israel after finishing high school, and why I would go back after finishing college, and why I continue to go back, even now. To lose the kind of Zionism with which I was raised was to lose my religion. Which meant that as it fell away I would need to return to the sources of the tradition and observance, to Torah, Talmud, Jewish philosophy, to reinforce my Judaism on more solid ground.

IfNotNow

Amid the 2014 war, I received a text from a friend. He was a graduate student at Princeton, and we had taken a philosophy seminar together the previous spring. He had a background in labor and community organizing; he had worked at J Street in the early 2010s. He told me a new group called IfNotNow was starting up to protest the war and American Jewish communal support for it. They were planning a demonstration.

IfNotNow held its first organized act of civil disobedience outside the Madison Avenue offices of the Conference of Presidents. We gathered in a Midtown corporate park and talked out the plan in the cool summer morning air. Part of the group set up posters outside and began to recite aloud the Mourner's Kaddish, the Jewish prayer for the dead, followed by the names of the Palestinians and Israelis who had been killed in the fighting. I was part of the group that went inside the building's lobby and began the sit-in. We linked arms, held on to each other tightly, and began to sing. Over and over, we chanted the Hebrew hymn, "Hinei Ma Tov," which draws its words from Psalm 133. In English, they say, "Behold how good and pleasing it is / For brothers to sit together in unity."

It was the first time I had sang these words in a group in years, even though the song had been a staple of my childhood. I suspect this was true for many of us that day. It was also certainly the first time most of us had sung these words as part of a protest against a war in Israel/ Palestine. Sitting on the cold marble floor, I felt my voice crack. The presence of the other protesters, some of whom would become close friends, strengthened me, but that could not stop the slow drip of foreboding in the back of my mind. By confronting a Jewish establishment institution like this, we had crossed an unspoken line. Organized Jewish life prized the value of unity; we had transgressed it. We wanted to change Jewish life. It seemed just as likely, if not more, that we would end up excommunicated instead.

The NYPD soon arrived, zip tie handcuffs hanging from their belts. They asked us to leave; we refused and kept singing. They arrested us. They cuffed our hands behind our backs, marched us out of the building, along the street, and into two patrol cars that were waiting around the corner. We were processed at a Midtown precinct, then taken to the Manhattan Detention Complex, colloquially known as "the Tombs." We spent the night there, in a fetid holding cell with more than twenty other people, and were released the next morning.

Over the next month, IfNotNow protests spread across the country. Activists staged similar demonstrations in Boston, Chicago, and the Bay Area, in which they recited the Mourner's Kaddish for those killed in the fighting. The hashtag #IfNotNow on Twitter showed countless images of young American Jews tearfully calling for a stop to the war and for the end of American Jewish institutional support for the occupation. In early August, hundreds of people gathered in Brooklyn's Grand Army Plaza for an antiwar protest organized by IfNotNow that drew on the liturgy and ritual for Tisha B'Av, the day Jews traditionally mark the destruction of the Temple in Jerusalem. In 2014, this form of protest, the mix of traditional religion and radical politics, was not the commonplace performance it would become during the tumult of the Trump years and, especially, during the 2023–2024 war. In fact, it became so in large part because of IfNotNow.

The outpouring of interest in IfNotNow during the 2014 war in Gaza illustrated that there were many young American Jews who rejected the establishment's politics. They had disengaged from organized Jewish life, but they had not disengaged from Jewishness. They were seeking out expressions of Jewish identity and community that were untethered from Israeli militarism and that could be harmonized with support for human rights and concern for Palestinian suffering. At the time, it seemed the task of IfNotNow would be to harness this energy into an organized, effective political movement that could, at once, challenge the establishment's monopoly on Jewish identity and end Jewish communal backing for the occupation.

The group's strategic innovation was supposed to be that it would insist on the rhetoric of responsibility. While other left-wing Jewish groups seemed mainly to speak in the language of disavowal, IfNotNow began with Jewish particularity as the starting ground for a politics of compassion and solidarity with Palestinians. If you believed, as IfNotNow insisted back then (and as I still do today), that the mainstream Jewish institutions constituted an important pillar, albeit one among many, that sustained Israel's occupation, then shifting Jewish communal politics was a necessary part of bringing the occupation to an end. By contrast, if you disavowed your community—if you wrote them off entirely—then what reason would those inside still have to listen to you? The Jewish critique of Israeli policies could be leveled most effectively by those who possessed standing, even if tenuous, within mainstream communities. There was always the risk that this would fail, that dissent would appear as disavowal. To start with disavowal and disassociation, though—that was to scream into the void.

Through my early twenties, IfNotNow was my primary Jewish and political affiliation. Still in college during those years, I was not part of the group of disenchanted J Street alumni and Occupy Wall Street veterans who convened for the year following the 2014 protests, when the group suspended its public actions to strategize and build a multiyear plan. I was never a leader. But when IfNotNow reemerged, I rejoined the group's efforts. I helped ghostwrite op-eds and tweets for the group's leaders, older friends who had taken me under their wings. I punctuated hours of writing my senior thesis with video calls over strategy and messaging for the group's upcoming protests. With the hubris typical of a twenty-two-year-old, I believed that what we were doing had never been done before—that until IfNotNow no group had taken on the American Jewish establishment *from within* mainstream Jewish life.

Lost Precedents

Of course, that was not quite true. In 1973, after the Yom Kippur War, a group called Breira, "Alternative," emerged to contest the Jewish establishment's lockstep support for Israeli policies. Breira publicly opposed the construction of settlements in the occupied West Bank and proposed a two-state solution based on an Israeli withdrawal to the pre-1967 borders, to be achieved through direct negotiations with the PLO. While the group drew a segment of its ranks from the preceding decade's counterculture, many in Breira were young rabbis, Jewish professionals, professors, and prominent intellectuals.

The group, in other words, was not a creature of the radical left but a product of the American Jewish mainstream, even its elite. Its platform, designed to be in sync with the Israeli peace camp, was not especially radical either. "All this hardly constitutes a call to the barricades," the historian Jacques Kornberg remarked of Breira's two-state agenda at the time. "The question," he continued, "is whether there is room for this degree of dissent within the American Jewish community."

The answer was no. Breira faced vicious attacks from right-wing and Jewish establishment groups. The group's young rabbis, many of them leaders of campus Hillels, found their jobs threatened. In 1977, far-right militants from Meir Kahane's JDL broke into Breira's national convention, the only one it was ever to hold, and attacked its members. That same year, the Conservative movement's Rabbinical Assembly rejected two nominees for its executive council—Rabbi Arnold Jacob Wolf, then chaplain at Yale, and Everett Gendler, a leading Jewish environmentalist figure—because of their membership in Breira.

By openly opposing the Israeli government's policies—its construction of settlements, its refusal to negotiate with the Palestinians—Breira violated the taboo on American Jewish criticism of Israel in public. And in the eyes of the establishment, that meant it needed to be destroyed. "Dissent ought not to be made public," the Conference of Presidents declared in 1977. "The result is to give aid and comfort to the enemy and to weaken that Jewish unity which is essential for the security of Israel." Establishment groups like the Conference of Presidents succeeded in enforcing the mendacious diktat that Breira and its members were self-hating Jews who endangered Israel and abetted terrorism, and who therefore needed to be shunned from organized Jewish life. By the end of 1978, Breira was dead.

Although the energies that had fueled Breira diminished, they did not evaporate. In 1980, Jewish progressive activists, many of whom had been involved in Breira, founded the New Jewish Agenda. Israel/ Palestine—or "Mideast Peace," as the group named the issue—was only one of the areas on which NJA activists worked. They were pioneering Jewish feminists, advocates for nuclear disarmament, opponents of U.S. military intervention in Central America. For roughly a decade, NJA gave institutional form to the dissenting current in American Jewish life and at its peak boasted several thousand members. Yet, by the early 1990s, the marginality of the American left and the infighting that political isolation almost inevitably produces brought the group down. The result was that, by the mid-1990s, there was no real organized Jewish left to speak of in the United States. There was the magazine *Tikkun*, a lone institutional survivor of the 1980s progressive mobilization and refuge of the graying New Left generation. There were also independent intellectuals laboring on the margins of American life, scholars like Marc Ellis, who articulated a Jewish liberation theology that opposed Israel's occupation and rejected the transformation of Judaism into an ideology for the legitimation of the Israel exercise of military force, and diasporists like the brothers Jonathan and Daniel Boyarin. But unless one was already part of a left-wing activist milieu, sources of dissent were difficult to find. From within mainstream Jewish life, they could hardly be seen at all.

The Outside Game

One small group that did survive the political desert of the 1990s was Jewish Voice for Peace. It has since become one of the most visible

Jewish organizations within the Palestine solidarity activist ecosystem. Like IfNotNow, JVP grew dramatically in the late Obama years as young American Jews sought out new forms of Jewish identity and community against the backdrop of Israel's wars in Gaza and racial justice protests in the United States. Yet, for much of its existence, JVP had mainly been "more of a cultural exchange organization," explained Rebecca Vilkomerson, who led the group between 2009 and 2019. "It didn't have a super sharp politics."

That began to change with the outbreak of the second intifada. At first, JVP's more politicized members were largely secular baby boomers. They saw themselves firstly as leftists, veterans of the civil rights and anti-apartheid movements who happened to be Jewish. To the extent that they embraced their Jewishness publicly, it was in strategic, instrumental terms—"utilizing their Jewishness because they thought it would be more effective in criticizing Israeli policies," as Vilkomerson put it.

The thinking was that if Jews spoke out against Israeli policies as Jews, it would not only make them appear more credible; it would also neutralize the charge of antisemitism that establishment groups were quick to brandish against Israel's critics. (This, in fact, would not work.) For roughly a decade, this paradigm—epitomized by the slogan "Not in Our Name" on signs at JVP rallies—dominated the subculture of Jewish anti-occupation activism.

After Israel's 2008 war in Gaza, a cohort of younger activists bolstered JVP's ranks. Often the products of Jewish day schools and summer camps, they arrived with less ambivalence about Jewish ritual and observance than the older generation of staunch secularists and red-diaper babies. But what they shared with their predecessors was that they, too, had little interest in rejoining or changing communities that they had left. "From 2009 to 2014, the leading edge of JVP was actually more observant anti-Zionists," Vilkomerson said. "The reason they were able to be confidently anti-Zionist is because they had a Jewish practice." They felt at home in Jewish liturgy and texts. "They didn't need Israel to be Jewish." Which meant they didn't need the establishment's stamp of approval either.

The decision to forgo engaging with mainstream Jewish institutions was a strategic one. In the 2000s, JVP had sought acceptance within mainstream umbrella organizations in places like the Bay Area. Repeated rejections seemed to illustrate the futility of the inside game. "We made a very clear decision," Vilkomerson said of the change she instigated when she assumed leadership of the group in 2009. "We're not interested in the Jewish establishment; it is bankrupt. We are going to build our own establishment, one that allows people to be their full political selves, their full queer selves, their full convert selves, and their full interfaith selves." The underlying logic was that, beyond the communal institutions and the norms of conduct and affiliation that they enforced, there existed a silent plurality of alienated and unaffiliated American Jews who would flock to the antiestablishmentarian call. "Ultimately our theory of change was growth," Vilkomerson said. "The idea was to get big enough to wield actual political power."

And JVP did grow. Today, it claims thousands of members. Its social media accounts boast massive followings. It has a PAC and a presence on Capitol Hill. But within the mainstream Jewish world, it remains beyond the pale: barred from affiliating with campus Hillels, denounced by rabbis in sermons, portrayed by the establishment as a threat to the Jewish people. In May 2022, ADL CEO Jason Greenblatt described JVP as "the photo inverse of the Extreme Right." That stigmatization reflects the McCarthyist character of the Jewish establishment. But it is also, in part, the product of JVP's ideological choice, its adversarial approach, its commitment to the outside game. "I think people understood—and it was true—that our main responsibilities were not to the Jewish world," Vilkomerson said. "The critique was that we weren't putting Jewish life before universal principles. That maybe broke some rule of Jewish communal life."

In 2019, JVP announced that it was a doctrinally anti-Zionist organization, making it the only such group on the American Jewish landscape.

A Mixed Balance Sheet

By the late 2010s, groups like IfNotNow and JVP had succeeded in shattering the illusion of monolithic American Jewish opinion about Israel and Zionism. One could no longer claim in good faith that Israel was a matter of Jewish consensus. Zionism could no longer conjure a widely shared sense of pride.

Instead, Israel had become the greatest source of division in American Jewish life. At synagogues, on campuses, and at community centers, events about Israel became wellsprings of acrimony. Debates sometimes degenerated into threats of violence; protests of Israeli and right-wing figures were suppressed increasingly with real physical attacks. Division over Israel had, of course, been brewing for many years, long before IfNotNow and JVP's rise, but now the dissension had become explosive. Pushed from the right, then from the left, the pillar of Zionism, the substitute faith of American Judaism, was crumbling.

It turned out, however, that Jewish establishment organizations had long since insulated themselves from popular pressure. Funded and controlled by a small set of donors whose concerns differ vastly from those of most American Jews, the establishment proved impervious to the collapse of the old ideological consensus in American Jewish life. They have continued to operate as if on autopilot.

The organizations of the millennial-led Jewish left became incubators of vibrant progressive Jewish subcultures, but they have not come close to rivaling the wealth and political power wielded by groups like AIPAC and the Conference of Presidents. Neither IfNotNow's old strategy of connected criticism and campaigns of direct pressure nor JVP's prefigurative politics and counter-institution building translated into much influence in Washington. U.S. policy in the Middle East remains as supportive of Israeli government policies as ever.

Still, after Donald Trump descended his golden escalator in the summer of 2015, the establishment's disconnectedness from its putative constituents would work to the advantage of the growing movement of American Jewish progressives. Especially after Trump's election in 2016, the new Jewish left was well positioned to offer American Jews an outlet. Decades of domination by hawkish and conservative donors meant that no establishment Jewish group was going to back protests against Trump, especially since he promised to enact almost every line of their agenda when it came to Israel. IfNotNow and JVP, by contrast, were not held back by the small politics of big donors and wealthy boards and could therefore mobilize quickly. Much like other progressive, millennial-dominated groups such as the Democratic Socialists of America, IfNotNow and JVP's ranks swelled. Young American Jews were searching for a political community that they could not find within the mainstream institutions.

IfNotNow and JVP had both been founded with an explicit focus on Israel/Palestine, but amid the rise of Trump and the reappearance of violent antisemitism that accompanied it, the focus of their new members turned inward. They still cared about ending the occupation, but the Trump era had catalyzed a categorical shift in their political self-understanding. They now felt themselves to be victims in America, threatened by the same right-wing, ethnonationalist forces that threatened Black and brown people. Before Trump, the new Jewish left had predominantly advanced a critique of Jewish state power as embodied by Israel. Now they became preoccupied with Jewish vulnerability and the dangers posed by antisemitic white nationalism. After years of learning to decenter themselves in activist spaces, young American Jews found that the Trump era had enabled them to dwell on their own experiences, and there was something exhilarating, even freeing about this.

For these young Jews did not simply want to protest as concerned citizens or abstract individuals; they wanted to protest Trump and the surging far right *as Jews*. IfNotNow and JVP had already been experimenting with forms of public Jewishness and protest, with slogans and banners that drew on liturgical Hebrew. During the Trump years, the embrace of Jewish victimhood and vulnerability further catalyzed the deployment of Jewish imagery and language as part of a broader cultural swing, another return to identity, to roots. Signs emblazoned with Hebrew and Yiddish, invoking past heroic periods of Jewish struggle, would become fixtures of anti-Trump protests. An alternative to the plutocratic, right-wing Zionist politics of the establishment took living form in the streets. Perhaps not since the 1930s had a left-wing Jewish politics claimed such a presence in American life.

The Generational War

There was no small irony here too. For decades, the leaders of the mainstream Jewish denominations had lamented high rates of disaffiliation among young American Jews. They had bemoaned what they saw as the growing disregard among young Jews for Jewish culture and practice. And yet, in the late 2010s, here they were: young American Jews protesting with IfNotNow against AIPAC in Washington, D.C., and against the Zionist Organization of America's embrace of Trump's consigliere Steve Bannon in New York City; young American Jews who felt fondly toward Jewish culture and practice and ritual and liturgy, who did not confine their Judaism to the synagogue but brought it with them into the streets. In another world, the young activists of the 2010s Jewish left should have represented the Jewish mainstream's dream. A wiser, more flexible, more compassionate Jewish institutional leadership might have tried, as the establishment did in the 1960s and '70s, to co-opt the youthful insurgents or induce them back into the communal tent.

That did not happen. Instead, the Jewish establishment anathematized an entire generational cohort of young American Jews. Major Jewish donors funded online blacklists, like the infamous Canary Mission, to track and shame anti-occupation and Palestine-solidarity activists. Establishment groups plowed vast sums of money into counterpropaganda and *hasbara* (pro-Israel rationalizations) that might have otherwise gone to better use, say, to rehabilitating the derelict infrastructure of non-Orthodox Jewish education. American Jewish leaders left no doubt that they would prefer to foreclose their institutions' futures than to give credence to the views of the people they claim to represent.

5

SHATTERING AND BUILDING

I.

Late in the 2010s, a certain myth of American goodness shattered, at least for those who still believed in it. In 2015 a white supremacist terrorist walked into the Mother Emanuel AME Church in Charleston, South Carolina, and shot nine Black churchgoers dead. In 2017 white nationalist and neo-Nazi supporters of President Donald Trump rallied in Charlottesville, Virginia, waving Confederate and Nazi flags and chanting "Jews will not replace us" during their torchlit march. In 2018 a white nationalist gunman, inflamed by President Trump's anti-immigrant and conspiratorial rhetoric, shot and killed eleven Jews while they prayed on Shabbat morning at the Tree of Life synagogue in Pittsburgh, Pennsylvania—the deadliest antisemitic attack in U.S. history.

What did it mean to be an American Jew when the country seemed on the verge of implosion? This was not a question that could be answered from within the mainstream of Jewish life. American Jewish identity had consolidated itself in the second half of the last century, in a much more hopeful period; it lacked the resources to confront an America where the overarching feeling was one of despair. Back then, America had seemed a haven for Jews, a place of openness and possibility, and for many American Jews this experience confirmed its generalizability: if America could enable the flourishing and inclusion of the Jews, who for so long had lived as a collective pariah, then it was only a matter of time before all other groups and minorities, no matter how oppressed, would enjoy the same. Yet by 2016 this optimistic trend line seemed to have frighteningly and rapidly reversed.

One response to this sense of crisis was protest. For those of us who participated in the countless marches, rallies, and vigils, the years between 2015 and 2020 blurred together into a single lugubrious sequence: marching down Broadway in Manhattan on a frigid December Saturday after a Staten Island grand jury declined to indict the NYPD officer who strangled Eric Garner; standing in a sunbaked Union Square Park the following summer as the crowd chanted "If we don't get justice, burn it down"; the next winter, standing, again, under a colorless sky, crushed in a sea of knitted pink hats on the National Mall. After 2016, the pace and intensity increased. We dashed to airports after President Trump announced his "Muslim ban," staged sit-ins at immigration detention centers, and gathered in public parks after the killing of another unarmed Black person by the police. The seasons changed, time passed, but the signs, the chants—the ritual—remained constants.

During these protests, there was often a moment when the entire mass of people would register in some ineffable yet palpable way an overwhelming feeling of disappointment coupled with disbelief: How could this be happening? *This* being the trajectory of the country that had swerved dangerously and dramatically downward. I, and I suspect many others born in the 1990s, had fully assimilated to the optimism of the decade in the middle of which I was born. Intellectually, I knew that history has no arc, certainly not a progressive one, but emotionally I still expected the world of my early adulthood to be better than my childhood. In my gut I still anticipated the gradual solving of once intractable problems, or at the very least that things would not seem like they were getting worse. Even the most jaded, seasoned of leftists—

who eons ago had internalized the reality that the American government perpetrated terrible, violent acts, that the myths that those in power told about America were, in fact, myths—shared in the feeling that something had gone terribly wrong.

Against this backdrop, and from within the largely youth-led activist movements that exploded during these years, a new kind of Jewish politics began to emerge. It took its cues from the Black Lives Matter movement, with which it insisted on standing in solidarity. Newly awake to the old and ongoing reality of anti-Black violence in America, many young American Jews exchanged the moral-triumphalist Americanism of their forebears for a deep pessimism about the American project. They focused instead on its "original sin" of slavery and sought to correct its lingering contemporary legacies.

After Trump's election, America began to appear so monstrous that these American Jews compared their government's policies—its detention and separation of migrant families at the southern border—to those of history's most terrible regimes. America ceased to be the great vanquisher of Nazi fascism and became its analogue. Soon, this darkened view of America extended to what they saw as the place of Jews within it. Jews now appeared among America's victims: white, but only conditionally so; stripped of their culture by assimilation and upward mobility; threatened by the same white nationalist violence that threatened other minorities. And from this renewed feeling of victimhood followed a reclamation of public Jewish identity and, to a degree, the rediscovery of forgotten Jewish histories and sources.

Jews for Black Lives

The killing of Michael Brown in Ferguson, Missouri, and the violent suppression of the protests that followed dealt a fatal blow to the dreams of national redemption on which Barack Obama's election had sailed. All the high-minded talk about the gradual dawning of a post-racial future, of the eventual overcoming of America's original sin, suffocated amid the tear gas fired by the Ferguson police and the Missouri National Guard. The protests laid bare the fact that beneath the glossy, self-congratulatory surface of Obama-era liberalism there remained a bleeding wound. They revealed that what the writer Ta-Nehisi Coates has called the "plunder" of Black America—the plunder on which the country was founded—had not stopped but was, in fact, ongoing, seemingly unarrested by the first Black presidency. The Black Lives Matter movement drew its power from this deep well of disappointment. With its minimal slogan, its politics of bare life, it toed the line of despair. That the worth of Black life was still a question seemed to indicate how little the post–civil rights decades had really achieved.

Among white people, American Jews were perhaps particularly invested in the optimistic narrative about America that Obama was to have represented. As true believers in America's exceptional goodness, many American Jews also took as axiomatic the possibility of transcending the matter of race and rectifying once and for all the legacies of slavery and Jim Crow. America was unlike Europe: it was not supposed to have ancient hatreds in need of extirpation. While anti-Black racism was, of course, embedded deep in American culture, even constitutive of a certain American whiteness, anti-Black racism was not supposed to be immutable. Obama's election buoyed the hope that it was only a matter of time before such racism went the way of American antisemitism and was banished from public life.

After Ferguson, this hope appeared foolish, naïve, even irresponsible. To many, the post-racial dream now seemed, at best, to be an illusion, and at worse an ideological screen that obscured the reality of persistent structural racism. American public life gradually became suffused with a vocabulary that had once lived mainly on the academic or activist margins: privilege, intersectionality, microaggressions. Soon, American Jews began to rethink their own place in the country's landscape of marginalization. Many hoped to show that they were allies to the emerging Black Lives Matter movement. They felt themselves to be.

But underneath this solidarity there was also a slow-burning, creeping anxiety. For much of the first half of the twentieth century, American Jewish groups understood their own struggle for civil rights in relation to that of African Americans. The much-vaunted Jewish involvement in the civil rights movement was, in no small part, motivated by self-interest as much as egalitarian commitment—the pragmatic calculation that if racism and discrimination were eliminated, not only African Americans but also Jews would benefit. What did it now mean, some American Jews asked, that the progress made by the civil rights movement appeared to be coming undone?

Of course, in reality, the relationship between Black and Jewish politics was never so straightforward. The often-imagined parallel destinies of Blacks and Jews is, in large part, a delusion. American Jews have enjoyed almost linear upward mobility and assimilation; most American Jews are white and have been counted as such in political terms since the country's establishment, even as they faced forms of civil discrimination through the first half of the twentieth century. The collapse of what some call the "Black-Jewish alliance" in the post–civil rights period reflected the fact that the divergent experiences of Blacks and Jews could not be managed within a shared political framework.

Moreover, beginning in the 1970s, the Jewish right and center began to take this divergence as the starting point for a politics of backlash and resentment. The neoconservatives, articulators of the inward turn, were the pioneers. For the neoconservatives, Jewish prosperity in America disproved the existence of structural racism, disproved the need for affirmative action, reparations, or any kind of race-based redistribution. In his book *Ethnic Dilemmas*, the sociologist Nathan Glazer claimed Jews had done just fine pulling themselves out of immigrant poverty without any of the programs the post-sixties civil rights movement was demanding. In the pages of *Commentary*, the neoconservatives reaffirmed the myth of America's inherent goodness and, as a corollary, centered political debate on the question: Why can't Black Americans be more like Jews? Even American Jews who rejected this understanding held on to the myth that progress was not only possible but inevitable; of all people, we should know.

Partly as a legacy of the right wing's takeover of Jewish institutions in the 1980s, American Jewish organizational support for the Black Lives Matter movement was, initially, not especially visible or widespread. The Jewish establishment largely kept its distance from the protests; their anti-systemic and often unruly character clashed with the sensibilities of the leaders of these groups, who were more comfortable with carefully stage-managed politics and bland consensual rhetoric. Jewish communal leaders may have liked to quote Martin Luther King Jr.—they may have even agreed with his remark that "a riot is the language of the unheard"—but if any demonstration even hinted toward a riot, they wanted nothing to do with it. Instead, they issued rote condemnations of property destruction and joined calls for a return to order.

There was also, for the Jewish establishment, the problem of the Palestinian connection. Israel's 2014 war on Gaza had begun just a few weeks before the uprising in Ferguson. As militarized police, guns drawn, bore down on unarmed Black protesters, comparisons to Israel/Palestine were immediate. Palestinian activists, watching from afar, tweeted advice to the Black Lives Matter protesters about how to handle tear gas and evade rubber bullets; they announced their solidarity. Black activists, in turn, began to describe the situation in Ferguson as a military occupation. It certainly looked that way. During those late summer nights, on the shaky live streams and in the grainy photos, Ferguson resembled Ramallah.

For establishment Jewish groups, even to entertain such a comparison was unacceptable. Columnists syndicated in Jewish newspapers accused the Black Lives Matter protesters of antisemitism. From 2014 until the George Floyd uprising in 2020, organizations like the Anti-Defamation League and the Jewish Federations would treat the surging Black-led movement with a suspicion that barely masked their silent contempt.

But while these establishment groups withheld their support for the movement, there were many young American Jews who wanted to join the protests. For the most part, they were neither discouraged nor menaced by the open parallels between American and Israeli versions of apartheid and the visible displays of Black-Palestinian solidarity. In fact, these young American Jews often seemed to want to participate in the Black Lives Matter protests visibly as Jews. They brought signs bearings Hebrew letters and held aloft banners that read, "Justice, Justice You Shall Pursue." Ahead of one protest later in the summer of 2014, I debated with a friend about whether he should wear his kippah specifically to show that Jews were showing up to back the movement. It was the first of many such conversations about public Jewishness and protest that I would have over the next several years.

Why might a young American Jew want to attend a Black-led protest visibly identifiable as a Jew? My friend's answer was an amalgam of half-formed notions and good intentions; in this, I don't think he was unique. It presupposed a belief, even if unsayable, that the optimistic myth could be saved by a wholesome gesture, that what felt like the beginning of a terrifying slide backward could be arrested by the force of goodwill. Some, I think, also wanted to demonstrate that there existed "Jews of conscience"—Jews whose political commitments had not narrowed merely to Israel advocacy, who still believed in a broad conception of justice for all people, and who were not content with a garrisoned, defensive organized Jewish community set apart from the rest of American society. Others seemed to believe that any display of Jewish solidarity with the Black Lives Matter movement might help to repair the long-running rift between Jewish people and Black people in this country.

In retrospect, there was also, to no small degree, a desire for exculpation at work here. For many, embracing Jewish particularity seemed a way to dilute the sting of the charge of white privilege. Jewish particularity reconnected one with the long history of Jewish suffering. Even those who knew that most American Jews experience the world as white insisted that Jews are also, in important ways, different from other white people. After all, we, too, had a history of oppression. We, too, had suffered as the ultimate "Other" at the hands of a brutal state.

A (Old) New Jewish Left

It turned out that this structure of feeling was shared by many other American Jews, waiting to be mobilized. In some parts of Brooklyn and the Bay Area, it sometimes even seemed like it was on its way to becoming a dominant sensibility. Young American Jews, especially, began to seek out more ways to become politically involved and support the protests. Suddenly, the ranks of groups like New York City's Jews for Racial & Economic Justice (JFREJ) began to grow.

Founded in the 1990s, JFREJ is an archetypical stalwart of New York's left-wing activist scene. It was the political home of Jewish gay and lesbian activists who had survived the AIDS epidemic, old-school Jewish communists who kept the language and culture of Jewish dissent alive, veteran feminists who'd given their lives to the struggle for reproductive rights. In the late 2010s it experienced something of a revival. It became a beacon for young American Jews looking for a more radical alternative within a Jewish organizational landscape that had flattened into an array of pro-Israel groups and anodyne, nominally philanthropic initiatives.

Like the country as a whole, JFREJ was "extremely transformed by the movement for Black Lives," said Dove Kent, who led the group from 2011 to 2017. "We were started by lesbians and queers and that's who we were for a long time," she said. After Ferguson, and especially after Trump's election, the range of people attending JFREJ meetings began expanding dramatically. "We hit some weird barometer where all of a sudden a whole roomful of cis men are, like, 'JFREJ is my home,'" Kent said, laughing.

Many existing progressive groups underwent similar shifts. As the American promise appeared to be fading, groups like JFREJ provided people, especially young Jews, with a theoretical framework to understand what was happening and provided ample opportunities—marches, meetings, pickets—to put that theory into practice. Because many of these older groups had been involved in racial justice and solidarity work for years, they also had close ties to grassroots Black-led and anti-racist organizations. At a time when protest politics were becoming increasingly disorganized and semi-spontaneous, mediated by algorithm instead of personal connection, such real and rare ties gave groups like JFREJ an aura of legitimacy.

Sophie Ellman-Golan, today JFREJ's director of strategic communications, was part of the post-Ferguson influx to the group. A self-described "Park Slope, New York, Jew," her path to progressive activism was one that many other young American Jews followed during the years after 2014. (In other regards, Ellman-Golan's trajectory was exceptional: she was the deputy head of communications of the Women's March at twenty-six.)

What brought her to JFREJ, she said, was that the group embodied an expression of Jewishness that she had not found anywhere else: "fundamentally feminist, anti-capitalist . . . in addition to being anti-racist." Most of all, the activism felt to her vibrant, dynamic, suffused with meaning compared to the dull routines of conventional communal life.

Raised in a practicing Jewish home, the daughter of a liberal rabbi, Ellman-Golan had drifted away from organized Judaism as she entered college, where she majored in African American studies. She described the Jewishness practiced by her family as centered on singing together, liturgy, and identification with historical Jewish struggles for justice. On campus, by contrast, Jewish life seemed shallow, focused on Israel advocacy, Birthright trips, and summer camp nostalgia. "It just didn't feel like me," she said. What did feel like a better fit was the kind of Jewishness represented by JFREJ, which she encountered during a march on Staten Island after the killing of Eric Garner. Ellman-Golan recognized the group's signs and joined them. "I was like, 'Oh, we are out here as Jews and we are proudly saying we are Jewish and marching for Black lives,'" Ellman-Golan said. "For the first time, I was proud to be publicly Jewish."

There was, during those first years of the Black Lives Matter movement, both a mournfulness and an optimism that could be felt during the protests. Soon, though, the optimism faded. Police killings of unarmed Black people did not stop after Ferguson. To the contrary, they seemed to become more frequent and more visible. Horrifying videos of Black people's last moments were recorded on cell phone cameras and circulated widely on social media. There were days and weeks when images of Black death felt ubiquitous. And while this feeling fueled the righteous rage that powered near-continuous protest, it also began to erode the conviction that the problems of racialized police violence and inequality could be mitigated at all. If, as some Black radical theorists argued, racism was inexorably encoded in the country's DNA, if the original sin could never be atoned for, then the problem was not just racism. The problem was America. Increasingly, American progressives, among them progressive Jews, began to fear that America could not be redeemed.

The emergence of Donald Trump as a Republican presidential candidate and the accompanying surge of openly racist animosity greatly deepened this fear. The forces of bigotry, intolerance, and violence seemed far more powerful than previously imagined. The depth of white resentment toward what the Obama administration represented appeared surprisingly great. The intensity of white anger toward Black Lives Matter for insisting on the reality of ongoing racial oppression began to overflow the container of conventional politics and find expression in the beatings of protesters at Trump rallies and in the American right's open celebration of these assaults. This was only a preview.

II.

After Trump's election in 2016, the sense of emergency that the Ferguson uprising had induced among progressive activists engulfed American life as a whole. For many American Jews, Trump's election was especially jarring because it was accompanied by the reappearance— for the first time in recent memory—of open and sometimes violent antisemitism in U.S. politics. The president egged on the alt-right and dog-whistled to neo-Nazis. He indulged in antisemitic rhetoric even when he tried to praise the Jews he claimed he admired. In the common American Jewish myth of America's exceptional goodness, the country was supposed to have been basically immune from what pundits called the "virus" of antisemitism. But now the country seemed to be very sick.

Most American Jews are also liberals, and like their fellow liberals they debated—endlessly, exhaustively—the question: What, really, did the rise of Trump and the resurgence of antisemitism mean? Was it all an aberration, a terrible but temporary deviation from the American norm? Or was it all a great, final act of unmasking, the culmination of the pathological injustices that had afflicted the republic since its beginnings? Was it business as usual, just under new and more colorful management? Or was fascism on the horizon? At protests and on social media, some people declared indignantly, "This is not who we are," as if simply saying these words could make them true. Others replied to them, "No, this is what we have always been." It was hard to argue against the latter group because they seemed to have most of U.S. history on their side.

And if Trump was "the first white president," as Ta-Nehisi Coates wrote, what were the implications for Jews? For much of the American Jewish century, Jewish organizations had lobbied for the incorporation of Jews into the dominant conception of whiteness in the hopes of evading the fate of immigrants classified as nonwhite. In 1909 the American Jewish Committee even successfully pressured Congress and the Census Bureau to remove the racial category of "Hebrew" from the census forms. To a great extent, the efforts at whitening succeeded. To no small degree, this is what made the affluence and stability that defined the American Jewish century possible.

The presence of Jews in prominent positions within the Trump administration complicated matters further. Trump's own son-in-law Jared Kushner, Trump's senior advisor and speechwriter Steven Miller, and Treasury secretary Steven Mnuchin—to name only a few—all made Trump's flirtation with antisemitism more vexing by giving his administration very public Jewish cover. Trump and his surrogates frequently boasted that his administration was "the most pro-Israel in history"—and yet, at the same time, it seemed the most openly tolerant of white nationalism. It was a confusing combination of visibility and vulnerability that seemed redolent of previous centuries in Europe, when select Jews occupied powerful positions as advisors to princes and doctors to kings, while the Jewish masses faced down expulsion and violence at the hands of their peasant neighbors. That the same dynamic, albeit updated for the digital age, now seemed to define American Jewish life appeared as another warning sign that America's promise might prove false—that it was not, in fact, exceptional after all.

The cumulative effect of such fears and the renewed sense of victimhood was, perhaps counterintuitively, the reanimation of Jewish communal life. Paradoxical though this may sound, Donald Trump was a gift to American Judaism at the very moment when it appeared, again, to be losing its sense of purpose. Disaffiliation and disengagement had for years been the norm, and while these trends did not reverse themselves, American Jews did begin to reengage with their Jewishness in new ways. They seemed to return to their heritage, their history, and, yes, some, although not most, even returned to shul. It was as if the reappearance of American antisemitism had tripped an old, instinctual Jewish wire.

Rabbi Marc Katz was working at Brooklyn's Congregation Beth Elohim, the borough's largest Reform temple, at the time of Trump's inauguration. A thoughtful, passionate speaker, he described an enormous outpouring of political energy within the community in the election's aftermath. When the temple held its first meeting to strategize about how best to respond to the Trump presidency, "the whole neighborhood turned up," Katz said. "There was a line up around the block of people who couldn't get in" because the sanctuary was filled. "And 1,200 people can fit in that sanctuary," he added.

The postelection boom seemed to shake liberal American Jews out of their complacent, Obama-era slumber. "People really woke up," said Rabbi Jill Jacobs, CEO of T'ruah, a rabbinic human-rights NGO. They were also newly curious about alternative modes of Jewishness. "People [were] looking for some kind of connection" to Judaism, and "it just might not look like what it used to look like," Jacobs, who was ordained by the Jewish Theological Seminary, told me. If prayer could no longer get liberal American Jews through the synagogue doors, it now seemed like protest could.

Even within once lethally somnolent Jewish congregations, politics did not just inflect and restructure religion; politics became an expression of religion itself. Among the many norms the Trump era demolished was the convention that partisan politics ought to have no place in dignified, respectable congregational life.

This had been a long-standing, even fundamental assumption of postwar synagogue culture. For decades, especially in the more conservatively inclined suburban congregations, rabbis had insisted on the assiduous separation of politics and the pulpit. Israel, of course, was an exception, being the transcendent cause of Jewish life and, as such, presumed to be above political dispute. According to this quietist line of reasoning, congregants were not coming to synagogue to hear a gloss on the *Times* op-ed pages but instead to be spiritually enlivened by a *drash* on the week's Torah portion. In practice, this meant that in many congregations religious life was almost hermetically sealed off from current affairs. In places like the community where I grew up, the general evasion of politics also reflected the uneasy truce between Democrats and Republicans. For the sake of communal unity, the clergy preferred that some things go undiscussed.

After 2016, more and more rabbis appeared willing to rethink the old, conventional relationship between rabbinic practice and activism. Of course, this rethinking was most prevalent in Jewish communities that were predominantly liberal. But it was not restricted to them either. After all, the country had veered into a period of disorienting crisis. For many rabbis, this meant that they had an obligation to speak to the times.

"The wrong question is: Should we preach politics," said Rabbi Sharon Brous, the founder and spiritual leader of IKAR, a nondenominational community in Los Angeles. "The right question is: What is the role of the moral or faith leader in a time of moral crisis?"

Brous had insisted on synthesizing progressive activist politics with traditionalist liturgy since long before Trump's election. IKAR—known for its artsy, hippie aesthetic and, for much of its life, the lack of a building of its own—took a commitment to social justice as one of its core tenets. "We were, as a community, deeply enmeshed in the conversation" about racial justice and immigrant rights, she said. After 2016, Brous seemed to insist even more strongly on linking the political and the religious. On Rosh Hashanah in 2017, she delivered a sermon titled "Our Country Was Built on a Stolen Beam," in which she made the case for reparations for slavery.

For other congregations, however, the Trump-era pivot was not as seamless. While "in mainstream Jewish spaces there was a growing awareness that this administration [Trump's] and these ideas were unprecedented or dangerous and demanded a kind of moral clarity in response," Brous said, the lingering effects of the old apolitical model of Jewish leadership meant that many communities were at first unprepared to respond to an American president who seemed hostile to Jews and non-Jewish minorities alike. Because many mainstream Jewish organizations "had essentially sidelined that [activist] part of the Jewish experience," Brous said, "there wasn't a muscle tissue that had developed."

Nor was everyone satisfied by the activist turn in liberal Jewish life. Right-leaning Jewish figures often griped that support for the Democrats had replaced belief in God as the core of liberal Judaism (and there is, regrettably, some truth to this, although the same could also be said of some right-wing, Trumpist congregations). But for Brous, such dissatisfaction only attested to the absurdity of trying to maintain distance from the political during the Trump years. She recalled the story of a rabbinic colleague whose board members had, after Trump's election, forbade him from invoking Pharaoh in order to respect the ideological divisions within the community. "He couldn't say the word 'Pharaoh' because it could be read as an implicit critique of Donald Trump!" Over the course of Jewish history, Brous said, "we did not run into burning buildings to pull out these scrolls in order to mute them and make them irrelevant precisely at the moment when they matter most."

Yet if Brous represented the vanguard of liberal rabbis as they confronted the cruelties of the Trump era, her politics also exemplified the new ambivalences of Jews who had begun to despair over the fate of America. Brous, it seemed, wanted to refashion American Judaism into a religion of protest. But American Judaism had, since its arrival on these shores, taken shape as a religion of empire.

For almost all of American Jewish history, Jewish leaders have understood themselves as willing and sometimes enthusiastic participants in what they saw as America's special earthly mission. Early Jewish advocates in America spoke of America's "providential" qualities and described the country as the real promised land. The belief in the exceptional and inherent goodness of the American project was fundamental to much of modern mainstream Judaism, embraced by Reform, Conservative, and Modern Orthodox thinkers alike. With a few exceptions, even those Jewish leaders who joined social movements in America did so under the banner of pushing America to fulfill its promise. What did Jewish activism mean when that promise seemed illusory or, worse, a lie?

Of all the horrors of the Trump presidency, perhaps none challenged this old and deeply held tenet of American Jewish life more than the 2018 Tree of Life synagogue massacre in the Pittsburgh neighborhood of Squirrel Hill. The antisemitic attacks that marked the Trump era reanimated fears that many American Jews had, for the most part, long relegated to the back of their collective consciousness. America began to appear much less like the promised land it seemed to be for nineteenth- and twentieth-century rabbis and more like another site of exile, of diaspora—another place where Jews could be oppressed. America looked less like the *goldene medine* of American Jewish myth and more like the dark regimes of the *alte heym*.

III.

These Are Camps

In the summer of 2018, reports began to circulate of inhumane conditions at detention facilities along the country's southern border. Journalists described seeing children in cages, huddled under large foil sheets given to them as blankets, separated from their parents. As days and months went by, it turned out that thousands of parents and children, many from Central America, had been torn from each other's arms. Even after the Trump administration issued an executive order reversing its policy of family separation, the practice continued. When a *New York Times* reporter visited a detention center in Clint, Texas, where children as young as seven and eight were being held, she described "a chaotic scene of sickness and filth."

The Trump administration's draconian immigration detention policies proved to be, for many American Jews, the ultimate test of their belief in America. And for many, it was a test that their faith would not survive.

Since Trump's announcement of the Muslim ban in January 2017, immigrant rights had been a major focal point of Jewish anti-Trump activism. Yet the policy of family separation at the border struck at something very deep within the American Jewish consciousness. In the South and Central American immigrants facing hostile border patrol officers, many American Jews could see a version of their own forebears: people who had also fled poverty and oppression, who had crossed borders, sometimes without the requisite papers. Even if they did not engage deeply with scripture, they knew the biblical injunction that first appears in the book of Exodus: "You shall not oppress a stranger, for you know the feelings of a stranger, having yourselves been strangers in the Land of Egypt." Everything about the Trump border policy ran counter to this commandment.

In the summer of 2019, a new Jewish group called Never Again Action, which had grown out of IfNotNow, began to stage sit-ins and acts of civil disobedience outside of immigration detention facilities. The group's rhetoric and name—invoking the post-Holocaust imperative to prevent at all costs its repetition—drew a direct parallel between the U.S. government's treatment of immigrants and the Nazi Reich's treatment of Jews. In a matter of a few months the group seemed to take off. In July and August, hundreds of American Jews protested outside of an ICE detention facility in Elizabeth, New Jersey. More than 1,000 protesters shut down traffic in Boston, where eighteen people were arrested.

Never Again Action and smaller, similarly aligned groups staged protests in New York City, Philadelphia, Providence, Los Angeles, San Francisco, and Washington, D.C. The group's message—and, surprisingly, the comparison that it implied—seemed to resonate widely.

That was an indication of how disenchanted some American Jews had become with the country under Trump. The underlying, less-than-subtle argument that Never Again Action put forth was that the Trump presidency had taken the country in a Hitlerian direction. "The military camps where my people are being held today are concentration camps; just like the camps my people were held in 75 years ago were concentration camps," said Tae Phoenix, a Jewish Latina activist-artist, in a statement released by the group that summer. For an older generation of American Jews, the United States was the moral antithesis of Nazi Germany. For these largely millennial Jewish activists, by contrast, the United States now appeared to be Nazi Germany's moral parallel.

By making such a comparison, the Never Again Action organizers broke with the view of the Holocaust that mainstream Jewish institutions had long promulgated and defended. Under the old model, groups like the Anti-Defamation League maintained that the Holocaust was "unique" and "incomparable" to any other human event. Establishment Jewish leaders often charged that to make such a comparison was an affront to the memory of the victims and the survivors, even that it was antisemitic.

For the Never Again Action protesters and other Jewish immigrants' rights advocates, the memory of the Holocaust implied a different moral imperative: not to let the kind of suffering that Jewish victims endured under the Nazis befall any other people. These activists hoped to resignify Jewish suffering as a bridge to solidarity with other historically marginalized communities.

Just as significant, the comparison between the United States under Trump and Germany under Hitler reflected the continuing reevaluation of the Jewish relationship to America. Postwar Jewish identity had come to rest on the understanding of the United States as a beacon of freedom and tolerance. In the postwar Jewish consensus, the U.S. role in World War II made the country into the liberator of concentration camps and the global guarantor of human rights. America claimed for itself this image and consecrated it through institutions like the U.S. Holocaust Museum constructed on the National Mall—a national museum to an atrocity that happened elsewhere.

Now, in the rhetoric of many progressive Jewish activists, America appeared as a fascist, totalitarian, even murderous regime. Perhaps not since the Vietnam War had so many Jewish activists denounced the United States in such terms or hewed to such a catastrophic, pessimistic view of its history. One crucial difference, though, between the antiwar protests of the 1960s and '70s and the anti-Trump movements of the late 2010s was that in the latter the Jewish participants also saw themselves among the victims of the U.S. state. In the view of many millennial Jewish activists, while America under Trump threatened, first and foremost, Black and brown people, it posed a significant threat to Jews too.

Reclaiming Suffering

Through their rediscovery, so to speak, of Jewish victimhood, progressive Jewish activists during the Trump years scrambled older political convictions. Since the 1960s, if not earlier, a politics centered on Jewish suffering had, for the most part, been the hallmark of the Jewish right. The muscular Zionism of the Jewish establishment and Israel advocacy infrastructure, the anti-communism of the Soviet Jewry movement, and the vigilantism of Meir Kahane's Jewish Defense League—all these political tendencies valorized, even sacralized, Jewish strength and Israeli military might in the present to compensate for Jewish weakness in the past. Their slogan was "Never Again," as if any lapse in vigilance might enable a second Holocaust. Within the arena of U.S. politics, these partisans of Jewish suffering often conceived Jews as in competition with other minorities, especially African Americans, for the state's attention and for redress. Their politics of suffering was competitive, zero-sum: the recognition of one's group past oppression necessarily came at the expense of the other's.

Progressive Jewish activists rejected this kind of politics. They sought to articulate a Jewish victimhood that was not competitive but, rather, comparative, outward reaching, and solidaristic. While many progressive Jewish activists asserted a Jewish stake in the fight against the structural injustices exacerbated under Trump, they were also careful about the perils of comparison. They were especially cautious to avoid being seen as eliding the differences between antisemitism and anti-Black racism. "Who is currently at the tip of the knife when it comes to colonialism, imperialism, white supremacy—that may have been an ancestor of mine three generations ago; it's not me now," said JFREJ's Dove Kent. "But I am still in the fight against those forces because I don't want this to happen to anyone. And I want to reclaim my history for my people."

In turn, the emphasis by many progressive activists on reclaiming suppressed or overlooked parts of Jewish history prompted a rethinking of the meaning of assimilation; this, too, constituted a profound break with the postwar Jewish consensus. "There's more awareness of the ways in which assimilation wasn't just benign, that [there are] much more insidious aspects to it," said Aryeh Bernstein, a Chicago-based longtime Jewish educator and anti-racist activist. In the 1960s, a small group of self-described "radical Jews"—many of whom would later go on to hold important roles in Jewish life—had also revolted against their comfortable suburban upbringings. Yet the prevailing American Jewish self-understanding still stressed the successes of Jewish integration and celebrated the *Americanness* of American Jews. Within the mainstream institutions, that remains the dominant view today.

Under Trump, many progressive Jewish activists felt this self-understanding was no longer viable. With the rise of sporadic antisemitic violence, some American Jews began to feel less American and more Jewish. They also began to understand their Jewishness as opposed to the right-wing forces that Trump and his party represented. "The emergence of an explicit fascist movement caused Jews to wake up and see their Jewish identity as one of their primary political identities," said Isaac Luria, a veteran progressive Jewish organizer who ran a Jewish community center in Brooklyn. It catalyzed "a reclamation of the centrality of Jewishness in our politics," he added. Embracing one's Jewishness as part of public protest against the Trump administration thus became for some progressive Jews a means of distancing oneself from America, or at least the vision of America that Trump represented.

Not-White-ness

For Alyssa Rubin, like many on the millennial Jewish left, the catalyst was Trump. "When the 2016 election happened," she said, "that was honestly the thing that pushed me over the edge." The experience of fear, the sense of peril, was also radicalizing and identity building, she said. "I had this feeling—*I want to be with Jews right now* . . . Which I had never felt before." Rubin quickly joined IfNotNow that fall and marched in the demonstrations organized by IfNotNow, JVP, and JFREJ through the winter of 2017. By the summer of 2019, she was an organizer coordinating Never Again Action's demonstrations outside ICE detention centers.

Rubin's path to progressive Jewish activism was an increasingly common one for young American Jews who grew up on the edges, or outside, of mainline affiliated life. She described growing up in a small town in central Connecticut, in a family that belonged to a "very small" Reform community. Judaism "felt like something we left the house to do," attending synagogue only on High Holidays, she said. "It wasn't really a deep part of my life." So much so that when Rubin left for college, Jewish community was not a factor on her list, she told me. "I think for a long time, I had just been, like, 'I don't see any form of Judaism that reflects my values or the things I care about, so I guess I'm not Jewish.'"

That all changed as the new Jewish protest movements of the late 2010s took flight. Their rhetoric was invigorating, their cause just. Suddenly, being Jewish appeared viable again to Rubin and many other young Jews who had found themselves increasingly alienated from mainstream Jewish life. Unlike the establishment groups that reacted to the outrages of the Trump presidency with feeble, manicured statements, groups like IfNotNow, JVP, and JFREJ seemed better suited to the moment.

Their message was "We're here because we've seen this before—it's not despite our Judaism but because of it," Rubin said. "This was extremely new for me." So, too, Rubin added, was the feeling of togetherness she felt while marching with other progressive Jews in the physical act of protest. "I had this extremely transformative experience walking through the streets of Boston, singing in Hebrew" as part of the anti-Bannon demonstrations in the winter of 2017, she told me. "That you can be Jewish and have these politics" had not seemed possible before.

The use of Hebrew and Yiddish chants and banners became, and remains, a hallmark of the new Jewish progressive activism. Such public displays of Jewishness during protests have served several purposes: to perform dis-assimilation and reject the old consensus. As many progressive Jewish activists imagined it, the manifest Jewishness of their demonstrations was intended to establish distance between themselves and ordinary American whiteness. Against the backdrop of intermittent Black-led protest and the emergence of organized white nationalist violence, many American Jews' relationship to whiteness had come to feel more fraught, more uncertain. "Going out on the streets, singing songs in Hebrew, and chanting Aramaic liturgy is a really good way to be, like, 'What you're seeing on TV is not me,'" said Rabbi Alissa Wise, former deputy director of Jewish Voice for Peace and a longtime activist.

Yet it wasn't all about exculpation. Many American Jewish activists knew that they were white, but they also did not feel part of the white America that, in the last years of Obama's presidency and into Donald Trump's, seemed to reassert violently its exclusionary interests. As one activist described it, there were not very many spiritual tools within the "homogenizing American whiteness" that American Jews could use to grapple with their new situation: the constant whirl of outrage and the seemingly endless cycle of horror. Instead, they sought solace and resilience in Jewishness—and this was even, or perhaps especially, the case for those Jews who previously had not spent very much time in synagogue or given much thought to what being Jewish meant. Wise explained, "There's a nothingness to whiteness, and reconnecting to a really robust cultural mooring—there's a groundedness to that, which can provide meaning when it feels like just a white existence is very isolating and meaningless."

By the late 2010s, Old World ethnicity was hardly a living presence in most Jewish communities: the Yiddish-speaking generation had almost entirely passed from the scene; nationalism in both its American and Zionist forms had, especially for a growing number of progressive Jews, become untenable. So in their place, Jewish activists turned to the last available form of Jewish expression, religion. They took ritual from the place of prayer into the space of protest. And even those who were not technically Jewish were often encouraged to participate. "Jewish particularism is on the wane," Wise said, "but Jewish practice as a way to connect wider and wider is on the rise." Progressive Jewish activists almost never asked whether those who attended the protests that they organized were, in fact, Jewish. In our post-ethnic, multiracial age, doing so, for many, was probably unthinkable.

Such radical openness sometimes posed problems of theoretical coherence. If Jewishness was something someone could affiliate with simply by participating in a ritual or protest, what did this mean for the pervasive rhetoric of generational and familial trauma? The notions that defined this new progressive Jewish identity could sometimes seem, at least to me, confusingly postmodern. On the one hand, the binds of identity were often described as timeless, inescapably inherited, almost ontologically definitional. On the other, it seemed that what governed identity formation was less ancestry, history, or memory than self-identification, which could be revised and discarded as one pleased. The new Jewish activists seemed uncertain if Jewishness was ultimately a matter of familial inheritance or—more often, it seemed—merely of personal choice.

Hereness

There was no single manifesto or text that captures the full spirit, the total worldview, of the new Jewish activists. On the more radical edges, some began to advocate for reviving the notion of "hereness"— in Yiddish, *doykeit*—which had been the working philosophy of the Bund, the socialist, Yiddish political party that had animated tens of thousands of Jews in early twentieth-century eastern Europe. In the 1990s, JFREJ founding leader Melanie Kaye/Kantrowitz herself attempted to revive the term to describe progressive Jews' commitment to fighting, first of all, for justice in the communities in which they lived. "*Doykeit*," she wrote, "means Jews enter coalitions wherever we are, across lines that might divide us, to work together for universal equality and justice." It was to be an alternative to the parochialism, chauvinism, and Zionism that dominated mainstream Jewish life, a Jewish entry point into intersectionality.

In a 2018 essay, then *Jewish Currents* publisher Jacob Plitman called for a reclamation of Kaye/Kantrowitz's *doykeit* for the age of Trump. "Hereness isn't just about place but about people: centering our politics and spiritual practice around those nearest to us," he wrote. "Hereness demands that we learn our local histories and resurrect hidden ones of our own. Hereness means we refuse to disappear into the interiority of our liturgy, and equally refuse to stop being Jews in public." As a corollary to the embrace of "hereness," Plitman called for a rejection of "thereness"—the centrality of Israel and Zionism to Jewish identity and politics. Opposition to Israeli government policies and human rights abuses would still be part of "hereness," as Plitman saw it, yet that was to be only one struggle among many.

It is hard to overstate how central the embrace of "hereness" and the rejection of "thereness" was to the new Jewish movements that emerged during the Trump years. Bundist slogans appeared, as if resurrected from the archive, on pins and posters and patches; old Yiddish iconography found a new life in the online avatars of digital activists. The idea of "hereness," Sophie Ellman-Golan said, "is not just an antidote or counterbalance to Zionism; it's anti-nationalist fundamentally."

But at times it also seemed less like a practicable politics than a kind of wish fulfillment. While the anti-Trump campaigners and immigrant rights activists mostly stayed mute about Israel and Zionism, many privately argued that Israel's treatment of the Palestinians was indefensible. They felt that Israel's existence as an ethnonationalist, militarized, even apartheid state sullied what had once been, before 1948, an otherwise old and robust Jewish tradition of fighting for justice. They increasingly saw any connection to Israel as an obstacle to American Jewish participation in the struggles for freedom and equality at home. Some believed Israel itself was entirely illegitimate. Perhaps unbound to Israel by ties of family or community, they could indulge in political fantasy. They hoped Israel would go away. "My dream Jewish identity," Rubin said, is that "we just exist not in relation to a nation-state."

IV.

Durham, North Carolina

The progressive Jewish revival of the Trump years was not limited to the liberal coasts. Grassroots groups sprouted quickly around the country, sometimes outstripping the capacity of national organizations that sought to provide constructive order to the upsurge of protest. Social media allowed for the spread of images of slogans that perhaps first appeared in LA or New York, which were then picked up by activists elsewhere. A new kind of Jewish political culture was growing across the country, novel and rediscovered forms of Jewish identity taking shape in unlikely places.

In the South and the Midwest, progressive Jewish organizers adapted to conditions very unlike those on the coast. In many cases, these Jewish communities were smaller, less ideologically diverse, and more precarious, more dependent on Jewish establishment organizations for funds to sustain them. In general, there was less room to maneuver.

In North Carolina, a small group of largely Durham-based activists founded Carolina Jews for Justice (CJJ) in 2013. By the late 2010s, the group had chapters in several counties across the state. It was, as many of the new progressive Jewish groups were, one part protest movement, one part Jewish outreach. CJJ was a place where people who had not found a Jewish home within the mainstream Jewish community might do so. "For the majority of the people who are involved in CJJ, CJJ *is* their Jewish community," said Rabbi Salem Pearce, who led the group in 2020. "They're not affiliated . . . more than half, probably, are not affiliated with any mainstream Jewish institution."

Yet the absence of a robust alternative Jewish infrastructure could be an opportunity for progressive Jewish organizers. In most of the conventional Jewish communities in North Carolina, there was "a very parochial and very narrow window of acceptable discourse," Pearce said. "There aren't any davening [prayer] spaces that won't say the prayer for Israel here, or maybe very few." Jews interested in a Jewishness decoupled from nationalism and instead invested primarily in local struggles for racial and economic justice therefore needed to look elsewhere. Compared to New York, where there is a smorgasbord of progressive Jewish options, North Carolina's offerings are sparse. "We are it," Pearce said.

Pearce's life story is a still relatively uncommon one on the new Jewish left (although, increasingly it seems, less so). She was born in Houston, Texas, and grew up in an evangelical Christian household. In college, Pearce met a Jewish man and converted. "My joke is that he and I didn't last, but the Judaism did," Pearce said. She was ordained as rabbi by the nondenominational, Boston-based Hebrew College after years working with Jewish social justice organizations. "Being an American Jew in the twenty-first century is just the most amazing thing in terms of the creativity and passion and the incredible Torah," Pearce said. "I just feel grateful daily for being able to be a Jew in this time and place."

Talking with Pearce, I began to think that perhaps the texture of American Jewish life was changing much faster than I had realized, especially within liberal and progressive communities. Pearce, and the new progressive activists more broadly, offered a Judaism that was all about social justice and spirituality; it had none of the nationalism or tribalism that I was familiar with. It strived to be open-minded, flexible, inviting, at least when it came to ritual and to people. It was as exacting in its politics as it was loose in its approach to Jewish law.

For decades, many Jewish leaders, especially those right of center, had derided this kind of Judaism. They referred to it as "*tikkun olam* Judaism," which was meant to signal its intellectual thinness, undemandingness, and liberalism. For the most part, the progressive Jewish activists showed little concern for the establishment's critiques. When prompted, Pearce offered a rebuttal of her own to their charges. "The mainstream institutions are offering what I would consider to be a very thin Judaism," she said. "I would turn that accusation back on them and say, 'If all you have is Israel and endogamy—no, that's not thick. That's not enough to sustain community.'"

St. Louis, Missouri

In 2019, Hannah Rosenthal, a social worker and organizer, helped found Progressive Jews of St. Louis (ProJo). Rosenthal had grown up in the city, left to attend college at Princeton (where she was a few years ahead of me; we knew of each other), and returned to her hometown after a stint in Chicago. During this same period, the Windy City had become something of a hub for left-wing Jewish activism. It was where the rabbi and activist Brant Rosen had established what he called the first openly anti-Zionist synagogue. Rosenthal said she hoped to build a similar kind of community. "I came to St. Louis wanting a lefty, Jewish base where I could be my full Jewish self," she said. Since there was no existing lefty Jewish organization, she realized she would have to start one herself.

The conditions were not the most genial. The St. Louis Jewish landscape shares many of the features that define Jewish life outside of the major coastal cities: there are fewer Jews, fewer young Jews, and fewer spaces where progressive politics and Jewish practice easily mix. "St. Louis doesn't necessarily attract all the young lefties," Rosenthal said, "but there's so many strong, typical Jewish establishment institutions here." Conventional synagogues and the Jewish Federation dominate the scene. Establishment funds bankroll most Jewish initiatives in the city, so contravening political red lines could jeopardize crucial resources.

All this meant that the more confrontational, oppositional tactics that might have worked in New York or the Bay Area needed to be modified. Rosenthal said that while Progressive Jews of St. Louis had relationships with members of national organizations like JVP and IfNotNow, by remaining unaffiliated with any of them, ProJo intended to maintain a flexibility and an attentiveness to the city's particularities. "[The national organizations] missed the local context sometimes," she told me. "We don't have to do what they think is best for us."

ProJo, Rosenthal acknowledged, is not a large group. "We're really scrappy. Five to six organizers." But the group takes a wide range of issues as its mandate, from racial and economic justice—Ferguson is next door—as well as Israel/Palestine. When the issues have intersected, ProJo members have jumped into the fray. And because of the relatively small size of the engaged Jewish population of St. Louis, just a few voices can go a long way.

One intense moment of activity for ProJo came during the 2020 Democratic primaries. Black Lives Matter activist and nurse Cori Bush was challenging ten-term incumbent William Lacy Clay for the congressional seat representing the city of St. Louis. The scion of a Black political dynasty, Clay had held his seat for two decades—a seat that his father, a founding member of the Congressional Black Caucus, held from 1969 until 2000. Clay embodied the Black political establishment. Bush, by contrast, was running as an insurgent, backed by activists in the street.

The contest was thus a proxy fight between the competing wings of the Democratic Party—a fight that had been ongoing, with significant acrimony, since the first Bernie Sanders campaign in 2016. Centrist Democrats like Kamala Harris and Nancy Pelosi lined up behind Clay, while Bush had the support of the remnants of Bernie's coalition and groups like Justice Democrats, which helped recruit and back progressive politicians like Alexandria Ocasio-Cortez and Rashida Tlaib, who made up the "Squad." Toward the end of the campaign, as Bush appeared to be leading in the polls, Clay's campaign sent out bluntly Islamophobic mailers, ominously depicting Bush with Palestinian American activist Linda Sarsour, who wears a hijab, and the text, "Cori Bush Has an Anti-Israel Agenda." It was a last-ditch effort to provoke negative press for Bush and an attempt to sway Jewish voters toward Clay by playing on Jewish fears.

The move did not have its intended effect. According to Rosenthal, members of ProJo had relationships with people involved in the Bush campaign and were ready to "collaborate with and support them" in fighting the attempt to tar Bush as antisemitic. "I don't think that would necessarily happen in another city," she said, where "a more established organization" would have likely stepped in. Bush's Jewish allies took to social media to rebut the Clay campaign's criticism and turned the issue back onto Clay. They also stressed that criticisms of Israel and Israeli policies were not antisemitic, that they were legitimate, and that there were Jews who agreed with Bush's position of solidarity with the Palestinian cause.

The Clay campaign's gambit seemed to have backfired even beyond the ranks of progressive activists. Tasha Kaminsky, a St. Louis Jewish community professional, said that the mailers had prompted her to switch her vote from Clay to Bush. She said that she was "taken aback" by Clay's attempt to use Israel as a wedge issue within the Jewish community. The flyer "played into a lot of assumptions about Jewish people" and helped perpetuate "the myth that we have dual loyalty," Kaminsky said. "We're not voting on Israel—we're voting on St. Louis."

And Bush, unlike other Black candidates who recanted pro-Palestinian statements when under pressure, did not soft-pedal her stance on Palestinian rights. With the support of the city's progressive Jewish activists, she didn't need to. When I asked Bush about her support of BDS in the summer of 2020, she explained that it was motivated by the same principles that had led her to protest on the streets of Ferguson. "The core of all the work that I've done, period, is love—love of people, love of humanity—and it's justice for all," she said. "My thing," Bush added, "is we have to show up not only for what our own issues are, but we have to show up for people who are oppressed differently than us." In January 2021, she was sworn in as the first Black congresswoman to represent the state of Missouri.

Chicago, Illinois

In 2015, Rabbi Brant Rosen did something strange and, from an economic standpoint, extremely ill-advised. He started a synagogue, and not only that—an explicitly non-Zionist one. When he founded what became Tzedek Chicago, Rosen was working full-time for the American Friends Service Committee (AFSC), a Quaker human rights group. Before that, he had been a congregational rabbi, first in Denver, then in Evanston. "Organizing was always a big part [of the work] and also a big attraction for becoming a rabbi," Rosen said. "I was very involved in advocating for Palestinian statehood and a two-state solution back when that was considered a pretty edgy thing to do." But for the most part his politics stayed within the boundaries of mainstream Jewish acceptability—"always very much on the left edge of Zionism," he said.

During Israel's Operation Cast Lead in 2008, Rosen's politics began to change. "That was kind of the final straw," Rosen told me. "I would argue it was not that just for me; it was a pretty significant turning point for a lot of people." In the ensuing years, Rosen became a popular blogger criticizing Israel and Zionism from a left-wing Jewish perspective. He dove into Palestine solidarity organizing, helping to found JVP's rabbinical council with Rabbi Alissa Wise while maintaining his congregational obligations. "I give the leadership of the congregation a lot of credit," Rosen said, for enabling him to remain a visible advocate for Palestinian rights while working as a rabbi. But it was an arrangement that could not last. Against the backdrop of Israel's war in 2014, Rosen said he became "much bolder" in his approach. "I was suddenly not the rabbi they hired."

Rosen described his resignation from his post at Chicago's Jewish Reconstructionist Congregation with some residual sadness. "Everything within that congregation just sort of crumbled," he told me. "Sooner or later, I would have needed to go," but the knowledge of that fact did not cushion the blow, he said. The career change, to a senior role at AFSC, was "very dramatic." It looked like his time as a rabbi was over. "I didn't think there was any congregation that would hire me," Rosen said. "I never considered starting my own congregation." But when a group of former congregants began to meet, led by

Rosen, for services and spiritual guidance, a new possibility emerged. In addition to his full-time job, Rosen launched Tzedek Chicago with a critical mass of supporters but, he added, with "no strategic plan" and "no sense of what the future would be."

By 2018, Tzedek Chicago was big enough that Rosen could leave AFSC to lead the congregation as his full-time job. Tzedek was not like other congregations, and not only because of its disavowal of Zionism. "We crafted our core values," Rosen said, "before we recruited one member." It was not going to be another liberal synagogue where the euphemism of a "broad tent" would describe its congregants' views. There were enough synagogues like that, Rosen said. What was missing, in his view, was a synagogue that left no doubt about where it stood on political issues, even if that might turn potential members off. "Our approach was 'This is who we are; we are not for everybody,'" Rosen said. "'But if we're for you, and you dig what we're doing, please join us.'"

According to Rosen, Tzedek Chicago's membership grew "dramatically" during the pandemic as synagogue services went online. Now, members no longer needed to live in the city to participate. "During those first five years I would always get emails from people all over the country—all over the world, actually"—who wanted to know if there was anything like Tzedek Chicago closer to their homes, Rosen said. "And I would always say, 'No, sorry.' But now I don't have to do that," he said, smiling. "We're not a local congregation anymore."

All the trend lines sketched by sociologists of American Jewry would have suggested that this was impossible. Fewer and fewer American Jews belong to a synagogue—the most recent Pew survey puts the number at less than a third. The number of self-identified Jewish anti-Zionists in polls tends toward the single digits. Perhaps Rosen and Tzedek Chicago are simply the exception that prove the rule.

More likely, however, it seems they represent the cutting edge of the profoundly changing character of American Jewish religious practice and the ideological possibilities of a synagogue untethered from

Zionism. The minority of non-Orthodox Jews who seek out ritual life are no longer looking for the conventional, consensus Judaism of the last century. They may be looking for something else—for something radically different.

As disillusionment with Israel increases, especially among Jewish millennials now entering what sociologists once considered the prime years of synagogue membership, it would only make sense that they would seek out the kinds of shuls compatible with their broader politics. For Rosen, the surprising success of Tzedek Chicago reflects this process. "The Zionist narrative is crumbling," he said, "especially with a younger generation of Jews who see it as a settler colonial, apartheid movement." And while these younger Jews "identify deeply as Jews, and in many cases spiritually as Jews," Rosen added, they are increasingly unwilling to compromise on their politics to participate in Jewish communal life. "They just don't want their spiritual life to include apartheid and settler colonialism," Rosen said. These are, after all, young American Jews whose vision of Judaism is one of social justice, of a commitment to helping the downtrodden and the oppressed. Why, Rosen asked, should they be expected to make an exception when it comes to Palestine?

What would seem utterly counterintuitive and contradictory to an older generation of American Jews appears to many in the younger generation as obviously unproblematic. "Whether it's through text or liturgy or ceremony," Rosen said, people are "seeking to find Jewishly, religiously authentic ways to express their solidarity with the Palestinian people." The kinds of modifications and appropriations common to Jewish protest movements like JVP and IfNotNow are no longer restricted to strategic deployment in the streets but have become the foundation of a new kind of grassroots, Jewish ritual expression. They have entered synagogue life.

At Tzedek, for instance, Rosen said they had replaced the prayer celebrating Israel's Independence Day, common in almost all but ultra-Orthodox synagogues, with a mournful prayer for Nakba Day, commemorating the expulsion of roughly 700,000 Palestinians during Israel's founding. "Writing prayers that actually sanctify standing in solidarity with Palestinians, as opposed to celebrating their dispossession—that's really important," he said. Other groups of left-wing Jews have rethought the rituals of Sukkot to demonstrate solidarity with Indigenous peoples of North America.

Rosen is not illusioned about the size of the broader movement of which his synagogue is a part. "I think it will always be a dissident movement," he said. As much as progressive activism has become more visible and popular, "these kinds of movements by definition tend not to be hegemonic," he added. But there is no question that the guardians of the establishment have grown alarmed by the reappearance of non-Orthodox anti-Zionism as a Jewish politics and form of religious expression after more than half a century of nearly unbroken consensus.

V.

Throughout the late 2010s, not only did antisemitism return as a force in U.S. politics; its meaning also became more politically contested, and accusations of antisemitism, like those of the Clay campaign, became political weapons. On both the right and the left, the stakes of defining antisemitism were taken to be nothing less than the determination of where Jews would fit in a fragmenting America.

The American Jewish establishment's first concern, however, was about Israel. Slowly, over the course of years, Israel advocacy organizations had promulgated and tried to codify, in U.S. states as well as countries in Europe, a definition of antisemitism intended to quash strident criticisms of Israel. Named the International Holocaust Remembrance Alliance (IHRA) definition, it listed among its examples of antisemitism "claiming that the existence of a State of Israel is a racist endeavor" and "applying double standards by requiring of it a

SHATTERING AND BUILDING   *195*

behavior not expected or demanded of any other democratic nation."
According to the definition's own author, Kenneth Stern, an attorney
and longtime American Jewish Committee operative, the IHRA was
never intended to be used as an enforceable speech code; it was, Stern
wrote, "created primarily so that European data collectors could know
what to include and exclude" in their monitoring efforts.

But turning the IHRA definition into hate speech code was exactly
what the Trump administration did. In December 2019, Donald
Trump signed an executive order that made the IHRA definition us-
able as criteria to adjudicate anti-Jewish discrimination on college
campuses under Title VI of the Civil Rights Act. The unambiguous
intention of the order, as Jared Kushner himself wrote in the *New York
Times*, was to crack down on Palestine solidarity and anti-occupation
activists on campus, and on the BDS movement in particular. In practice, this created the conditions for an absurd yet all-too-imaginable
scenario in which a granddaughter of a Palestinian refugee expelled
from the Galilee in 1948 could be held to have violated a fourth-
generation American Jew's civil rights for claiming that Israel was
"racist." Instead of allowing students to argue over the politics of
Israel/Palestine, and even to be wrong, the Trump administration
clamped down on free speech and tried to foreclose the argument.

The codification of the IHRA definition was, however, only one
battle in what had become a much larger fight. Jewish establishment
organizations, in tandem with right-wing groups like the Zionist Organization of America and politically aligned pundits, tried to make the
case that the progressive left was responsible—as much if not more so
than the Trumpian right—for the renewed salience of and threats
posed by antisemitism. Establishment leaders like ADL CEO Jonathan
Greenblatt repeatedly attacked the members of the "Squad," the cohort of mostly young, female congresswomen of color elected in 2018—
and specifically Representatives Ilhan Omar, Rashida Tlaib, and
Alexandria Ocasio-Cortez. And not only when it came to Israel. Greenblatt denounced Ocasio-Cortez for calling the Trump administration's

detention facilities at the southern border "concentration camps." Conservative writers like Bari Weiss charged that "anti-semitism that originates on the political left is more insidious and perhaps more existentially dangerous" than antisemitism on the right.

Such claims were more fantasy than fact. Progressives were not asking Jews "to commit cultural genocide, to abandon their traditions and to worship false idols," as Weiss claimed. To the contrary, during the Trump years, Jewish organizations played active, visible roles in campaigns against mass incarceration and in support of immigrants' rights, women's rights, labor, and civil liberties. For the most part, Jewish difference was tolerated and often welcome; it certainly was not suppressed. Moreover, throughout the late 2010s, right-wing extremists and white nationalists carried out the vast majority of antisemitic violence. The equivalence between right- and left-wing antisemitism suggested by figures like Weiss and Greenblatt was a false one.

Yet many of the accusations of antisemitism on the left, even if sometimes exaggerated or wielded in bad faith, reflected something real. Some prominent progressives seemed unwilling or incapable of speaking about Jews with the sensitivity with which they would have been expected to speak about any other racial or ethnic minority. In 2018, the Women's March imploded, with two Women's March leaders standing behind their support for the virulently antisemitic Louis Farrakhan. There was Ilhan Omar's "All about the Benjamins, baby" tweet, which evinced not just poor political judgment but ignorance of how such statements rhymed with old antisemitic sentiments. There were many other examples, which reflected a reality that I, and I suspect other progressive Jews, either consciously or unconsciously ignored: that being a Jew on the left often meant shrugging off casual antisemitic remarks from other activists. It was a cost of "doing the work."

I struggled for a while to admit this. For many years, I chalked it up to a matter of education or training or strategy. I wanted to be charitable. If some racial justice or antiwar activists seemed unable to speak without indulging in subtle bigotry when denouncing housing policies in New York or Israeli government policies abroad, perhaps they just needed to be taught, engaged with, brought "into dialogue"— I even knew people who did this for a living. But over time, the pervasiveness of certain strands of antisemitic rhetoric simply could not be attributed to incompetence or ignorance.

The reactions of some on the left to the October 7, 2023, attack revealed with disturbing clarity the extent to which antisemitic thinking had found a home in my own political camp, even among erstwhile allies. Cheers for Hamas gunmen, glee at the killing of Israeli civilians, grotesque conspiracies of Jewish global control—all have appeared at pro-Palestine demonstrations. And to ignore this reality, as some prefer, is to do a disservice to the movement that is rightfully outraged over Israel's brutal war in Gaza. Acknowledging the reality of antisemitism on the left is, in fact, wholly compatible with opposing Israeli war crimes.

Antisemitism on the left takes a different form than on the right, but it is no less real. Right-wing antisemitism imagines Jews as a threat to the authentic members of the organic nation; it figures Jews as a foreign, malign influence, usurping and corrupting the *Volk*. Contemporary left-wing antisemitism, by contrast, envisions Jews as the quintessential oppressors—the puppet masters and chief beneficiaries of capitalism, imperialism, and even white supremacy. In January 2024, for instance, the leader of the People's Forum, a left-wing NGO, articulated this lunatic strand of politics when he declared, to applause, that "when the state of Israel is finally destroyed and erased from history, that will be single most important blow we can give to destroying capitalism and imperialism in our lifetime." Not only is this an antisemitic fantasy of Jewish political influence, imagining Israel as the hinge point of global systems of exploitation; it is also bad analysis—capitalism and imperialism existed long before Israel's creation, and would persist even if Israel were to disappear.

But what both left-wing and right-wing antisemitism share is that they traffic in exaggerated visions of Jewish power, whereas other forms of bigotry and racism usually denigrate their subjects of disdain as inferior. Of course, this dichotomy does not always pertain. Nazi antisemitism rested on an idea of Aryan racial supremacy while fanning fears of a "Judeo-Bolshevik" enemy. On the left, the construal of "the Jews" as a stand-in for powerful, exploitative forces also has a long history; the structure of conspiracy has frequently proved a simpler, populist vehicle for channeling class conflict than nuanced analysis. For this reason, the German social-democratic leader August Bebel denounced antisemitism as "the socialism of fools" in the 1890s. More recently, some have called contemporary conspiracies of Zionist global dominance, like those expressed at the People's Forum, "the anti-imperialism of fools."

Still, part of what made, and still makes, discussing antisemitism such a fraught feature of U.S. politics is because of how mainstream pundits and right-wing groups alike have manufactured antisemitism scandals, which they amplify to political ends. In truth, while many reporters ignored this fact, the instrumentalization of antisemitism was an explicit part of Republican Party strategy. In 2019, Norm Coleman described his party's plan as aimed, in part, at convincing Jews that they "will be much more comfortable in the Republican Party." Other veteran Republicans, like Trump surrogate Jeff Ballabon, launched the Astroturf "Jexodus" initiative, which claimed to be leading American Jews out of a Democratic Party that had turned irrevocably anti-Israel and therefore intrinsically antisemitic. Israel was, in the mind of Republican strategists, the wedge issue that could split Jews off from the Democrats and bolster the Trumpian coalition.

They were wrong. The efforts to peel Jews off from the Democratic Party were often hampered by Trump's frequent use of antisemitic rhetoric. Trump thought himself entitled to Jewish support because of his support for Benjamin Netanyahu's hard-right government. He seemed to delight in toeing the line between philosemitism and antisemitism, once telling an audience at the Israeli American Council,

"You're brutal killers" in real estate. He described American Jews who voted for Democrats as showing "either a total lack of knowledge or great disloyalty"—both to his administration and to Israel. On this, many on the Jewish right and many within the American Jewish establishment agreed with Trump. He was a vehicle, however imperfect, for their agenda of continued settlement expansion in the occupied West Bank and the elimination of any possibility of creating a Palestinian state.

Much to the establishment's frustration, few American Jews turned out to share their views. Less than a quarter of American Jews voted for Trump. But this also wasn't just about Trump. Most American Jewish voters do not choose their candidates based on their positions on Israel. While that was certainly common in the community where I grew up, it was highly unrepresentative of American Jewish voting behavior. Polling has consistently showed Israel to be a low electoral priority for most American Jews. According to J Street's election night polls, in 2016 just 9 percent of Jewish voters chose Israel as one of their top two voting priorities; in 2018, that number decreased to 4 percent. In polls conducted by the Jewish Electorate Institute in October 2018 and May 2019, Jewish voters ranked Israel as the lowest of sixteen policy priorities. While most American Jews, in other polls like the Pew survey, affirmed the importance of Israel to their identities, such importance was, for the most part, imperceptible in U.S. electoral politics.

At the time, it seemed that even for many self-described "pro-Israel" Jewish Democrats, Israel itself had become a problem of sorts. Trump's embrace of Netanyahu endeared him mainly to those who were already on the right. But for most American Jews, Netanyahu's personal corruption and turn to a right-wing populist brand of politics made him appear little better than the president that they loathed. Throughout the Trump years and into the Biden presidency, liberal Jewish discontent with Israel only grew. As the Netanyahu government pursued its agenda to dismantle the country's judiciary, that discontent seemed to reach unprecedented levels—until the outbreak of the Israel-Hamas war in the fall of 2023 undid this brief thaw in Jewish communal discourse.

Tuning Out

It may seem unthinkable now, but for a stretch of years many American Jews preferred not to think about the situation in the Middle East. Rabbi Marc Katz, who moved from Congregation Beth Elohim to Temple Ner Tamid in Bloomfield, New Jersey, told me in 2021, "People are not talking about Israel." Katz described his "pretty liberal" congregants as torn between a deep feeling of connection to Israel and the recognition of a tension "between unabashed support for Israel" and their liberal values. He said they also felt dismayed that supporters of progressive causes, like Black Lives Matter, which they supported, had begun to echo strident criticisms of Israel. "People are just so confused. They don't feel like they've got the tools to deal with the nuance," he said. Ambivalence, confusion, shame—these feelings had never before defined mainstream Jewish opinion on Israel.

The cause was, in large part, the undeniable reality on the ground in Israel/Palestine: an Israeli government uninterested in peace, an occupation that went on with no end in sight, an increasingly vocal and extreme Israeli right. Yet the malaise that washed over parts of American Jewish life during these years also had to do with the fact that there was no space for nuance, no space for discussion. For decades the American Jewish establishment had expelled dissenting voices, and now there was hardly any form of acceptable criticism of Israel within mainstream Jewish life.

The practical effect was the neutralization of debate about Israel to such an extent that American Jews no longer knew how to discuss it constructively. "The American Jewish establishment completely and very recklessly shut down honest discourse for many years out of fear and trauma," Rabbi Sharon Brous said. "And so there was no room for us to engage responsibly and to openly push for the kinds of solutions that would be necessarily in order for there to be a just society there."

Brous herself had run up against the hard limits of mainstream discourse. During Israel's brief war on Gaza in 2012, she had been disturbed by the intolerance and hateful rhetoric, the bellicose embrace of violence and the encouragement of killing Palestinians in certain parts of the community. "I saw a celebration on Facebook [pages] and it was disgusting," Brous said. "I was sick over it. I wanted people to at least hear a rabbi saying, 'This is not okay. We don't celebrate killing, even if it's a terrorist.'" In a letter to the IKAR congregation, Brous outlined these concerns, described her moral anguish, and called for an end to the fighting.

The response was vitriolic. Rabbi Daniel Gordis, a prominent Conservative rabbi now living in Israel, denounced Brous in a widely read blog post on the *Times of Israel*. Gordis was no stranger to Brous: he was a former teacher of hers; she had babysat for his children. Gordis described Brous as a traitor to the Jewish people. "The need for balance is so pervasive," Gordis wrote, critiquing the tendency he took Brous to represent, "that even an expression of gut-level love for Israelis more than their enemies is impossible. Balance has now bequeathed betrayal." The message Gordis sent was that established figures with significant platforms would show no qualms intimidating and shaming other rabbis who stepped out of the tightly policed boundaries.

It also seemed that some seized on Gordis's accusation as justification for threats of violence. "I had to put security on my children and was called into my kids' school because they were scared for my kids . . . I got so many credible death threats and rape threats," Brous said. "What happens in a community when you shut down discourse to that extent? Well, people leave the conversation." But where do they go when they leave?

At least, for a contingent of young American Jews: into activism, into the left, into the streets.

6

THE DIASPORIC DOUBLE BIND

I.

On the first day of May 2006, the Israeli novelist A. B. Yehoshua stood before a distinguished audience of Jewish leaders assembled in the Library of Congress and told them that if the Jewish diaspora were to disappear in a century, he would not shed a tear. Yehoshua, who died in 2022 at the age of eighty-five, had been invited to deliver an address as part of an event commemorating the centenary of the American Jewish Committee (AJC), one of the oldest of the self-defense organizations that today comprise the American Jewish establishment. As one of Israel's greatest living authors at the time, rivaled perhaps only by Amos Oz, Yehoshua had been placed on a panel with several other Jewish luminaries—the novelist Cynthia Ozick; the rabbi, mystic, and Talmud translator Adin Steinsaltz; and the editor Leon Wieseltier. The broadcasting giant Ted Koppel moderated. It was supposed to have been a festive symposium. But when Yehoshua took the podium, the event veered wildly off course.

He delivered a jeremiad, taking aim at what he saw as the shallowness, the partialness, of American Jewish identity. He compared the Jewishness of American Jews to a jacket, which one can take on and off, while his own Israeli Jewishness was more robust, more permanent. "Israeli is my skin, it's not my jacket," he said. "You are changing jackets . . . changing countries like the Jews have done all the time." By virtue of his being Israeli, Yehoshua claimed that he had made an eternal commitment to the Jewish future, while American Jews' commitment was more equivocal. "The difference between you and me [is that] I'm married, and you are . . . to be nasty about it . . . playing with the idea of marriage," he said. Compared to Israeli Judaism's task of ensuring Jewish survival, American Judaism, Yehoshua charged, lacked both substance and stakes. "You're playing with Jewishness—plug and play," he said. In Israel, "Jewish decisions" were made about life and death, statecraft and political economy, "as it was in the time of the Bible or the time of the Second Temple." In the United States, by contrast, American Jews were "not doing any Jewish decisions . . . All the decisions that you're doing are done in the American framework," their meaning diminished by virtue of their existence outside the Jewish state.

Yehoshua was an equal-opportunity denigrator. He took aim at those American Jews who professed their fealty to Israel too. "You are living with all your loyal feelings to Israel," he turned and said to Cynthia Ozick. "[But] you are living in myth about Israel, and not in [the] history of Israel."

For weeks, a fury raged in response to Yehoshua's speech. A barrage of op-eds appeared in Jewish newspapers and magazines. American Jewish leaders railed against Yehoshua's hubris and lamented his seeming lack of appreciation for all the Israel-advocacy work for which they had enlisted their communities. In Israel, the reaction was more laudatory. Peaceniks and hawks alike celebrated Yehoshua speaking tough love to an American audience more accustomed to coddling than critique. Eventually, Yehoshua was forced to apologize personally to Alfred Moses, a longtime Democratic operative who had chaired the AJC event, and published an essay in *Haaretz*, the liberal Israeli daily, clarifying that he had not meant to insult American Jews, simply to stress the centrality of the concept of homeland in the life of the Jewish people.

But Yehoshua was not contrite. In his follow-up essay titled "The Meaning of Homeland," he returned to the claims he had made in his AJC speech. To live in Israel was to live in a total Jewish reality, he charged, whereas Jewish life in America was fragmented and circumscribed. "Jewish-Israeli identity has to contend with all the elements of life via the binding and sovereign framework of a territorially defined state," he wrote. "And therefore the extent of its reach into life is immeasurably fuller and broader and more meaningful than the Jewishness of an American Jew, whose important and meaningful life decisions are made within the framework of his American nationality or citizenship." For the American Jew, Yehoshua continued, "His Jewishness is voluntary and deliberate, and he may calibrate its pitch in accordance with his needs." It was precisely the voluntarist nature of Jewish life in America, the cordoning off of Jewishness from questions of existential weight, which, Yehoshua argued, made American Jewish identity appear to him feeble and insufficient. In one of the essay's most memorable lines, he wrote, "Jewish values are not located in a fancy spice box that is only opened to release its pleasing fragrance on Shabbat and holidays, but in the daily reality of dozens of problems through which Jewish values are shaped and defined, for better or worse"—problems, as he saw it, that could only exist in a sovereign Jewish state.

As many pointed out at the time, nothing Yehoshua said was particularly new. He himself had said many similar things before. In large part, he had recapitulated an old Zionist position—*shlilat ha-golah*, "the negation of the diaspora." It was long a Zionist article of fate that Jewish life in the modern age faced dual threats to its survival: assimilation ("moral and spiritual" destruction) or persecution (physical destruction), both of which could only be avoided through the establishment of a national Jewish home. In the writings of many classical Zionist thinkers, the view of the diaspora as lowly and degenerate often accompanied such pessimistic determinism as well. "Either the Jewish people shall redeem the land and thereby continue to live," the

Belarusian-born Zionist philosopher Jacob Klatzkin wrote, "or we shall remain in exile and rot away." As Klatzkin saw it, "the Judaism of the Galut [diaspora] is not worthy of survival . . . Galut can only drag out the disgrace of our people and sustain the existence of a people disfigured in both body and soul."

Ironically, only a half century before Yehoshua's speech, in 1950, Jacob Blaustein, the president of the AJC at the time, had flown to Israel to negotiate with David Ben-Gurion "an understanding" over a modus vivendi for the new Jewish state and what was then the world's largest and most affluent Jewish diaspora. Blaustein had sought to stop Ben-Gurion from exhorting American Jews to make aliyah and denigrating, in typical Zionist form, diaspora life as hollow, compared to the fullness of Jewish national existence that Israel offered. In return for an ideological truce, Blaustein offered to use his power as president of the AJC, which was not yet a Zionist organization, to shore up American support for Israel. The Blaustein–Ben-Gurion Agreement set the rough parameters of the Israel-diaspora relationship for the next three-quarters of a century.

That is, roughly until the 2000s, when once-suppressed expressions of brashness, even hubris, among Israelis seemed to reemerge. In a reflection on Yehoshua's performance for the *Jerusalem Post*, the novelist Hillel Halkin, once eager to play "the role of the fire-eating Zionist to the hilt" himself, remarked that most Israelis had come to realize that there was no way to convey to American Jews the contrasts between the Israeli and American Jewish realities without insulting them. "Perhaps this is why American Jews think we all vanished with Ben-Gurion," Halkin wrote, "when all we've really done is become more polite." Yehoshua had broken with such politesse, and he was not the only one. In part, that was because Israeli public opinion had hardened toward the outside world against the backdrop of the second intifada. It was also, in a more subterranean way, because of a new demographic triumphalism. Israel's Jewish population reached parity with America's in the early 2000s. After U.S. dominance for much of the twentieth century's second half, Israel now rivaled America as the center of global Jewish gravity and would, almost inevitably, surpass it.

The Diasporic Double Bind

I heard Yehoshua give a version of his speech as a teenager one summer in Israel. As part of what had become a kind of masochistic ritual, American Jewish organizations increasingly sought out Yehoshua after his 2006 address, bringing new audiences of current and future Jewish leaders to be pricked by the novelist's sharp truths. Yehoshua's words agitated me then when I saw him in 2011. If he was right, and Israel was the place where Jewishness was expressed in its totality, that seemed to me as much a tragedy as a triumph. If Yehoshua was indeed saying, as I understood him, that Israel's actions—and, specifically, its brutal treatment of the Palestinians—flowed from its Jewishness, this reality was not to be celebrated but mourned. I rejected the idea that there was anything Jewish about the occupation of the West Bank and the siege of Gaza. I saw Israeli state violence as a desecration of the Jewish ethical tradition, not its consummation. I still do.

But Yehoshua's speech lingered with me for many years after. I thought of it often as I dove into the new Jewish social movements of the late 2010s. He became a nagging voice at the back of my mind. Marching at protests under Yiddish banners that few in the crowd could really read, or singing liturgical poems in the streets when few of us went to shul, I wondered if Yehoshua's metaphor of the spice box didn't apply. Were we really doing something Jewish in its essence, or were we merely sprinkling a Jewish fragrance onto things that we probably would have done anyway—demonstrate against an unjust war, a bad president, an inhumane law—whether we were Jewish or not? Wasn't it inconsistent, if not even a little hypocritical, to brandish our Jewishness in public in service of our politics while neglecting Judaism's most basic tenets in our private lives?

In the whirl of the Trump years' cascading crises, I mainly brushed these thoughts to the side. There was an urgency to these protests, what felt like strategic necessity and moral imperative. And besides, that so many of us chose to make our protests Jewish reflected a yearning for a Jewishness that connected to the central concerns of our young lives, something that the conventional expressions of mainstream Jewish life could not do. Perhaps, I thought, we might produce a new kind of Judaism for the current age of crisis through praying, as Abraham Joshua Heschel famously put it, with our feet.

Yehoshua's voice was stubborn, though. It was easy to imagine him sounding off on other matters too. For all the new Jewish left's talk of reclaiming *doykeit* and diasporism, its historical fetish for the old socialist Bund, and its preoccupation with slotting Jews and antisemitism into theories of intersectionality, we spent most of our time talking about Israel. Seemingly no matter what the issue, domestic or foreign policy, Israel seemed to exert an unshakable gravitational pull. The fights over the 2016 "Vision for Black Lives," the 2018 implosion of the Women's March Leadership, the 2020 presidential campaign— all seemed to illustrate the stubborn intrusion of Israel/Palestine into U.S. politics at almost every level, threatening the cohesion of activist movements and multiracial coalitions.

Many left-wing American Jews, who perhaps had never been to Israel, who had no family there, found themselves closely following developments in Israeli politics. In part, the salience of Israel/Palestine in U.S. politics was because Republicans and the right had decided to use Israel and antisemitism as a wedge issue in the (naïve) hope of peeling some American Jews out of the Democratic Party. Between 2018 and 2020, the politics of Israel/Palestine in America dominated the headlines, and this was a time when there were no major Middle East wars. Faced with persistent and often gratuitous attacks on progressive figures by Jewish establishment organizations like the ADL for their strident criticism of Israeli policies, left-wing Jews felt compelled to respond, and to do so as Jews.

The inescapability of Israel also reflected an inexorable reality. Israel claims to speak on behalf of all Jews, and so we found ourselves compelled to dissent as Jews. Even as some of us envisioned ourselves as doing the work of disentangling Judaism from Zionism, deprogramming ourselves out of the Israel-centric Jewishness with which we had been raised, we remained preoccupied with Israel and its actions. In our devotion to our anti-occupation politics, we were, I sometimes thought, not so different from the communities of our childhoods, only instead of Israel as the shining homeland, the location of Jewish self-actualization, we had flipped the valence: Israel became the place that sullied our Jewish values, made us ashamed and angry. Our activism did not, in fact, lead to a disentangling from Israel, but to an intensified connection through opposition. Anger, after all, is a modality of attachment.

Such is the diasporic double bind. As long as the state of Israel exists, American Jews will find themselves pulled within its orbit. That is the case whether they respond to this fact by affirming Israel's centrality to Jewish existence, as mainline affiliated Jewish communities do, or by rejecting Israel and agitating for its dismantling, as the growing but still marginal Jewish anti-Zionist tendency does. The reality of a sovereign Jewish state imposes its own logic onto global Jewish existence. There can no longer be a meaningfully autonomous Jewish politics outside of it. Diaspora politics is therefore, by necessity, reactive, always a response to a first move made by Israel, under conditions primarily determined by Israel's sovereign prerogatives.

About this, too, Yehoshua seemed undeniably right: When American Jews fight about politics, the consequences remain confined within the American political framework. We can, perhaps, influence U.S. politics, but that usually requires coalitional work. On our own, as Jews, our reach is rather circumscribed. By contrast, the consequences of Israeli politics flow with a sometimes-shocking immediacy out of the Israeli political arena and into the American one. The choices, even remarks, of Israeli leaders condition the durability of

activist coalitions here in the United States. A war in Israel can fracture American politics, and thus reshape the conditions of American
Jews' lives.

The relationship is not reciprocal. American Jews must live with
the fate that, in part, Israeli Jews impose upon them. But American
Jews exert no such power over Israeli reality. Israeli leaders must, of
course, concern themselves with American public opinion. But when it
comes to matters of statecraft and strategy, American Jews might as
well not exist.

II.

If Yehoshua gave his speech at a moment of Israel-diaspora parity, we
are now living amid an even more fundamental shift in the global distribution of Jewish life. We are on the cusp of a new—and, in Jewish
history, unprecedented—demographic reality.

By many accounts, Israel has already surpassed the United States as
home to the largest single population of Jews in the world. According
to the demographer Sergio Della Pergola, today Israel's Jewish population hovers around 7 million, while America's Jewish population sits
roughly at 6 million. By the year 2050, Israel is projected to be home
to the *majority* of the world's Jews. According to a 2015 Pew survey,
by mid-century Israel's population "is expected to be significantly
larger than the U.S. Jewish population." Israel will be home to 8.1
million Jews; the United States will be home to around 5.4 million.
Between 2010 and 2050, Israel's Jewish population is projected to
grow by 2.5 million. The U.S. Jewish population, by contrast, is projected to decline by about 330,000.

In raw numerical terms, the eclipse of American Jewry by its Israeli
counterpart marked the end of the American Jewish century. From
1945 until the early 2000s, the long postwar period during which
American Jewish identity as we know it took shape, the United States

claimed the majority of the world's Jews. No longer. The future of American Jewish life will unfold at a time when American Jews make up a shrinking portion of the world's Jewish population.

There have been other no less consequential shifts in the global distribution of Jewish life. On the eve of World War II most Jews lived in Europe, with smaller but still significant communities in the Middle East and North Africa. Even after the first decades of the twentieth century brought roughly 2 million mostly eastern European Jews to the United States, in 1939 there remained more than 3 million Jews in the Soviet Union alone.

The Holocaust destroyed European Jewry, and with it the world the European Jews had made. In the aftermath, the United States emerged as the demographic center of global Jewish life, while the new state of Israel claimed to be the Jewish people's spiritual core and its national and physical future. In light of this new reality, many American Jewish leaders spoke of there being "two poles" or "two centers" of Jewish life. The Hebraist and scholar Simon Rawidowicz proposed imagining the Jewish people as "two that are one," or "as an ellipse with two foci, the Land of Israel and the Diaspora of Israel."

For ordinary American Jews, however, Israel mainly made being Jewish easier by allowing them to jettison the pesky rituals and obligations of religious observance for political nationalism. With assimilation imagined by American Jewish leaders as the only alternative, Zionism's replacement of religion seemed a reasonable means of sustaining Jewish identity in a secular age, and the dual-centered model thus appeared as a mutually beneficial arrangement. Most Israeli leaders, however, imagined this situation as merely an interim one. As they saw it, the day Israel surpassed America as the global center of Jewish life—when the diaspora would indeed finally be negated—was only a matter of time.

The emergence of Israel as the homeland of the majority of the world's Jews will mark more than a simple demographic shift—it will constitute a revolution in the most basic conditions of Jewish existence. Diaspora defined Jewish life from 70 CE onward. Centuries of exile constituted Judaism and gave rise to the rabbinic tradition, to the chain of interpretation that stretches back to when the ancient sage Yohanan Ben Zakai, borne out of Roman-occupied Jerusalem in a coffin, settled in Yavne to rebuild the faith. By 2050, for the first time in two millennia, most Jews will live in a sovereign Jewish state. It is not just the American Jewish century that will have ended, but an entire era of Jewish history.

American Jews today live in the slipstream of this epochal transformation. The turbulence and incoherence of Jewish life in 2024 owes much to the interregnum in which we find ourselves, the time-space between two paradigms of Jewish existence, increasingly dominated by Israel as the author of the collective Jewish fate.

It is a reality to which few have adequately managed to respond. Neither the American Jewish establishment nor the anti-Zionist left offers sufficient avenues for navigating the diasporic double bind. While the former carries on as if nothing has changed, ignorant or inured to the suffering in Israel/Palestine, some on the left hope to escape their condition by fantasizing of Israel's destruction. But neither complicity nor renunciation will work. Israel's rapid emergence as the global Jewish center of gravity imposes upon us a set of challenges—political, theological, and ethical—which, I believe, we must not evade.

Complicity

Already constructed through the postwar period with Israel at the center of its activities, the mainline affiliated Jewish world has embraced Israel as the unitary geographic center of global Jewish life. While this emergent reality has not necessitated any paradigm shift on the part of these communities, it has nonetheless altered the total communal terrain. In the political realm, establishment groups such as the ADL have pushed for measures, like codifying the IHRA antisemitism, that equate anti-Israel politics with anti-Jewish animus, and anti-Zionism with antisemitism. Of course, there is no shortage of expressions of anti-Israel or anti-Zionist sentiment that are also antisemitic. Yet the IHRA is not aimed primarily at combatting antisemitism. Instead, as its backers freely admit, the aim is to quash criticism of Israel at a time when Israel's moral standing has never been more sullied by its government's actions.

The construal of Israel as a stand-in for the Jewish people as a whole reflects a deeper, ideological, even theological change that has grown out of the dawning demographic reality. Increasingly, establishment Jewish leaders articulate the view that the modern state of Israel represents the natural telos of Judaism rather than a historical contingency, the result of this worldly human activity. They are engaged in a substantial revision of a religion that long precedes the advent of the modern nation-state. Theirs is a peculiar kind of religious Zionism, or neo-Zionism, according to which Jewish destiny culminates, and was always meant to culminate, in a Jewish air force, army, and tank corps. It is an ideology that sacralizes secular state power, that finds inspiration in the deeds of kings instead of the words of the prophets.

The rejection of the prophetic tradition in favor of sovereignty's harsh logic has significant ethical consequences. Mainline Jewish organizations have demonstrated little concern for the grim results of Israel's actions—neither for the tens of thousands of Palestinian civilians killed by its army during the 2023–2024 war in Gaza, nor for the millions who have lived for more than half a century under Israeli military rule. The most generous interpretation for this moral myopia is that, having outsourced the entire content of Jewish identity to Israel, mainstream Jewishness has become so brittle that it cannot accommodate the truth of the Israeli government's actions without risking disintegration. But while that may be true for a great many ordinary American Jews to whom Israel remains less a place than an idea, the establishment Jewish leaders have no such excuse. These figures have not simply been indifferent or blind to the Jewish establishment's complicity in the current undemocratic one-state reality in Israel/Palestine. They have enthusiastically cheered Israel on, shielding it from criticism and consequences, as it has barreled toward the ethical abyss.

Renunciation

Against this backdrop, a growing though still small segment of American Jewish progressives expressly rejects the idea of Israel—not just as a state that ought to exist but also as the center of global Jewish life. For the first time since before World War II, Jewish anti-Zionism has become a visible political force in American Jewish life. At the very moment the diaspora has been eclipsed, some left-wing American Jews have sought to reinvest it with meaning.

Yet if the American Jewish mainstream prefers a sanguine fantasy vision of Israel over reckoning with its grim reality, the most radical forms of anti-Zionism now exhibit a cruel disregard for the lives of Jews in Israel; in the aftermath of October 7, some went as far as to suggest that killing Israeli Jewish civilians might be necessary, and even justified, for a free Palestine. For its part, diasporism in its nostalgic neo-Bundist form is plagued less by ethical failure than a failure of analysis. It opts for a peculiar kind of conservatism: repulsed by Israel's actions, it fantasizes of turning back the clock, arresting the historical process that is leading to the diaspora's demographic eclipse.

Post-Holocaust diasporism boasts eloquent and convincing spokespeople in addition to youthful, social-movement energies. Its lineage is one of dignified iconoclasm, a genealogy of stubborn resistance to the regnant Jewish communal common sense. In a now famous 1985 essay titled "Our Homeland, the Text," the literary critic George Steiner celebrated Jewish text-centeredness as "the instrument of exilic survival," the "indestructible guarantor, the 'underwriter' of the identity of the Jew: across the frontiers of his harrying, across the centuries, across the languages of which he has been a forced borrower and frequent master." For Steiner, the creation of the state of Israel was an absurdity, even a kind of sacrilege—by assimilating into the oppressive nation-state form that had been the cause of much of the Jews' suffering, Judaism, Steiner wrote, "has become homeless itself."

More recently, the philosopher and theorist Judith Butler published *Parting Ways: Jewishness and the Critique of Zionism*, in which she attempted to compose a counter-canon of non- and anti-Zionist thought, to separate Judaism from Zionism, drawing largely on European-Jewish thinkers, as well as Palestinian intellectuals such as Mahmoud Darwish and Edward Said. And in his newest book, an essay collection titled *The Necessity of Exile*, the scholar Shaul Magid argues for recovering exile as an ethical ideal to aid in "rebuilding a humble and non-proprietary Jewish relationship to the land between the Jordan River and the Mediterranean Sea." Many of their analyses, if not their proposals, strike me as compelling.

But when translated from the abstract realm of philosophy to the concrete realm of the political, the meaning of diasporism becomes more confused and less certain. Despite the rhetorical bark of some contemporary diasporist theorists' strident critiques of Israel, their proposals for Israel/Palestine more closely resemble dissident or forgotten Zionist tendencies. For instance, while Butler begins *Parting Ways* by calling for "an end to political Zionism," they devote much of the book to exploring the possibility of forms of "less than wretched binationalism"—correctives to the current unjust one-state reality—drawing extensively on the work of Hannah Arendt. Magid, in his attempt to "sever Zionism as an ideology from Israel as a nation," describes himself as a "counter-Zionist." Yet by this he means that he is "not against the State of Israel"; he is simply "not in favor of it functioning as an exclusively 'Jewish' state." Neither suggest a return to a Jewishness disconnected from the sovereign Jewish experience or propose severing the ties between Jews in Israel and Jews abroad. To the contrary, both maintain Israel at the center of their approaches to Jewishness: for Butler as an object of "a critique of nationalism and militarism," with the hope of transforming it; likewise, for Magid, as the place where the reenvisioning of the concept of exile might contribute to creating a more just polity.

Closer to the streets, diasporist activists have embraced a truncated form of Jewish peoplehood that valorizes Jewish group identity in the United States in isolation from, or even opposition to, the Jewish experience in Israel. In this view, the experience or threat of antisemitism constitutes the common denominator of American Jewish collectivity; statelessness becomes not just a historical condition suffered by Jews for two millennia but *the* essential Jewish condition and prerequisite for any ethical form of Jewish existence.

There is, however, a fundamental flaw at the core of this soft diaspora nationalism. It cannot accept the demographic reality of Israel as the global Jewish center of gravity. Faced with this dilemma, some American Jewish diasporists simply prefer to ignore this fact. Their concern, they say, is what happens close to home—that is, after all, the meaning of *doykeit*, of "hereness." But others make dismantling the state of Israel core to their putatively Jewish politics. They describe their relationship to Israel as analogous to that between abolitionists and slavery or feminists and patriarchy. They appear unconcerned by what Israel's destruction would mean for Israeli Jews. Theirs is, perversely, a Jewish politics that revels in its callousness toward the lives of other Jews, whose ancestors happened to flee to the embattled, fledgling Jewish state instead of the United States.

Responsibility

Today, Israel is failing the ethical test of sovereignty. The Israeli armed forces' recent punishing, indiscriminate bombardment of the Gaza Strip has killed tens of thousands of innocent civilians. Entire families have been wiped out; untold children left as orphans. Millions of Palestinians have been internally displaced from their homes. Within Israel, politicians call for ethnic cleansing, the resettlement of Gaza by

Jewish settlers, and even the expulsion of all Palestinians living under Israeli control. Long before the gruesome October 7 attacks by Hamas that ignited the most recent war, Israel/Palestine had become the site of a unitary, Israeli-controlled regime defined by variegated hierarchies of laws, privileges, and rights determined by ethno-national identity. As of this writing, the region has plunged into a catastrophe that far exceeds the death and destruction wrought by the war of 1948.

I understand those who look at this situation and want nothing to do with it—who, in their rage, dream of dissolving the ties between their Jewishness and Israel. But for me and, I imagine, for many American Jews, this is not possible. And it would not be morally right even if it were. As opposed to the Jewish establishment's complicity, on the one hand, and the diasporist and anti-Zionist impulse toward renunciation, on the other, I prefer the position of responsibility as a response to Israel's actions. My humanism means that I am appalled by Israel's carpet-bombing of the Gaza Strip and mourn the lives of the Palestinians whom Israel has killed; my membership to the Jewish people, the plurality of whom now live in Israel, means that I am aggrieved by what my people have done.

But I cannot disavow our bounds of faith, language, and heritage. I will not renounce my belonging to our collectivity, nor will I adopt a pose of radical hard-heartedness toward the fate of Israeli Jews, as some on the American left have done. I do not chant "not in my name," but prefer to accept that because Israel is increasingly home to most of the world's Jews, I am, as a Jew, implicated in its crimes. I want to speak to my fellow Jews, to beseech them—if necessary even to force them through sanctions or conditions imposed on future U.S. support—to pursue justice and seek peace, instead of occupation and endless war. Our fates *are* inextricably entangled, so it is my obligation.

We live in the age of what some Jewish theologians call *hester panim*—in the age of God's hiddenness. The divine does not intrude into human events. And human beings, by the same token, have no power to hasten the end. "Any messiah that comes," the great Israeli philosopher Yeshayahu Leibowitz once quipped, "is a false messiah." Israel's founding was not an act of providence, nor was it the dawning of the period of redemption, however miraculous its creation may have seemed.

But while an event of mundane history, the establishment of a sovereign Jewish state and the imminent return of most Jews to the Land of Israel nonetheless marks a significant turning point—a *Wendepunkt*, as German philosophers say—in the experience of the Jewish people. The ethical task of global Jewish life is now to make the modern experiment in Jewish sovereignty a just one. Neither the Jewish establishment nor the most radical left offers paths to meeting this challenge. The establishment's willful blindness to Israel's deeds is a form of moral abdication. Likewise, the pursuit of exculpation and clean hands through renunciation is to shirk our great collective responsibility.

The locus of the Jewish people's historical drama is now there, in Israel, whether we like it or not. Indeed, some of our tradition's sources convey an ambivalence about political sovereignty; human kingship appears as a lowly, even corrupted form of governance, a suboptimal substitute for the sovereignty of the divine. In his commentary on the book of Samuel, the medieval biblical commentator David Kimhi, known as the Radak, observes that the children of Israel desired a king to be "like all the other nations," so that they might throw off the yoke of the commandments. The Torah also warns of the potentially grave consequences that the Jews will face if we fail so horrifyingly and spectacularly to uphold our own ethical precepts. "You shall observe all my laws and regulations," the God of the Bible warns in the book of Leviticus, "lest the land to which I bring you to settle in vomit you out."

III.

Of course, from across the Atlantic, the pitched debates about Zionism and anti-Zionism that roil American Jewish life look much different. To most Israelis, they barely register. When such matters do pierce through to Israeli popular consciousness, they appear, in the main, as baffling curiosities, symptomatic of the identity-related anxiety that diasporic existence generates. Or, more uncharitably, as the last tortured gasps of a historical condition destined to fade away.

In 2019, an Israeli academic named Yossi Shain published a book called *The Israeli Century*. A bestseller in Hebrew, the book contains a blunt and, from the Israeli perspective, triumphalist argument—American Jewry is over. Shain does not mean literally that there will be no more American Jews, although he intimates that such an extinction could very well be possible in the future. Instead, he means that the era when American Jewry could claim to represent the Jewish people on the world stage—the era when American Jewry could exert a determinate pull on collective Jewish destiny—has ended.

"Jewish sovereignty will overshadow—even define—all other modes of life in the diaspora," Shain writes. "Israel has displaced the United States as the center of global Jewry and as the long-term definer of the Jewish people's interests and identity." His argument has found readers in high places. In 2021, Shain boasted, *The Israeli Century* was photographed on former Israeli prime minister Naftali Bennett's desk.

The "Israeli Century"

Such pessimism about the viability of diaspora life has long been part of Israeli Zionism: it is, of course, among classical Zionism's most basic tenets. Yet for many in Israel, this belief is no longer simply a matter of philosophy; it has begun to determine Israeli state policies. The sense of diaspora Jewry's demographic decline has dovetailed with the growing perception that U.S. global power has begun to diminish as well. Mainstream Israeli thinkers, journalists, and politicians have started to imagine a future not only without American Jews but, in some sense, also without America. The post–October 7 reality, in which Israel found itself utterly dependent on U.S. support, highlighted the folly of what had been, until then, the ascendant post-American fantasy. But while the Israeli hope of decoupling from America has been chastened, it has not disappeared.

I spoke with Yossi Shain by phone during a stay in Tel Aviv in the summer of 2022. He couldn't meet; he was too busy, he said. When I called, he was in his car, circling Ben-Gurion airport, waiting for his daughter to retrieve lost luggage. In the years since his book had appeared in Hebrew, Shain had entered Israeli parliamentary politics. He was nearing the end of his tenure as a representative of Avigdor Liberman's right-wing secularist party Yisrael Beitenu (Israel Is Our Home). Once closely aligned with Netanyahu's Likud, Liberman's party had joined the anti-Netanyahu opposition the year before—a wild-card move that had thrown the entire Israeli political system into disarray. Although it was an extraordinarily fractious moment, Shain was easy to reach and eager to talk. Israel may be one of the few countries where parliamentarians freely give out their own phone numbers in response to interview requests.

An ebullient, good-humored speaker, Shain assured me that his skepticism of American Jewry's future was not borne of animus. To the contrary, and unlike many on the Israeli right, he said, he feels great affection toward American Jewry. He doesn't hate us; he just thinks our time has passed. Shain speaks as someone to whom America feels intimately familiar. He has a PhD in political science from Yale and taught at other universities in the United States; his daughter was born there. American Jewry "was the most amazing experiment in Jewish life," Shain told me. "Until the Israeli century was brought in." His willingness to appreciate American Jewry's accomplishments puts him in opposition to the hard right, "the religious and ultra-nationalist Israelis," he said, "who basically despise American Jewry."

On the contemporary Israeli right, antipathy toward American Jewry has become almost de rigueur, part of a larger anti-liberal worldview. Representatives of the ultra-Orthodox parties frequently disparage the Reform Judaism practiced by many American Jews, which they view as a desecration of traditional religion and a threat to Judaism's survival. Moshe Gafni, a member of the Haredi United Torah Judaism Party, once denounced Reform Jews as "a group of clowns who stab the holy Torah," in response to the Israeli government's (still unrealized) plan to create a non-Orthodox prayer section at the Western Wall. Especially, but not exclusively, among Israeli territorial-maximalists, American Jews—correctly identified as overwhelmingly liberals—are often seen as harshly critical of Israel or even as self-hating Jews, willing to put their belief in human rights above Israeli security. Netanyahu himself holds this view. As Alon Pinkas, a former Israeli consul general in New York, once observed, what liberal American Jews fail to realize about Netanyahu is that to him, "you are his nemesis, not his fellow Jews."

Despite his avowals of amity, Shain is not free from some of these sentiments either. He describes widespread American Jewish support for a negotiated compromise between Israel and the Palestinians as hopelessly naïve. "They don't get what's going on here," he said of American Jewish liberals, echoing a common refrain. While the demand that Israel reach a peace agreement with the Palestinians is understandable in theory, it will not be possible anytime soon. "Who will build [a Palestinian] state?" Shain asked. "No one. Chaos will prevail." As Shain sees it, the Palestinian Authority cannot be trusted to assume power without threatening Israeli lives. To suggest otherwise, he said, is to "impose Western values that we all cherish" onto a reality where they do not apply. In a comparison that raised my eyebrows, Shain said it was "like when Americans wanted to impose 'freedom' on Afghani women."

Disagreements about the two-state solution aside, Shain's main point in *The Israeli Century* is that the American Jewish experiment was a victim of its own success. It was too good to last. "The *goldene medine*, it came to solve all your problems," he said. "In America you could be anything you want, you can be like the rest of the population." But while many American Jews celebrated the liberty they found in the United States, it was also double-edged. America's freedom hastened the decline of religious commitment and ethnic identity. Today, most Jews do not pray regularly or attend synagogue. They do not speak Hebrew, Yiddish, or Ladino. They no longer have living ties to the Old World. "There is very little, think about it, if you're not a religious practicing or ethnically involved Jew," Shain observed. And for him this is a problem that only Zionism can solve.

Having grown up in the autumn of American Jewish culture, I found it hard to disagree with much of Shain's analysis here, even if I bristled at most of his proposals and reject his politics. I could not deny that nonobservant Jewish identity seems to be tottering on the relics of the last century, lacking in substance and vitality. The situation has become so dire that some Jewish academics, out of desperation, have suggested that attending museum exhibits on extinct forms of Jewish life ought to be considered a form of Jewish practice. What is left of American Jewish culture appears to have lost its distinctiveness and its bite, devolved into mere kitsch and cliché: no more Saul Bellow novels, only Seth Rogen movies.

In *The Israeli Century*, Shain astutely diagnoses this cultural malaise too. Shain observes that Israel has become central to the works of the best-known contemporary American Jewish novelists. Jonathan Safran Foer, Nicole Krauss, Nathan Englander, Joshua Cohen—all have, in their own ways, turned to Israeli characters or encounters with Israel, as if the material of American Jewish life has exhausted itself. American Jews, Shain told me, "can hardly detach themselves from Israel, even if they wanted to."

I thought again of the diasporic double bind. American Jews find themselves in a situation in which Israel increasingly defines the terms of Jewish identity. Even attempts at articulating alternative kinds of

Jewishness—diasporist or anti-Zionist—end up placing Israel at the center of attention and activity, whether through contradistinction to Israeli-ness or opposition to Israel as a state. It seems there is no escaping Israel's orbit.

A Post-American Israel

Unlike those Israelis who are alarmed by signs of disillusionment with Israel among some young American Jews, Shain is unperturbed. Once an important resource to Israel in its attempts to shore up U.S. support, American Jews, according to Shain, are simply no longer needed. "American-Israeli relations are not built on diaspora-Israel relations," he said. Israel can make its geostrategic appeal to the United States on its own terms, without American Jewish mediation. And besides, Shain added, "the component of the diaspora in U.S. foreign policy is on the decline. American Jewry is less and less significant, less and less critical."

Shain is far from alone in the view that Israel no longer has use for American Jews. In May 2021, Ron Dermer, then Israel's Florida-born U.S. ambassador, made headlines for declaring that Israel should be "spending a lot more time doing outreach to evangelical Christians than to Jews." Known as "Bibi's brain," Dermer was not being provocative. Instead, he was expressing the actual strategy of the Netanyahu government. In a November 2022 article for *Haaretz*, Alon Pinkas attempted to illustrate the Netanyahu government's approach to American Jews, including even its supporters. In Netanyahu's Israel, American Jews had "become obsolete," Pinkas wrote. "You're like a cassette recorder, a Kodak camera, a BlackBerry phone. You've been replaced."

Not only have some Israeli leaders begun preparing for a future without American Jews—they have begun to imagine a future without America too. When I spoke with Shain in the summer of 2022, American global power had never looked more brittle. President Joe Biden had landed in Israel looking feeble, mouthing the usual slogans. He was the first U.S. president in decades to present no plan for the future of Israel/Palestine. The region barely appeared on his administration's agenda—an oversight that would prove disastrous in the fall of 2023. Israeli policymakers were all too aware of "the declining stature of the United States in world affairs," Shain said. Before Israel's humiliating total reliance on the United States after October 7 made such pronouncements appear painfully hubristic, the Israeli century, as Shain imagined it, was also to be a post-American century.

The Failure of Decoupling

On the Israeli right, this was supposed to be a good thing. A Middle East where the United States plays a less active role has long been a dream of Israeli hawks, who view Israeli reliance on the United States as a strategic constraint and liability. In 1996, a group of neoconservative think tankers lead by Richard Perle, who would later join the Bush administration, published a paper titled "A Clean Break: A New Strategy for Securing the Realm," which outlined steps for how Israel, during Netanyahu's first term as prime minister, could "forge a new basis for relations with the United States." According to the "Clean Break" authors, Israel could gain "greater freedom of action and remove a significant lever of pressure against it" if it were able to "cut itself free" from U.S. support.

The policies of Bibinomics aimed to turn this aspiration into a reality. Under successive Netanyahu administrations, economic liberalization was the method. Aggressive privatizations of banks and utilities, tax cuts and sharp decreases on public spending, and anti-union measures helped to transform Israel from a middling, state-dominated economy into an affluent, military- and surveillance-tech exporting regional power, even as inequality within Israel deepened. Under Netanyahu—first as finance minister in Ariel Sharon's government, then during his second stint as prime minister—Israel reversed its long-standing trade deficit and began to accumulate vast foreign currency reserves. The stronger Israel became economically, the less it required direct economic grant aid from the United States, which ceased in 2008. Even U.S. military aid to Israel, though it still amounts to the enormous sum of $38 billion allocated over ten years, mostly comes in the form of a discount for Israeli purchases of U.S. arms and missile-defense funding—essentially a subsidy to U.S. arms manufacturers.

In the 2010s, Netanyahu also began to turn away, at least symbolically, from the United States and its allies. He started to cultivate relationships with proudly illiberal governments such as Viktor Orbán's Hungary and Jarosław Kaczyński's Poland as an insurance policy against potential measures the European Union could take toward Israel. Netanyahu boasted of his good working relationship with Russia's Vladimir Putin—2019 Likud election campaign posters showed Netanyahu shaking hands with Putin under the slogan "In a League Above." Throughout Russia's war on Ukraine, Israel has held out on supplying missile defense systems to Ukraine and kept criticism of Russian conduct to a minimum.

In what was perhaps the most telling sign of wariness of U.S. decline, Israel began to cultivate closer ties with China. In 2021, as part of China's Belt and Road initiative, Israel granted the state-owned Shanghai International Port Group a tender to operate the Haifa Bay shipping terminal, which manages roughly half the country's freight. Chinese companies also worked on major Israeli infrastructure projects, such as the new Tel Aviv light rail system.

But on October 7, all the talk of decoupling and the ostensible "self-reliance" Netanyahu claimed to have achieved proved to be a farce. Netanyahu's Israel found itself in need of rescue by Joe Biden. Amid the threat of a broader regional war, Israel appeared more reliant than ever on its U.S. sponsor, which in the early days of the war sent two aircraft carrier strike groups to deter Iran-backed forces from even greater escalation. Israel has depended on the United States for everything from small arms, such as automatic rifles, to key components of the Iron Dome system. The United States sent three-star general James F. Glynn of the U.S. Marine Corps to advise the Israeli general staff on how to conduct urban counterinsurgency. Secretary of State Antony Blinken and Secretary of Defense Lloyd Austin both sat in on Israeli cabinet planning meetings to counsel their Israeli counterparts.

Shain and others were not totally wrong, though, about the reality of American decline. Even as the Biden administration moved swiftly to back up Israel, U.S. global power has appeared precarious. For all its support for Israel's war, the United States has never appeared more diplomatically isolated and unpopular. The empire seems stretched too thin. At the same time, Israel failed to achieve the strategic independence of which its leaders had boasted. In large part thanks to Netanyahu, Israel has never appeared more like a client state of America. Hoping for a clean break, it got the worst of both options, chained to the hegemon that has entered its last days.

Out with a Shrug

Two days after my conversation with Shain, I traveled to the quiet north Tel Aviv neighborhood where Shmuel Rosner lives. A former U.S. correspondent for *Haaretz*, Rosner is a prolific writer and commentator on Israeli affairs. In his book #*IsraeliJudaism: Portrait of a Cultural Revolution*, co-authored with the late Israeli pollster Camil Fuchs, Rosner argues that a new form of Jewish identity, what he calls "Jewsraeli," has emerged in Israel, synthesizing the practices of religious tradition with the civic obligations of the Israeli state. I wanted to discuss with him what the emergence of the Jewsraeli might mean for the relationship between Israel and the diaspora. I arrived late to Rosner's door, where he greeted me and led me inside, then downstairs to his modernist study that doubles as a podcast recording studio.

I had sought out Rosner, as I did Shain, because I wanted to talk, and argue, with Israeli public intellectuals who saw themselves as part of the country's mainstream. I know the Israeli left and its moribund peace camp well. They are my friends and comrades. But they have no power. They set no policy. The future of Israeli politics—and thus in some sense the future of American Jewish politics—would instead be determined by the articulators of the Israeli consensus.

For Rosner, like Shain, there's no question that Israel has become the determining force in Jewish history. Israel is in the driver's seat, and American Jews are welcome to come along for the ride. If they're unhappy with its direction, they can get off at any time. "If you think Israel is worthy of your effort, then fight for it," Rosner said. "If you don't think it's worth your time . . ." He shrugged.

Rosner is not worried by the perennial warnings that Israeli and progressive American Jews are on the precipice of a great divergence. As he surely knew, I told him, American Jewish leaders agonize over what they fear is a growing "distance" between American Jews and Israel. Over the last several years, Jewish establishment figures have become so worried that they have openly lamented that Israel's turn to right-wing populism under Netanyahu has chilled American Jewish opinion about Israel. Rosner replied that this was only natural. "Since circumstances in Israel and in the United States are very different for Jews here and there," he said, "it should be expected that we will have different views, different practices, and a different interpretation of what Judaism means."

In contrast to Shain, Rosner believes it is not so much that Israel has absorbed or overwhelmed American Jewry as much as the two have parted ways. American Jewry, therefore, would have to resolve its own identity riddle for itself. "I'm not deluding myself into thinking that Israel is powerful enough to fight against cultural trends in the United States," he said. Intermarriage, disaffiliation, distaste for Israel— these, Rosner told me, were problems for American Jewish leaders to address.

And if they expected Israel to change to make their jobs easier, they would be sorely disappointed. American Jews might balk at Israel's treatment of the Palestinians and its ongoing occupation of the West Bank and siege of Gaza. Anti-democratic legislation might make it harder for American Jewish groups to defend Israel in the public sphere. It might be harder for Jewish educators to convince young Jews that Israel matters. But according to Rosner, that was not Israel's problem. "If you tell me, well, *I* need to evacuate all the settlements from Samaria," he said, using the biblical name for the northern part of the occupied West Bank, "because otherwise *you* cannot educate *your* children, well, tough luck, this is something I cannot do for you."

In a 2014 *New York Times* op-ed, Rosner staked out an even stronger line. As Israeli warplanes bombarded the Gaza Strip, American Jewish liberals—liberal Zionists, for the most part—wrung their hands despondently about how the scenes of carnage would harm Israel's image among American Jews. Rosner took aim at what he saw as the self-importance of these liberal critics and their inflated view of American Jewry's importance. "They seem to believe that the implied threat that Israel might lose Jewish supporters abroad will somehow convince the government to alter its policies," he wrote. "This is a self-aggrandizing fantasy."

The Contemporary Challenge

I disagreed with much of what Rosner said. We argued at length, more than I had with Shain. Rosner had been generous with his time. But while I disputed almost all of his political claims, by the end of our conversation I found myself agreeing, begrudgingly, with his analysis of the dilemma facing many young and progressive American Jews. "For most liberal young American Jews, God isn't an option, halacha isn't an option, making aliyah isn't an option. Tell me, what is?" Rosner said. "It's a great challenge, and also a very interesting challenge—to try to reimagine or reinvent American Judaism or diaspora Judaism for the twenty-first century."

After I said goodbye, I alighted on the bus back to south Tel Aviv.

The late-summer sun set over the wide, intra-city highway. I turned Rosner's and Shain's words over in my head. They had not shocked me. But they had unsettled me. There appeared to be no way out of the diasporic double bind, short of outright disavowing one's Jewishness. Indeed, some left-wing Jews, driven by outrage over Israel's actions, or uncommitted to any fragment of ritual and text, had begun to contemplate full disavowal—an old and distinguished Jewish tradition itself, but hardly an option for most American Jews.

It seemed to me that commentators like Shain and Rosner were right about this one very important thing. Non-Orthodox American Judaism faces a profound, fundamental crisis of content and purpose. The secular Jewishness of the immigrant generation had departed the scene, and Zionism had emerged to replace it. But now the practices of sovereign Jewish power generate as much ambivalence, even disgust, as celebration. Having outsourced nearly all its content to Israel, American Jewish life can no more evade Israel and Zionism than choose to dissolve. If it doesn't find a new foundation on which to stand, it might anyway collapse.

PART THREE

THE TRANSFORMATIONS OF LIBERAL JUDAISM

I.

On Yom Kippur in September 2021, I found myself, rather incongruously, at a boutique winery in Sullivan County, New York. It was the end of the second summer of the pandemic, and social life, indoor gatherings, and non-remote work had begun their slow, stuttering return.

A group of mask-wearing volunteers, dressed in white, stood at the stolid wood door to the winery's main hall. They handed out small suede yarmulkes and colorful booklets filled with short meditations on the holiday printed in a big, inviting font. Their contents were not strictly spiritual fare but broad, breezy discussions—on the relationship between *teshuvah* (repentance) and racial justice, and on what the Jewish tradition might have to say about matters like climate change and trans rights.

Even after roughly a decade moving in and out of various American Jewish communities, I felt, and still feel, surprised when I meet people for whom combining the liberal causes of the day with Jewish liturgy seems to be second nature—for whom *this* is what Judaism is and always has been. The Judaism of my childhood was different.

During the years I lived in Israel, I had also seen Judaism transformed into a weapon. On holidays like Simchat Torah and Purim, I watched public celebrations of Jewishness become outbursts of racist violence, when young Jewish revelers pelted the cars of Arab taxi drivers with rocks or surrounded them and banged on their windows. For a time, I worried that *this* was what Judaism had become.

My reasons, then, for being at a Sullivan County winery on Yom Kippur were not purely journalistic. On the recommendation of activist friends who had found their spiritual home among his flock, I had sought out Rabbi Amichai Lau-Lavie and Lab/Shul, the "artist-driven, everybody-friendly, God-optional, experimental community" which Lau-Lavie founded in 2013. These activist friends assured me that there would be no nationalism at Lau-Lavie's Lab/Shul. He understood all too well, they said, the challenge of wresting Judaism's definition from its most chauvinist, exclusivist, and intolerant interpreters. Yet they also cautioned that Lab/Shul's Yom Kippur would not be from the traditional service I was used to.

I entered the main hall and met a cross section of liberal Jewish New York. Middle-aged TriBeCa dads with expensive haircuts and designer sneakers swayed, holding small children; in the rows behind them, young adults with tattoos and facial piercings looked down somberly at their Doc Martens; surprisingly, given Lab/Shul's public-facing aesthetic, at least half the attendees appeared to be retirees, the only people really dressed as if they were attending an ordinary synagogue. But this was not an ordinary synagogue.

When the service began, I recognized the motifs of familiar melodies. The liturgy and the arrangement, however, had been dramatically changed. There was no gendered language about God, none of the typical references to the "Almighty King" or "He who sits on high." There was hardly any mention of God at all. On the *bima*, or front stage, there were at least three guitarists, two female cantors, two African American ministers, and a Palestinian percussionist. In the break before the start of the evening service, two gay Zen monks, a married couple, performed a guided meditation by Zoom.

If many of the Lab/Shul attendees seemed utterly unsurprised by the possibility of this syncretic, experimental form of Judaism and seemed to take for granted the synthesis of liberal politics and Jewish practice, Lau-Lavie did not. He was born in Israel to a family that is part of the country's religious establishment; its rabbinic lineage, he says, stretches back centuries. His uncle, Yisrael Meir Lau, was the Orthodox Ashkenazi chief rabbi of Israel. His father, Naphtali, served as Israel's general counsel in New York. Lau-Lavie's early life followed the trajectory of Israel's religious nationalist elite: yeshiva study in the West Bank settlement of Alon Shvut, then military service as a paratrooper.

Yet there was one fact that would take Lau-Lavie on a different path from the one into which he was born. By his bar mitzvah, he said, he knew he was gay, and in Israel's Orthodox, Zionist world, this was a problem.

Lau-Lavie's story is unique in its particulars, but it is far from anomalous. Increasingly, the liberal Jewish world functions in large part because of people like him: Jewish leaders, many of them gay and lesbian, who confronted exclusion and marginalization personally, but instead of leaving Jewish life behind, set out to change it. Their sense of commitment powers their transformation of the contours of liberal Jewish life. It is the force behind their reinvention of ritual and liturgy and their redefinition of Jewish identity in the process.

Lab/Shul's Yom Kippur service exemplified many of the tendencies of contemporary, non-Orthodox Jewish life's avant-garde. It was inclusive not just of racial diversity and the full range of sexual identities but even beyond religious lines, with non-Jewish clergy participating in the prayers. At the same time, it was at its core an *experience*— something that everyone on the grounds of the winery that day had paid for and opted into because of what they thought it would do *for them*. My own attendance was no exception. While some sense of community was, of course, part of this experience—after all, Jewish prayer requires a group—the emphasis was more on the subjective experience of contemplation and mindfulness for the individual. The service's internal logic resembled that of secular rituals, like yoga, that define the lives of affluent professionals. Indeed, Lab/Shul's proposal seemed to be that one could *do* Jewish just the way one might *do* yoga.

Put differently, Lab/Shul embodied at once both liberal Judaism's most substantial achievement and the greatest challenge to its continued existence as a living practice. On the one hand, it showcased the opening of Jewish practice to those once excluded from it—the metamorphosis of Judaism into a religion of universal emancipation. On the other hand, it reflected the transformation of ritual practice into an experiential, fungible commodity that must compete in the market for buyers.

At stake in liberal Judaism's navigation of these two forces is whether liberal Jews can build and sustain vibrant and substantively committed communities, or if the future of non-Orthodox Judaism will resemble occasional aesthetic experiences with Jewish themes: Burning Man meets Yom Kippur.

Torah in Drag

A few months after the Yom Kippur service, I met with Lau-Lavie in a Senegalese café near his apartment in Harlem on an overcast, wintry afternoon. Lau-Lavie is stocky, with short-cropped, graying hair and a mischievous grin. When he moved to New York City in the 1990s, he said, he made two important discoveries.

The first was the city's gay underground activist community. In the Radical Faeries—a queer countercultural movement known for ecstatic gatherings that melded neo-paganism and radical environmentalism—Lau-Lavie found something appealing. "Reverence, irreverence, ritual," he said. "We're laughing, but actually no—it's like, this is shamanism." It turned out that the edge of humor and seriousness, of play and worship, was a place he liked to inhabit. It allowed for a mode of being, he said, "where the queer is able to be the court jester, but also deliver truth."

The second discovery was that mainstream, liberal American Judaism was terribly, stultifyingly boring. For most American Jews, large parts of Saturday morning prayers were inaccessible and unintelligible. The Torah service, which forms the centerpiece of Shabbat morning davening, was, for many, alienating and literally incomprehensible. Most American Jews could neither read nor understand the original Biblical Hebrew. Their attendance in synagogue was more reflex and habit than the product of any connection to the texts. As a result, services were almost listless, rote gestures, the full meanings of which had become obscure.

In 1999, Lau-Lavie launched a traveling religious theater initiative called Storahtelling, aimed at enlivening the Torah-reading experience. It took off quickly—and took on an almost evangelical quality. Lau-Lavie went on tour with the project, bringing the show on the road to synagogues in need of a jolt of youthful, radical-theater-informed energy. One can still find old Storahtelling videos on the internet. Somehow, all at once, they are earnest enactments of scenes from the Bible and over-the-top comedy, total musical productions and fully serious religious ceremonies. It turned out that the edge of worship and play was a place many American Jews wanted to inhabit too. Or perhaps they could no longer tell the difference.

Storahtelling gave birth to Lau-Lavie's enduring theatrical drag alter ego, the Rebbetzin Hadassah Gross. Bedecked in a full wig and costume jewelry, discoursing on Kabbalah in a heavy Hungarian-Yiddish accent, "Hadassah was completely immersive," Lau-Lavie said. Appearing as Hadassah in a 2007 televised interview with Israeli journalist Yair Lapid, who would later serve as Israel's prime minister, Lau-Lavie didn't break character, even when asked about what his mostly Orthodox family thought of the act. "Becoming Hadassah was a way to own both my queerness and my Jewishness," Lau-Lavie told me, "through a lot of makeup and heels."

There was a serious theory behind all this spectacle, Lau-Lavie explained. The idea for Storahtelling built on a contemporary interpretation of what was, in fact, an ancient practice. For centuries, the traditional reading of the Torah in Jewish communities had been accompanied by a simultaneous translation of the biblical text. There was even a name for the person who had done the translating: in Hebrew, the *metargem*. By reviving the practice through theatrical reenactment, Lau-Lavie said he found both "a way of talking back" to the text—of "queering it," altering its meaning from the original—and of making that meaning more immediately accessible to the modern Jew. "The adaptation is built in [to the tradition]," Lau-Lavie said, laying out the grounds for his practical innovations. "Without it, you got a museum piece that is frozen in time."

In 2013, Lau-Lavie transformed Storahtelling further into a more institutional form when he started Lab/Shul. The new ritual community would be occasional by definition—a "pop-up," borrowing the word from the world of hipster fashion. It would emphasize the experiential "gathering" aspect of worship. To this day, Lab/Shul has no building. Instead, it stages its services in venues across the New York area. For the progressive, artsy, and new-agey crowd that it draws, the immersive Torah-as-performance-spectacle model appears to give them what they want. In 2019, Lab/Shul filled New York's Hammerstein Ballroom on Rosh Hashanah. In 2020, its Purim holiday event was co-hosted by House of Yes, a trendy queer cabaret in Bushwick. Instead of having Judaism compete with the dance club, Lab/Shul proposed, why not bring Judaism to the club, merge the two together?

Still, for all the levity and play that marks Lab/Shul's ceremonies, it also appeared to me that Lau-Lavie held some real pain when it came to his relationship with the tradition, visible in moments during his performances and prayer leading. Toward the end of our conversation, I asked Lau-Lavie why he had chosen to stay in the Jewish world: Why hadn't he left when it had been so closed and hostile to him? "This is my vocabulary; this is my birth language," he replied. He added that he felt called "in deep ways" to create a new practice of Judaism, "which includes queering and feminizing and challenging the masculine Godhead and rabbinic obstructionist attitudes," and that doing so required working the tradition. Ultimately, he said, "to change the text you need to know the text."

Several years into Lab/Shul's operation, at the age of forty-seven, Lau-Lavie—who has made his name for the unconventional—did something very conventional indeed. He became a Conservative rabbi. Lau-Lavie said that he felt he would not have had "the tools to be a change agent" if he remained an artist. Besides, the title didn't hurt either. "It was also ego," he said. "I wanted to be the other Rabbi Lau." He received ordination from the Jewish Theological Seminary, the flagship institution of Conservative Judaism, in 2016. If there was anything remarkable about this, it was how unremarkable JTS's ordination of a gay, drag-performing rabbi now seemed.

II.
Judaism's "Pink Line"

It is hard to overstate the magnitude of the cultural and institutional change that made Lau-Lavie's ordination possible. Only a decade earlier, the Conservative movement's ordination of a vocally out gay drag-performing rabbi would have been unthinkable. At the time, American Jewish life, like America as a whole, was divided by a "pink line," to borrow South African journalist Mark Gevisser's phrase. On one side were the even more liberal Reform and Reconstructionist denominations, which were already open to ordaining LGBTQ clergy. On the other side were the traditionalists, the Conservative movement among them, and the Orthodox, who maintained that Jewish law strictly prohibited homosexuality. It was not until 2006 that Conservative

Judaism lifted its ban on ordaining gay and lesbian rabbis, and only after a long and intense period of debate.

Over roughly the last fifteen years, Conservative Judaism's position on homosexuality has gone the way of the other non-Orthodox denominations. Today, LGBTQ acceptance and inclusion is not simply the norm; it is an explicit tenet of communal life. Openly gay and lesbian rabbis lead Conservative congregations around the country. By some accounts, close to half the students in recent JTS rabbinical school classes identify as queer. These changes within the denomination that long saw itself as representing the American Jewish religious "center" reflect in miniature the revolution in gender and sexual identity that has swept America and, with it, American Judaism. While homophobia no doubt persists, non-Orthodox synagogues have never been more inclusive or more sensitive to those once on the margins of Jewish life.

And yet the victories for liberal inclusion arrived at an inopportune time in the history of non-Orthodox Judaism—in the midst of the liberal denominations' precipitous collapse. By the time LGBTQ Jews finally gained a foothold in the mainstream Jewish institutions, these institutions were in the throes of decline. The steady drop in synagogue membership in the twentieth century turned into a dramatic plunge in the early twenty-first. Over the last twenty years, more than one-third of Conservative synagogues and one-fifth of Reform synagogues have closed. The leaders of both denominations have begun to speak in barely veiled terms of managed obsolescence.

More than the other non-Orthodox denominations, perhaps, the Conservative movement encapsulates both the gains and losses of the last quarter century in American Jewish life. The gay and lesbian rabbinical students who fought for a place in the Conservative seminaries created, through their refusal to give up on the tradition, the possibility—for the first time in Jewish history—of an inclusive, progressive Judaism that also seeks to maintain its commitment to halacha. They demonstrated, contrary to the claims of their detractors, that there is no inherent contradiction between LGBTQ acceptance and adherence to the normative framework of Jewish law. The tragedy of contemporary liberal Judaism is that they may be the ones to turn off the lights in the buildings that once tried to keep them out.

A Place in the Middle

Since the turn of the twentieth century, Conservative Judaism has aspired to represent the practical and theological middle ground of American Jewish life. Solomon Schechter, the great biblical scholar and the movement's architect (and for whom the day school I attended was named), believed in both the binding nature of halacha *and* the need for its interpretation to adapt to the lived realities of existing Jewish communities.

Initially, Conservative Judaism was slow to gain adherents when it arrived on U.S. shores in the century's first decades, but in the postwar years its membership ballooned as the descendants of the eastern European immigrants fled the cities for the suburbs. My great-grandmother Bessie lived and died an Orthodox Jew. My grandmother Charlotte belonged to a Conservative synagogue she only rarely entered.

In the 1950s and '60s, the number of Conservative Judaism's adherents grew rapidly as Jews sought to conform to the norms of respectable middle-class life. Conservative Judaism became, as the sociologist Marshall Sklare put it, the Jewish "ethnic church," an institutional parallel to the Protestant and Catholic model. "At once religiously authentic and amiably inoffensive," historian Jonathan Sarna writes, Conservative Judaism seemed "well-suited to this cultural moment and felt in touch with the times." By 1970, Conservative Judaism represented the plurality of American Jews—42 percent—with close to 2 million members. (Today, by contrast, it claims roughly only 8 percent of Jews under age thirty.) The movement appealed to Jews who had no desire for the stringency of their Orthodox forebears but who also did not want to abandon the traditional liturgy and ritual observance for the Americanized Reform Judaism, which seemed to them unfamiliar.

At once open to and skeptical of change, Conservative Judaism responded slowly to the revolutions of the 1960s and their aftermath, especially when compared with the other non-Orthodox denominations. Reform Judaism, by contrast, responded the fastest and with the most enthusiasm. Feminism, in particular, remade almost every facet of Reform Jewish practice. Jewish feminists catalyzed the growth of women's Torah study groups, changes to prayer books, and, most significantly, the ordination of women rabbis. In 1972, Hebrew Union College, the Reform Movement's flagship seminary, ordained its first female rabbi. In 1974, the Reconstructionist Rabbinical College—which had split from the Conservative movement largely over feminism— ordained its first woman. Conservative Judaism would not ordain a woman rabbi until 1985.

The evolution of the liberal denominations followed a similar trajectory when it came to homosexuality. In 1981, Congregation Sha'ar Zahav, a gay synagogue in San Francisco, affiliated with the Reform Movement. In 1989, HUC ordained its first openly gay rabbi. The Jewish Theological Seminary, by contrast, would not graduate an openly gay rabbi until 2011.

At the Limit of the Law

The Conservative movement's internal reasoning for how it chose to address homosexuality centered on its putative commitment to Jewish law. While Reform and other liberal denominations made no pretense that halacha constituted a divine, binding system of commandments, Conservative Judaism—or at least its leaders—did.

In practice, this commitment to halacha meant that the movement's rabbis felt they needed to justify religiously any decision to deviate from the biblical prohibition on homosexuality. It was not a challenge they took lightly. In the 1990s the movement began the debate, which would last for more than a decade, about the place of gay people in Jewish life.

But there was much more to the Conservative movement's trepidation on the issue than concerns with conformity to Jewish law. After all, the movement's internal Jewish jurisprudence had proved rather flexible on just as serious matters before. Famously—or infamously, for the movement's traditionalists—the Conservative leadership had ruled in 1950 that congregants could drive to synagogue, even though doing so constituted an unambiguous violation of the laws of the Sabbath. They feared that barring driving risked letting Jews drift away from synagogue, from Judaism itself, and into the permissiveness of secular American society. Better to violate the law, they argued, than to lose the tradition altogether.

This also meant that "they [the Conservative movement] had the justification frameworks, the plausibility structures" to make the shift on gay rights, explained Rabbi Steven Greenberg, the founding director of Eshel, an Orthodox LGBTQ advocacy group, and the author of the 2005 book *Wrestling with God and Men: Homosexuality in the Jewish Tradition.* "What they didn't have was the broad ability to deal with gay desire," he added. "It's extremely important not to forget that the resistance was not merely an atavistic commitment to literalism."

Widely considered the first openly gay Orthodox rabbi, Greenberg has approached reconciling Jewish law and homosexuality by writing frankly about the challenge posed by queerness to core elements of the Jewish tradition. "If the continuity of your civilization rests on reproduction, what does it mean that the reproductive framework of love and attraction fails for you consistently?" Greenberg asked. At the heart of traditional Judaism's resistance to homosexuality was, he added, "the legitimate fear that the life centeredness of the Jewish people will be harmed by a lovemaking that doesn't serve life."

At the same time, Greenberg has insistently argued, LGBTQ inclusion can be reconciled with a commitment to the normative framework of Jewish law. The work of doing so, he explained, was twofold. Traditionalist communities had "to give gay people the sense that God did not hate them, that they could be members of the *brit* [the Jewish covenant]," Greenberg explained. They also had to recognize their communal obligation to LGBTQ Jews as Jewish people. "You make them responsible for the human beings that they claim to be responsible for," Greenberg said. "You make them take responsibility for the broken lives."

The First Try

Through the 1990s, however, the Conservative movement proceeded along a different path than the one Greenberg might have suggested, even as some rabbis drew on similar arguments. This was much more a dispute among the Conservative rabbinical leadership, some of whom resisted ordaining gay and lesbian students, than it was a matter of live debate among the movement's laypeople, who like much of liberal America were becoming increasingly supportive of LGBTQ rights. Intense disagreement divided the rabbis responsible for the movement's religious-legal rulings, the members of its Committee on Jewish Law and Standards (the "Law Committee").

On the side staunchly opposed to accepting LGBTQ students was Rabbi Joel Roth. A well-regarded scholar of halacha, Roth argued not only that gay and lesbian students could not be ordained but also that Conservative congregational leaders could bar them from working as synagogue educators. At the more liberal end was Rabbi Bradley Shavit Artson, a California-born rabbi who argued that the biblical prohibition of homosexuality referred to coercive sexual acts and should not apply to loving, monogamous homosexual relationships—a type of love that, he claimed, was unknown to the ancient world.

Artson—now the dean of the Ziegler School of Rabbinic Studies, the movement's West Coast seminary—had become an advocate for LGBTQ rights while a student at JTS in the 1980s. "My sister came out the week I went to rabbinical school," he remembered. "So I felt like I needed to know what I thought." Artson chose to write a final paper for a Jewish law class in which he argued for ordaining LGBTQ rabbis and creating LGBTQ wedding ceremonies. "I became instantly the most unpopular person at JTS," Artson said. "Literally, I would be in the cafeteria, sipping my soup, and a pair of pants would come up to me. A voice from above would say, 'Are you Brad Artson?' And I would say yes without looking up," he recalled. "Then they'd just be yelling up there."

In 1992, after much deliberation, the Conservative movement issued a "Consensus Statement on Homosexuality." Charitably viewed, it was a gesture toward compromise. The Conservative movement would still not ordain LGBTQ rabbis—Roth's position had, in this sense, won out over Artson's. But the statement also left the employment of LGBTQ educators up to the discretion of synagogue leaders and affirmed that gay and lesbian Jews would be "welcome in our communities." In practice, the message was "Welcome, but we're not going to do anything to show that you're welcome," said Rabbi Daniel Nevins, a former dean of JTS's rabbinical school who supported LGBTQ inclusion within the movement.

"I remember the day that Joel Roth's paper passed and mine failed," Artson said. "I went up to him and I said, 'Today is the best day your position will ever have, and it will get worse every day forward. It is the worst day for mine, but it will get better every day.'" He added, "That happened way quicker than I thought."

The Swift Victory

American political culture was changing fast. During the Bush years, the fight over LGBTQ rights took center stage. After the Supreme Court's 2003 decision in *Lawrence v. Texas* dismantled anti-sodomy laws, Massachusetts became the first state to legalize same-sex marriage. Connecticut followed two years later. Throughout the early 2000s, cities in liberal-leaning states like San Francisco, Portland, and New York began to issue marriage licenses. In response, the Christian right tried to stop the wave of liberalization. In 2004, President George W. Bush called for a constitutional amendment banning gay marriage.

The majority of Conservative Jews then, as now, voted for Democrats. And as the issue of gay rights polarized along party lines, the denomination's leadership recognized it would need to reconsider its opposition to ordaining gay rabbis in the current climate. "This led to almost three years of talking about nothing else," said Rabbi Elliot Dorff, the current chair of the Law Committee and rector of the American Jewish University in Los Angeles, home to the movement's West Coast seminary. "A lot of things were happening in America on the gay and lesbian issue," he said, and not only in politics. There was a new visibility of openly gay and lesbian characters on television; public figures were coming out of the closet.

If Conservative Judaism didn't change, it risked becoming dangerously out of step with the people it claimed to represent. For a denomination premised on the adaptability of Judaism's normative framework coupled with adherence to it, proving that obligation to halacha and LGBTQ inclusion could be reconciled was a necessity. The argument for doing so also raised questions about what commitment to Jewish law as a normative framework really meant and what kind of reasoning could justify a break with precedent.

Yet, ultimately, it was not the heady argument based on halacha that provided the impetus for the denomination's shift but something perhaps more rudimentarily human. Not only had America changed; people could also no longer bear being cruel to those they cared about. The issue of LGBTQ rights was not theoretical. For many, it was personal. That was true of Artson, and it was true of Dorff too. In 1991, his daughter, the oldest of his four children, came out. "I remember saying to people all the time, if you know members of your family, or friends of yours, are gay or lesbian, it's hard to hate people that you love," Dorff recalled.

In 2006, Conservative Judaism's Law Committee convened to vote on a new position on gay and lesbian Jews. The range of opinion was wide. Some rabbis opposed LGBT acceptance and endorsed "reparative" therapy for changing sexual orientation; others called for rejecting the biblical prohibition on homosexuality entirely. "It got ugly," Daniel Nevins remembered.

The twenty-five members of the Law Committee could not reach a consensus. Instead, they ratified three separate decisions, in keeping with the Conservative denomination's stated committed to pluralism. Communities could now choose which decision to follow. Only one of the three allowed for ordaining gay and lesbian rabbis. But that was all that was needed to bring the ban down.

Dorff, Nevins, and another rabbi, Avram Reisner, were the authors of the decision that opened Conservative Judaism's doors to gay and lesbian students. In their paper, *Homosexuality, Human Dignity, and Halakhah*, they argued that the halachic principle of *kavod habriot*, or human dignity, superseded the rabbinical interpretations of the biblical prohibition on homosexuality that had barred gay and lesbian Jews from engaging in Torah study and thus from becoming rabbis. They argued that preventing LGBTQ people from becoming rabbis was itself discriminatory and humiliating, and therefore a violation of the principle of human dignity as well.

Within the movement's institutions, the transformation was almost instantaneous. Immediately, Conservative Judaism's West Coast seminary began ordaining LGBTQ rabbinical students. Throughout the deliberations, members of the Law Committee feared that any ruling on homosexuality risked splitting the denomination between liberal and less liberal wings, as had happened in the 1980s when the movement began to ordain women rabbis. No such schism occurred. When

Arnold Eisen—at the time, JTS's chancellor—surveyed the denomination's members, he found that roughly two-thirds of Conservative
Jews in America supported Dorff, Nevins, and Reisner's decision.

For many of the staunchest LGBTQ rights advocates, however, the
victory was only partial. It did not reject the verses from Leviticus but
found a way to work around them, Nevins explained. It maintained
not only the stigma on homosexuality but also the prohibition on anal
sex. It implied that bisexual Jews should live their lives as heterosexu-
als if they could, since Judaism believed in the control and suppression
of certain desires. It also left its position on same-sex marriage open-
ended.

But it was only a matter of time before the process that began in
2006 was, in a way, completed. Six years later, in 2012, as the Supreme Court prepared its ruling in *United States v. Windsor*, JTS filed
an amicus brief in favor of marriage equality. That same year, the denomination enumerated its guidelines for same-sex marriage ceremonies. The "pink line" in American Jewish life had shifted decisively.

In the Institutions

Rachel Isaacs was the first openly lesbian woman to graduate from
JTS. She entered the seminary shortly after its 2006 ruling. She had
been enrolled in the Reform Movement's seminary, Hebrew Union
College, but felt that Conservative Judaism was her real religious
home. "I actually believe in the halachic system and in the binding
nature of Jewish law," Isaacs told me. That was not the approach to
Jewish law in HUC, where Jewish law was thought to be akin to
guidelines for ethical behavior. When the possibility of transferring
arose, Isaacs took it.

In the years immediately following the 2006 ruling, JTS was not an
easy place to be for out gay and lesbian students. There were still faculty who supported the use of "reparative" therapy. At the denomination's affiliate in Israel, where students were required to spend a year,

LGBTQ students faced open and sometimes strident homophobia. "You can't admit gay and lesbian students and send them to an institution where the dean is talking about homosexuality as an illness," Isaacs said. The seminary's leaders seemed to have thought that accepting LGBT students was enough. But "all these demographic changes can't happen without real sensitivity to how things need to be changed and adopted," Isaacs said.

Aaron Weininger was the first openly gay man admitted to JTS as a first-year student under the new policy. He and Isaacs have remained close friends. "He was more the activist," Isaacs remembered. "Then there was me, trying to do things internally."

In college, Weininger had been an outspoken gay rights organizer. He had few illusions about what he was getting into when he enrolled at JTS. That didn't make the experience easier. "It wasn't a horrible place," he said of JTS during those years, "but it wasn't an affirming place." During his fourth year of rabbinical school, Weininger worked as a rabbinical intern at a synagogue in Florida, where he helped students prepare for their bar mitzvahs. "The coming-out process there was quite challenging," he said. The Florida congregation's president created a "veto policy" that allowed bar mitzvah families uncomfortable with the presence of an openly gay rabbi to request Weininger's absence.

Under difficult circumstances, Isaacs and Weininger shared an uncommon determination. Both were raised in the Conservative movement's institutions—its synagogues and summer camps—and had maintained their commitment to its philosophy of Judaism, despite the ways it had excluded them. Both had insisted on their right to exist in a denomination that at first rejected, then only ambivalently accepted, their presence. Instead of leaving for other, more liberal denominations, or leaving Judaism entirely, they fought for their place and transformed American Judaism in the process. "Change often involves staying in relationship and witnessing people opening up to new ideas," Weininger reflected. "Rather than run away from messiness," he added, "I find it more helpful to say, 'Okay, this is uncomfortable—I'm going to be in it *more*.'"

His life would seem to bear out the wisdom of this strategy. In 2006, when Weininger was a senior in college, his childhood synagogue invited him to address the congregation during Friday night services, but the rabbi rescinded the invitation when he learned that Weininger had come out as gay. His family subsequently left the synagogue for a different one. "But for me that didn't mean leaving the Conservative movement," he said. Roughly a decade later, Weininger received an invitation to return to the same synagogue and deliver its "Pride Shabbat" sermon, an address to the congregation that had not previously existed.

The pace of change "has been unbelievably rapid," Isaacs said. Today, openly gay rabbis hold Conservative pulpits around the country: from New York and Chicago to St. Louis and Des Moines. "Basically, where there are Jews, there's gay clergy," Nevins said. Weininger is slated to become the senior rabbi of his Minnetonka, Minnesota, synagogue—the first time the board of a major Conservative shul has voted to invest an openly gay senior rabbi. Both Isaacs and Weininger have served in institutional leadership roles within Conservative Judaism. "There are more and more queer people at the table," Weininger said. When Isaacs talks to current JTS rabbinical students about what she went through, she said, "the world that I am explaining to them"—the world of the 2006 decision—"is beyond their comprehension."

III.

In the years just before LGBTQ rabbis assumed their seats at the mainstream institutions' tables, those same institutions had begun to wither. Isaacs remembered being asked when she transferred to JTS if she was sure it was a good idea, in light of the denomination's diminishing stature. Conservative Judaism has been a shadow of its mid-century self for so long that its decline has become the subject of a kind of gallows humor. Its existing members are rapidly graying. Its synagogues are closing, even in former strongholds like the suburbs of Long Island and New Jersey. The only consolation, perhaps, is that this process of attrition is less a testament to the denomination's ideological weakness than a reflection of the sociological phenomenon that Jewish demographers call "the shrinking Jewish middle"—the thinning ranks of mainline affiliated Jewish life.

On the right wing of Conservative Judaism and among its traditionalist critics, the explanation for this decline, sometimes framed in sexist and homophobic terms, is that the movement's social progressivism eroded the denomination's foundations by deviating too far and too consistently from Jewish law—that when faced with an ostensibly zero-sum choice between inclusion and halacha, the movement chose the latter and condemned itself to irrelevance. These right-wing critics argue that people want "the real thing"—Jewish authenticity and "serious" religion. They point to the rapid growth of Orthodox communities as proof.

This explanation is wrong. As generations of Orthodox feminists have argued, there is no inherent incompatibility between the greater inclusion of women and LGBTQ people and a commitment to the normative framework of Jewish law. Blu Greenberg famously argued in her pathbreaking book *On Women and Judaism: A View from Tradition* that "where there is a rabbinic will, there is a halakhic way"—not that everything is permitted, but that where there is a desire to maintain adherence to Jewish law, adaptation and innovation are, in fact, possible. Within Conservative Judaism, progressive voices like Rabbis Artson and Nevins were right that commitment to halacha as a binding set of obligations could be maintained while expanding its boundaries to include LGBTQ people within it.

In this spirit, a small but growing group of Modern Orthodox rabbis even began to officiate same-sex marriage ceremonies in 2020. These are generally not marriages according to the halachic definition, but they are significant rituals nonetheless. In most cases, the rabbis have avoided the traditional *kiddushin* (betrothal) ceremonies of heterosexual weddings, opting instead to invent commitment or partnership ceremonies of their own. In an op-ed explaining why he decided to break with Orthodox precedent and perform a same-sex marriage, Rabbi Avram Mlotek wrote that, while understanding the prohibition in Leviticus of homosexual sex, "I also believe that the Torah does not want human beings to live alone, and supports a covenantal relationship between parties as they build a faithful Jewish home."

Still, one of the most common liberal explanations for the decline of the traditionalist though non-Orthodox Judaism that the Conservative movement represented is also wrong. According to prominent liberal voices within the denomination, it could have avoided its current fate if it had responded sooner and faster to feminist and gay and lesbian demands for equality. If this were true, and the moderate-traditionalist orientation toward Jewish law remained popular, then it would have been reasonable to expect a return of the disillusioned to the movement after it opened its doors to the previously excluded. The opposite has happened. As Conservative Judaism has jettisoned more of its traditionalist trappings, its decline has only accelerated.

The Rise of the "Nones"

To focus on one denomination or even one religion is to miss the scope of the shift in the place of religion in public life and the far-reaching diminishment of institutional religion in the United States.

Among the non-Orthodox Jewish denominations, the Conservative movement is far from unique in its troubles. Even as the more liberal Reform Movement has declined less rapidly in terms of self-identification (roughly a third of American Jews still identify with Reform), its institutions are not substantially healthier than its slightly more traditionalist counterpart. In 2020, against the backdrop of the pandemic, Rick Jacobs, leader of the Union for Reform Judaism, acknowledged that the eventual merging of Reform with other liberal denominations like Conservative and Reconstructionist Judaism was "a very real possibility." In 2022, the Reform Movement shuttered its historic seminary campus in Cincinnati, Ohio.

Disaffiliation is a top-down as well as a bottom-up phenomenon. Enrollment at the existing Reform and Conservative movement seminaries has dropped in tandem with synagogue membership. The numbers can appear shocking. Across its Los Angeles and New York campuses, the 2022–2023 Hebrew Union College rabbinical student class had only fourteen students. At the Conservative JTS in New York, the same year's first-year rabbinical class had only seven.

At mid-century, the Reform and Conservative movements were mammoth organizations and, like the mammoths, seem headed toward extinction—not tomorrow, but inevitably. For now, they still boast sizable endowments, multiple campuses, libraries, and archives. Hundreds of synagogues remain affiliated with them, although what that affiliation counts for has become increasingly unclear. But the statistical trends all point to a grim and fast-approaching future. The once vast suburban architecture of liberal Jewish life is becoming a mausoleum to a religious civilization that has now passed.

While this process was already ongoing when the COVID-19 pandemic hit, years of social distancing and Zoom services greatly accelerated it. Many of the Reform and Conservative rabbis I spoke to said that even after reopening their synagogues, the congregants are not coming back. Their congregations struggle to make a prayer quorum on Saturday mornings, if they can at all. Even Friday nights, the more popular time for non-Orthodox service attendance, have lackluster attendance.

The pandemic did not supercharge just liberal Jewish institutions' decline; it did so for institutional religion more generally. It seems that rather than prompt a return to faith, the pandemic eroded it. Recent studies by Pew and the Public Religion Research Institute show that church attendance has not returned to its pre-COVID numbers. And not only are fewer Americans attending religious services regularly; they are also reporting that religion is less significant in their lives.

But this, too, is the result of a process that has long been underway. In 1999, the literary scholar Harold Bloom could still write that "no Western nation is as religion-soaked as ours." The comparison may remain true, but America is less religious than ever before. While as recently as a decade ago three-quarters of Americans identified as Christians, today the number is less than two-thirds. Some scholars estimate that in the United States "somewhere between 6,000 and 10,000 churches close down every year, either to be repurposed as apartments, laundries, laser-tag arenas, or skate parks, or to simply be demolished." Surveys by Pew and Gallup also show that a historically unprecedented three in ten American adults describe themselves as atheists or agnostics or identify with "nothing in particular"—what scholars of religion call "the rise of the 'nones.'"

After Yiddishkeit

Already more secularized than most other American religious traditions, Judaism has, in some sense, become a religion of "nones." According to a 2020 Pew survey, a full 27 percent of American Jews identify as among the "nones," and for young Jews ages eighteen to twenty-nine, the percentage jumps to 40 percent. While these Jews were raised Jewish, have a Jewish parent, or consider themselves to be ethnically Jewish, they said that they had *no religion* when asked by the survey. Even among Jews who identify as Jewish religiously, 15 percent say they belong to "no particular branch."

A century ago, the prevalence of unaffiliated Jewishness might not have been surprising. As the eastern European Jews made their way to the United States, many abandoned their faith. They stopped attending synagogue and let old rituals fade away. But they did not abandon their Jewishness—their Yiddishkeit. Some exchanged religion for ideologies like socialism, communism, or anarchism, while others put their faith in Yiddish itself as the iron tie between the Jewish people. These immigrants had, for the most part, been born into traditionalist Orthodoxy even if they had rebelled against its strictures. While flouting religious norms, they observed them in the negative, like the Yiddish-speaking anarchists who sought to provoke their faithful brethren by organizing Yom Kippur balls. They did not worry about profaning the sacred because they carried it with them on their tongues, in their language, which could not avoid invoking the tradition even, or perhaps especially, in rebellion against it.

American Jews today do not have recourse to this effortless secular Jewish culture. But what, then, *do* we have? Mainly, it seems, vestiges— of Yiddishkeit, but also of religion, ghostly remainders of once robust traditions. When Pew asked American Jews what they believe is essential to being Jewish, most said "remembering the Holocaust," "leading an ethical life," "working for justice/equality," and "being intellectually curious." Few, by contrast, named "being part of a Jewish community," "eating traditional Jewish foods," or "observing Jewish law" as essential to being Jewish.

Such a list of important yet nonetheless rather vague and universal-minded dispositions would have seemed to most American Jewish leaders and intellectuals, even just half a century ago, a strange set of core convictions for Jewish life. Even if they disagreed with his philosophy, many would have recognized the truth in the Yiddish educator Leibush Lehrer's argument that "our creed is a constitution of commandments," that its "core is not theological but normative." The scholar Saul Goodman was an ardent advocate of secular Jewishness, but even he stressed that "in Judaism the essence is not theological but legalistic; not metaphysical sanctions but sociological functions; not whether you have faith in God but whether you observe the sancta (mitzvot) . . . that the true substance of Judaism is expressed in folk-ways, observances, in culture, in tradition, in Law."

In other words, for most of Judaism's existence, being Jewish meant recognizing Judaism's binding framework, even if one struggled with, bristled at, or neglected, whether with guilt or relish, its stipulations. Contemporary American Jewish life, by contrast, appears to rest on a roughly opposite axiom. While most American Jews describe themselves as proud to be Jewish, they also seem to believe that such a declaration exists independent of any set of obligations—that it requires no adherence, let alone knowledge, of Jewish law. Jewishness today has become more of an identity to be professed than a coherent set of practices. Self-gratification and individual preference have supplanted commandedness and commitment to community.

It is this liberal-individualist mentality—not queer inclusion or gender egalitarianism—that is responsible for mainline affiliated Judaism's demise. And even "pop-up" Jewish initiatives like Lab/Shul, intended to avoid the pitfalls of institutionalism, cannot escape its corrosive force. "The rent-a-rabbi stuff really rubs me the wrong way," Lau-Lavie said, describing increasing requests for him to perform ceremonies as a kind of contract ritual worker coming from outside of his intentionally amorphous, progressive, hybrid-virtual community. "Consumerism," he added. "That's the name of the game."

During my conversations with Lau-Lavie, Isaacs, Weininger, and many of the other rabbis I interviewed, I was often moved and even challenged by their words. Contrary to the more dismissive critics of American liberal Judaism, there is no shortage of sensitive, intelligent, and inspiring rabbis. They all ought to be leading vibrant synagogue communities. They all ought to have students and congregants with whom they can share their learning and creativity. Instead, after fighting for a seat at the table of mainstream Jewish life, they are likely to be among the last ones left.

IV.
Crumble Before the Crash

If dynamism has begun to dissipate within the mainstream Jewish institutions, where might it still exist? Increasingly, it appears, in the places once seen as marginal—in the small, independent minyanim and progressive learning groups, in the pop-up ritual projects and text-study retreats, in forms more occasional than fixed, more virtual than brick-and-mortar. As the old patterns of Jewish life have fallen away, new forms have emerged, not so much in their place as in their wake. And not only have the organizational containers of Jewish life transformed, so, too, has the shape of Jewish identity. The meaning of Jewishness—its content and its boundaries—is being remade, sometimes radically, sometimes almost unrecognizably, by those who have chosen to continue embracing it.

A "radically traditional yeshiva" that teaches Talmud through "the lens of queer experience," the Chicago-based Svara may be the most influential start-up–style Jewish learning initiative to emerge over the last decade and a half. Founded in 2003 by Rabbi Benay Lappe, the organization began with no paid staff and no operating budget. "It was just me, Benay Lappe, with a lot of smoke and mirrors for the first ten years of our existence," Lappe said, laughing, when we spoke by Zoom. Today, Svara boasts an operating budget of roughly $1.7 million, eight faculty and staff, and some forty teachers in its extended educational network.

Within the progressive Jewish world, Svara is best known for its popular, weeklong Queer Talmud Camp. A sample schedule includes dedicated prayer time, during which participants can choose between "Creative and Songful" or "DIY traditional" options, and classes with titles like "Gettin' Tied Up: A Queer Lens on Tefillin, Liberation, and Bondage." For many of the camp's participants, it is often their first encounter with the ancient Jewish legal compendium. Increasingly—and ironically, given Lappe's anti-institutional bent—Svara is also the first step for many future rabbinical students at the country's liberal seminaries. "Svara is powering a lot of queer Jews now in rabbinical school," said Elaina Marshalek, Svara's director of programs. Several faculty members at JTS confirmed that it was common for students to have become interested in rabbinic ordination after encountering Svara's programming.

As Lappe and Svara's other faculty see it, part of the organization's "radically traditional" ethos is its pedagogical approach. Many if not most of the Queer Talmud Camp participants arrive with little Jewish background. Some arrive without knowing how to read Hebrew at all. That lack of knowledge is the starting point, though, not an obstacle. As soon as participants arrive, they dive into the Hebrew and Aramaic of rabbinic law. The method is slow, deliberate, philological: word by word, root by root. The students learn to read as they learn the content. They keep their Bible concordances and Aramaic dictionaries at the ready. Few leave with the ability to "learn" a full, untranslated page of Talmud on their own, one instructor at a non-Orthodox rabbinical school told me. But what they do leave with is a feeling, which they did not have before—a sense that few non-Orthodox Jews grow up with—that the Talmud has something to say that is relevant to their lives.

Laynie Soloman, Svara's associate rosh yeshiva, explained that when it came to queer issues, older models of Jewish education tended to focus on the passages in Jewish texts where queer people appear excluded or stigmatized and then try to grapple with or change them. "That's the dysphoric approach," they said. "The text is other than us, it dominates us. It defines who we can and cannot be."

Svara, by contrast, is trying to create what Soloman called a "euphoric" alternative approach to Torah for queer people. "Once we assume that we can do more, we can actually find moments of freedom, liberation, expansion, and serious euphoria," they said. According to Soloman, Svara's radicalness lies not in an emphasis on *how to queer* the Jewish tradition, revising old texts with new meanings, but in its insistence on the ways Jewish tradition *is already queer* for those who want it to be. Or, as Soloman wrote in a reflection on getting top surgery and halacha, "Instead of asking 'What are the points of dissonance between our tradition as it has been practiced and trans realities?' we must ask 'What are the profound opportunities for revelation that trans people can offer our learning communities and legal tradition?'"

One of Soloman's favorite "euphoric" texts is a passage from the Talmud that deals with the permissibility of feeding a sick person on the fast day of Yom Kippur. According to the Mishna, the oral law to which the Gemara is a commentary, a sick person can eat on Yom Kippur, although ideally under the supervision of experts or doctors. Amid the discourse on whether a doctor can deny a person despite their stated medical need for food, the anonymous voice in the Talmud known as the *stamma* (other statements are attributed to various sages) declares that a sick person who feels they must eat can determine to do so without expert approval, quoting as justification the proverb, "The heart knows the bitterness of its soul."

For Soloman, this passage provided textual grounding for crowning the individual as the chief sovereign of their own experience, as opposed to precedent, custom, or top-down authority. "Our rabbis centered the experience that is found within the person," they wrote. "In this text," they added, "I found a witness to my experience. I found ancestors who elevated self-determination over conventional expertise."

After Inclusion

It is not only in textual interpretation that Svara's approach challenges established modes of thought. In a way, the entire project emerges out of a great skepticism toward institutionalist thinking and existing Jewish institutions.

Lappe, for instance, rejects the entire framework of LGBTQ inclusion of the kind that Isaacs and Weininger fought for at JTS in the 2000s. "Once upon a time, inclusion was as good as it could get, so we all settled," she said. "Inclusion is over. Very few people are satisfied within inclusion now." According to Lappe, what changed was not only that a new generation of queer people grew up expecting more than simply to be tolerated; it was also that the mainstream institutions were, at their core, built without queer people in mind. "Queer inclusion is not a revolution," Lappe said, leaning easily back in her chair. Shelves filled with Talmud tractates and rabbinic commentaries lined the wall behind her. "It is a sustaining innovation of the status quo."

In Lappe's view, the mainstream institutions can never truly become places where queer people can thrive. Repression is built into the institutional DNA. "The people who are doing the including think that they're benefiting the included," she said. "But they don't question the assumptions, the values, the culture, the goals of the space into which they're including people." Without fundamental, thoroughgoing change that would render such institutions all but unrecognizable, "they will never significantly benefit from the inclusion of queer people," Lappe said, "and queer people will have to sit nicely and assimilate even to be moderately happy in those spaces." In other words, Lappe seemed to argue, queer integration into the mainstream institutions would never suffice; and, besides, the institutions also might not be worth saving.

More than most, Lappe's anti-institutionalist bona fides are hard-won. Lappe received rabbinic ordination from JTS in 1997, a decade before the seminary began admitting openly LGBTQ students. Prior to enrolling, Lappe had been an out lesbian and activist. She had even appeared in her activist capacity on *Oprah*. But those were the days before Google, so to become a student at JTS she opted to go back into the closet and hide her sexuality for the next six years.

Three days before she was to receive her diploma, Lappe was called into the office of a JTS dean and asked point-blank if she was gay. Lappe recounted the experience in a remarkable essay titled "Saying No in the Name of a Higher Yes," published in a 2001 anthology on lesbian rabbis. It was a scenario she had prepared for. "I knew I could be called in at any moment and rehearsed what would be my instantaneous response," Lappe wrote, "the way soldiers are trained in battle without having to think, to automatically do what is necessary to save their lives and the lives of their soldiers." After an interrogation that lasted several hours—a violation of the ethics code that Rabbi Elliot Dorff had written in the early 1990s barring "witch hunts" against closeted students at JTS—Lappe replied that, no, she was not lesbian and was permitted to graduate. Her answer, she said, was "a form of halachic disobedience."

Living in the Crash

Both Lappe's experiences within the institutions of mainstream Jewish life and her analysis of their shortcomings led Lappe to articulate a theory of the crisis of American Jewish life, which she encoded into Svara's organizational identity. Called Crash, Lappe's theory is part management consulting, part religious history, part Kuhnian history of science. The basic contention of Lappe's Crash theory is that every tradition has a meta-narrative, or "master story," that provides answers to fundamental questions of life and existence and gives the tradition its coherence and order. Yet every tradition is also mortal, and "will eventually, inevitably" collapse. Its answers become implausible, metaphysically, morally, sometimes both; an event unmoors it from the socially and historically specific context in which it made sense.

When a tradition begins to crash, Lappe argues that its adherents face three options. Option one is to deny that the collapse is happening, to double down on the tradition as it is, to "build a 'wall' around it," Lappe writes, and carry on as if all is normal. Option two is radical acceptance of the tradition's crisis of legitimacy and a rejection of the traditional entirely; after all, the world that made it meaningful and coherent is gone. Option three is to revamp the "master story," to revise it so that it can meet the changed world and new metaphysical reality, to retell the story and emend the answers it provides.

According to Lappe's reading of Jewish history, what we know of as Judaism today was a product of such a crash. After the destruction of the Second Temple in Jerusalem by the Romans in 70 CE, the creators of rabbinic Judaism faced a religious crisis of the most fundamental kind: how to maintain the Jewish religion without what had, until then, been its ritual core, the Temple and the sacrifices and sacraments that were performed there. They responded by writing down the Oral Law, which would develop into the Talmud, and by adapting Judaism to center not on the sacrificial rites of the Temple but on textual learning and worship wherever Jews might be. (In time, this would give rise to the institution known as the synagogue.) As Lappe sees it, the early sages' flexibility, imagination, and willingness to break with precedent enabled Judaism to survive after the Roman conquest and through the millennia of exile. Even more importantly, she argues, the ancient rabbis embedded within the new textual tradition guidelines for its continued adaption and change. They set out qualifications required of a person who could authorize changes—that they must demonstrate learnedness (*gamirna*) and moral intuition (*savirna*). Svara draws its name from this idea.

Much like the rabbis of the first century CE, Lappe charges, American Jews today are living amid a serious conceptual crash. The Jewish tradition, Lappe writes, "is in many ways no longer morally plausible": its definitions and restrictions, especially on matters of gender identity and sexuality, no longer correspond to contemporary life. The aim of Svara, Lappe explained, is to provide an option three model of Judaism—to give Judaism the radical update it needs to remain alive and relevant in a new reality.

As proof of concept, Lappe cites Svara's burgeoning popularity and the emergence of initiatives like it. When a tradition's grand narrative begins to "crash," it is, she writes, "the queerest folk" who tend to catch on first. Lappe calls this anticipatory stage "the crumble-before-the-crash," when the previously excluded, historically margin-alized, and nonconformists gather "in small communities, in alternative spaces, and begin learning the old tradition and reinterpreting it." Eventually, gradually, the once marginal will supplant the mainstream.

When "option three" Judaism represented by Svara has succeeded, there will no longer be such a thing as "queer Torah" or "queer Juda-ism" juxtaposed to normative Judaism, Lappe wrote. "They'll just call it Judaism."

A Flower amid the Ruins?

The Svara-niks' vision can sometimes appear as hazy as it is ambi-tious. When I asked Soloman what success might look like in practice, they replied that the future of Jewish life would most likely not center on formal institutions at all. "I think we're going to see a lot of rabbis doing powerful ritual work for people who don't see themselves deeply rooted in an institution," they said. Citing the demographic surveys showing that a large portion of Gen Z identify as queer, Benay Lappe said, "Our target audience has pretty much become *the next* Jewish demographic," and added, "We're out to do to Svara what the last generation did with *tikkun olam*."

As sympathetic as I am to Svara's project, these struck me as curi-ous aspirations. While the rejection of existing institutions made sense to me on a political level, should not reformers and revolutionaries seek to build counter-institutions to take the place of the old ones? And how can Judaism, which requires community, survive if religious practice becomes decoupled from the life of the group, and if the role of the rabbi becomes reduced to that of a mere ritual worker, putting on occasional ceremonies with a religious aesthetic for interested con-sumers instead of being the anchor of religious life?

Likewise, while over the last several decades *tikkun olam* has certainly become an important concept in American Jewish life—for many, it is one of the few Jewish precepts (or even the only one) with which they identify—and while there is no shortage of Jewish social justice groups that claim to fly *tikkun olam*'s banner, it does not seem like the concept has catalyzed much of a substantial, wide-reaching revival in Jewish practice, religious text study, or community building. Most often it appears as a slogan brandished much more by individuals as a vague ethical commitment than the foundation for a new, integrated, encompassing form of Jewish life.

As I considered Lappe's vision in the weeks and months after we spoke, I wondered if it was at once too sanguine and too amorphous. What if the "option three" Judaism that Svara sought to represent proved to be less a successor to the old forms of American communal practice than a lone flower growing amid the ruins? Or what if in trying to fit Jewish tradition into contemporary categories, something essential about traditional Judaism—its untimeliness, its inconvenient practices, the friction observance introduces into modern life, its challenge to liberal individualism and the idea of a sovereign self—gets lost?

Disassimilation Theology

One need not embrace every part of Lappe's Crash theory and its aims to recognize that Svara's recent success has been buoyed substantially by the emergence of the new Jewish social movements over the last decade and the crises to which they have aimed to respond. Amid political uncertainty and the backlash to gains by racial and sexual minorities, many young Jews have recently looked for comfort within a tradition that they knew was theirs but had only minimally explored. Svara—maximally inclusive, despite Lappe's distaste for the word—became an important conduit in their search.

Many participants arrived at the group's Queer Talmud Camp after reexperiencing Judaism through movements like IfNotNow, explained

Marshalek. The encounter with traditional liturgy during protests made them rethink the place of Judaism in their lives. "People who might have never been comfortable [with ritual] or who never thought it was a meaningful act to say Kaddish realized that it did have meaning," Marshalek said, when they chanted it at a protest, and that catalyzed a new desire to reengage with tradition. Svara bolsters the movements, which in turn bolster Svara, because both are "about subverting the status quo," she added. "It's about looking to the rabbis [of the Talmud] as having given us tools to radically subvert what is happening and claim that is what's been happening all along."

Many of Svara's students have thus found in its teachings a new Jewish language and textual warrant for queer and transgender experience—yet an equal number also appear to have found a new way to claim Jewish authenticity and mark out Jewish difference. "Jews, especially white Jews, are trying to uncover patterns of assimilation by rebooting tradition," Soloman told me. They're interested in "fighting white supremacy by revisiting and recovering their own culture." In other words, like the Jewish revival of the long 1970s, the return to Jewishness mirrors the upsurge of Black radical politics. It is at once a move toward self-exculpation—*we Jews are not those other white people*—and a gesture toward cultural reclamation that also contains an implicit critique of assimilation's cost—*this knowledge is what we Jews gave up to become like those other white people.*

Svara, then, is another instance of the trend that Rabbi Alissa Wise identified when she observed that "Jewish particularism is on the wane, but Jewish practice as a way to connect wider and wider is on the rise." This "practice without particularism" involves the embrace of Jewishness as an aesthetic, as an identity, and sometimes as a language, but often without what progressives recoil from: the tradition's difficult obligations; the priority of familial and ethnic ties.

V.

Practice without Particularism

Wise's observation about waning particularism and waxing practice might be said to define contemporary liberal Judaism. Outside of Orthodoxy, American Judaism seems to be trending not only post-God (as Lau-Lavie or the "nones" would have it) and post-gender (as Svara's teachers would have it), but also post-ethnicity.

A new logic of identity reigns. Its rule: "I feel myself to be, therefore I am, or must become." And this seems to have begun reshaping Jewish life, even if the effects of such a transformation remain temporarily subterranean. Whether in New Jersey or Minnesota, rabbi after rabbi that I interviewed about the shifting norms of gender and sexuality also said, unexpectedly, that they were guiding more people than ever before in processes to become Jews, some through formal conversions, others not. "It's incredible," Rabbi Marc Katz said of the heightened demand for "Introduction to Judaism" courses and conversions. "Rabbis are dealing with just an influx of people that they're carrying at any given time."

What accounts for the increased interest in Judaism on the part of non-Jews? And what does this shift mean for American Jewish identity, which for so long has rested on ethnicity, shared history, and family inheritance?

In the rabbinic tradition, rabbis are supposed to discourage converts, who must prove their willingness to overcome this barrier. In its modern history, Judaism has not been a proselytizing religion. The Reform Movement does not send solicitors to knock on doors in the hopes of bolstering the ranks of its faithful. The Reconstructionists do not set up booths in public parks to disseminate the good word contained in Rabbi Mordecai Kaplan's works. Even Chabad-Lubavitch's ubiquitous emissaries seek mainly to bring people who are Jewish back to traditional observance. There had to be other reasons why it appeared that more non-Jews were seeking out "Introduction to Judaism" courses and inquiring about the requirements of non-Orthodox Jewish conversions than ever before.

But the nature of American Jewish life also meant that ascertaining these reasons would not be easy. There is no centralized Jewish organization that keeps track of conversion numbers, nor is this a number that the various denominations keep track of in any systematic way. Especially within the more liberal denominations, which do not operate within the halachic framework, major aspects of the conversion process are often determined at the discretion of the supervising rabbi; for instance, while Orthodox and Conservative conversions require submersion in the mikvah, or ritual bath, many Reform rabbis do not. In fact, in some Reform congregations, non-Jews, even those with no intention of converting, can take part in every ritual aspect of Jewish life. Significant hard data, then, on these "Jews by choice" would be impossible to come by.

America's Most Liberal Monotheism

To get a better sense of the terrain, I went the more qualitative route and reached out to Rabbi Julie Zupan, the Union of Reform Judaism's director of Jewish engagement. Zupan oversees the Reform Movement's vast "Introduction to Judaism" program, which includes in-person classes conducted by synagogue congregations and online courses conducted over Zoom. Roughly 630 people participate in the online courses each year, Zupan said, and roughly 78 percent of participants "checked as one of the reasons they were taking the class, 'I am considering conversion,'" although there is no way to know if, in the end, they converted.

Perhaps more striking was that, according to Zupan, while many of the program participants had arrived at the course after being referred by a rabbi, a full half had not. Instead, they had sought out

"Introduction to Judaism" of their own accord, largely through key word searches on Google.

Zupan explained that this reflected a paradigm shift in how people were deciding to become Jewish. Under the old model of conversion, she said, it was typically couples, working within the framework of synagogue membership, who sought to have the non-Jewish member convert to participate more fully in communal and religious life. That still happens, but less so, in part because many congregations allow unconverted spouses to participate in ritual and, just as significant, in part because the nature of identity has changed. In the Jewish world, as in American culture more broadly, "religious identity, and identity period, is less about the identity of the family and more about the identity of the individual," Zupan said. "We're seeing more people come to these classes as individuals, as opposed to partners who are doing this with their partner."

And if liberal Judaism has become one equal option among many for people looking for spiritual fulfillment in the American religious marketplace, that seems to stem from the impression that the non-Orthodox streams of Judaism constitute America's most liberal form of monotheism—especially when it comes to the embrace of LGBTQ people and its openness to other minority identities. "A lot of the people [in the Union of Reform Judaism courses] tell us that they have felt harmed by their [non-Jewish] religious upbringing," Zupan said. "They feel that Judaism is a place where they can be accepted . . . as bringing their whole selves." Rabbi Marc Katz echoed the sense that the increasing number of people seeking to be Jewish is linked to Judaism's acceptance of LGBTQ people: "A huge percentage of people who are looking to convert are LGBT," and, especially, identify as transgender, even though gay, lesbian, and transgender people account for only a small percentage of the Jewish, and general, population.

Although predominantly a phenomenon expressed within the non-Orthodox denominations, even Modern Orthodoxy has seen a surprising increase in the demand for conversions. "I have seen a profound and overwhelming interest," said Rabbi Avram Mlotek, who in 2020 helped open an independent *beit din*, or religious court, to facilitate Orthodox conversions outside of the existing Orthodox rabbinical establishment. In a *Jerusalem Post* op-ed Mlotek wrote with two other Orthodox rabbis involved in the project—Adam Mintz and Jonathan Leener—they charged that the old attitude of skepticism toward potential converts "does not reflect the multicultural societies that we live in, where we appreciate the richness and diversity of people's experiences." Since January 2020, the *beit din* has converted more than 325 people—potentially more, Mlotek added, in one year than the Rabbinical Council of America, the central Modern Orthodox organization.

Protestant, Catholic, Jew

But perhaps it should not be surprising that the contours of American Jewish identity have shifted just as the conception of identity in the United States has undergone a revolution.

Only a century ago, albeit on a different continent, Jewishness was a synonym for unluckiness, a fate to be suffered rather than chosen. Some of that old misfortune followed Jewish immigrants to the United States in the early twentieth century. But it did not persist for long. Already in 1955, the sociologist Will Herberg could proclaim Judaism as one of America's three great religions, alongside Protestantism and Catholicism. And while that may have been a premature elevation of Judaism at a time when antisemitic discrimination still very much existed, Judaism's apparent contemporary position as a coequal option among the various Christian streams—and, indeed, sometimes a preferred option among non-Jews seeking out religious meaning—would have far exceeded even Herberg's most sanguine predictions.

Of course, conversions have always been part of Jewish tradition:

on the holiday of Shavuot, Jews read from the book of Ruth, considered by some to be Judaism's first convert. But in its strictly traditionalist and Orthodox forms, Jewish identity draws its meaning from collective belonging, from membership in a community bound by divine commandments. For this reason, in most Orthodox communities, conversion also involves a separation from the convert's old identity and community. They receive a new name. They are reborn into their new tribe. They proclaim their singular obligation.

Contemporary liberal Judaism, by contrast, embraces the multiplicity of heritages. Certainly in practice, many non-Orthodox communities do not consider Jewish belonging as mutually exclusive with membership to another faith tradition. As a corollary of this expansive pluralism, the ultimate arbiter of identity has also shifted. It is no longer the community that ratifies belonging but the individual who chooses where they want to belong. In this sense, perhaps, Judaism's Americanization has also involved a certain protestantization. Increasingly, becoming a Jew is now mainly a matter of faith alone, though less in God than in what one takes oneself to be.

Toward "Post-Judaism"?

Talking with countless liberal rabbis over the last several years, I found that these shifts in the texture of liberal Judaism vexed and even challenged me, if only because this emergent form of liberal Jewish identity felt hard to reconcile with the sense of Jewishness with which I was most familiar. I have always felt Judaism as something to struggle with—that its weight, its claim on me, derives from the very fact of its un-chosenness. Judaism in all its familial, tribal, and communal complexity imposes itself upon me. While I've sometimes resented this, often delighted in it, I had not seriously contemplated Jewishness as something that could be taken on and off at one's will.

Contemporary Jewish life now operates according to a different logic. And this new direction is not only a product of the shift in the locus of identity from the group to the self over the last quarter century. It is also because, at the same time, new social movements have emerged within Jewish life, buoyed by and accelerating this shift, that endeavor to challenge much that has been taken for granted as inherited or immutable and highlight the oppressive quality of binaries and boundaries.

In their deconstructive ambition, they appear to push for consistency. They seem to ask that if there can be fluidity in gender, no longer understood as dual in nature, then why can there not be fluidity between gentile and Jew? If the program is practice without particularism, then is it not such a stretch to decouple religious ritual from fixed and mutually obligating community? Why can't Judaism be syncretic, multireligious (Bu-Ju or Hin-Jew), nontheistic or multi-theistic, a performance or play, and why does it matter if the people doing all this are Jews by birth or Jews by choice, converted or unconverted?

But there is a part of me that wonders, were all these changes to occur, would this still be Judaism? That seems to be the basic, unresolved question facing the most experimental, radical edge of non-Orthodox Judaism, as well as the unaddressed shadow of Lappe's Crash theory. What if the rupture with precedent, of which classes on bondage and tefillin are both product and catalyst, leads not to a reformulation of Judaism but, in a way, to its supersession? Likewise, at what point will the rejection of basic religious categories—and there are perhaps none as fundamental as gentile and Jew—mean that the lived ritual practice of many self-identified American Jews has transmogrified into . . . something else?

According to some scholars of religion, it already has. In his 2013 book *American Post-Judaism*, scholar of religion Shaul Magid writes that "the inclusion of non-Jews in Jewish communities" as well as "the ways in which post-ethnicity has contributed to Jews defining their Jewishness by constructing/performing their Judaism outside of any normative framework—including free and open expressions of religious syncretism and borrowing—has moved Judaism into . . . a 'post' state." Unmoored from traditional anchors of inheritance, family history, or halacha, "post-Judaism" is Magid's label for a Jewishness defined by voluntarism rather than obligation, affiliation rather than ascription, and multiculturalism rather than cultural particularism.

It is hard, though, to see anyone whose practice or identity that matches this label using the term Magid has invented for them. While much contemporary non-Orthodox practice ignores the halachic framework, knowledge or concern for Jewish law has in many cases so diminished that this fact often no longer even registers as religious transgression or "post-"; instead, for these practitioners, it is just Judaism as they know it. At the same time, in many alternative and activist Jewish communities—and in established Reform and non-Orthodox synagogues as well—the replacement of a Jewish normative framework by an anything-goes ethos of liberal pluralism has been so thoroughgoing that few who count themselves as members would see Magid's description of their religious identity as a critique.

Put differently, then, this is another, and no less serious, challenge to liberal Judaism: at the very moment it has actualized its liberal values—inclusion, voluntarism, pluralism—it also risks abandoning the most ancient, constitutive, normative framework, without which it is unclear Jewish religious life can persist. The gamble of a group like Svara is based on the conviction that, yes, in fact Jewish practice can live on and even thrive in unabashed, exuberant rebellion against normativity.

Once inclined to view this as an entirely salutary development, I am these days more ambivalent. The larger project represented by the new, alternative Jewish initiatives and movements remains indispensable—opening of traditional texts to those previously excluded from their study, expanding our understanding of the tradition beyond the sociological realities of the time of its creation. But it is hard to imagine the possibility of sustaining a vibrant Jewish community over the long term in the absence of a strong, binding normative framework. That does not mean that such commitments cannot involve reinterpretation; indeed, they must. Judaism has developed, and remains alive, because of the unceasing attempts by Jews to bring Judaism into conversation with their times.

But there can be no reinterpretation without a canon, no reconstruction without a foundation, no continuity without a normative core. If the primary and ultimate impetus for Jewish religious participation narrows completely to individualism, then what will become of the religious obligations that are hard, inconvenient, uncomfortable, or even unpleasant, as some of the most important ones happen to be? And if religious experience devolves into merely one more consumer experience for which one might pay, then how will it ever compete in the late-capitalist market of sensation and entertainment?

At their best, the alternative and activist Jewish communities I visited crackled with the energy of building something new. Just as often, I left with a sense that I had been a spectator to a well-rehearsed performance, more a ticket buyer than a community member. There is no necessary relationship between this often ersatz quality of liberal religious life and the inclusiveness of the spaces in which it lives; normative Judaism can be made inclusive for those who want it. But I fear that without any normative framework, so much of what makes Judaism distinctive—the commandments that define it and the proscriptions that perpetuate it—might be lost.

8

THE ORTHODOX ALTERNATIVE

I.

As a child, I often slept over with my more religious first cousins at our grandparents' apartment. Under Bubbie's watch, we would play marathon games of Scrabble and, if we were lucky, get treated to ice cream with "brickle," the shards of hardened toffee that I only ever encountered there. At night, in our shared room, I'd watch one of my older male cousins fold his tzitzis with care and place his black felt kippah gently on the white laminate bedside table. I, too, wore a kippah most of the day, not out of sincere religious obligation but simply because those were the school's rules. Unlike my cousin, I did not make sure to pray when I woke in the morning—I read a book while he davened. But before bed I did, like him, make sure to say the Shema. It was only as a teenager at sleepaway camp—and a Jewish one, no less—when I stopped, no longer afraid that if I failed to recite the prayer, I wouldn't wake up in the morning.

Through these cousins on my father's side, I grew up with a passing familiarity with stringent Orthodox Judaism. During Hanukkah and Sukkot, the two holidays when we usually saw each other, I tried to absorb, the best I could, the halachic debates, the rules and regulations, the rhythms of a discussion that was comprehensible but still rather distant. Over time, I learned to find my way. Though not as often, perhaps, as I would have liked, we prayed together, celebrated together, and mourned together. Their bar mitzvahs and weddings were the first I remember, and they set the bar for a serious, rigorous religiosity that, I always felt, the Judaism I learned in school, and certainly at home, sorely lacked.

They were, I felt, the real deal, and we were not. Even if still relatively observant compared to most American Jews, we compromised. We picked and chose which rituals worked and which did not. We fit Judaism into the mold of a liberal, secularized, Americanized lifestyle according to no coherent logic, our choices inflected with apathy and ignorance. They, by contrast, made Judaism the center of their lives. It seemed that for them there was nothing outside Judaism. I often envied their certainty. Even more, I envied the depth of their textual knowledge, their intentionality, their commitment to a tradition to which my community also claimed to be committed, and yet, I could not deny, seemingly less so.

Bessie's great-grandchildren, too, my cousins have, in a way, charted a trajectory parallel to mine—a different path through the end of the American Jewish century—although more recently our lives have converged in a few unexpected ways.

Over the years of writing this book, I came to know the Orthodox—and specifically the ultra-Orthodox, or Haredi, world—much more intimately through my wife, who grew up in Lakewood, New Jersey's ultra-Orthodox community. The more time I have spent there with her loving family, which has become my own, the more I have begun to understand the town, and to a degree the community, from the inside. The experience has confirmed my sense of how, in a deep and fundamental way, Haredi Judaism constitutes perhaps the strongest and most viable alternative to the now fading American Jewish consensus.

Orthodoxy will thrive long after the old mainstream institutions fade away. While most branches of American Judaism exhibit the same trend—declining affiliation, diminishing engagement, a growing sense of irrelevance—Haredi Judaism stands apart. In the Brooklyn neighborhoods of Borough Park and Williamsburg, in the New York townships of Monsey and Kiryas Yoel, and in the sprawling New Jersey suburbs like Lakewood, synagogues do not struggle to make a minyan. Instead, communities fill sports stadiums like Citi Field and the Wells Fargo Center for massive religious events. The main concern of these communities is not how they will weather decline; it is how they will build new houses and schools fast enough to accommodate the constant growth. Liberal Jewish leaders plow vast sums into desperate schemes to make Judaism appear relevant to the secular eye. Meanwhile, Orthodox leaders reassert commitment to Jewish tradition as it was lived, they insist, since time immemorial.

Haredi life rests on entirely different pillars from the old communal consensus, and that may well be the reason for its comparative vitality. Whereas non-Orthodox American Jews typically view their lives and culture as synonymous and in sync with the broader American culture, most Haredi Jews understand the values to which they are committed as distinct, and often diametrically opposed, to the currents of secular American life. Of course, ultra-Orthodox Jews seek to be tolerated, even respected by their fellow Americans. But they also seek to keep secular America—in particular its materialism, its sex obsession, its liberalism—at a great distance from their homes.

Opposition to liberalism is fundamental and has been ever since ultra-Orthodoxy emerged in Europe in the nineteenth century. The centrality of divine commandments and the transcendent bonds of family and community place strict limits on individual choice and autonomy. Self-gratification is nowhere a virtue in Haredi life; instead it is a vice to be combated and reined in. The overcoming of desire is discussed daily in homiletics printed in newspapers. There is only one path to self-actualization: the Torah's.

Yet there has also long been a paradoxical quality to Haredi Judaism's opposition to liberalism, especially in the Jewish diaspora. The enemies of liberalism in the West have, in most cases, been hostile to Jews as well. When it comes to politics, this has often meant that the ultra-Orthodox way was the pragmatic one, less concerned with ideology than with securing the community, although, in places like eastern Europe, Orthodox separatism sometimes led to strange political bedfellows.

In today's United States, as political polarization has fractured public life along ever-deepening partisan lines, even communities that pride themselves on their closedness to wider American pathologies have been unable to escape the inexorable churn of animus and division. Indeed, in their attempt to shield themselves from what they perceive as liberalism's excesses, some Haredi communities have been Americanized, aligning themselves with the anti-liberal and Trump-y American right. It is a treacherous bargain. For the same political forces that some Orthodox communities now support also threaten the elements of American society—its openness, its tolerance, and, indeed, its liberalism—that have enabled religious Jewish communities to flourish here.

In the Yeshiva Velt

On a blisteringly cold November day, one of my brothers-in-law guided me a through a tour of Lakewood's Beth Medrash Govoha, or BMG, as it is known in the community. The largest yeshiva in America and the second-largest in the world, BMG boasts some 8,000 male students who pore over rabbinic texts in its several *batei midrash*, or study halls, at the center of the town. Since its founding in 1943, BMG has transformed Lakewood from a small resort community into a series of dense tract housing developments, with a bustling, city-like downtown. Today, Lakewood is home to roughly 130,000 people, the majority of them Haredi Jews. It is, perhaps, the most Jewish place that most American Jews have never been to—and BMG the biggest Jewish institution most have never heard of.

We arrived in the parking lot and parked as everyone else had. Which is to say, we blocked in several other cars and left the key inside, so whoever's car we'd obstructed would be able to move it later. I laughed and looked at my brother-in-law incredulously when he explained the system. "This is what you can do when everyone in the community trusts each other," he said. If you needed to get your car out, you could simply get into another person's car and move it. No big deal. What surprised me wasn't just that the car—that private, inviolable kingdom of the solitary American—carried no sanctity here. It was also that the sense of security, the belief in one's neighbors, was so deep, so different from the paranoias of theft and deceit that grip regular American life.

In general, the community practices a soft collectivism when it comes to private property. It is more kibbutz than conventional suburb. The social ramifications of this fact are most immediately perceptible. Children roam unsupervised in and out of each other's homes, sometimes introducing themselves to a mother they've never met before, who will ask them, as good Jewish mothers do, if they would like anything to eat. Lakewood on Shabbat afternoons may be one of the last places in suburban America where spontaneous, free-for-all games of baseball still unfurl for hours in the middle of the street. It is a universe apart from the New Jersey suburb where I grew up, just an hour's drive away, where parents and nannies furiously shuttle children to untold extracurriculars, and neighbors don't know each other's names, even after years of sharing the same street.

The economic aspect of Lakewood's communitarianism is no less striking. There are *gemachs*, charity funds or free loan banks for almost anything. (*Gemach* is a Hebrew acronym for *gemilut chasadim*, or acts of kindness.) Not just money but ritual items like mezuzahs and even wedding dresses for brides. In Lakewood it is a norm, following the religious commandment, to give 10 percent of one's annual income to charity. Many give more. These funds often go to the communal social safety net, which also includes free food delivery for those who need it, free tuition for school, and apartments to stay in when a relative is in the hospital. The system is far more generous than the American welfare state, and far more expansive than anything my leftist friends who talk about mutual aid could ever dream of. At the same time, such generosity extends, for the most part, only to other Jews.

———

When we entered one of the yeshiva's main buildings, the first thing that greeted us were cell phones. Rows of battered flip phones and aged Nokia soap bars rested along the vestibule's crown molding, balancing precariously on the ledges outside the doors of the *beit midrash*. The "kosher" phone—either a dumb phone or a smart one with filters installed to block certain apps and web browsing—serves as a bulwark against the secular, liberal culture of America, against the immorality and pornography that live on the internet. Also, more prosaically, against distraction. Even the strictly kosher dumb phone is forbidden inside the *beit midrash*. "Just the feeling of your phone in your jacket," my brother-in-law said, "it makes it hard to learn."

And learning, in Lakewood as in the Haredi world more broadly, is one of the most important, most exalted things a young man can do. In Orthodox parlance, "learning" refers specifically to the study of religious texts, and in BMG, as in every Orthodox yeshiva, the focus is on the Talmud, the central text of Jewish law. Traditionally, Talmud is learned out loud and argumentatively in a study duo called a *chavruta*. A second bloc of yeshiva study is the *chabura*, a larger group of students led by an older scholar or rabbi, who sets the subject and pace of learning. At BMG, taped beneath the cell phone ledge are diagrams that organize seating in the study hall according to *chabura*, each demarcated in its own highlighter color, light blue for one rabbi's class, green for another. There are no grades or examinations. In the *chabura* is where progress, comprehension, and excellence are judged. The reward is the learning itself.

We opened the doors into a packed *beit midrash*. The late morning sun glowed through a massive set of windows. A low thrum of conversation rose and fell. Most of the men looked to be around my age, somewhere in their twenties, although there were also older, white-bearded men who sat alone, bent over *shtenders*, their book stands, in places throughout the hall.

I tried to catch a glimpse of what the nearest *chavruta* was learning. Subtly as I could, I glanced over their shoulders. They were reading part of Masechet Nedarim, a tractate of the Talmud that deals with the making of vows. But I was not close enough to make out their conversation over the murmuring in the hall and too shy to ask them directly which passage they were mulling over. I was already self-conscious about standing out. The dress code for religious men is a clear one: white shirt, black pants, black felt yarmulke. I was not in flagrant violation, but I wasn't really in compliance either. My black yarmulke was knitted, my black pants too fitted, my shoes too brown. To have adopted the full dress code seemed to me wrong, as if religiosity were a costume to take off and on. So I wore my own clothes, dressed almost as I would have on any other day. Still, the ambivalence of nonconformity weighed on me.

Back in the hallway outside the study hall, a few pairs stood together, learning animatedly. The method of Talmudic disquisition is not simply to read or memorize the text but to internalize it through singsong argumentation. One duo was immersed in a *sugya*, or Talmudic passage, gesticulating and deconstructing the argument in rapid-fire speech. They spoke, almost rapped, in a mix of Hebrew, Aramaic, English, and Yiddish. They paced around each other, shuckled back and forth, pulled at their beards. They were, it seemed, exhilarated; this was not academic learning but a devotional act. The Yiddish term for this is "shteiging," which comes from the German root, *steig*, to ascend or rise.

The town of Lakewood has taken shape to allow as many young men as possible to shteig as their full-time occupation. Eventually, most will leave the yeshiva to make a living. Only a few, the elect, remain in yeshiva their entire lives. But even those men in the working world make time for learning, whether through a few hours at night or regular classes at the yeshiva. Commitment to regular learning in one's free time outside work is considered an important marker of good character.

Accordingly, the town operates largely according to the rhythms of BMG. The day is divided into three sections, or *sedarim*: morning, afternoon, and evening. Sixth Street, Lakewood's main artery, functions as a kind of anthropic sundial. In the morning, the *jungerleit*, or young married male students, make their way to the yeshiva. In the late afternoon, they—or their wives, if they have only one car—drive back home, especially if they have young children. During these hours, Sixth Street becomes a train of modest black sedans and minivans. If learning is the first occupation of the young man, raising a family is the second. The yeshiva is the community's physical center, the family, its most fundamental social infrastructure.

Torah, family, community—these are, more or less, the pillars on which the life of the town rests. They are the transcendent goods that each aspect of life serves. Everything else is secondary. In the official-practical ideology, no individual's wants or preferences supersede these sets of interlocking obligations.

Departure

At the end of the morning seder, we were standing on a street corner, squinting in the late fall haze, when we learned that a well-respected rabbi had died. Almost at once, men began to step out of houses and *shtiblach*, small synagogues and study halls, and into the streets, making their way toward the yeshiva, where the funeral service was to be held. Soon hundreds of men were hurrying to pay their respects. It was an obligation that the living owed to the dead, to guide him to his final place of rest, a commandment that superseded carrying on with the weekday routine.

We arrived too late to find spots inside the yeshiva, so we stood with the crush of mourners in the vestibule. A rabbi read the customary funerary psalms over the loudspeaker, his voice quavering through the end of Psalm 121: "God will guard your coming and going, from now and all eternity." Next he read the man's Hebrew will: the deceased rabbi requested that there be no eulogies, only that his books stand as a testament to his work on Earth. Then, the chanting of El Malei Rachamim, "God Full of Mercy," which asks God to watch over the soul of the dead. The men beside me removed their glasses and wiped away tears or looked up at the ceiling watery-eyed. The final act was to accompany the bier to a van, which would take the coffin to the airport, then to Israel for burial. It is an important mitzvah, my brother-in-law said, to accompany the dead as far as possible on this last trip. We stepped outside again into the cold and walked in silence through the parking lot.

The sun began to dip beyond the peaks of the narrow, gray-paneled houses. It was past 3:00 p.m., and we had not yet prayed minchah, the afternoon prayer service. My brother-in-law wanted to make sure he could do so with a minyan, so we stopped at a small shul in the basement of an acquaintance's home. The priority of prayer challenged my notion of time. As an aspiring academic and journalist, I live my life, for the most part, to the chimes of Google Calendar, preoccupied by productivity and writing deadlines. Here, by contrast, there is hardly a moment that is not structured by service to others—and to God.

It did not take long to make a minyan. The prayers were brisk and businesslike but for a few men who stood at the very front near the ark, lost deep in passionate prayer, swaying back and forth, hands extended, beseeching God. I prayed with them.

I felt jealous of their faith. While I have spent years of my life praying each morning, I have never felt a connection to the divine the way some of these men did. God, for me, has always been much more an awful absence, a commanding void, than the source of all things, of good, of life.

By now I was also exhausted by the day's intensity, by what felt like constant davening, by the gravity and intentionality with which each moment was lived. On our way out of the shul, old, bearded men with tattered hats waved credit card readers in our direction. They were meshullachim, or collectors, the beggars who, in Lakewood, are vetted by a communal organization. We were to follow one mitzvah with another.

II.

In the Beginning

The story of today's Lakewood starts with the arrival of Rabbi Aharon Kotler in America in 1941 from what is now part of Belarus. Considered a Talmudic genius by his teens, Kotler had, by the 1920s, become one of the leading rabbis of the most exacting branches of eastern European Orthodoxy, defined by the centrality of Talmud study and dogged opposition to the ecstatic, mystical worship of the Hasidism.

Kotler's was an Orthodoxy that did not seem to have much of a future in the early twentieth century. While many of the immigrants who arrived during the great migration of 1880 to 1924 came, like Kotler, from the heartlands of the yeshiva world in the czarist Pale of Settlement, many sought not to perpetuate their faith but rather to abandon it. A common image in Jewish immigrant narratives of arrival was that of a man aboard a ship docking in New York who casts his phylacteries into the sea.

For this reason, and others, Rabbi Yisrael Meir Kagan, known as the Chofetz Chaim, one of the almost saintlike figures of Haredi Judaism, warned religious Jews that moving to America would test and ultimately erode their faith. Many rabbis issued similar warnings. Rabbi Jacob David Wilovsky, the rabbi of Slutsk, denounced America as so *treyf* that "even the stones are impure." I suspect this sensibility accounts, at least in part, for why my great-grandmother's sister Nesha and her husband, Leyzer, arrived in New York only in the 1920s, once the conditions in eastern Europe had become unbearable.

The kind of Orthodoxy that did exist in the United States at the time was, largely, a residual folk practice. With a few exceptions, it was a nostalgic holdover for those Jews who had not yet abandoned the tradition but who also could not bear the innovations of the non-Orthodox streams. Its practitioners were not especially learned, and the lack of serious yeshiva education meant that even the caliber of its rabbis was low. When Wilovsky traveled from Slutsk to visit New York City in 1900, he denounced the rabbis there in the harshest terms. "There sermons contain no true guidance for the Jewish people," he despaired. "If these practices will not cease, there is no hope for the continuance of the Jewish religion."

Wilovsky, of course, turned out to be wrong. And his words should serve as a reminder of Simon Rawidowicz's now-famous observation, in his essay "Israel, the Ever-Dying People," that while each Jewish generation imagines itself to be the last, there is always another, however unrecognizable it may be to its predecessors, that follows. Yet it took some time for history to refute Wilovsky's prediction.

Especially when viewed from the perspective of today's extremely punctilious ultra-Orthodoxy, the Orthodox Judaism that evolved through the early decades of the century was sometimes strikingly lax on issues now seen as central to religious life. The separation of genders, the definition of modest dress for women, secular studies—all were less stringently policed than today. Through the 1950s and '60s, congregants in some Orthodox communities drove to synagogue on the Sabbath, and men and women sometimes even sat together in shul. It seemed, then, that Orthodoxy in America was running out of time, that Wilovsky's warning would prove right, that Orthodoxy was but the remnant of a world destined to disappear.

During these very years, Kotler set about staging a quiet Haredi counterrevolution, slowly laying the foundations of traditionalist

Orthodoxy's revival. He founded BMG in the building of an old hotel with roughly a dozen students. Soon it began to grow, and with it, Lakewood's religious Jewish community.

For much of his life, Kotler appeared to many American Jews as the representative of an atavistic, even outmoded Judaism. He would not live to see the yeshiva, the town, and, in a sense, the Orthodox world transformed in his ideology's image.

A Corner That Stands Apart

From BMG's inception, Kotler articulated the yeshiva's guiding spirit as in total opposition to the dominant currents of mainstream American Jewish life. In his view—still upheld by his grandsons, who lead the yeshiva today—the emendations proposed by the non-Orthodox denominations to adapt Judaism to the times (vernacular liturgy, halachic leniency) were destined to fail. Even if such measures were to succeed, the product would be such an intellectually and spiritually impoverished form of religion that it would only exacerbate the problem—diminishing adherence to traditional Judaism—that the "modern" denominations had set out to address in the first place.

Perhaps most importantly, they were also religiously prohibited, in keeping with centuries-old Orthodox precedent. The Hatam Sofer, the Hungarian rabbi who was among the forefathers of ultra-Orthodoxy in the late eighteenth and early nineteenth centuries, famously declared "*Chadash assur min haTorah*"—"Innovation is forbidden by the Torah." Resistance to the new has been a cornerstone of Haredi Judaism ever since.

Not only opposed to religious and philosophical innovation, ultra-Orthodoxy was, and remains, defiantly anti-pluralist. Inclusivity is not part of its vocabulary. It holds that religious life can only reproduce itself if anchored by total devotion to God's Torah and its strictest interpretation—that it can only survive, only deserves to survive, if oriented in the world by divine obligation, even if that limits its adoption to a few select adherents, to the faithful remnant, *shearith hapletah*, who would preserve the tradition when all others have abandoned it. There is a reason that keeping the mitzvot, God's commandments, is referred to as accepting "the yoke of the Torah."

And such a life of devotion, a life under the yoke, would also require a particular environment, which is why Kotler proposed a staunchly separatist way of life. In his view, the values of secular America were incompatible with strict Torah observance. Its materialistic soil—in Yiddish, its *chumriusdiker bodem*—was hostile to the spiritual focus for a life of Talmudic study. So instead of New York City, where there were many more Jews, Kotler chose to build the yeshiva in Lakewood. It was better to be isolated than surrounded by heresy and immorality. A widely read hagiography of the rabbi recounts that what Kotler wanted was to "create a *'reineh vinkeleh'*—a corner that stands apart . . . pure, clean, free of any taint of *goyishkeit* [non-Jewishness], of secularism, of materialism." To this day, the recognition that the values that define Orthodox Jewish life are incompatible with those that belong to secular American culture is central to the ideology of Haredi Judaism.

There were other elements to this Haredi critique of secular decadence. One was the embrace of asceticism. While Judaism, unlike Christianity, has no monastic orders, the Lithuanian mussar tradition is perhaps the closest thing Judaism has to a living, ascetic tendency. Kotler inveighed frequently against *gashmiyus*, materialism, and sought to set a personal example of simple, nonmaterialistic living. The popular hagiography details how he ate "without pursuing pleasure," that his household furniture was "battered and decrepit" and mismatched.

Yet this was not simply austerity for its own stake. The corollary of the refusal of self-gratification was the cultivation of character, the core of the mussar tradition—the constant focus on ethics, the virtues of modesty, charity, and loving-kindness. Kotler, according to the legend that makes him an exemplar, described his rejection of material comfort as not only the elevation of the spiritual realm over the physical but as an empathetic protest of a world where poverty exists. "*Kol Zman es iz doh ein yid in der velt vos hut nisht tzu essen ken ich azoi nisht lebben*," he is believed to have said—in English, "As long as there is even one Jew in the world who doesn't have food to eat, I can't live that way."

Today, however, ascetism of any intensity is a value much more honored in the breach than the daily observance. One of the ironies of contemporary Lakewood is that a place founded in opposition to 1950s bourgeois domesticity has preserved the domestic suburban idyll in amber: the female homemaker, the child-centered home, the front-yard baseball game.

More recently, money has begun to flow in as men have gone to work in well-paying jobs, like medical billing, law, and finance. The houses have grown bigger, the clothing more expensive, the vacations, kosher all-inclusives, more lavish. The rise in conspicuous consumption has begun to erode the community's resistance to the values of the secular world. Indeed, the community's embourgeoisement has reached such a level that it has produced a reaction in the form of a group of BMG yeshiva students calling for a rejection of material comforts now commonplace in the town. Once, Haredi Judaism connoted poverty, and there are still many poor Orthodox Jews. Lakewood, though, is not an impoverished shtetl. It is a thriving middle-class town.

For Its Own Sake

By far the most important element of Kotler's vision was the idea of learning Torah for its own sake, *lishma*. It is, in the words of one of Kotler's daughters, "the raison d'être of Lakewood." The idea was unheard-of, countercultural when Kotler brought it to the United States, and remains so. The notion of noninstrumental learning contravenes something basic in the American creed, which elevates the pursuit of wealth and idealizes self-interest. In America, everything is a commodity, and if it cannot become a commodity, it might as well be worthless.

That common mentality was the challenge Kotler faced when he arrived in America. Learning *lishma* "was against the spirit of the country," his son, Rabbi Shneur Kotler, told the late sociologist William Helmreich. "People asked, what's the *tachlis* [the point] of studying Torah? What can be gained from it? This was the attitude. It was hard to explain that sometimes the most lasting things seem to come out from things which seem to have no purpose."

Today, it is precisely this noninstrumental quality of Torah study that continues to draw the greatest ire from ultra-Orthodoxy's critics. The apparent unproductiveness of yeshiva education and its curriculum's indifference to the secular world contravenes the common American understanding of the purpose of an education. In the secular imagination, the yeshiva *bocher* often appears almost as a Jewish transmogrification of the Reaganite welfare queen, feasting on government funds while shirking the capitalist duty to increase the GDP.

Lakewood is far from exceptional in the centrality of Torah learning in its communal life. It is, perhaps, the place where more young men devote their lives to learning Torah than any other in America, but it is far from the only place where they do so. Learning Torah *lishma* is the cornerstone of Haredi life broadly.

In Haredi communities across the United States, a new American Orthodoxy has taken shape that is entirely unconnected to the institutions of mainline Jewish life. And as these institutions have begun to totter, Haredi communities have only grown stronger. Having rejected the postwar Jewish consensus, Haredi Judaism can thrive as it collapses. Orthodoxy's future is not dependent on its survival.

But, at the same time, Haredi Judaism has been affected by the postwar Jewish consensus even without embracing its central pillars. Orthodoxy sought separation from Americanism, yet it also flourished because of America—because of the country's remarkable hospitality to religious sects and communities, because of the autonomy it grants to those who seek self-seclusion. While ultra-Orthodoxy rejected liberalism within its communities, it has survived because of the liberalism of American society—because of the constitutional defense of religious liberty and the almost sacrosanct value of tolerance.

III.

The Costs of Community

There are, however, real costs to the maintenance of ultra-Orthodox communal life. From the liberal-secular perspective—axiomatically opposed to a life centered on divine command—these are almost too numerous to name. Conformity: on matters from dress down to thought. Insularity: a disinterest in, and even hostility to, the non-Jewish world beyond its walls. Collectivism: the concept of the individual is one that, when acknowledged, must always be in service of the group. Patriarchy. Sometimes, for these reasons, people leave. But even for those who do not seek to depart, the strictures of traditionalist community can become sources of friction.

As in most religiously conservative cultures, there is a clear and circumscribed role for women in Haredi life. The family is their first and primary locus of self-definition. Unlike in other traditionalist societies, however, it is often Haredi women, and not men, who work outside the home and receive a better secular education. They can be schoolteachers or health-care workers or work in any number of businesses and charity organizations within the community. But they can never be leaders, Talmudic scholars, or public-facing figures. To be sure, there have been some recent hints of a slow shift underway: the election of Rachel "Ruchie" Freier, the first Hasidic Jewish woman on New York's Supreme Court; in 2020, the founding of an all-female EMT corps, Ezras Nashim, in Borough Park.

But these are exceptions, not the rule. More characteristic gender roles can be seen in a video released by Lakewood's BMG to honor the wives of its yeshiva students. Set to dramatic music, the video mainly shows disembodied women's hands waking up children, doing laundry, wiping countertops, on a steering wheel, cooking pasta, answering phones, making grocery lists, tucking children into bed. (Out of concern for modesty, women's faces cannot be shown.) "It's you—the crown of our town," the popular Haredi singer Baruch Levine croons. The message: these forms of women's labor make men's learning in yeshiva possible.

At least officially, the concept of homosexuality exists only as a biblical prohibition in Orthodox life. While there are, presumably, gay and lesbian people in every Haredi community, public acceptance of those forms of desire, let alone living openly, is an impossibility. The commonplace attitude is that adherence to halacha demands the repression, even elimination, of many forms of desire, and homosexual desire is no exception. What kind of bad *yetzer*, or inclination, matters less than the need to suppress it. For preserving the traditional community is paramount, and the suppression of such inclinations is what the community demands. "The choice to accept oneself as gay is seen by many, if not most, as a full-fledged rejection of the Torah," Steven Greenberg writes. In the past, if such desire could not be absolutely repressed, then, more lenient rabbis tacitly allowed, it must be actualized far away, outside the communal bounds. Gay people, Greenberg recalls, were "often told to 'dress in black and go violate the law in another city,' meaning 'Do what you will, but dress in black as a sign of sadness and mourning and go to a place where you are not known so your sinful depravity will not become a public scandal.'"

Few prices are too great for what is perceived as the maintenance of communal integrity. The mentality is a defensive one: that the forces of secular liberalism, combined with the ambient antisemitism of the non-Jewish world, threaten the survival of authentic Jewish life. And such defensiveness entails a raft of consequences beyond strict social conservatism.

For instance, it makes exceedingly difficult holding accountable those who commit forms of abuse. There is a powerful taboo against involving secular authorities—police and courts—in such matters out of fear that scrutiny by the non-Jewish world will damage the image of the community. "Reporting abuse to the authorities is something that just isn't done," said Asher Lovy, the Brooklyn-based director of Za'akah, an organization that raises awareness about child sexual abuse in Orthodox communities. "It's called *mesirah*, 'informing,' and it's absolutely forbidden."

In practice, Lovy explained, this means that the challenge of combating abuse within many Orthodox communities is twofold. It is, in part, that people fear repercussions for speaking out. They also take seriously the religious prohibition on informing to secular authorities—even if it means inaction in the face of knowledge of a terrible crime. "When people are raised thinking all sin is sin," Lovy said, "they have a hard time understanding why certain sins are worse than others," especially when they fear reporting on misdeeds might harm the community. But, even more significant, is the problem of authority. The people with the power in many ultra-Orthodox communities—leading rabbis, rabbinic boards, or vaadim that govern religious communities—prefer not to draw attention to the issue at all. They are also willing to discipline those who try to, usually through pressure and shaming. "Until there's systemic change at the top," Lovy said, "this is going to be a problem."

The Fight over the Schools

Even the recent and highly public fight over yeshiva education—played out in the pages of the *New York Times*—has, at its root, the incompatibility of the values of liberal society and the prerogatives of preserving Haredi life. Over the last ten years, a group called Young

Advocates for Fair Education (YAFFED) has doggedly campaigned for expanding the secular education offered in New York's Hasidic schools, the largest conglomeration of ultra-Orthodox institutions in the country. YAFFED began by arguing that many Hasidic yeshivas were failing to comply with the state-required secular studies that were "substantially equivalent" to the education provided in New York public schools. But as the years went by, and the organization intensified its public advocacy work—lobbying the city government to investigate yeshivas' failure to comply with the law, helping to source *New York Times* exposés on educational malfeasance in Hasidic yeshivas—the organization put forward a more comprehensive critique of Haredi education.

YAFFED charged that Hasidic schools in New York were setting up students to fail in the secular world—that these schools were denying students their rights by making it all but impossible for them to gradate with a high school diploma. In the early 2020s, the fight became visible on the radar of the secular public as well as that of Hasidic communities, and before long yeshiva education became another culture war issue, fought out in the pages of magazines as much as in the halls of power.

For Naftuli Moster, YAFFED's founding executive director, the issue is personal. Born to a Yiddish-speaking family of seventeen children that is part of the Belz Hasidic sect, Moster recalls that he only realized he had not received a full education when he attempted to go to college. "When I was about nineteen, twenty, I began having this itch to become a psychologist," he said. "They had me write an essay; I didn't know what that was. Even the little math quiz that they gave me I couldn't do without any help," he continued. "So that was my first awakening to my own poor education." In a story that Moster likes to tell, even after he managed to get into college, he found himself so woefully unprepared that he arrived in an intro biology class having never heard the word "molecule" before.

It is no secret that Haredi and Hasidic yeshivas typically offer little secular education. For boys, any real formal instruction in English and math often ends after fifth grade, while girls receive more time learning secular studies because they are expected to enter the workforce. In many boys' yeshivas, after sixth grade the two or so hours a day, if that, allotted for non-Jewish learning is often considered a time to let off steam and fool around. "In elementary and middle school, we had a maximum of ninety minutes of secular education a day, and it happened at the very end of the school day," Moster said. "Once we entered high school, we got cut off completely from secular education. There was no English, there was no math, there was no science, there was no social studies for all our high school years."

Because many of the yeshivas in New York receive funds from the state, Moster and YAFFED observed this was not just an internal Hasidic matter but a broader political one: the yeshivas were in violation of the law. YAFFED's proposal to rectify this was, on its face, simple: if the law requires "substantial equivalency," the yeshivas must comply. They also argued that there was no inherent contradiction between the strictest Orthodoxy and learning basic English and math. The fact that girls' schools offer a better secular education proved that a better balance could be struck. "My sisters went to the Belz Hasidic girls' schools," Moster told me. "If Naftuli Moster got the same education as his very own sisters got, there would be no YAFFED." This is also the logic of YAFFED's backers: the aim is not to dismantle the yeshiva education system but to improve it.

Yet, contrary to the popular framing, the absence of secular studies in Hasidic yeshivas is not a product of neglect. It is an intentional product of a Haredi ideology that sees secular knowledge as a mortal threat to the traditional Jewish way of life. The idea is as old as ultra-Orthodoxy itself, even constitutive of it. Ultra-Orthodoxy emerged as a self-conscious rejection of modernity and the Enlightenment. In the late nineteenth century, a leading Hungarian rabbi once likened secular knowledge to a disease so virulent that if a person fell ill with desire for it, the guards outside the quarantine doors would be at risk of catching it too. In the czarist and Austro-Hungarian empires, Orthodox Jewish communities determinedly resisted attempts by secular authorities to reform yeshiva curricula. Today these are stories of heroism, remembered and retold in many Haredi communities. New York's Hasidic leaders often frame their fight against the state as another iteration of a timeless Jewish struggle.

"This society has a right to retain its unique way of life," said Frieda Vizel. A tour guide and blogger who grew up in the Satmar Hasidic town of Kiryas Yoel, Vizel argues that, for many Haredi communities, refusing state demands and pressure to change yeshiva education is a matter of communal survival. "If you mess with the boys' education—especially because the boys' education is one of the foundations of the systems of socializing Hasidic children, then I think you do, potentially, entirely dismantle the system," Vizel said.

In this sense, the fight over yeshiva education is about much more than curricula: it is about fundamentally different ideas about the purpose of an education. For YAFFED, Hasidic schools are failing to provide a secular education, and this prevents students, especially male students, from finding livelihoods outside the community. The restriction of life options violates a core part of the liberal sensibility, which values self-making, autonomy, and the ability to choose a life course from a menu of options. From the perspective within Hasidic communities, that is precisely the point: the lack of secular studies, the denial of a range of life options, is not a failure. It is a success.

IV.

The Rise of Heimish *Populism*

For all the Haredi world's talk of the need to keep the influence of secular America at bay, it began to seem that this distancing was not uniformly upheld, especially during the fall of 2020, when it came to politics. In the lead-up to that year's election, what at first appeared to be a continuation of many Orthodox communities' support for Republican candidates began to morph into something more: not only their explicit alignment with Donald Trump's agenda, but also their adoption of his political style. The Haredi embrace of Trump stemmed in large part from its opposition to liberal America—to progressive support of LGBTQ rights and the perceived anti-religious ethos of the left. Yet the intensity of Orthodox support for Trump also reflected a kind of Americanization process of its own: an Americanization without liberalism.

By the fall of 2020, far more than any U.S. president, Trump had won widespread adoration in Orthodox communities. At the grassroots level, this enthusiasm took on unprecedented, almost cultlike enthusiasm. A well-known Hasidic singer penned a Yiddish ode to Trump. A synagogue served whiskey and cake to celebrate the president's birthday. Religious sleepaway camps hosted Trump impersonators. The Orthodox pop star Yaakov Shwekey reworked his hit song "We Are a Miracle," a schmaltzy ode to Jewish resilience, into "We Love America," a pro-Trump anthem. (The new lyrics, Shwekey told the Haredi web outlet Vos Iz Neias?, had been written for a Trump campaign fundraiser early that summer at the New Jersey home of the late Stanley Chera—a Trump donor and friend of the president who died of COVID-19.)

Across Orthodox media, coverage of Trump tended to be fawning. In November 2019, a headline in the glossy Orthodox weekly *Mishpacha* proclaimed Trump "the first heimish president." The literal meaning of the Yiddish word *heimish* is "homey." But in the colloquial speech of Orthodox communities in the United States, it has come to mean something like "one of us."

Of course, Orthodox support for the Republican Party is nothing new. Since the Bush years, when Orthodox communities were courted as potential members of the "value voters" coalition, it has only increased. The Obama presidency solidified this alignment. Many in the Orthodox world viewed the Obama administration, which clashed openly with Israeli prime minister Benjamin Netanyahu, as insufficiently supportive of Israel. The perception that Republicans are more supportive of traditional religious values has also helped bring conservative-leaning Jews further into the party's fold. Following the 2016 election, a survey commissioned by the American Jewish Committee found that while Trump won just 18 percent of all American Jews, he won 54 percent of the Orthodox vote, with even higher levels of support in Haredi communities.

The Trump presidency only made Orthodox identification with the Republicans stronger and adulation of Trump more fervent. "Some people have become so hyper-partisan, so whipped up into a frenzy because of that guy," *Mishpacha* columnist Eytan Kobre told me in the fall before the 2020 election. And while hyper-partisanship and polarization "are not new problems," he said, Trump "has exacerbated them to the zillionth power."

"He's a Gvir*"*

There is no single explanation for this phenomenon. It is, at least in part, due to the perception that Trump delivered on key Orthodox priorities. His administration's embrace of a pro-settlement, territorial maximalist position endeared him to many in the Orthodox world. So did his domestic policies. The 2018 tax bill signed by the Trump administration enabled college saving plans to be used for private and religious day schools—a change lobbied for and celebrated by groups such as the Orthodox Union and Agudath Israel, which boasted of close ties to U.S. secretary of education Betsy DeVos. Trump elevated Orthodox officials—among them his son-in-law Jared Kushner and his personal bankruptcy lawyer David Friedman (former U.S. ambassador to Israel)—into positions of power, and he diligently courted Orthodox groups unaccustomed to such a warm welcome at the White House. Trump commuted the sentence of Sholom Rubashkin, an Iowa kosher meatpacking executive sentenced to twenty-seven years in prison for money laundering, who had become an Orthodox cause célèbre. And when the Trump administration convened a meeting with Jewish groups on issues "impacting the community," Orthodox groups such as the Orthodox Union, Agudath Israel, and American Friends of Lubavitch received an invitation. The leaders of the three largest (and liberal) Jewish denominations did not.

There is also the undeniable element of Trump's personality. The combination of common causes and the president's own apparent proximity to Jewish culture earned him a kind of familiarity among Orthodox Jews that no other U.S. president has enjoyed. Trump is seen as someone who "gets" Jews, as Williamsburg businessman Yoel Klein told *Mishpacha*. The former president's Orthodox supporters point out that Trump has Orthodox Jewish grandchildren and that he spent much of his professional life working alongside Jews in the New York real estate business. He is a recognizable archetype: the gruff, ill-mannered businessman who nonetheless puts his money behind the right causes. When asked by *Mishpacha* deputy editor Yisroel Besser about his support for Trump, given "the fact that the current president is sometimes less than a positive role model," Rabbi Shmuel Kamenetsky, a prominent Haredi leader, replied, "That's because he's a *gvir*, a wealthy man . . . Wealthy, powerful people have a way of speaking and acting that is not refined. That's not a reason not to vote for him."

And then there was the simple fact that many in Haredi communities saw Trump as an ally in their battle against liberals and progressives. Communal leaders and laypeople alike freely acknowledged Trump's personal failings. But the pervasive sense that he was on their side, fighting the same fight, was enough to persuade people to overlook them. "The Orthodox have always seen themselves as us versus them," explained Samuel Heilman, a professor of sociology at Queens College. And in many instances Orthodox communities share the same adversaries as Trump. "Among America's Orthodox Jews, a primary fear propelling support for Trump is the rise of the progressive left," wrote *Mishpacha* editor-at-large Binyamin Rose in a pro-Trump op-ed for the Jewish Telegraphic Agency. "Orthodox Jews see Trump as their man on the street, standing up for the causes they believe in."

In Every Generation . . .

The feeling that religion and the traditional way of life are under siege runs deep in the Orthodox world, where collective memory of persecution is strong. And this abiding sense that they are under siege by hostile forces from without—whether secularism or the left-wing agenda—has been massively amplified by the Orthodox mediasphere, which, unlike other American media, has thrived in the last half-decade. The Haredi daily *Hamodia* boasts a readership of hundreds of thousands in North America; the glossy weekly *Mishpacha*, a print readership in the United States of more than 175,000; the newspaper *Yated Ne'eman*, a print circulation of more than 20,000 in the New York metro area. Then there are the frum clickbait ventures such as Matzav, Yeshiva World News, and Vos Iz Neias? (What's New?), as well as more locally focused papers, like Long Island's *5 Towns Jewish Times*. These are only the English-language outlets; there is a lively Yiddish media world of newspapers and radio hotlines with reaches in the tens of thousands. While there is a degree of ideological diversity, their coverage of U.S. politics and Israel leans—often hard—to the right.

"*Mishpacha* has been a little more balanced, but largely the Orthodox media has created a hermetically sealed information bubble," Kobre told me. *Yated Ne'eman*, he added, "could just as well be a wholly owned subsidiary of the Trump campaign." A characteristic news analysis for *Yated Ne'eman* by Rabbi Avrohom Birnbaum painted a grim picture of the threat posed by the "ultra-totalitarian" left to Jewish religious life. "Now, simply put, you are not allowed to even voice an alternative opinion to the Leftist orthodoxy that is in vogue, and if you do, you have no *zechus kiyum* [right to exist]," Birnbaum wrote. ". . . Religion is one of the next things on the chopping block. When religious sensitivities that are *halachically* [in terms of Jewish law] non-negotiable are deemed 'archaic,' 'racially insensitive,' 'chauvinistic,' 'xenophobic,' 'insufficiently sensitive to minorities,' and 'improperly cruel to animals,' we will not be given a choice. We will be thrown under the bus like dogs . . ."

In *Community Connections*, a popular weekly circular that serves the largely Hasidic communities of Monsey, New Square, and Spring Valley, Yiddish exhortations to vote in the 2020 Democratic primaries described the stakes in stark, existential terms. "Remember, the future of Judaism in NY is on the ballot," one ad declared. "If the radical progressives win and implement their dark anti-religious agenda, a Jew will not be able to live in NY in a couple of years." Another ad played on the long history of Orthodox antipathy to left-wing causes, stretching back, long before their absorption into the GOP coalition, to nineteenth- and twentieth-century conflicts with socialists and communists in Europe. "The local candidate for Congress is Mondaire Jones, who refers to himself as a socialist and member of the Democratic Socialists of America (DSA)," the ad warned. "We don't need to tell you how dangerous the socialist tendency is. Just take a look at the dozens of countries where they came to power to see that their cruel agenda is a catastrophe for Judaism."

Against the backdrop of decades-long tension with neighboring Black communities, issues of race have also become a prong of Orthodox support for Trump. Trump's opposition to the Black Lives Matter movement has resonated with many in Orthodox communities, where BLM is seen as pushing a political program that is hostile to Jewish interests. When racial justice protests swept the country in the wake of George Floyd's killing by Minneapolis police in May 2020, they were met in many Orthodox communities with a combination of suspicion and, at times, coarse hostility. On the Kol Mevaser Yiddish radio hotline in early June, two radio hosts, Velvel Shmeltzer and Rav Yitzchok Shlome Dresdner, discussed the Black Lives Matter protests in blunt terms. "The plundering," Shmeltzer said, referring to reports of looting during protests, showed the difference between a Jew and a gentile. "When a Black man was killed and the response, the justice that they do is to rob shops," he said. "The gentile when he has a chance his animalistic behavior comes out and he starts to act like a beast, simply like an animal! Would a Jew have done this?"

The Collapse of the Pragmatist Paradigm

As right-wing ideological imperatives have gathered strength within Orthodox communities, they have also come into tensions with concerns of realpolitik, jeopardizing the long-standing pragmatism of Haredi political leaders.

The vast majority of Orthodox Jews in the United States live in cities and states run by Democrats, one Orthodox political operative explained. For a long time, Orthodox communities managed to navigate this disjuncture by remaining registered Democrats in order to vote in local and state Democratic primaries, leaving them free to vote Republican at the presidential level. But as Orthodox communities have grown to identify more with Trump and the Republicans, relationships between Orthodox representatives and their local Democratic politicians have become increasingly strained. At stake is the ability of many Orthodox communities, long reliant on good relations with local officials, to preserve their much-prized autonomy and pursue communal interests.

Ezra Friedlander, a veteran Haredi political consultant from Borough Park with close ties to Democratic politicians, has long been sounding the alarm about the consequences of growing Orthodox hostility to the Democratic Party since the emergence of the Trump phenomenon. He said he fears that Orthodox disaffiliation from the Democratic Party could render Orthodox bloc voting impossible— and jeopardize the influence Orthodox communities have been able to exert in New York politics. "Yes, I realize that many of the electorate who either registered as Republicans or chose not to vote feel that the mandate that defines the current Democratic Party is anathema to them," Friedlander wrote in an op-ed for Yeshiva World News in July 2020. "But we are making a big mistake," he continued. "By registering as Republicans we have essentially opted out of the system. We may be making a statement or standing on principle but in the end we have abdicated our voice in the conversation."

"I think we have to work with the local Democratic infrastructure," Friedlander told me. "Politics is about being strategic. If you're in politics just for the sake of being an ideologue, you're going to achieve nothing." What too many people seemed to misunderstand is that "it's not the Democrats who need your vote. It's you who needs your vote," he continued. "The Orthodox Jewish community [in New York City] has the power to sway the election for a candidate they support in a citywide election," which means that politicians have a reason to pay attention to Orthodox interests, Friedlander explained. "But why would people pay attention if you don't vote for them?"

This essentially nonideological approach has long been the modus operandi of New York's Haredi communities. It has paid off. In exchange for consistent and disciplined support at the ballot box, city officials have given Orthodox communities broad autonomy to run their own parallel education system. On issues from school funding to affordable housing to religious practices—including controversial ones—Orthodox communities, with the promise of votes, have been able to move elected officials in their favor. Yet such pragmatism "is falling on deaf ears," Friedlander said. "It's becoming increasingly difficult for people to make the distinction" between their ideological preferences on the level of national politics and the strategic demands of local political realities, he added. "I think people should be able to separate themselves nationally and locally."

What blossomed in many Orthodox communities around the country since Trump's 2016 election was not just the rise of a new, right-wing Orthodox populism. It was also a break with a much older, arguably foundational mode of Orthodox politics, one that has its centuries-old roots in eastern Europe. "A very basic part of the Ortho-dox movement is the idea that we're in *galus* [exile], that we have to be extremely careful about the way we speak and act in a non-Jewish host society," Kobre told me. "We dare not do the things that draw the ire of the people around us. We believe that an outbreak of violent anti-semitism is no more than a short distance away."

Damage Control

For this reason, the Haredi establishment has sought to quash the community's more rambunctious Trumpian spirits. In August 2020, Rabbi Avi Shafran—a writer who also serves as the director of pub-lic relations for Agudath Israel of America, a century-old Orthodox umbrella organization—published an open letter subtitled "Sinai, Not Washington" on his personal blog, calling for a return to rhetorical moderation and civility. The letter, which was signed by several other Orthodox rabbis and writers, decried the rise of "partisan posturing" within Orthodox communities and cautioned "against the reflexive identification of Orthodox communal interests with any particular party or political philosophy."

Though it did not mention Trump, the letter was clearly meant as a rebuke of the Orthodox alignment with the Trumpian mode of poli-tics. But this was not a critique from the left. Like those Christians who have criticized widespread evangelical support for the president, the letter's signatories stressed that they were motivated by their com-mitment to conservative religious values. "Shameless dissembling and personal indecency acted out in public before the country are, in the end, no less morally corrosive than the embrace of abortion-on-demand or the normalization of same-gender relationships," the letter stated. "If we don't seriously consider the negative impact of our com-munity's unhealthy relationship with the current political style," it warned, "we risk further erosion of our ability to live lives dedicated to truly Jewish ideals."

Ironically, the call for a return to more civil discourse sparked intense, and occasionally acrimonious, debate across Orthodox media. Shafran and the letter's signatories were accused of defending the Democrats, of singling out Trump and the Republicans for criticism, and of attempting to push voters toward Biden. "The letter was decrying partisanship and clearly stated it was not intended to change anyone's vote," Shafran told me. "That the critics somehow overlooked those salient facts was, to me, evidence itself of the need for what the letter was pleading for." (Shafran stressed that he signed the letter in an individual capacity, and not as a representative of Agudath Israel.)

In November 2022, Rabbi Aharon Teitelbaum, Satmar Grand Rebbe of Kiryas Yoel, issued his own rebuke of Trumpist enthusiasm in the Haredi community. "This Trumpism has twisted the minds of so many yiden [Jews]," he warned. The Trumpists, he said, "have brainwashed people" into thinking that Orthodox Jews stand to benefit from the MAGA movement. In reality, the opposite was more likely—that Jewish support for Trump and Trumpists could end up harming Jewish interests. The wiser course of action, the Satmar Rebbe counseled, was to return to the traditional Haredi political stance—to keep a distance from America and view politics as only instrumental to ensuring communal flourishing. "We are not going to fix America. We are in galus [exile], and we are not allowed to fix anything. We can only protect ourselves," he said. "We cannot fix America—if we say we are going to send a message, what if they send us back a message? It will be very painful if they send us back a message."

Viewed in this light, the populist turn in Orthodox politics appears as a revolt—both against the rabbinic establishment and the class of Orthodox political operators, the *askanim*. Contrary to those who link greater religious stringency to increasingly right-wing politics, the preoccupation with secular affairs and electoral politics in fact reflects a certain leniency, a kind of opening to the broader world, an opposition to one form of Americanism through the embrace of another.

One afternoon in Lakewood, I asked one of my brother-in-law's friends if he had heard the critiques of political involvement like Shafran's and the Satmar Rebbe's. He said he had, then he offered a traditionalist spin of his own. Obviously, the Hasidic leader was no liberal, he said. What concerned him was that people were taking politics into their own hands, when it should really remain the purview of a select few leaders. A religious person should be focused on Torah, on learning, and on family. It wasn't appropriate to be so concerned with secular affairs. While this remains the official position in many Haredi communities, populist enthusiasm increasingly challenges it.

The incorporation of many Haredi communities into the political culture of the Trumpist right would perhaps be less worrying if the stakes of U.S. politics did not currently seem so high. As the Satmar Rebbe observed, one of the sad ironies of Orthodoxy's alignment with right-wing populist and anti-liberal forces in America is that, were these forces to win out, the America they might create would almost certainly be less hospitable to Jews. Already the surge in right-wing antisemitism can be felt, and most acutely by Orthodox Jews. Too few among the Trumpist Haredi cadres recognize that while white Christian nationalists and Catholic integralists may appear to be strategic partners in fighting "gender ideology" or "wokeness" or BLM, the place of observant Jews in a future dominated by these tendencies will be much less certain. Orthodoxy in America has flourished as much because of liberalism as despite it.

Still, it would be a mistake to see the emergence of such dilemmas as new. How to insulate tradition from secularism and liberalism is a question as old as Orthodoxy itself. So, too, are the practical considerations about which side of the political spectrum might provide traditionalist Judaism's best allies. In the Hapsburg Empire, Orthodox political actors found common cause with other national minorities—including their nationalist, populist, and sometimes even antisemitic representatives. In the German Empire, a more moderate German Orthodoxy found common cause with German Catholics, who also saw their religious rights as jeopardized by a consolidating, Protestant-dominated German Empire.

The placid contours of postwar American Jewish life meant that these questions largely disappeared. But only for a time. They are back. And while previous generations of American Jewish leaders insisted on the perfect compatibility, even the synonymity, of Judaism with Americanism and liberalism, the rise of new kinds of anti-liberal Americanism and the growing strength of Orthodoxy have shattered such once self-evident convictions. As the old American Jewish consensus collapses, Orthodoxy is in position to definitively shape whatever takes its place.

———

There is a great deal I admire about Haredi Judaism: its intentionality, the centrality of transcendent values, its commitment to community and family. There is not a moment of life left unstructured by divine command. Everything, from the forming of one's character to the food that one eats, is the subject of a constant, permanent process of study, contemplation, and practice.

But I was also left wondering if the social conservatism and the thickness of community required each other, whether the closedness and the emphasis on obligation needed to go together. Could a community expand its circle of concern to those outside its boundaries, to the broader world, without sacrificing its cohesion or its unity, the organicness that gives it its strength? Can only faith in God and devotion to one's people enable the kind of attention to the well-being of others and the generosity on display every day in Haredi communities? Can a community that seeks to protect its way of life ally itself with other minority communities on the basis of solidarity instead of with xenophobic forces, if only because they seem to share the same enemies? I want the answer to be yes. I'm not sure.

In the twentieth century, the grand ideologies, the old political faiths, could compel remarkable, and terrible, feats—of community and nation building, self-sacrifice, and devotion. But despite those heralding its end, the post-ideological age persists. For now, Orthodoxy remains the only living Jewish alternative to liberal capitalist culture on offer.

FOUR PATHS FOR THE FUTURE OF AMERICAN JEWISH LIFE

I.

In the spring of 2023, my great-aunt Estelle passed away just shy of her one hundredth birthday. The older sister of my maternal grandfather, who died young, she was like a grandmother to me. She grew up the child of the acculturated yet traditionalist Jewish bourgeoisie of the Bronx: apartment off the Grand Concourse, live-in maid, piano lessons during the week. She was the eldest daughter of my great-grandfather, after whom I am named—Isidore, an urbane physician of Lithuanian origin, doctor to the New York area's various rabbinic luminaries, and a small-time artist who sketched dancing Hasids on business cards in his free time. Unlike my paternal grandmother Charlotte's, Estelle's life—marriage to another dapper physician, Milton, who died tragically young too—led her out of New York and over to Connecticut, where she worked as the receptionist in her daughter's dermatology practice until she no longer could.

Her life spanned the entire American Jewish century: the journey from the clamor of the old ethnic neighborhood to the quiet of the new affluent suburb; the anxiety of the Second World War, the start of which she heard broadcast on the radio; the dawning realization of the Holocaust's real magnitude; the drama of Israel's war of independence, and its subsequent wars of survival and conquest; the inward, conservatizing turn in American life; and finally, the slow unraveling of U.S. politics, with its ghoulish nadir in Trump's election.

She was among the last living members of an American Jewish culture that increasingly exists only in memory. This Jewish culture supplied the idioms, rhythm, taste, and texture of what we think of when we think of American Jewish identity. It took shape in the early decades of the twentieth century, just as America closed its golden doors, bloomed in full by mid-century, and, in our own time, has withered.

In what one might call its classical form, this was a secularist, rationalist, and sometimes even intellectually elitist culture. Far more than God, it worshipped education, which it imagined as the path to uplift. Its affect was essentially Yiddish, despite—or perhaps because of—the determined efforts of its members to transcend their Yiddishkeit, their particularity, and to achieve some imagined quantum "universal" civilization.

Yet in the same breath it could be intensely tribal. It certainly became more so as it aged. Toward the end of his life, my grandfather and Estelle began a book club to read the latest Israeli fiction in translation together. Their old, peeling paperbacks of Amos Oz, A. B. Yehoshua, and Shulamith Hareven now rest on the basement shelves of my childhood home. Estelle and I argued lovingly over Israeli politics. "I disagree with every word you write," she told me the last time I saw her, days before her heart finally stopped. But that meant she read every word too.

An incendiary yet generative tension powered this American Jewish culture until its force abated. What is often remembered as the golden age of American Jewish creativity owed its remarkable dynamism to the conflict between the draw of America's capitalist phantasmagoria and the weight of Jewish family, history, and tradition. At a time when the comparatively hospitable climate of America made Jewish life more comfortable than ever before, Jewish novelists and filmmakers made the angst of assimilation into art. Jewish comedians and entertainers felt sufficiently at home in America to bring their unabashed Jewishness into the mainstream, but still confident enough in the meaning of their patrimony that they could rebel against it. Today, these conditions no longer pertain.

———

The family buried Estelle on a hazy April afternoon in the Hebrew Sick Benefit Association Cemetery—a relic of that dense network of Jewish organizations and mutual aid societies now lost to oblivion. Because she had belonged to this once proud and self-sustaining Jewish culture, she had not felt it necessary to join a synagogue. She was not a spiritually inclined person. She did not seek out the guidance of rabbis.

So the funeral home the family had contracted to take her to the grave provided one. A rent-a-rabbi arrived with what seemed to be a standard "old Jewish woman eulogy" template, into which she plugged the details of Estelle's life and the adjectives my bereaved cousins had asked her to use. The rabbi then proceeded to botch this basic task. She repeatedly and incorrectly said that Estelle had been born and raised in Brooklyn, not the Bronx, as if she had forgotten to update her script since the last dead Jew. She struggled through the Hebrew of El Malei Rachamim, the prayer for the soul of the departed. She offered not consolation but perfunctory gestures toward its simulacrum.

Estelle would not have cared much about the botched Hebrew. A keen critic of all things, she would have detested most the incompetence, although, at the other extreme, she would have equally derided zealousness if she'd had the opportunity. "When did we become so Orthodox?" she would often chide me when I vigorously led Passover seders for my mother's side of the family. The uniqueness of the secular Jewish culture that she embodied was such that Jewishness could exist independent of piety or religious conviction. It lived in her accent, in her wit, in her shrug. No mediocre rabbi could take that away from her.

For me, however, the farce of the eulogy added insult to the grief. It aggravated my personal loss and denied Estelle the final dignity I thought she deserved. It also left me with a deep foreboding about the disappearance of a culture into which I, too, had been born, the death of which I had understood intellectually as a possibility but had not yet internalized as fact. It painfully illuminated for me the necessity of tradition and the chasm of unmeaning left by a living culture's absence: how life's inevitable sufferings become less bearable when the bonds of a common way of life fray; how the passage of generations begins to feel senseless without the spiritual scaffolding—the texts, the practices, *the language*—that instructs us in what we owe to those who came before us and those who will come after.

People often say that we Jews are "good at death." What they mean is that our protocol for mourning softens the blow of the loss. The daily recitation of Kaddish carves out fixed space for contemplation. Shiva turns bereavement from a solitary misery into the work of collective memorialization. But as time passes and connection to the tradition attenuates, these rituals become less accessible to increasing numbers of Jews. For many, such practices have already taken on a strange and foreign quality. They know they need to do them, but they are no longer sure how. They are left with the hollow, stilted procedure of religion, devoid of the core, of substance—with the disenchanted shell of something that was once alive.

The Autumn of American Jewish Culture

Born in the mid-1990s, I can only remember an organized Jewish community that appeared to be on the downslope of inexorable decline. While I was still a teenager, the YMHA where I had grown up playing floor hockey, where my beloved Hebrew teacher's husband sold pizza out of the "Jerusalem Café," was bought out by its Christian equivalent and folded into the YMCA. The small religious day school I attended had always appeared on the brink of insolvency, its enrollment never more than 120 students. In 2022, it finally closed.

"Nobody Wanted to See This Happen," read the headline in the local Jewish paper. The synagogue to which my parents belong, where my father and I walked to on countless Shabbat mornings, can no longer consistently make a minyan. These days, when I come home, it feels all but inevitable that the shul is next to go.

"Decline is a fact," the literary scholar Jed Esty writes. "Declin*ism* is a problem of rhetoric and belief." For much of the last half century, a certain strain of declinism has been the dominant affect, even ideology, of mainline affiliated Jewish life. From the 1970s, when *Look* magazine foresaw the "vanishing" of the American Jew, onward to the 1990 National Jewish Population Survey, which found that most American Jews were marrying outside the tribe, the leaders of the Jewish establishment have warned of an impending demographic collapse. Employing the language of existential threat, they describe an American Judaism in the throes of "a continuity crisis," its survival imperiled by insufficient levels of endogamy. To a large extent, the entire Jewish communal apparatus reorganized itself with the aim of resolving, or at least arresting, Jewish demographic diminishment as its central goal. Yet despite all the talk, the real process of decline has not stopped.

As much as possible, I have tried in this book to avoid discussing "the continuity crisis" and its attendant woes. That is not only because the issue has so dominated the Jewish discussion over the last few decades, but also because it has always seemed to me a subject without substance. To obsess over intermarriage is to mistake a symptom for a cause.

But this, then, is one of the consequences of American Jewish declinism. As a rhetoric, it obscures the real reasons for the problems it aims to solve. American Jewish declinism is a prophylactic to thinking. It deflects from hard questions in favor of easy solutions. To understand what it means to live in the autumn of American Jewish culture, we must first uncover what the discourse of declinism has occluded. Only then can we confront the inexorable reality of decline for what it is and begin to ask what might be required of us to live within it as people—and as Jews.

Within the Jewish institutional world, the fear of American Jewish demographic collapse has produced intensive, even manic activity to study and reverse the problem. American Jewish organizations have commissioned—and continue to commission—innumerable surveys on the statistical minutiae of American Jewish life, only to come away from each examination of the crosstabs even more alarmed. These organizations have become obsessed with the calculus of reproduction—birth rates, marriage rates, life span—in the hope of shoring up chances for group survival. Jewish leaders seem to believe they can return American Jewish life to the long-gone mid-century norm, as if it were possible through sheer force of funds and will.

As a consequence, sociology has become not merely the dominant but the sole discourse of organized Jewish life. Debates over demographics have eclipsed whatever unresolved theological questions or rabbinic quandaries remained. Around a Shabbat dinner table in a mainline Jewish community, one is probably still more likely to find a spirited debate about intermarriage than a learned disquisition on the week's Torah portion. Prominent Jewish figures often seem more concerned about who young Jewish people date than with what they know of their tradition or whether they can even read the sacred texts.

If the demographic obsession is one symptom of decline, in the realms of art and culture pervasive repetition attests to a larger creative, even spiritual exhaustion. There are few better ways of evading the present than nostalgia. Broadway revived *Fiddler on the Roof* twice within the span of a decade, perhaps so that the story of Tevye might do the work for Jewish families that long-since deceased Old World relatives no longer could do. Across the country, fading Jewish delis like the Upper West Side's Barney Greengrass have become tourist traps, interactive gravestones to a lifeworld that has faded away. Writers and filmmakers vulturously pick through the Holocaust's archive of horror, driven as much by the imperative to remember as the knowledge that it remains a story guaranteed to sell.

Stagnation is "the predicament" of a people "estranged from the future by collective nostalgia," Esty observes. In American Jewish life, such stagnancy results from attachment to outmoded forms—to the old consensus, to the time before the current polarization and division, and to the way of life that made it possible. We are doomed to live among the relics of a sunsetting Jewish culture unless we can find a way to reckon soberly with where we currently find ourselves.

Judged against this metric, the rhetoric of American Jewish declinism has been immensely counterproductive because it holds out hope that the trends it fears might still be reversed. To borrow again from Esty's schema, which he derived to analyze American culture more generally, mainstream American Jewish declinism is "too deterministic about the catastrophic results" of Jewish demographic eclipse, but "not deterministic *enough* about the likelihood of that eclipse." In other words, American Jewish leaders and demographers imagine Jewish demographic decline as extinction—indeed, Michael Steinhardt, the billionaire hedge funder who cofounded Birthright, once likened Jews to an "endangered species." But they also imagine that through the right combination of outreach initiatives and well-directed donor cash, they might be able to catalyze the production of enough new Jewish babies to solve the continuity crisis they so greatly fear. American Jewish declinism is thus at once a pessimism and a grandiose fantasy of near omnipotence.

What might happen, though, if we instead take the irreversibility of decline as a starting point, while recognizing that most of us, and probably our children too, will live out our lives alongside decline's long course? If we accept that there will be no return to any semblance of communal consensus, nor any mass religious revival that will bring American Jews back to now shuttered synagogues and schools? If we properly mourn the disappearance of a living secular Yiddish culture, and with it its humor, its food, and its folkways, so that the pain of the loss doesn't mire us in perpetual melancholic attachment? At the very least, we might be able to see what American Jewish life in its autumn will actually look like.

II.

Prognostication is a dangerous art, but I will hazard it here. What follows is by necessity schematic. It seems to me that there are four main paths forward in American Jewish life, four primary political-religious tendencies that have begun to emerge. They coexist uneasily; sometimes they conflict directly. I have called them, respectively: the dying establishment; prophetic protest; neo-Reform; and separatist Orthodoxy.

These paths are not exhaustive. Instead, they are meant to suggest a different way of thinking about the fissures within American Jewish life beyond the usual denominational framing. They are not all equal in power or size: the establishment institutions remain the best funded and the largest, even if they have become shadows of their former selves. Nor can any single path claim the majority of American Jews, for to be part of them requires intentional and sustained activity—participation in ritual life, in community, or in study—which few American Jews profess to do with any real consistency. Contrary to the contemporary catechism, identity cannot be mere self-affirmation. Judaism is a religion of practice. We are defined by what we do.

The Dying Establishment

The architects of what became the American Jewish establishment built their institutions with posterity in mind. Founded in the early twentieth century, organizations like the American Jewish Committee, the Anti-Defamation League, and the Jewish Federations transformed fundraising and philanthropy into the quintessential American Jewish activity over the course of a few decades. To be a good Jew in the age of the postwar consensus was not necessarily to attend synagogue, observe Shabbat, or study Torah; it was to donate, usually to Israel-advocacy organizations. And while many of the funds raised by establishment organizations went to cover day-to-day concerns, campaigns, and, for the federations, community services, they were also intended to guarantee the Jewish future. "In the 1960s and 1970s," historian Lila Corwin Berman writes, "Jewish philanthropic organizations gained new tools to build financial strength through endowment vehicles and, simultaneously, to render Jewish identity through the prism of financial perpetuity." That these organizations remain standing today—even as they have become dominated by big donors and, at the same time, more detached from the lives of most American Jews—reflects the success of the establishment founders' vision, as well as their savvy navigation of the shifts in American capitalism. On the local and synagogue level, too, the philanthropic model predominates.

At the core of mainline Jewish life is the logic of affiliation through contribution. Donations, dues, memberships—these constitute the foundation of the establishment institutional edifice. Without them, the communal organizations, synagogues, schools, foundations, and community services would not survive. The prerogatives of fundraising, in tandem with the Jewish holidays, set the calendar: fund drives and galas, telethons and 5Ks. But affiliation is not only financial. Affiliation also entails those old-fashioned values of dedication to community, long-term commitment to institutions, even brick-and-mortar buildings in which to gather—values all denigrated in today's popular culture. It provides a concrete means by which one demonstrates belonging to one's people, which is also why so much of mainline affiliated life revolves around fundraising for Israel. Affiliation is also an ethos as much as a practice. If it were not for those dedicated and very often older congregants who trek each weekend to services out of habit, or who show up first to help set up for events, American Jewish communities would be in much worse shape.

What keeps the establishment locked into its old ways is also what has gotten it here in the first place. Mainstream Jewish organizations are often painfully unable to adapt or meaningfully deviate from the tracks laid decades ago. Such rigidity risks condemning organized Jewish life not to the immediate catastrophe that demographers fear, but to slow diminishment in the long run, as the social base of the legacy institutions wither. The often single-minded focus on intra-communal affairs and self-perpetuation further limits the ability of mainstream organizations to speak to the issues that most concern many of their would-be members. And as Israel becomes ever more embattled, its actions increasingly impossible to justify on liberal or humanistic terms, this, too, puts mainline affiliated life on the gradual yet near-certain track to obsolescence. In response to the rising millennial and Gen Z cohorts that reject unequivocal support for Israel, mainline affiliated Judaism has no coherent or compelling proposition to offer. That won't matter materially in the decades immediately to come, before the full generational turnover. But it will eventually.

Prophetic Protest

In 2008, the then-young editors of the Brooklyn-based literary magazine *n+1* surveyed the state of American Jewish culture in the wake of September 11 and found it lacking. The attacks, they wrote, had thrust American Jews "into history once again, not as a successful group looking backward to historical catastrophe and sideways to a distant troubled country, but as contemporary actual living Jews." For a moment, the real and novel vulnerability of Jews in America had cast aside the previously dominant retrospective and vicarious concerns that had defined the old communal consensus. And yet, the *n+1* editors lamented, instead of generating new, vital, ambitious, or critical modes of Jewish art and thought, the traumatic wake of September 11 had given rise mainly to a donor-funded Jewish cultural landscape notable only for its conservativism, shallowness, and sterility. For the *n+1* editors, this was perhaps a sign that the Jewish cultural enterprise was finally running out of gas. "The greatness of this people was that it once believed its experience of oppression to be a universal one, and its fortunes tied to all those who are oppressed," the *n+1* editors wrote. "There are many ways back to that belief, including through ethnic particularism, if one wants to find that way." Otherwise, they continued, "secular Jews deserve to become like people of Scottish descent: to wear yarmulkes twice a year like kilts, and toot shofars like bagpipes, calling no one back to righteousness."

It took about half a decade, but a cohort of mainly young millennial activists rediscovered the Jewish call to justice in the early 2010s. Fueled in large part by the long-burning idealism of Occupy Wall Street and bitter disillusionment with the American Jewish establishment's support for Israel's occupation, they coalesced in new organizations like IfNotNow and Never Again Action, and reinvigorated existing ones like JFREJ and JVP. At their best, these activists embody Judaism's prophetic impulse in the Heschelian sense of the word. "The prophet was an individual who said No to his society, condemning its habits and assumptions, its complacency and waywardness," Abraham Joshua Heschel wrote. "The situation of a person immersed in the prophet's words is one of being exposed to a ceaseless shattering of indifference." The practitioners of contemporary prophetic protest are righteously horrified by pervasive racialized police violence, by the quotidian sadism of America's immigration regime, and, most of all, brought to desperate grief by Israeli human rights abuses and oppression of the Palestinians. Prophetic protesters account for a statistically small segment of American Jews—less than a quarter, even by generous accounting. What they lack in number they make up for in volume.

The Judaism of prophetic protest, however, has yet to find stable ground. Painfully, almost violently, aware of global injustice, it finds too little to affirm in the world. A popular front brought together by shared oppositions, it defines itself much more by what it is against than what it is for: a deficiency that has afflicted almost all social movements over the last decade. Indeed, in this sense and others, the Judaism of prophetic protest may not be prophetic enough. It is too comfortable in the rhythms of late-capitalist life. While prophetic protesters occasionally convene in real-life demonstrations—strategic deployments of politicized ritual—the natural home of this tendency is on social media. In practice, its notion of community is often more virtual than concrete. Its commitments are less deliberated or reached through consensus than proclaimed in 240 characters or illustrated by Instagram slides. Likewise, because its use of ritual and liturgy is almost always in service of an urgent political action, it has no coherent approach or explicit commitment to religious observance for when the demonstration is over and the marchers have returned to their atomized lives in cramped city apartments. Sometimes, those engaged in protest even resent the idea that they ought to have a more substantive vision of the relationship between the religious and the political. They are radicals, but they are also liberals—in the private realm, they believe, anything goes.

Neo-Reform

While born in Germany in the early nineteenth century, Reform Judaism is perhaps the most authentically American of the Jewish denominations. On the comparatively free soil of the United States, the Reform Movement was able to realize in total its vision for a Judaism fully in sync with what it perceived to be the demands of modernity.

The movement's 1885 Pittsburgh Platform, although supplanted by later statements, encapsulates the theologically radical sentiments professed by many of Reform Judaism's adherents from its earliest decades and up to the present. The Pittsburgh Platform repudiated Judaism's exclusive claim to divine truth in favor of a universalist ethnical monotheism and recognized "in every religion an attempt to grasp the Infinite one." It threw off the yoke of halachic obligation and proclaimed that it would reject "all such [laws] as are not adapted to the views and habits of modern civilization." It deemed kashruth and the laws of ritual purity as having "originated in ages and under the influence of ideas altogether foreign to our present mental and spiritual state." Most provocatively, the authors of the Pittsburgh Platform declared Jews "no longer a nation but a religious community." While this platform has ceased to be official movement doctrine, it is nonetheless likely that many of the platform's claims would be embraced by congregations across the liberal Jewish denominations.

The inheritors of the radical Reform's spirit are today's ritual innovators and liturgical experimenters. They can be found in the liberal and nondenominational rabbinical schools, in the bevy of new-age and spiritualist entrepreneurial ventures, and in organizations like Svara. Like their predecessors, the neo-Reformers aim to revise the tradition and its texts—to edit, rewrite, replace, or disregard any element that fails to fit within the contours of today's social reality. They have transposed Reform's universalism into a more contemporary, postmodern key; whereas the old radical Reformers spoke of "universal culture" and "monotheistic and moral truth," today's neo-Reformers have raised "inclusion" and "accessibility" as the highest of religious values. Also like their predecessors, they reject not only peoplehood but also particularism. For neo-Reformers, Judaism is not just for Jews, nor does it have any exclusive claim to validity. Neo-Reformers delight in intermingling Judaism with other traditions in strange and syncretic (and, sometimes, frankly ridiculous) amalgams of religious expression. While sometimes participants in acts of prophetic protest, the neo-Reformers have a distinct mission. Prophetic protest takes Jewish ritual and brings it into the secular world of politics; neo-Reform, by contrast, takes the world of politics and brings it into the synagogue. Its guiding principle is that there should be no discrepancy between the values and norms outside and those inside.

Neo-Reform Judaism faces many of the predicaments common to liberal religion. When inclusion without qualification becomes the highest good, it becomes difficult, if not impossible, to assert why one way of doing things—why one tradition—is more worthy of observing than another. And if the tradition is not in some sense closed but is, instead, entirely open-ended and up for debate, it likewise becomes hard to argue why some practices should be permitted while others ought to be emended or suppressed. Such is the challenge of a non-foundationalist Judaism. If it incorporates too many outside sources and ideas into its corpus, it risks growing heavy with additions and falling out of the Jewish orbit. Or, put differently, if it sands down its distinctiveness until all that remains is a shining, unadulterated universalism, then it loses its distinctiveness and, with it, its raison d'être: Why not just be a Unitarian? Finally, the glorification of individual autonomy comes at the expense of the thick sense of obligation that perpetuates community over the long term. Too calibrated to mainstream American culture—with its tendency toward hybridity and its worship of choice—neo-Reform is at perpetual risk of getting lost in the current of the times.

Separatist Orthodoxy

Were it not for the Holocaust, there would hardly be Orthodox Judaism in the United States. The destruction of the European Jews was, in sheer numerical terms, also the extermination of the traditionalist masses of eastern Europe. They were not only gassed in the mechanized death factories of Auschwitz and Treblinka, but massacred, shot in pits, buried in ditches, flung into ravines—hundreds of thousands alone in Babi Yar (Ukraine), Ponary (Lithuania), Maly Trostenets (Belarus, today an hour's drive from Slutsk). Only a few of the great religious leaders, Torah sages, and rebbes of eastern European Jewry's pious population made it out of the Nazi charnel house, but those who did changed the trajectory of religious Jewish history. Whether representatives of Lithuanian yeshiva learning (Rabbi Aharon Kotler, Rabbi Moshe Feinstein) or leaders of Hasidic courts (the Satmar Rebbe Yoel Teitelbaum, the Lubavitcher Rebbe Menachem Mendel Schneerson), they all arrived in the United States with a common dream in mind. They would return their faithful remnant to its former glory. They would encourage their communities to grow so that they might make up for the lives that had been lost. They would rebuild the world of Torah devotion that had been destroyed. And they would make it even better than it had been in Europe: more single-mindedly focused on rabbinic learning and spiritual elevation, more set apart from the malign influences of secular society, and even more punctilious in the observance of the mitzvot. They succeeded—perhaps more than they ever could have imagined. Today's ultra-Orthodox are, in this sense, survivors twice over: first of the Nazi mortal threat, then of the liberal capitalist culture on American shores.

In its own religious terms, the purpose of Orthodox life is to serve Hashem, God, in every moment. In sociological terms, it is to live within a Jewish totality, to maintain a total Jewish existence. And the only way to make this vision a living reality is to cordon off the surrounding non-Jewish world. The success of separatist Orthodoxy owes not simply or primarily to its demographic prowess—separatist Orthodoxy is thriving because it is the only form of Judaism today that defines itself in opposition to mainstream American culture. Whereas the unspoken rule in secular American life is a value-neutral relativism that views theological commitment with skepticism, the Orthodox Jew knows with certainty exactly what he believes. While the crass materialism of secular life induces us to gratify our needs—whether through unearned affirmation ("treat yourself") or as therapeutic salve (self-care)—the urge to self-gratification for the Orthodox Jew is an evil inclination to be combated and repressed. Mainstream American ideology puts the individual at the center; for the Orthodox Jew, the center of life is Torah and, consequently, obligations to God, family, and community. These commitments are what have enabled Orthodoxy's unlikely ability to flourish, more than any other stream of American Judaism, during secular modernity's apogee.

To be sure, though, separatist Orthodoxy faces challenges of its own, including ones beyond the obvious pitfalls often so evident to secular liberals peering in from the outside. Despite the ubiquity of social media and the plagues wrought by Big Tech, Orthodoxy has managed to maintain communal integrity and insulate itself from many of the worst pathologies of secular life. But it is far from immune to all of them. There is a fine line between separatism and chauvinism. In many ways the crassness of U.S. public discourse is leaving its mark on Orthodox life. With the passing of the great immigrant rabbis, there are no longer any towering religious authorities to guide communities through today's political turbulence and fast-moving technological changes. In the coming years, separatist Orthodoxy is poised to assume a much more central role in setting the tone of organized Jewish life and politics, but no new religious leader has emerged who can speak to Orthodoxy's enlarged responsibility for the future of American Judaism. And as affluence increasingly appears to be the main form of pseudo-assimilation within the strictures of a Torah-true life, opposition to conspicuous consumption has lessened dramatically. Many in separatist Orthodox communities have become wealthy, and with wealth comes new, market-manufactured needs. In the end, the iPhone finds us all.

Each of the four paths has something to teach us. While the affiliated mainstream appears to have been dethroned from the position of near-total hegemony that it enjoyed during the years of the postwar consensus, it remains an object lesson in institution building. Although we have entered a post-denominational, even post-institutional age of American Judaism, the establishment organizations, with their outsize bureaucracies and architectural contributions to match, will serve to remind future generations that it was not always so. They will become monuments to what a mode of Jewish life that is passing from the scene was able to achieve.

In many ways, the Judaism of prophetic protest arose as a rebuke to the complacency embodied by mainstream organizational life. In the decade since its emergence, this new Jewish left has almost single-handedly revived and recovered streams of oppositional Jewish politics that had nearly been forgotten—Jewish socialism and anarchism, diasporism and anti-Zionism. At a time when the diminished yet still powerful Jewish establishment has tried to quash almost all criticism of Israel, and when some prominent Jewish organizational leaders have found common cause with the hard right (in America and, of course, in Israel), prophetic protesters have offered an alternative form of Jewish politics in the streets—one committed first and foremost to solidarity with the marginalized and the oppressed.

In synagogues around the country, neo-Reformers have staged a different sort of revolution. Having made inclusivity into a sacred virtue, they have transformed liberal Judaism into America's most welcoming monotheism. Step into almost any neo-Reform–style congregation and one will find exemplars of open-mindedness and attentiveness to difference. Because of the premium that the neo-Reformers place on acceptance, their ranks are well-positioned to grow through the next century. Its flexibility about what makes a person Jewish, its capacity to contain and even celebrate other ethnic and religious traditions—these features will make neo-Reform a potential home for the growing number of Jews from multi-faith and multiethnic backgrounds.

Among all these varied paths, none approaches separatist Orthodoxy's practice of communal solidarity. It is only within Orthodox communities where a distinctly Jewish social safety net still exists. Free wedding gowns for brides, subsidized religious day school, organizations that help cancer patients find health insurance and cover the cost of treatment—all are features of an internal Haredi welfare state, of a religious society unaware of its own socialist tendencies. A remarkable emphasis on giving charity and on cultivating the virtues of character makes a system like this one possible. The world of separatist Orthodoxy is a parallel universe—spiritually and practically—to the rest of American Jewish life.

III.

Many people, I suspect, will find that they don't fit easily into these four categories. I know I don't either. But by virtue of my family and the course of my life, I have walked through, or sometimes along, these different paths. I was born and raised within the institutions of mainline affiliated life, but also with a background consciousness of the alternative that Orthodoxy offers. As a teenager I began to bristle at the political conformism and moral compromises that mainstream Jewish life entailed and departed toward the path of prophetic protest. In many ways I came of age within the new Jewish social movements of the 2010s. Through those years of intense political activity, I met, learned from, and lived with people who had grown up, or joined belatedly, other paths too. I sat with them over Shabbat lunch tables, marched with them in demonstrations, studied with them in classes, and prayed with them in their shuls.

The process of working on a book can be transformative, and that has been the case for me. I have not ended this project in the same place, or on the same path—religiously, politically, personally—as I started. I suppose that is only natural given how much has happened during the roughly three years that have passed. Today, I live on the border between some of the different paths in Jewish life, or, perhaps more accurately, at the points of their jagged intersection.

The years of writing deepened my commitment to Jewish observance. I had already been a practicing Jew, a kosher-keeping vegan and synagogue attender, with a long-running, regular *chavruta*, learning rabbinic texts as is traditionally done in a pair. But daily immersion in the details of Jewish history and politics and halachic and theological arguments illuminated for me anew not only the undying merit of the tradition into which I was born but also its truth, in the sense of the word as the theologian Stanley Hauerwas has used it: "I mean that I am willing to die for it." After years of excuses and half measures, telling myself I would get around to it one day, I began to keep the Sabbath and all other holy days in strict accordance with Jewish law, don tefillin each morning, and wear a kippah, as I had been instructed as a child in school. I have also been lucky that I found a partner to walk with me in a shared life lived with commanded-ness at its core.

As part of my reimmersion in normative Jewish practice, I began to rethink how to navigate political differences in Jewish life. For much of my twenties, I refused to pray alongside people with whom I disagreed deeply or whose views I found abhorrent, especially on Israel/Palestine. I could not bear the thought that as we directed our intentions heavenward, they were petitioning for divine intervention in ways I believed would cause great injustice. There were times when I needed a synagogue but felt I could not go, because this would have meant endorsing a politics that I reject. Now, I prefer to pray with those I disagree with; I find that I have more to learn from them than I realized.

In retrospect, I had placed far too much value in speech acts and offhand comments and undervalued the small acts and often unacknowledged deeds that shape the fabric of Jewish community life. I was too young to fully grasp that virtue is not expressed through bold declarations of uncompromising ideology but through subtle acts of kindness and service without reward. It is now obvious to me that some of the people whose stated politics I find most objectionable are

exemplars of communal and familial devotion, caring and gentle people, while others whose politics I once found unimpeachable live, by
comparison, oriented mainly around the pursuit of pleasure and the
whims of the self.

This does not mean that I abandoned my politics—the opposite. It
turned out that by self-exiling from Jewish spaces where I assumed I
would not be welcomed because of my views, I had missed out on opportunities to discuss, explain, and even persuade other people. I had
so demonized people I perceived as my ideological opponents that I
could not fathom that they might be willing to hear what I had to say.
To my surprise, many are. By remaining cloistered mainly among
those who share their views and lifestyle, many progressive Jews, especially young ones, forgo the important work of making themselves
comprehensible to the people whom they would hope to recruit to
their cause.

Increasingly, I have begun to wonder, what if all of us who had
distanced ourselves from religious life because of our opposition to the
occupation of the West Bank and Gaza were to insist, simply by virtue
of our presence, on the compatibility of anti-occupation politics with
halachic observance—despite, or rather because of, the discomfort
this would entail? Of course, there are already people doing this (many
of my friends), enough to cause concern among those on the right, like
the historian Gil Troy and refusenik-turned-politician Natan Sharansky, who have labeled critics of Israel who remain "deeply involved
Jewishly" as "un-Jews." What might happen if there were more of us?

But my shift in outlook is the result of disappointment as much as
inspiration. I emerged at the end of this project acutely concerned with
the pernicious effects of mainstream American culture, especially on
non-Orthodox Jewish life. I had embarked on writing in the hope of
debunking the pervasive narrative of decline. I wanted to show that
the in-house *gevalters* of organized Judaism had misread the landscape. Instead, I may have ended up even more pessimistic than they

are. Except for the pockets of dynamism that I chronicle in this book, I found a mainline affiliated Judaism sunken into indifference, satisfied with its shallowness, and unaware of the extent of its own religious ignorance.

It seems to me that separatist Orthodoxy is right to identify the inducements of consumerism, the worship of individual choice, and the celebration of self-gratification as lethal threats to the virtues that make vibrant and committed forms of Jewish community possible: a sense of obligation to the tradition; generosity and kindness toward others; willingness to subordinate one's own needs for the good of the whole. Likewise, the compulsive power of the smartphone and the ubiquity of social media menace the text-centeredness of the Jewish tradition that is responsible for our people's unlikely survival. As early as four decades ago, the late literary scholar Harold Bloom could recognize that what most endangered the character of Jewish life was not exogamy or faithlessness but the American culture of the image, enthrallment to the televisional spectacle. "If American Jewry, of the supposedly most educated classes, assimilates and all but vanishes," Bloom wrote, "it will be because the text—all text—is dying in America."

Protecting the values core to Jewish tradition therefore necessitates consciously staking out a great distance from the mainstream of American cultural life. Yet this is something few American Jewish leaders outside of Orthodox communities have been willing to do. Most, in fact, have done the opposite. They have celebrated Jewish contributions to American culture, high and low; some have even gone as far as to ascribe religious meaning to these putative "achievements." Many have imagined their Judaism and their Americanism as one and the same. Indeed, even as more Jews, and especially progressives, have embraced foundational critiques of the American project, the structure of feeling that historian Jonathan Sarna calls "the cult of synthesis"—"the belief that Judaism and Americanism reinforce one another, the two traditions converging in a common path"—remains predominant in much of American Jewish life.

Historically, then, the task of drawing the boundary between an imperial culture and religious life has fallen instead to Christian neo-Orthodox thinkers, such as Hauerwas, and before him, H. Richard Niebuhr. (Heschel, in his moments, and Will Herberg were perhaps exceptions to the rule.) In a way, this is ironic, for these Protestants read to a Jew like me as irrepressibly American. But it also makes sense. For most of U.S. Jewish history, our place in this country felt too tentative to reject its culture so openly, to denounce Americanism the way these Christians do, as a form of idolatry. Perhaps, though, with the American Jewish century's end, we are now sufficiently comfortable to defend our tradition from the forces that would dissolve it. For two millennia the Jewish people survived as a minority everywhere by recognizing where their Judaism ended and where the values of the surrounding society began. American Jews should learn to do so again.

The Radical Potential of Traditional Judaism

Most of all, I have become convinced of the radical potential of traditional Judaism. Of course, I believe that a life centered on the commandments, on mitzvot, is a good life in and of itself. In our current moment, it is also a profoundly and radically countercultural one.

"The very being of Judaism consists in its imposing a distinctive regime on the everyday existence of the Jew," Yeshayahu Leibowitz writes. "This system of norms is constitutive of Judaism." At its core, in other words, Judaism is a religion of limits and obligation—two concepts utterly opposed to the dominant currents of contemporary life. Our liberal capitalist culture celebrates boundless growth, infinite choice, and instant gratification. Traditional Judaism, by contrast, teaches the merits of long-term commitment, patience and restraint, and contentment with one's lot. Whereas liberal capitalism glorifies the individual while condemning him to an atomized and isolated existence, traditional Judaism requires that life be lived with and for others—in obligated community. Liberal capitalist culture sets the pace of life according to the market; traditional Judaism breaks the market's hold by insisting on the priority of Shabbat and Yom Tov.

Especially in times like ours, I understand that these may seem like conservative values. In a sense, they are. But I have arrived to them through my left-wing convictions, not despite them. Or, more specifically, I have found myself drawn back to traditionalism because the ambient culture of many progressive spaces and, in particular, progressive Jewish spaces has felt inadequate to the ends that they hope to pursue. Progressives talk frequently about community, but we also want to feel free to opt out of what doesn't speak to us or what seems inconvenient, archaic, or demanding. We say often we're proud to be Jewish, yet we want our Jewishness not to require too much, or even to ask anything of us at all. For all our posturing about mutual aid and ending capitalism, when was the last time any of us gave *ma'aser*, tithing the religiously required tenth of our salary to charity, or, much more uncommon, fulfilled the mitzvah of taking the poor stranger into our home?

To be clear, I don't think embracing tradition means relinquishing important progressive commitments like feminism, anti-racism, or opposition to the occupation of the West Bank and Gaza. It simply means realizing these commitments differently. The long hegemony of liberalism in American culture has meant that those who dissent to patriarchy, homophobia, and bigotry in Jewish life often end up leaving it. The associational logic of religion in America means that the cost of exit is low. That is not a bad thing. But exit should not be the only option. There are, in fact, many people committed to living out their progressive values, to fighting for them, from within the normative framework of traditional Judaism. It is not easy. But that is, I think, the point.

A series of questions has motivated the writing of this book. Is it possible to live a life defined by Judaism and, at the same time, guided by progressive values? How does one maintain one's Jewishness while grappling with the gruesome reality in Israel/Palestine? What does it take to sustain community in an era of disintegration and flux, at the start of a new cycle of large-scale geopolitical turbulence and war? I do not have all the answers. Far from it. But it is my hope that I have, here, provided a starting point to begin to formulate them.

The American Jewish Legacy

Every great diaspora has made its own epochal contribution to the chain of Jewish history. In the legendary Babylonian yeshivot of Sura and Pumbedita, in present-day Iraq, the ancient sages began to compile and codify the Oral Law, what would become the Talmud. Before their expulsion, the Jews of Golden Age Spain produced beautiful and enduring Hebrew commentary, liturgy, and poetry—much of what we know of as Jewish prayer took shape during this period. Despite facing pervasive discrimination and constant suspicion, German-speaking Jewry attempted to marry the arts and sciences of Western civilization with the traditions of Judaism and in the process produced much of what we know of as modern Jewish thought.

It is unlikely American Jewry will leave behind any enduring textual legacy. Instead, American Jewry's historical contribution will almost certainly be its diversity and its pluralism. No historic Jewish civilization has ever contained such a variety of Jewish expression and identity. No historic Jewish civilization has proved itself as accepting of non-Jews, as ritualistically malleable, even syncretic, as twenty-first-century Judaism.

But now American Jewish life has entered a period of dramatic uncertainty. The relative stability that marked the postwar years has fallen away, replaced by a violent fractiousness. The underlying conditions that shaped what we know of as American Jewish identity no longer apply. How will American Jewry fare at a time when the ground of communal life has begun to crack?

The old consensus was an anomaly. It is not coming back. But that, I think, is not a reason to mourn. A living community is a community that finds things worth fighting over. When we cease to fight, we begin to die.

ON OCTOBER 7, MOURNING, AND RESPONSIBILITY

I.

On the morning of October 7, I was on the couch in a New York City apartment, recovering from a surgery. It was the holiday of Simchat Torah, so my wife and I were not using our phones. The doctor's order of bed rest meant that I was not in synagogue; I did not hear the worried talk of those trying to piece together fragments of the news. Only after the holiday's end did I begin to understand the scale of what had happened. Even then, it was not yet possible to grasp the enormity of the attacks.

For days immediately after October 7, my wife and I huddled on the sofa for hours, glued to a livestream of Israeli TV, and cried. We were pulled into a tunnel of grief. We lost track of time. We forgot to eat. The news was a blur of devastating testimony: babies and toddlers torn away from their families; hundreds of young people gunned down at an outdoor rave; corpses mutilated, desecrated, incinerated; hostages, including the elderly, dragged back to Gaza, tortured and assaulted.

Each WhatsApp notification brought with it the fear that someone we knew was missing or had been killed. We frantically texted our closest people in Israel. They all were safe, but several acquaintances had been killed—a few at the rave, another in his home. Everyone we knew seemed to have lost someone or knew someone who had. My Facebook feed was an infinite scroll of mourning: friends posting and reposting images of lost or murdered loved ones, plaintive calls for help.

In those early days, before Israel's massive invasion of the Gaza Strip began, the responses of some on the U.S. left, including people I knew personally, shocked me. It turned out that people who were supposed to have been interlocutors, self-professed human rights defenders, and even would-be colleagues supported and justified Hamas's unspeakable acts. Progressive writers declared "glory" to the Hamas fighters or proclaimed October 7 a day of "celebration." Lawyers who made their careers criticizing Israel's violations of international law twisted themselves in defense of Hamas's war crimes.

Yet, looking back, perhaps I should not have been surprised. Although I had only allowed myself to admit such fears in fleeting journal entries or the dark of a sleepless night, I had long dreaded a moment like this.

Over the previous two years, I had reported from Israel/Palestine several times, trekking in and out of the occupied West Bank. The situation there was already volatile. The Israeli army had killed more Palestinians in 2022 than in any year since the second intifada. Settler violence displaced entire hamlets in the area of the south Hebron Hills, while in Palestinian towns like Huwara and Turmus 'Ayya, radical hilltop youths carried out a series of vicious pogroms. New groups of young Palestinian militants, unaffiliated with any political faction, were carrying out bold shooting attacks on Israeli settlers and checkpoints. An explosion seemed just around the corner. Like most observers—even Israeli military intelligence—I assumed that when everything ignited, the epicenter would be the West Bank. Fatally, Gaza was an afterthought.

There seemed to be a high probability that, sooner or later, a mass-casualty event would claim the lives of dozens, maybe even hundreds of Israelis. That was the scale on which, before October 7, we measured such things. I imagined it would resemble the terror attacks of the second intifada, against the backdrop of which I had come of age: suicide bombers detonating on buses, restaurants shredded by shrapnel.

But I knew that whatever form this looming attack took, when the bomb went off the Jewish left would face its most serious test. For reasons of moral integrity and political strategy, we would need to find a way to oppose the killing of innocent Israeli civilians, to mourn with our Jewish families—and, at the same time, remain resolute in our opposition to Israel's occupation and prepare to protest what was all but guaranteed to be the Israeli army's disproportionate and devastating response. We would need to do this even if it meant angering the Palestinian activists who would see any grief for dead Israelis as politically unacceptable, and even if it meant drawing the ire of those on the left who believe that any action taken in an anti-colonial struggle, no matter how ghastly its civilian toll, is justified.

The alternative would mean severing the ties between our movement and the people in whose name we spoke. To refuse to mourn the deaths of Israeli Jews as Jews would, in effect, mean denying our membership in the broader Jewish people, the plurality of whom live in Israel. It would be an untenable, even perverse kind of disavowal. How could we continue to protest Israel as Jews, a relationship of antagonism that nonetheless also presupposed some sense of identification—that was, after all, the strategic rationale—and yet be unable to grieve for our fellow Jews?

On October 7 and the days that followed, a vocal segment of the Jewish left did precisely this. They failed the test. For instance, one Jewish left-wing historian argued that there was no way to mourn dead Israeli civilians without "tithing ideologically to the IDF." And since their deaths had already been "pre-grieved," in his ugly turn of phrase, by virtue of the West's guilt for the Holocaust and consequent support for Israel's actions, there was, he claimed, no reason to mourn anyway. Many people seemed to agree with him, never mind that there was no shortage of left-wing Israelis, among them prominent Palestinian citizens of Israel like Ayman Odeh—leader of the socialist, Arab-led Hadash Party—who managed to do what some American leftists claimed was impossible.

In the immediate aftermath of October 7, having become barely distinguishable from one another, IfNotNow and JVP mobilized to protest Israel's anticipated massive retaliation. Yet in doing so they likewise could hardly muster a word about the 1,200 dead Israelis or the more than 250 held hostage. When they acknowledged at all that some Jews might be grieving—for friends, for family, for their people—it was, for the most part, only to argue that such grief ought not be used to justify the impending war.

According to Jewish tradition, mourning is a collective endeavor. We mourn the dead as a member of a community and as a member of a people. Kaddish, the prayer for the dead, can only be said with a quorum. But by insisting that no public expression of grief for Israeli Jews was acceptable, some on the left demanded from those of us who were mourning what was tantamount to communal and familial renunciation: that we accept that our friends and loved ones be killed and tortured—acts imagined by erstwhile comrades as part of some cleansing, liberatory event—and that we not speak of their deaths. This was a cruel demand that no differential of power, even one as great as that between Israelis and Palestinians, made acceptable. It also seemed to me that this demand would not have been made of any other people, nor was it one to which any self-respecting member of a people could possibly agree.

The pose of radical hard-heartedness was, and remains, the easy way out—an abdication of moral judgment costumed as sober realpolitik. The exceedingly difficult but morally imperative task of the Jewish left is to hold our particular people to act in accordance with the universalist values we find within the sources of our tradition. The "Jewish" part of the label means we begin from the place of a broad, if fractious, sense of Jewish collectivity; the "left" part means we are committed unflinchingly to the belief in the inherent, even divine, worth of every human life. Instead of framing Israel's instrumentalization of Jewish grief in the service of war crimes as inevitable and inexorable, it was—and still is—our responsibility to demonstrate that it need not be. That grief is political does not mean it only serves power, or that some victims are unworthy of it because of the power that grief serves.

II.

As I write this, Israel's war on Gaza still rages. Its punishing bombardment has killed more than 30,000 Palestinians, most of them civilians. An estimated 70 percent of homes in Gaza, an unthinkable sum, have been damaged or destroyed. Some 2 million people, most of them already the descendants of refugees, have been displaced from their homes again. The dry calculus of suffering cannot capture the horror this war has wrought.

Entire neighborhoods have been leveled and entire extended families wiped out. A man named Khaled al-'Azayzeh lost twenty-six members of his family when their home was bombed; in the al-Zeitoun neighborhood of Gaza City, fifteen members of the extended al-Dos family were killed by an Israeli air strike, including an eighteen-month-old baby; twelve members of the Hijazi family were killed in another strike, among them three young children. Repeated sieges and shelling of hospitals eviscerated Gaza's already fragile health system. Doctors have been forced to operate without anesthesia, with vinegar for antiseptic and rags for bandages. The morgues are filled, and health officials have reportedly resorted to storing bodies in ice cream trucks, or to burials in mass graves.

Each day, a new artifact of sadism appears to surface on social media. Israeli soldiers grinning as they detonate an apartment block. A montage of stripped and blindfolded men, piled into the backs of pickup trucks, set to electronic dance music, and uploaded to You-Tube. Soldiers, again, posing triumphantly in front of a home they have set on fire. Adherents of the Chabad-Lubavitch movement dropping a banner, staging the mock opening of a Chabad house over a pile of smoldering ruins. Elite combat units, decked out in balaclavas and night-vision goggles, scrawling Jewish stars and Hebrew verses on the walls of blown-out homes. The images do not stop. They have documented themselves meticulously. They seem proud of what they have done.

Israel has prosecuted this war with no coherent strategy. At the outset, the Netanyahu government proclaimed two mutually exclusive goals: the destruction of Hamas in the Gaza Strip and the return of all the hostages. So far it has achieved neither. Even after more than six months of fighting, Hamas can still launch rockets at Israeli cities and towns. More than once, the Netanyahu government has rejected ceasefire proposals, arguing that only a "total victory" can assure the hostages' return. Meanwhile, over one hundred Israelis remain in captivity; according to a recent intelligence estimate, around a third might already be dead. The indefinite prolongation of the war has, for Netanyahu, also served the convenient purpose of delaying the day when he will be called to account for the enormous failure that occurred on his watch.

One could be forgiven, then, for thinking that the stated goals were beside the point—that the goal, mainly, has been vengeance itself. In early October IDF spokesperson Daniel Hagari said that the army was "focusing on maximum damage." Leading Israeli politicians have spouted eliminationist rhetoric. "We are fighting human animals and must act accordingly," current defense minister Yoav Gallant declared. Deputy speaker of the Knesset and Likud member Nissim Vaturi called to "Burn Gaza." Former defense minister Avigdor Liberman proclaimed, "There are no innocents in Gaza." That South Africa has taken Israel to the International Court of Justice for the charge of genocide, no matter what the verdict turns out to be, is a mark of shame and a bitter historical irony—that we, the victims of last century's emblematic catastrophe, now find ourselves accused of committing the same crime.

As appalling as Israel's response to Hamas's attack has been, it also has not been surprising. In recent years, Israeli political life took a sharp turn to the right. Some of the most extreme and violent settlers rose to positions of power, boosted by Netanyahu in his desperate bid for political survival. Israeli politicians made increasing threats to carry out a second Nakba, a dangerous symptom of the mounting support for the forced expulsion of the Palestinians and a decisive, apocalyptic conflagration. More than half a century of military rule over another people corroded the moral compass of Israeli society. The stage seemed set for a new catastrophe.

If the U.S. left failed morally on October 7, against this backdrop of mounting horror, the organized American Jewish community has failed even more spectacularly. It had already grown indifferent to Palestinian suffering over years of unequivocal support for Israeli government policies. After the gruesome Hamas-led attack, its dehumanization of Palestinians has reached new heights. Prominent American Jewish leaders, among them self-professed liberals, now assert that there is no amount of death that might lead them to reconsider the justness of the war and call for the fighting to continue indefinitely. Jewish establishment figures have thrown their weight behind hysterical attempts to censor and expel advocates for Palestinian rights from the U.S. public sphere, further fueling a culture war that was already at fever pitch. They have instrumentalized accusations of antisemitism in ugly public spectacles, making the fight against real and resurgent antisemitism in U.S. politics even harder.

But what the American Jewish establishment fails to understand is that far more than Hamas's rockets, or left-wing pro-Palestinianism on U.S. campuses, the real threat to Israel's survival is a return to the status-quo ante—to the undemocratic one-state reality. The October 7 attacks proved that the occupation-management paradigm is unsustainable and guarantees only the loss of future lives. With Israel increasingly isolated on the world stage, maintaining the occupation also risks burning whatever shred of international legitimacy Israel has left. Ending military rule in the West Bank and the siege of Gaza is necessary not just because Palestinians deserve to live with freedom and dignity; it is also necessary because it is the only way Israelis will not be forced to live forever by the sword.

III.

The American public's perception of Israel has shifted in an unprecedented way. You can feel it in the streets and coffee shops, on college campuses and in office suites. "Stop the Genocide" appears graffitied on Forty-Second Street in New York. The keffiyeh has become a ubiquitous accessory on Yale's quad. Palestinian flags now hang in the crenelated windows of expensive Brooklyn brownstones. For now, a canyon-sized generational divide prevails between those under twenty-nine, most of whom believe Israel is carrying out a genocide, and those over fifty, most of whom still say they take Israel's side. As those whose image of Israel remains an idyll—a small, embattled social democracy surrounded by hostile countries—depart the scene, the material consequences of this shift will begin to be felt.

For Israel, this change in U.S. public opinion constitutes a major geostrategic challenge. It is hard to overstate how utterly dependent Israel has been on America in fighting its war. The United States has sent Israel billions of dollars in emergency military aid on top of its already substantial non-wartime backing and supplied Israel with thousands of missiles, tens of thousands of artillery shells, and tens of thousands of M16s. Of course, Israel has weathered earlier periods of much more tepid U.S. support. But if, in a future war of the same or even higher stakes, a much less friendly U.S. government refuses to supply Israel with the armaments it needs, then the Jewish state may truly find itself in existential jeopardy.

One surprising consequence of the current war is that it has, even if only temporarily, revived talk of a two-state solution after years when many, including myself, assumed it was dead. Squandering this unforeseen opportunity will supercharge the already growing calls for Israel to democratize the unitary regime it currently maintains between the river and the sea by dissolving itself. This may be the last chance.

At the same time, the low hum of ambient antisemitism seems to grow steadily louder. Famous racial-justice activists tweet to their hundreds of thousands of followers about the danger of "Zionist doctors" and the alleged connection between Jeffrey Epstein and the Gaza war. In Brooklyn, my wife's cousin was beaten by a group of five people shouting "Free Palestine," his black hat violently knocked off his head.

As a Jew and a progressive, I often feel closed in on from both sides, pinched between great shame and great fear. I am infuriated by the crimes of the state that acts in my name, and more worried than I have ever been by the rising acceptability of conspiratorial thinking and the demonization of Jews. It often feels like an impossible place.

But it is the place that we must hold. I understand my friends and former colleagues who wish to renounce Israel with finality and disavow any connection between their Jewish identity and the Jewish state. Yet I believe that doing so would be both a moral and political mistake. The power of our protest grows from our connection. And while Israel and Zionism are not the sum or telos of Jewishness and Judaism, thinking and acting Jewishly also requires recognizing that Israel, more than any other place, is where Jews live. To change our people, we must be with them. That is our responsibility.

ACKNOWLEDGMENTS

I would not have written this book were it not for Gary Morris and Maya Ziv, who took a chance on a twenty-six-year-old journalist with hardly a print clip to his name. Gary and Maya saw this project's potential long before I did, and they understood what I was trying to do even when I didn't. I am immensely grateful for the care and patience with which they have guided me through the process. I never imagined that I would "have" an agent, but I cannot think of a better one than Gary. Maya pushed me to write about my own life, even when I resisted, and in doing so helped me discover a voice I didn't know I had. I cannot express my thanks enough.

My great-uncle Ken and great-aunt Audrey generously spoke to me at length early in the process; without them, I would not have been able to write the book's first chapter, let alone get the small details right. Audrey's narrative of our family, "Two Sisters," provided essential inspiration for those early sections and, most of all, taught me at an early age about where I come from.

I am extraordinarily grateful to the family and friends who read drafts of the book in full and offered much-needed suggestions. Steven Mufson provided careful line edits. Daniel Judt read the whole thing and somehow saw exactly what was missing; without his insight, this book would have been much worse. Daniel Roth helped me zoom out and remember the questions I had set out to ask; his generosity was more than I could ever ask for. Raphael Magarik read the manuscript with his unbeatable eye, offered invaluable criticism, and helped save me from some of my worst impulses. Yossi Ort helped me sharpen my thoughts in places where it mattered most.

Many other people read chapters, sections, and offered guidance; this book is better because of them. From the proposal stage to copy-editing, Gabriel Fisher, my oldest friend, believed in me and pushed me to write for a broader audience; as in so much of my life, listening to his advice works. Edo Konrad parsed the book's ideological contradictions; just as important, he has had my back in hard times. Uri Ort offered constant encouragement and watched out for my best interests. My long-running *chavruta* with Maya Rosen laid the ground for much of the analysis here and helped me conceptualize the book's framing. Conversations with Pinny Huberman over the years in New Haven have enriched my life, and thus this book.

I am grateful to the editors and publications that have given my writing a home over the years. A few sections of this book first appeared as segments of essays and reporting in their pages. The idea for a political history of late twentieth-century Jewish life first took shape in an article for *The Baffler* titled "Led Astray," published in March 2020. The coverage of Cori Bush's congressional race was adapted from an article in *Jewish Currents*, published in June 2020. The interviews that appear in the section on yeshiva education were conducted as part of a recording for the *Jewish Currents* podcast, *On the Nose*. My analysis of right-wing populism in Orthodox communities appeared in an earlier form in a November 2020 *Jewish Currents* article. Finally, parts of the afterword were first developed in essays first published in *Dissent* and *The New York Review of Books*.

Writing this book while in graduate school was probably unwise, but I have been lucky that my advisors have been continuously compassionate and unfailingly supportive. David Sorkin has contributed to this book more than he probably knows. Samuel Moyn has been a model of scholarly and polemical engagement. Carolyn Dean helped me realize what I wanted to study and constantly pushes the boundaries of my thinking. Elli Stern's wise guidance has helped orient me in the world of academia. Bryan Garsten taught me to return to the classics.

Over the course of writing, I joined a family that has utterly changed my life for the better. To begin to describe the virtues of my mother-in-law, Manya Ort, would be to fail from the get-go; watching her live her values with such steadfastness inspired many parts of this book. Shabbos in Lakewood has been a refuge, and a place to learn and talk with the rest of the Ort crew. Yitzy Ort took me on the tour of the town that freezing November day; his interest has been a source of constant encouragement. Dovy Ort showed me the ropes in BMG; many of the rabbinic references in this book I owe to him. Chamim and Rabbi Eliezer Hirsch have made Philadelphia into a second home and helped me get the cover and the title right. Eliezer has shown me what true devotion to Torah and community looks like; his wisdom, I hope, graces many pages in this book. It is not possible for me to convey the extent of my thanks here to the rest of the family for welcoming me beyond any measure I could have possibly imagined. *Zachiti.*

My parents, Laura and Bennett, and my sister, Nina, put up with me turning our lives into material for this book. They have always supported my writing; I was lucky to have grown up with their tireless encouragement. Without them, none of this would have been possible. I have tried to follow their ways. I have aspired to their work ethic, conscientiousness, and commitment to family. It was they who taught me that virtue is expressed in subtle acts of kindness and service without reward. I hope this book will make them proud.

Most of all, to Shaindy, my *shutafa l'derekh*—this book is as much yours as it is mine. You read every word, at least three or four times. You talked through everything, dealt graciously with my insanity. You helped me be brave. I treasure the life we are building together. I am so looking forward to our future. I still have so much to learn from you. I love you beyond words.

NOTES

INTRODUCTION

1 **for having slapped an armed soldier:** Edo Konrad, "An Israeli and a Palestinian Slap a Soldier. Guess Who's Still in Prison?," +*972 Magazine*, March 25, 2018, https://www.972mag.com/an-israeli-and-a-palestinian -slap-a-soldier-guess-whos-still-in-prison/.

2 **epicenter of an unarmed popular resistance movement:** Ben Ehrenreich, "Is This Where the Third Intifada Will Start?," *New York Times Magazine*, March 15, 2013, https://www.nytimes.com/2013/03/17/magazine/is-this -where-the-third-intifada-will-start.html.

2 **But by 2018, when I was there, the weekly protests had largely ebbed:** Haggai Matar, "Hundreds Protest in Nabi Saleh to Demand Freedom for Tamimi Women," +*972 Magazine*, January 13, 2018, https://www.972mag .com/hundreds-protest-in-nabi-saleh-to-demand-freedom-for-tamimi -women/.

2 **left the village in some way changed by what they saw:** Lisa Goldman, "Nabi Saleh Is Where I Lost My Zionism," December 24, 2017, https:// www.972mag.com/nabi-saleh-is-where-i-lost-my-zionism.

8 **"the American century":** Henry R. Luce, "The American Century," *Diplomatic History* 23, no. 2 (Spring 1999): 159–71.

9 **"the concordance of Judaism and Americanism":** Kaufmann Kohler, "The Concordance of Judaism and Americanism," in Paul R. Mendes-Flohr and Jehuda Reinharz, eds., *The Jew in the Modern World* (New York: Oxford University Press, 1980), 372–73.

10 **"to postpone that inner reconsideration of 'Jewishness'":** Irving Howe, *World of Our Fathers: The Journey of the East European Jews to America and the Life They Found and Made* (New York: Bantam, 1980), 625.

12 **exclusionary oaths and religious tests:** David Sorkin, "Emancipation," unpublished draft of chapter for *Oxford Handbook of American Jewish History*.

12 Jews in the home and men on the street: Yehuda Leib Gordon, "Awake, My People," from Michael Stanislawksi, *For Whom Do I Toil?: Judah Leib Gordon and the Crisis of Russian Jewry* (New York: Oxford University Press, 1988), 49–50.

13 "vast sacramental heritage" . . . "subjectively possible to accept": Stephen J. Whitfield, *In Search of American Jewish Culture* (Hanover, NH: University Press of New England for Brandeis University Press, 1999), 198.

13 began to articulate a more conservative liberalism: Samuel Moyn, *Liberalism Against Itself: Cold War Intellectuals and the Making of Our Times* (New Haven, CT: Yale University Press, 2023).

14 affirmative action and busing met resistance from many American Jews: Jonathan Rieder, *Canarsie: The Jews and Italians of Brooklyn Against Liberalism* (Cambridge, MA: Harvard University Press, 1987).

14 For some, like the neoconservatives: On the making of the neoconservatives and their break with their political pasts, see, for instance, Benjamin Balint, *Running Commentary: The Contentious Magazine That Transformed the Jewish Left into the Neoconservative Right* (New York: PublicAffairs, 2010).

15 "permission to narrate": Edward Said, "Permission to Narrate," *Journal of Palestine Studies* 13, no. 3 (Spring 1984): 27–48, https://doi.org/10.2307/2536688.

16 by 2050 . . . the *majority* of the world's Jews will live in Israel: "The Future of World Religions: Population Growth Projections, 2010–2050," Pew Research Center, April 2, 2015, https://www.pewresearch.org/religion/2015/04/02/jews/.

17 "Destruction" . . . "is both liberation and risk": Gershom Scholem, *On Jews and Judaism in Crisis: Selected Essays* (New York: Schocken, 1978), 34.

18 "the nullification of the Torah may in fact be its upholding": Yitzchak Hutner, *Pachad Yitzchak: Chanukah*, Chapter 3.

CHAPTER 1: UP FROM RIVINGTON STREET

24 "a forgotten corner on the edge of Slutsk": Rachel Feigenberg, "My Town Is No Longer," in *Slutzk and Vicinity: Memorial Book*, ed. N. Chinitz and Sh. Nachmani (Tel Aviv: "Achduth" Cooperative Press, 1962), 201 [Hebrew].

24 no train station; it was connected to Slutsk only by a dirt road: Zvi Assaf, "Lyuban as I Remember It," in *Slutzk and Vicinity: Memorial Book*, 214 [Hebrew].

24 To the extent that there was industry: Feigenberg, "My Town Is No Longer," 201.

24 to serve as maids in the homes of the wealthier Jewish families in nearby cities like Babruysk: Feigenberg, 201.

24 "The town began to move, torn from its place": Feigenberg, 202–3.

25 "to describe grandfather or great-grandfather": Arthur Hertzberg, *The Jews in America: Four Centuries of an Uneasy Encounter* (New York: Columbia University Press, 1997), xi.

25 A response to the crisis of the traditional way of life: Mordechai Breuer, "Orthodoxy Between Retreat, Resistance, and Creativity," *HaMaayan* 4, no. 39 (Tamuz 5759): 17–30 [Hebrew].

26 mussar teaching associated with the Novardok Yeshiva: For this quote and an English-language introduction to the mussar movement, see Alan Morinis, *Everyday Holiness: The Jewish Spiritual Path of Mussar* (Boston: Trumpeter, 2008), 48.

26 a well-known story about Rav Yeruchom: Morinis, *Everyday Holiness*, 73–74.

26–27 "without a passport or visa it's impossible to go anywhere": See his collection of Hebrew sermons, *Meori Orot Ha-Mussar*.

27 the *Ostjuden*, whom right-wing nationalist and antisemitic political movements in Germany sought to keep out and expel: Til van Rahden, "Words and Actions: Rethinking the Social History of German Antisemitism, Breslau, 1870–1914," *German History* 18, no. 4 (October 2000): 414–38, https://doi.org/10.1191/026635500701526633. See also Peter Pulzer, *The Rise of Political Anti-Semitism in Germany and Austria* (Cambridge, MA: Harvard University Press, 1988).

28 "a migration comparable in modern Jewish history only to the flight from the Spanish Inquisition": Howe, *World of Our Fathers*, 27.

28 "numberless ordinary Jews, the folksmasn": Howe, 27.

28 "to create a base for a rebirth of their religion, or to become the other front for Israel": Arthur Hertzberg, *The Jews in America* (New York: Simon & Schuster, 1989), 373.

29 The pogroms over the first decade of the century: Jeffrey Veidlinger, *In the Midst of Civilized Europe: The Pogroms of 1918–1921 and the Onset of the Holocaust* (New York: Metropolitan Books, 2021).

29 In 1920, the ominously named anti-Bolshevik general Stanisław Bułak-Bałachowicz besieged Slutsk and the surrounding shtetls: Walter Duranty, "Guerrilla Bands Raid Soviet Russia," *New York Times*, October 23, 1920.

29 "to murder the Jews, to take their property, and to erase them from the earth": Veidlinger, *In the Midst of Civilized Europe*, 300.

29 Bułak-Bałachowicz's men entered Lyuban and raided the shtetl: Binyomin Wolfson, "Slaughter and Murder," in *Slutzk and Vicinity*, 448–55.

30 what historian Timothy Snyder has called Europe's "bloodlands": Timothy Snyder, *Bloodlands: Europe Between Hitler and Stalin* (New York: Basic Books, 2012).

30 "anyone who emigrated to America was a sinner": Chaim Waxman, *America's Jews in Transition* (Philadelphia: Temple University Press, 1983), 7.

30 **the journalist Maurice Hindus:** Maurice Hindus, "Slutzk After World War II," in *Slutzk and Vicinity,* xv–xvii.

31 **Hindus described passing on the road:** Hindus, "Slutzk After World War II," xv–xvii.

32 **"destruction of memories":** Irving Howe, *A Margin of Hope: An Intellectual Autobiography* (New York: Harcourt Brace Jovanovich, 1982), 280.

32 **"it was with the shrug of resignation their fathers had taught":** Howe, *World of Our Fathers,* 640.

32 **"History," he said not long after the book's publication:** Howe, quoted in Natalie Gittelson, "American Jews Rediscover Orthodoxy," *New York Times Magazine,* September 30, 1984.

32 **"Inheritance is never a *given*, it is always a task":** Jacques Derrida, *Specters of Marx: The State of the Debt, the Work of Mourning, and the New International* (New York: Routledge, 2006), 67.

32 **"That we *are* heirs does not mean that we *have* or we *receive* this or that":** Derrida, *Specters of Marx,* 68.

34 **They encountered discrimination in housing, employment, and higher education:** David Sorkin, *Jewish Emancipation: A History Across Five Centuries* (Princeton, NJ: Princeton University Press, 2019), 348–50.

34 **"a whiteness of a different color":** Matthew Frye Jacobson, *Whiteness of a Different Color: European Immigrants and the Alchemy of Race* (Cambridge, MA: Harvard University Press, 1999).

34 **"the exhilaration of acceptance":** Eric L. Goldstein, *The Price of Whiteness: Jews, Race, and American Identity* (Princeton, NJ: Princeton University Press, 2006), 6.

35 **"Indeed, more Jews lived there than in any other city in all of Jewish history":** Hasia R. Diner, *Lower East Side Memories: A Jewish Place in America* (Princeton, NJ: Princeton University Press, 2000), 35.

35 **on Allen Street, sex workers took in customers:** Melech Epstein, *Jewish Labor in U.S.A: An Industrial, Political and Cultural History of the Jewish Labor Movement* (New York: Ktav Publishing House, 1969), 104.

35 **They endured "twelve-to-fourteen-hour days":** Annelise Orleck, *Common Sense and a Little Fire: Women and Working-Class Politics in the United States, 1900–1965* (Chapel Hill: University of North Carolina Press, 2017), 32.

35 **"'America, the thief'":** Hertzberg, *The Jews in America,* 1.

35 **"nothing but a shadow—an echo—a chimera of lunatics and crazy immigrants":** Anzia Yezierska, "America and I," *Scribner's Magazine* 71, no. 2 (February 1922): 161.

35 **"The long desert of wasting days of drudgery":** Yezierska, "America and I," 162.

36 **Karl Marx once likened capital to a vampire:** Karl Marx, *Capital: A Critique of Political Economy* (New York: Modern Library, 1906), 257.

36 On March 25, 1911, in the Asch Building: Richard A. Greenwald, "'The Burning Building at 23 Washington Place': The Triangle Fire, Workers and Reformers in Progressive Era New York," *New York History* 83, no. 1 (Winter 2002): 55–91.

36 "They crashed through broken glass": "141 Men and Girls Die in Waist Factory Fire," *New York Times*, March 26, 1911.

36 "For days after the fire": Greenwald, "'The Burning Building at 23 Washington Place,'" 66.

36 "Some vowed to avenge": Greenwald, 66.

37 In 1909, more than 20,000 garment workers had gone on strike: Epstein, *Jewish Labor in U.S.A.*, 387.

37 In 1910, the city's cloak makers staged a general strike: Epstein, 387.

37 "One by one, the sweatshops were assaulted and demolished": Epstein, 387.

38 In the early spring of 1892, two cloak makers named Sam Greenberg and Harry Lasker: Maximilian Hurwitz, *The Workmen's Circle: Its History, Ideals, Organization and Institutions* (New York: Workmen's Circle, 1936), 13.

38 "into a mighty oak with hundreds of branches and myriads of leaves": Hurwitz, *The Workmen's Circle*, 11.

38 The Workmen's Circle indeed expanded rapidly: Epstein, *Jewish Labor in U.S.A.*, 301.

39 another tension at the heart of that left-wing, working-class Jewish culture: Arthur Liebman, *Jews and the Left* (New York: John Wiley and Sons, 1979), 283.

39 the idiosyncratic Marxist intellectual Benjamin Feigenbaum: Epstein, *Jewish Labor in U.S.A.*, 301.

39 The Workmen's Circle declaration of principles: Epstein, 306.

39 It positioned itself: Epstein, 306.

40 the pragmatism of the Workmen's Circle would supplant its earlier radicalism: Liebman, *Jews and the Left*, 304.

40 "Though no less an idealist than the intellectual": Hurwitz, *The Workmen's Circle*, 14.

42 "The gradual disappearance of the Jewish working class": Epstein, *Jewish Labor in U.S.A.*, xlii.

42 Epstein had lived through the American Jewish working class's entire trajectory: Melech Epstein, *Pages from a Colorful Life: An Autobiographical Sketch* (Miami Beach, FL: I. Block Publishing Company, 1971).

42 "The classical Marxist doctrine": Epstein, *Jewish Labor in U.S.A.*, xlii.

42 "The Jewish labor movement, in its peak years": Epstein, xlii.

43 what Hasia Diner called the "main event" of American Jewish history: Hasia Diner, *The Jews of the United States: 1654 to 2000* (Berkeley: University of California Press, 2006), 206.

43 "lengthy and complicated process of middle-class Americanization": Diner, *The Jews of the United States*, 206.

43 "The Jewish community enclosed one": Irving Howe, quoted in Deborah Dash Moore, *At Home in America* (New York: Columbia University Press, 1981), 63.

44 "Almost everyone retained some strands of religious feeling": Howe, *World of Our Fathers*, 257.

45 "on Washington Avenue": Moore, *At Home in America*, 74.

45 "That poor worn synagogue": Alfred Kazin, *A Walker in the City* (New York: MJF Books, 1974), 40.

46 earlier generations of Jewish socialists: For more on the Yiddish schule movement, see Barnett Zumoff, "The Secular Yiddish School and Summer Camp: A One Hundred Year History," *Jewish Currents*, August 9, 2013, https://web.archive.org/web/20140417172522/https://jewishcurrents .org/the-secular-yiddish-school-and-summer-camp-a-hundred-year -history-19879. Zumoff was also my father's camp doctor at Camp Kinder Ring.

46 "It was not for myself alone that I was expected to shine": Kazin, *A Walker in the City*, 21.

46 "I was their first American child": Kazin, 21.

47 New York City in its fleeting social democratic heyday: See Joshua Freeman, *Working-Class New York: Life and Labor Since World War II* (New York: New Press, 2001).

47 "benign in intent, only a passport to the promised land": Vivian Gornick, *Fierce Attachments: A Memoir* (New York: Farrar, Straus and Giroux, 1987), 105.

47 "I lived among my people, but I was no longer of them": Gornick, *Fierce Attachments*, 105.

48 a Yiddish radio show called *Tsuris bay Laytn*: Interview with great-uncle, October 20, 2021.

48 they articulated a story of Jewish meritocratic achievement: Karen Brodkin, *How Jews Became White Folks and What That Says About Race in America* (New Brunswick, NJ: Rutgers University Press, 1998), 139.

49 the theory of the Jews as the American model minority: Brodkin, *How Jews Became White Folks*, 139.

50 "What is the difference between a bookkeeper in the Garment District and a Supreme Court Justice?": Ruth Bader Ginsburg, Senate Confirmation Hearing, Day 1, Part 1, July 20, 1993, https://www.c-span.org/video /?45719-1/ginsburg-confirmation-hearing-day-1-part-1.

50 "I am a first-generation American on my father's side": Ginsburg, Senate Confirmation Hearing, Day 1, Part 1, July 20, 1993.

50 In 1987, Saul Bellow sent a letter to Cynthia Ozick: Saul Bellow, *Letters* (New York: Penguin, 2012), 438–39.

50 found his generation lacking: For more on Bellow and the Holocaust, see Adam Kirsch, "The Wound," *The New Republic*, March 19, 2021, https://newrepublic.com/article/101693/saul-bellow-mr-sammler-planet.

51 three-quarters of American Jews were U.S.-born: Peter Novick, *The Holocaust in American Life* (Boston: Mariner Books/Houghton Mifflin, 2000), 113.

53 Father Charles Coughlin preached antisemitic conspiracy theories: See the classic by Alan Brinkley, *Voices of Protest: Huey Long, Father Coughlin, and the Great Depression* (New York: Vintage, 1983).

53 In 1939, the German American Bund: Sarah Kate Kramer, "When Nazis Took Manhattan," *Code Switch* NPR, February 20, 2019, https://www.npr.org/sections/codeswitch/2019/02/20/695941323/when-nazis-took-manhattan.

53 America claimed responsibility not only for defeating Nazi fascism but also for liberating the camps: Novick, *The Holocaust in American Life*, 63.

53 "None of this": Novick, 63.

54 "Much of the exuberance": Philip Roth, *The Facts: A Novelist's Autobiography* (New York: Vintage, 1997), 123.

54 "It's hard to imagine": Roth, *The Facts*, 23.

54 "the first free generation of Diaspora Jews": Eugene Borowitz, *The Masks Jews Wear: The Self-Deceptions of American Jewry* (New York: Simon & Schuster), 45.

55 "About being Jewish there was nothing more to say": Roth, *The Facts*, 31.

55 "The truth is that for most Jews the American way has become the real faith": Borowitz, *The Masks Jews Wear*, 60.

55 "There will be no death camps": Herman Wouk, *This Is My God* (New York: Little, Brown and Company, 1959), 281.

56 in 1990, survivors and their children constituted only an estimated 8 percent of American Jewry: Center for Israel Education, https://israeled.org/timeline/by-1990-holocaust-survivors-and-their-descendants-make-up-eight-percent-of-the-us-jewish-population-while-in-canada-they-constitute-between-30-and-40-per-cent-of-the-jewish-community/.

56 Bellow himself wrote a belated, manic attempt: Saul Bellow, *Mr. Sammler's Planet* (New York: Penguin Classics, 2004).

57 the last commonality shared by the vast majority: Novick, *The Holocaust in American Life*, 7.

57 I once asked my great-uncle: Interview with great-uncle, October 20, 2021.

57 one of the only reasons they can give: "Jewish Americans in 2020," Pew Research Center, May 11, 2021, https://www.pewresearch.org/religion/2021/05/11/jewish-americans-in-2020/.

57 "A community cannot survive on what it remembers": Will Herberg, quoted in Edward Shapiro, *A Time for Healing: American Jewry Since World War II* (Baltimore: Johns Hopkins University Press, 1992), 225.

CHAPTER 2: COMPLETE ZIONIZATION

61 **"the pivotal decade":** Judith Stein, *Pivotal Decade: How the United States Traded Factories for Finance in the Seventies* (New Haven, CT: Yale University Press, 2011).

61 **"the suburban frontier":** Marshall Sklare and Joseph Greenblum, *Jewish Identity on the Suburban Frontier: Study of Group Survival in the Open Society* (New York: Basic Books, 1967).

61 **"The Vanishing American Jew":** Thomas B. Morgan, "The Vanishing American Jew," *Look* magazine, May 5, 1964.

62 **Before the 1960s:** David Sorkin, *Jewish Emancipation: A History Across Five Centuries* (Princeton, NJ: Princeton University Press, 2019), 348–50.

62 **"Can Judaism survive in freedom?":** Jacob Neusner, *The Challenge of America: Can Judaism Survive in Freedom?* (New York: Garland Publishing, 1993).

62 **a thought they relegated to the rumination of a sleepless night:** See Lila Corwin Berman, "American Jews and the Ambivalence of Middle-Classness," *American Jewish History* 39, no. 4 (December 2007): 409–34.

64 **"the complete Zionization":** Norman Podhoretz, "Now, Instant Zionism," *New York Times*, February 3, 1974, https://archive.nytimes.com/www .nytimes.com/books/99/02/21/specials/podhoretz-zion.html.

64 **"So long as it goes hanging on":** Podhoretz, "Now, Instant Zionism."

65 **became a central theme:** See Jonathan D. Sarna, *American Judaism: A History* (New Haven, CT: Yale University Press, 2019), 333.

65 **Hannah Arendt's *Eichmann in Jerusalem*:** See Hannah Arendt, *Eichmann in Jerusalem: A Report on the Banality of Evil* (New York: Penguin Classics, 2006).

65 **While Jewish theologians debated:** See, for example, Emil L. Fackenheim, *To Mend the World: Foundations of Post-Holocaust Jewish Thought* (Bloomington: Indiana University Press, 1994). See also Richard L. Rubenstein, *After Auschwitz: History, Theology, and Contemporary Judaism* (Baltimore: Johns Hopkins University Press, 1992).

65 **"fundamentally vicarious":** Sorkin, *Jewish Emancipation*, 351.

66 **"the long 1970s":** Bruce J. Schulman, *The Seventies: The Great Shift in American Culture, Society, and Politics* (Cambridge, MA: Da Capo Press, 2002), xvi.

67 **"The mood that had engulfed the country":** Amos Oz, *In the Land of Israel* (San Diego: Harcourt Brace Jovanovich, 1983), 132.

68 **"Israel is the ultimate reality":** M. J. Rosenberg, "Israel Without Apology," in James Sleeper and Alan L. Mintz, eds., *The New Jews* (New York: Vintage Books, 1971), 82.

68 **a much larger reconfiguration of American liberal politics:** See Marc Dollinger, *Quest for Inclusion: Jews and Liberalism in Modern America* (Princeton, NJ: Princeton University Press, 2000), 203–5.

69 "In the past": Stokely Carmichael, "What We Want," *New York Review of Books*, September 22, 1966.
69 "The Jew is a white man": James Baldwin, "Negroes Are Anti-Semitic Because They're Anti-White," *New York Times*, April 9, 1967, https:// archive.nytimes.com/www.nytimes.com/books/98/03/29/specials/baldwin -antisem.html?fbclid=IwAR09N1nHAdgTseVmfOY_ypLQCbqp2RVauSJ4W _emCc80tR5j9sz8BcJS3KM.
69 "is singled out by Negroes": Baldwin, "Negroes Are Anti-Semitic."
69 "One does not wish": Baldwin, "Negroes Are Anti-Semitic."
70 "imperialistic Zionist war": Renata Adler, "Letter from the Palmer House," *New Yorker*, September 15, 1967.
70 "an incendiary spectacle, sterile, mindless": Adler, "Letter from the Palmer House."
70 It was also a model for what a self-confident politics: See Marc Dollinger, *Black Power, Jewish Politics: Reinventing the Alliance in the 1960s* (Waltham, MA: Brandeis University Press, 2018), 6–11.
70 "The legitimation of the assertion of the validity of distinctive group interests": Nathan Glazer, *American Judaism* (Chicago: University of Chicago Press, 1972), 174.
71 "The black example": Glazer, *American Judaism*, 174.
71 "active involvement in the civil rights movement was 'past nicht'": Adam Ferziger, "'Outside the Shul': The American Soviet Jewry Movement and the Rise of Solidarity Orthodoxy, 1964–1986," *Religion and American Culture: A Journal of Interpretation* 22, no. 1 (Winter 2012): 83–130, 102.
72 his group provided the shock troops: For an insider's account, see Yossi Klein Halevi, *Memoirs of a Jewish Extremist: The Story of a Transformation* (New York: Harper Perennial, 2014).
72 Kahane's followers staged a bomb attack: David Bird, "4 J.D.L. Members Held in Bombings," *New York Times*, June 17, 1972, https://www.nytimes .com/1972/06/17/archives/4-jdl-members-held-in-bombings-4-jdl-members -held-in-bombings.html.
73 political scientist Charles Liebman surveyed the metamorphosis: Charles S. Liebman, *Report to the American Jewish Congress Task Force on Priorities*, April 1979, https://www.bjpa.org/content/upload/bjpa/lieb/Liebman -ReporttotheAmericanJewishCongress.pdf.
73 "Israeli policy is one of unequivocal support for Israel": Liebman, *Report to the American Jewish Congress*, 42.
73 "survivalist" dialectic: Liebman, 56.
73 "A strong America and strengthening America's global position": Liebman, 57.
74 "the positions reflected in *Commentary* magazine": Liebman, 57.
74 They described the tumult of post-1960s America: Justin Vaïsse, *Neoconservatism: The Biography of a Movement* (Cambridge, MA: Belknap Press of Harvard University Press, 2010), 68–69.

74 **"I think that Jews must once again begin"**: Norman Podhoretz, "Is It Good for the Jews?," *Commentary*, February 1972.

74 **"a litmus test to all political judgments"**: Vaïsse, *Neoconservatism*, 68–69.

75 **Anti-Americanism appeared in the neoconservative mind as a surrogate for antisemitism**: Vaïsse, 69.

75 **roughly 40 percent of American Jews voted for Ronald Reagan**: Jonathan Sarna, "The Jewish Vote in Presidential Elections," *Shma* 42, no. 686 (January 2012).

75 **"Those Jews who had voted for [Reagan] did so"**: Norman Podhoretz, *Why Are Jews Liberals?* (New York: Doubleday, 2009), 181.

77 **"identity spirituality"**: Shaul Magid, *American Post-Judaism: Identity and Renewal in a Postethnic Society* (Bloomington: Indiana University Press, 2013), 8.

77 **Some people, of course, did become Orthodox**: For more on this phenomenon and its sociological basis, see Murray Herbert Danzger, *Returning to Tradition: The Contemporary Revival of Orthodox Judaism* (New Haven, CT: Yale University Press, 1989).

77 **a phenomenon with no precedent**: Danzger, *Returning to Tradition*, 2.

77 **"a case study in institutional decay"**: Marshall Sklare, *Conservative Judaism: An American Religious Movement* (New York: Schocken, 1972), 43.

77 **yeshivas and seminaries newly built in Israel**: Danzger, *Returning to Tradition*, 62–70.

77 **to devote substantial resources**: Danzger, 90.

78 **"if antimodernism has been one of modernity's most potent legacies"**: Matthew Frye Jacobson, *Roots Too: White Ethnic Revival in Post–Civil Rights America* (Cambridge, MA: Harvard University Press, 2008), 24.

78 **In his 1982 memoir**: Paul Cowan, *An Orphan in History: Retrieving a Jewish Legacy* (New York: Doubleday, 1982).

78 **"way home"**: Cowan, *An Orphan in History*, x.

78 **"search for [his] patrimony"**: Cowan, 22.

78 **"Many people who might have once explored"**: Cowan, ix.

78 **Protests faded to mantras**: For a survey of this phenomenon, see Stephen A. Kent, *From Slogans to Mantras: Social Protest and Religious Conversion in the Late Vietnam War Era* (Syracuse, NY: Syracuse University Press, 2001), 1–6.

79 **"inward turn"**: For the most extensive treatment of the turn inward, as well as left-wing and liberal opposition to it, see Michael E. Staub, *Torn at the Roots: The Crisis of Jewish Liberalism in Postwar America* (New York: Columbia University Press, 2002). See also Sarna, *American Judaism: A History*.

80 **what had been a sleepy, moribund Conservative synagogue**: Edward Abramson, *A Circle in the Square: Rabbi Shlomo Riskin Reinvents the Synagogue* (Jerusalem: Urim, 2008), 80.

80 **something of a *ba'al teshuva* himself**: Abramson, *A Circle in the Square*, 54.

81 chose Yeshiva University over Harvard: Abramson, 58.
81 lectures on Jewish approaches to sexuality: Abramson, 121.
81 the footsteps of the messiah: Abramson, 118.
81 "redemption had seemed near": Abramson, 118.
81 "Lincoln Square was exploding": Interview with Rabbi Ephraim Buchwald, December 14, 2021.
82 "It was a happening": Interview with Rabbi Ephraim Buchwald.
82 "was standing room only": Interview with Rabbi Ephraim Buchwald.
82 a cover story by the journalist Cathryn Jakobson: "The New Orthodox: A Jewish Revival on the Upper West Side," *New York Magazine*, November 17, 1986.
82 a young heterosexual couple: See cover, *New York Magazine*, November 17, 1986.
82 shot from an apartment in Lincoln Towers: Interview with David Eisner, January 5, 2022. Today, the view has since been blocked by Trump-owned real estate.
83 Riskin and Buchwald's leadership was charismatic, even ecstatic: Abramson, *A Circle in the Square*, 188–89.
83 Riskin would jump up and down: Abramson, 188–89.
83 Passover seders outside on the sidewalk: Interview with Rabbi Ephraim Buchwald.
84 "it was a vehicle to market Judaism": Interview with Rabbi Ephraim Buchwald.
84 something that one chose: See Danzger, *Returning to Tradition*, 327.
85 "Our parents prayed for a melting pot": Interview with Rabbi Ephraim Buchwald.
85 "to drive G-d out of the house of Israel": Elchonon Bunim Wasserman, *Epoch of the Messiah* (London: published for Histadruth Zeire Agudath Israel by Hachinuch Hebrew Publishing House, 1948).
85 a satanic test of the Jewish people's faith: Rabbi Yoel Teitelbaum, *Vayoel Moshe* (Hotzaas Yerushalyim, 2012) [Hebrew].
85 In 1958, Rabbi Schneerson: Joseph Telushkin, *Rebbe: The Life and Teachings of Menachem M. Schneerson, the Most Influential Rabbi in Modern History* (New York: HarperWave, 2014), 74.
85 "One must go to a place where nothing is known of Godliness": Telushkin, *Rebbe*, 74.
86 "parked Ryder trucks started to appear in Manhattan": Telushkin, 80.
86 a one-sided debate between Rabbi Buchwald and Chabad: Rabbi Buchwald claims he and the Lincoln Square community pioneered the mitzvah mobile before Chabad.
86 A militarist sensibility: See Telushkin, *Rebbe*, 80, 88.
87 debated the "religious meaning of the Six-Day War": Shear Yashuv Cohen, Norman Lamm, Pinchas Peli, Michael Wyschogrod, and Walter S.

Wurzburger, "The Religious Meaning of the Six Day War: A Symposium," *Tradition: A Journal of Orthodox Thought* 10, no. 1 (Summer 1968), 5–20.

87 cautioned against viewing the war through a messianic lens: Lamm in "The Religious Meaning of the Six Day War," 7.

87 "We are already on a very advanced stage of the Messianic era": Peli in "The Religious Meaning of the Six Day War," 11.

87 "we are now living in *yemot ha-mashiach*": Cohen in "The Religious Meaning of the Six Day War," 13.

87 "Singing the *Gemora* tune": Avraham ben Shmuel, "Watching the Airplanes," *Jewish Observer* 14, no. 9 (June 1980): 19.

87 "Praise the Lord and pass the ammunition!": Ben Shmuel, "Watching the Airplanes," 19.

88 The Messiah could not be reduced to a shift in geopolitics: Lamm in "The Religious Meaning of the Six Day War," 15.

90 took stock of the already visible changes: Bernard Rosenberg and Irving Howe, "Are American Jews Turning Toward the Right?," reprinted in Lewis A. Coser and Irving Howe, eds., *The New Conservatives: A Critique from the Left* (New York: Quadrangle/*New York Times*, 1974).

90 "an inward turn": Rosenberg and Howe, "Are American Jews Turning Toward the Right?," 87.

91 "There is no longer a proletarian majority": Rosenberg and Howe, 67.

91 "earn like Episcopalians but vote like Puerto Ricans": Joseph Berger, "Milton Himmelfarb, Wry Essayist, 87, Dies," *New York Times*, January 15, 2006, https://www.nytimes.com/2006/01/15/nyregion/milton-himmelfarb-wry-essayist-87-dies.html.

91 as the writer Leonard Fein: See, for instance, his essay *Smashing Idols: And Other Prescriptions for Jewish Continuity* (New York: Nathan Cummings Foundation, 1994).

91 The aftermath of the 1960s had left a heavy mark: Rosenberg and Howe, 74–75.

92 "we are witnessing a regrouping of forces": Rosenberg and Howe, 88.

92 American Jewish life was bifurcating: See Jack Wertheimer, *A People Divided: Judaism in Contemporary America* (Waltham, MA: Brandeis University Press, 1997), xvii.

93 "committed core": See Yehuda Kurtzer and Claire E. Sufrin, eds., *The New Jewish Canon* (Boston: Academic Studies Press, 2020), 90–96.

93 Jonathan S. Woocher's 1981 survey: Jonathan S. Woocher, "'Jewish Survivalism' as Communal Ideology: An Empirical Assessment," *Journal of Jewish Communal Service* 57, no. 4 (Summer 1981).

94 "Among communally active Jews today": Woocher, "'Jewish Survivalism,'" 296.

94 the new Jewish "civil religion": Jonathan S. Woocher, *Sacred Survival: The Civil Religion of American Jews* (Bloomington: Indiana University Press, 1986), 67–74.

94 "Conspicuously missing from the picture of civil religion": Woocher, *Sacred Survival*, 91.

94 "at once too hostile and too hospitable": Woocher, 114.

94 "the paramount moral importance": Staub, *Torn at the Roots*, 118.

95 "not only appropriate but ethical in its own right": Staub, 110.

CHAPTER 3: RABIN SQUARE

99 the shattering blow: For a discussion of the right's violent disruption of the consensus, see Steven T. Rosenthal, *Irreconcilable Differences: The Waning of the American Jewish Love Affair with Israel* (Hanover, NH: Brandeis University Press, 2001), 116–34. This chapter owes much of its framing to Rosenthal's analysis in this book.

99 spoke the loudest: Rosenthal, *Irreconcilable Differences*, 129.

100 Jewish establishment organizations wrote the playbook: Natasha Roth-Rowland, "The War That Canonized America's Hasbara Playbook," +972 *Magazine*, October 22, 2022, https://www.972mag.com/american-jews -israel-hasbara-lebanon/.

101 "is eroding the foundation of Israeli democracy": Yitzhak Rabin's last speech [Hebrew], November 1995, Rabin Center, https://www.rabincenter.org.il /speeches/%D7%94%D7%A0%D7%90%D7%95%D7%9D-%D7%94 %D7%90%D7%97%D7%A8%D7%95%D7%9F%EF%BF%BC/.

101 "one of history's most effective political murders": Dexter Filkins, "Shot in the Heart," *New Yorker*, October 19, 2015.

101 whether Rabin was a *rodef*: Dan Ephron, *Killing a King: The Assassination of Yitzhak Rabin and the Remaking of Israel* (New York: W. W. Norton, 2015), 94–95.

101 or a *moser*: Ephron, *Killing a King*, 94–95.

102 "Rabin will not die a natural death": Itamar Rabinovich, *Yitzhak Rabin: Soldier, Leader, Statesman* (New Haven, CT: Yale University Press, 2017), 221.

102 recommended that Rabin wear a bulletproof vest: Ephron, *Killing a King*, 145.

102 presided over rallies: "Netanyahu at War," *Frontline*, February 20, 2020, https://www.youtube.com/watch?v=7W-xxpXzAC0.

102 brandished posters depicting Rabin: "Netanyahu at War," *Frontline*.

102 "an attack on the basis of our existence": For a video of the speech, see https://www.youtube.com/watch?v=MgGqprMVR44.

102 tore the Cadillac symbol: Ruth Margalit, "Itamar Ben-Gvir, Israel's Minister of Chaos," *New Yorker*, February 20, 2023.

103 "the Rabin government was on a suicidal course": J. J. Goldberg, *Jewish Power: Inside the American Jewish Establishment* (Reading, MA: Addison-Wesley, 1996), 49.

103 "threatened to withhold donations": Goldberg, *Jewish Power*, 49.

103 Shield of David and the Maccabee Squad: Craig Wolff, "2 Bombs Left with Notes Fail to Go Off Near Offices," *New York Times*, January 6, 1994,

https://timesmachine.nytimes.com/timesmachine/1994/01/06/785431.html
?pageNumber=25.

103 **"Jewish civil war":** Lawrence Cohler, "Time Bomb: Are Jewish Radicals on the Right Turning Angry Rhetoric into Violence?," *New York Jewish Week*, January 20, 1994.

103 **death threats at Colette Avital:** Cohler, "Time Bomb."

103 **They pelted Itamar Rabinovich:** Cohler.

103 **"there is going to be a Jewish bloodbath":** Stewart Ain, "A Separate Peace: New Era or 'Dark Day in Jewish History'?," *New York Jewish Week*, September 29, 1995.

104 **a sit-in at a Carmelite convent:** A. D. Horne, "Polish Rabbi Protests Carmelite Convent at Auschwitz," *Washington Post*, September 1, 1989, https://www.washingtonpost.com/archive/politics/1989/09/01/polish-rabbi-protests-carmelite-convent-at-auschwitz/f513cfb1-f747-48c5-b3ca-5f99f527e828/.

104 **"Deep down, I loved Meir":** Avi Weiss, *Open Up the Iron Door: Memoirs of a Soviet Jewry Activist* (New Milford, CT: Toby Press, 2015), 68.

104 **"Rabin qualifies as an enemy":** Rabinovich, *Yitzhak Rabin*, 226–27.

104 **"national suicide":** Eric J. Greenberg, "No Regrets from Rabbis on Inflammatory Rhetoric: Orthodox Leaders Stand by Their Words About Rabin, While N. Y. Rabbinical Body Moves to 'Quarantine' Advocates of Murder," *New York Jewish Week*, November 17, 1995.

104 **complicit in murder:** Greenberg, "No Regrets from Rabbis."

104 **"Rabin Judenrat":** Gustav Niebuhr, "Peace Effort in Israel Leads to War of Words," *New York Times*, September 22, 1995.

105 **"destroyers and demolishers":** Niebuhr, "Peace Effort in Israel."

105 **"We are ashamed that you are not partners":** James D. Besser, "'We're Ashamed You're Not Partners': Jewish Leaders Respond to Rabin's Harsh Words Aimed at American Jewish Community," *New York Jewish Week*, October 6, 1995.

106 **Foxman to renounce his membership:** Niebuhr, "Peace Effort in Israel."

106 **"spurned repeated entreaties":** Lawrence Cohler, "A Time to Mourn: Even as They Grieve This Week, New York Jews Grapple with Areas of Darkness Within Themselves," *New York Jewish Week*, November 10, 1995.

106 **most American Jews:** "Only 9 percent of American Jews" opposed the Oslo Accords. See Rosenthal, *Irreconcilable Differences?*, 129.

106 **"yawning chasm of ignorance and mutual incomprehension":** Goldberg, *Jewish Power*, 7.

107 **"When there were rabbinic colleagues in our midst":** Greenberg, "No Regrets from Rabbis."

108 **15,000 people at New York's Madison Square Garden:** Lawrence Cohler, "Unity, After All: Compromise Efforts Succeed as Garden Fills with Jews of All Denominations, Views," *New York Jewish Week*, December 15, 1995.

108 "all specific references to the peace process . . . were prohibited": Cohler, "Unity, After All."

108 "purged of references": Cohler.

108 boycotted the memorial event: Cohler.

110 "It is wrong to remember and commemorate Rabin as a dovish leader": Rabinovich, *Yitzhak Rabin*, 243.

110 "Rabin was a centrist leader": Rabinovich, 243.

110 break the bones: "Colonel Says Rabin Ordered Breaking of Palestinians' Bones," *Los Angeles Times*, June 22, 1990.

111 "a soldier in the army of peace": Yitzhak Rabin, "Address by Prime Minister Rabin to the U.S. Congress," July 26, 1994, https://www.jewishvirtuallibrary .org/address-by-prime-minister-rabin-to-the-u-s-congress.

111 "will not return to the lines of June 4, 1967": Rabinovich, *Yitzhak Rabin*, 212–13.

111 "less than a state": Rabinovich, 212–13.

111 "the process would have continued": Interview with Yossi Beilin, August 20, 2022.

112 "nobody talked about a Palestinian state": Interview with Yossi Beilin.

112 "an instrument of Palestinian surrender": Edward Said, "The Morning After," *London Review of Books* 15, no. 20 (October 21, 1993).

112 "Israel has conceded nothing": Said, "The Morning After."

112 "Rather than becoming stronger": Said.

112–113 "Israel's enforcer": Said.

115 "Strictly speaking, there was never an Israeli offer": Robert Malley and Hussein Agha, "Camp David: The Tragedy of Errors," *New York Review of Books*, August 9, 2001.

115 more than 1 million bullets: Reuven Pedatzur, "More Than a Million Bullets," *Haaretz*, June 29, 2004.

116 "live forever by the sword": Barak Ravid, "I Don't Want a Binational State, but We Need to Control All of the Territory for the Foreseeable Future," *Haaretz*, October 26, 2015.

117 at the heart of McWorld: For the origins of this classic phrase, see Benjamin Barber, *Jihad vs. McWorld: Terrorism's Challenge to Democracy* (New York: Ballantine Books, 1995).

119 "America's war on terror merged with Israel's war against the Palestinians": Amy Kaplan, *Our American Israel: The Story of an Entangled Alliance* (Cambridge, MA: Harvard University Press, 2018), 244.

119 "The price of this flaccid toleration of terrorism": Mark Helprin, "What Israel Must Now Do to Survive," *Commentary*, November 2001.

120 "to pursue and obliterate the terrorist networks": Helprin, "What Israel Must Now Do."

120 "a note of schadenfreude": Kaplan, *Our American Israel*, 242.

120 the front-page headline: Gary Rosenblatt, "After 9/11, I Wrote a *Jewish Week* Headline Comparing the US to Israel. Here's Why I Regret It," *New York Jewish Week*, September 10, 2021.
120 later apologized in 2021: Rosenblatt, "After 9/11, I Wrote a *Jewish Week* Headline."
120 Americans had received a lesson: Gary Rosenblatt (editorial), "Terror Hits Home," *New York Jewish Week*, September 14, 2001.
121 "see the folly in its calls to use restraint": Rosenblatt, "Terror Hits Home."
121 "It's very good": James Bennet, "A Day of Terror: The Israelis; Spilled Blood Is Seen as Bond That Draws 2 Nations Closer," *New York Times*, September 12, 2001.
121 "Let's by all means grieve together": Susan Sontag, "Tuesday and After," *New Yorker*, September 16, 2001.
121 "Politics, the politics of a democracy": Sontag, "Tuesday and After."

CHAPTER 4: FALSE STABILITY
126 Thomas Friedman appeared on *Charlie Rose*: https://charlierose.com/videos/26893#.
126 Benjamin Netanyahu testified before Congress: https://www.c-span.org/video/?172612-1/israeli-perspective-conflict-iraq.
126 "little war": Michael Walzer, "What a Little War in Iraq Could Do," *New York Times*, March 7, 2003, https://www.nytimes.com/2003/03/07/opinion/what-a-little-war-in-iraq-could-do.html.
126 "What's good for Israel is good for America": Michelle Goldberg, "Why American Jewish Groups Support War with Iraq," *Salon*, September 14, 2002, https://www.salon.com/2002/09/14/jews_iraq/.
126 defend the open society: For a symptomatic text of this argument, see Paul Berman, *Terror and Liberalism* (New York: W. W. Norton, 2004).
126 "Islamofascists": Christopher Hitchens, "Defending Islamofascism," *Slate*, October 22, 2007, https://slate.com/news-and-politics/2007/10/defending-the-term-islamofascism.html.
127 "Mission Accomplished": Merrie Monteagudo, "From the Archives: 20-Years Later: 'Mission Accomplished' Speech," *San Diego Union-Tribune*, May 2, 2023.
128 "fiercely pro-Israel": Anne Gearan, "Neocon and Iran-Contra Figure Elliott Abrams in Line for State Department Job," *Washington Post*, February 9, 2017.
129 "supplies the amount of formaldehyde": Chris McGreal, "Row Erupts as Sharon Aide Says There Will Be No Palestinian State," *The Guardian*, October 6, 2004, https://www.theguardian.com/world/2004/oct/07/israel.
130 "a forceful resolution to the threat that Saddam Hussein poses": Goldberg, "Why American Jewish Groups Support War with Iraq."

135 Sarah Silverman appeared in an online video: Dave Itzkoff, "Message to Your Grandma: Vote Obama," *New York Times*, October 6, 2008.
136 "there is a strain within the pro-Israel community": Ron Kampeas, "Obama: Don't Equate 'Pro-Israel' and 'Pro-Likud,'" Jewish Telegraphic Agency, February 24, 2008.
137 Obama's Cairo speech: Barack Obama, "Remarks by the President at Cairo University, 6-04-09," The White House, June 4, 2009, https://obamawhite house.archives.gov/the-press-office/remarks-president-cairo-university -6-04-09.
137 "There's a lot of questioning": Shlomo Shamir, "Hoenlein: U.S. Jewish Leaders Deeply Troubled by Obama," *Haaretz*, June 15, 2009.
137 "[Jews] are genuinely very concerned": Shamir, "Hoenlein."
137 tens of millions of dollars: M. J. Rosenberg, "AIPAC Spent Millions of Dollars to Defeat the Iran Deal. Instead, It May Have Destroyed Itself," *Nation*, September 11, 2015.
138 a former Bill Clinton staffer: Ben Terris, "Jeremy Ben-Ami, Winning a Place at the Table for J Street," *Washington Post*, March 26, 2015.
139 "a voice missing from Washington's policy discussion": James Traub, "The New Israel Lobby," *New York Times Magazine*, September 9, 2009.
140 it was denied: Maya Shwayder and Sam Sokol, "Conference of Presidents Votes Against J Street Inclusion," *Jerusalem Post*, May 1, 2014.
140 "far worse than kapos": David Friedman, "Read Peter Beinart and You'll Vote Donald Trump," *Arutz Sheva*, May 6, 2016.
141 his 2010 essay: Peter Beinart, "The Failure of the American Jewish Establishment," *New York Review of Books*, June 10, 2010.
142 "uncomfortable Zionism": Beinart, "The Failure of the American Jewish Establishment."
142 "The painful truth": Peter Beinart, "Yavne: A Jewish Case for Equality in Israel-Palestine," *Jewish Currents*, July 7, 2020.
145 "to take whatever steps necessary": "Jewish Leaders Support 'Operation Protective Edge'; Condemn Hamas' Attacks on Israeli Civilian Population; Call on International Community to Stand with Israel," Conference of Presidents of Major American Jewish Organizations, July 8, 2014, https:// conferenceofpresidents.org/press/jewish-leaders-support-operation -protective-edge-condemn-hamas-attacks-on-israeli-civilian-population-call -on-international-community-to-stand-with-israel/.
152 "All this hardly constitutes a call to the barricades": Jacques Kornberg, "Zionism and Ideology: The Breira Controversy," *Judaism* 27, no. 1 (Winter 1978): 105.
152 "Dissent ought not to be made public": "Section 7: Breira: A Project of Concern in Diaspora-Israel Relations," Brit Tzedek v'Shalom (Jewish Alliance for Justice & Peace), n.d., https://btvshalom.org/movement-history /section-7-breira-a-project-of-concern-in-diaspora-israel-relations/.

154 "more of a cultural exchange organization": Interview with Rebecca Vilkomerson, April 4, 2022.

154 "It didn't have a super sharp politics": Interview with Rebecca Vilkomerson.

154 "utilizing their Jewishness": Interview with Rebecca Vilkomerson.

154 "From 2009 to 2014, the leading edge of JVP": Interview with Rebecca Vilkomerson.

155 "We're not interested in the Jewish establishment": Interview with Rebecca Vilkomerson.

155 "Ultimately our theory of change was growth": Interview with Rebecca Vilkomerson.

155 "the photo inverse of the Extreme Right": Joshua Leifer, "The ADL Goes Full Bully," *Nation*, May 6, 2022.

155 "I think people understood . . . our main responsibilities were not to the Jewish world": Interview with Rebecca Vilkomerson.

CHAPTER 5: SHATTERING AND BUILDING

164 the "plunder" of Black America: Ta-Nehisi Coates, *We Were Eight Years in Power: An American Tragedy* (New York: One World, 2018), 85.

166 comparisons to Israel/Palestine were immediate: For more on the extensive demonstrations of solidarity between Black and Palestinian activists, see Kristian Davis Bailey, "Black-Palestinian Solidarity in the Ferguson–Gaza Era," *American Quarterly* 67, no. 4 (December 2015): 1017–26.

168 "extremely transformed by the movement for Black Lives": Interview with Dove Kent, June 23, 2021.

168 "We were started by lesbians and queers": Interview with Dove Kent.

169 "We hit some weird barometer": Interview with Dove Kent.

169 "Park Slope, New York, Jew": Interview with Sophie Ellman-Golan, June 11, 2021.

170 "For the first time, I was proud to be publicly Jewish": Interview with Sophie Ellman-Golan.

170 as some Black radical theorists: See, for example, Frank B. Wilderson, *Afropessimism* (New York: Liveright, 2020).

172 to remove the racial category of "Hebrew": Eric L. Goldstein, *The Price of Whiteness: Jews, Race, and American Identity* (Princeton, NJ: Princeton University Press, 2006), 102–3.

172 "the most pro-Israel in history": Emma Green, "Is Trump Destroying Bipartisan Consensus on Israel?," *The Atlantic*, August 25, 2019.

173 "And 1,200 people can fit in that sanctuary": Interview with Rabbi Marc Katz, August 30, 2021.

173 "People really woke up": Interview with Rabbi Jill Jacobs, February 4, 2022.

173 "People [were] looking for some kind of connection": Interview with Rabbi Jill Jacobs.

174 "The wrong question is: Should we preach politics": Interview with Rabbi
Sharon Brous, January 11, 2022.

174 "We were, as a community": Interview with Rabbi Sharon Brous.

174 "Our Country Was Built on a Stolen Beam": Sharon Brous, "Our Country
Was Built on a Stolen Beam: The Call for a National Reckoning," Ikar,
September 22, 2017, https://ikar.org/sermons/our-country-was-built-on-a
-stolen-beam-the-call-for-a-national-reckoning/#:~:text=Sermons-,Our
%20Country%20Was%20Built%20on%20a%20Stolen%20Beam,Call
%20for%20a%20National%20Reckoning&text=We%20can't%20undo
%20the,A%20Jewish%20case%20for%20REPARATIONS.

175 "there wasn't a muscle tissue that had developed": Interview with Rabbi
Sharon Brous.

175 "He couldn't say the word 'Pharaoh'": Interview with Rabbi Sharon Brous.

175 "precisely at the moment when they matter most": Interview with Rabbi
Sharon Brous.

176 large foil sheets: Camila Domonoske and Richard Gonzales, "What We
Know: Family Separation and 'Zero Tolerance' at the Border," NPR, June
19, 2018, https://www.npr.org/2018/06/19/621065383/what-we-know
-family-separation-and-zero-tolerance-at-the-border.

177 "a chaotic scene of sickness and filth": Caitlin Dickerson, "'There Is a
Stench': Soiled Clothes and No Baths for Migrant Children at a Texas
Center," New York Times, June 21, 2019.

177 drew a direct parallel: Joshua Leifer, "The American Jews Invoking the
Holocaust to Talk About Trump's Migrant Camps," +972 Magazine, July
10, 2019, https://www.972mag.com/american-jews-camps-holocaust
-trump/.

177 hundreds of American Jews protested: Leifer, "American Jews Invoking the
Holocaust."

177 1,000 protesters shut down traffic in Boston: Leifer.

177 eighteen people were arrested: Leifer.

178 "The military camps where my people are being held": Leifer.

178 "unique" and "incomparable": For analysis of the discourse of uniqueness,
see Peter Novick, The Holocaust in American Life (Boston: Mariner Books/
Houghton Mifflin, 2000), 198. See also Walter Benn Michaels, "'You Who
Never Was There': Slavery and the New Historicism, Deconstruction and the
Holocaust," Narrative 4, no. 1 (January 1996): 1–16.

180 "Who is currently at the tip of the knife": Interview with Dove Kent, June
23, 2021.

180 "the ways in which assimilation wasn't just benign": Interview with Aryeh
Bernstein, January 12, 2022.

180 "radical Jews": See Matthew Frye Jacobson, Roots Too: White Ethnic
Revival in Post–Civil Rights America (Cambridge, MA: Harvard University
Press, 2008), 221.

181 "a reclamation of the centrality of Jewishness in our politics": Interview with Isaac Luria, June 30, 2022.
181 "I had this feeling": Interview with Alyssa Rubin, June 18, 2021.
181 "felt like something we left the house to do": Interview with Alyssa Rubin.
182 "so I guess I'm not Jewish": Interview with Alyssa Rubin.
182 "That you can be Jewish and have these politics": Interview with Alyssa Rubin.
182 "'What you're seeing on TV is not me'": Interview with Rabbi Alissa Wise, January 10, 2022.
183 "There's a nothingness to whiteness": Interview with Rabbi Alissa Wise.
183 "Jewish particularism is on the wane": Interview with Rabbi Alissa Wise.
184 "*Doykeit* . . . means Jews enter coalitions wherever we are": Melanie Kaye/Kantrowitz, *The Colors of Jews: Racial Politics and Radical Diasporism* (Bloomington: Indiana University Press, 2007), 198.
184 "Hereness isn't just about place but about people": Jacob Plitman, "On an Emerging Diasporism," *Jewish Currents*, April 16, 2018.
185 "not just an antidote or counterbalance to Zionism": Interview with Sophie Ellman-Golan.
185 "My dream Jewish identity": Interview with Alyssa Rubin.
186 "For the majority of the people who are involved in CJJ": Interview with Rabbi Salem Pearce, March 14, 2022.
186 "a very parochial and very narrow window": Interview with Rabbi Salem Pearce.
187 "We are it": Interview with Rabbi Salem Pearce.
187 "I just feel grateful daily": Interview with Rabbi Salem Pearce.
187 "what I would consider to be a very thin Judaism": Interview with Rabbi Salem Pearce.
188 "I came to St. Louis wanting a lefty, Jewish base": Interview with Hannah Rosenthal, March 16, 2022.
188 "St. Louis doesn't necessarily attract all the young lefties": Interview with Hannah Rosenthal.
188 "[The national organizations] missed the local context sometimes": Interview with Hannah Rosenthal.
189 "We're really scrappy": Interview with Hannah Rosenthal.
189 sent out bluntly Islamophobic mailers: Joshua Leifer, "Cori Bush's Message from the Grassroots," *Jewish Currents*, August 5, 2020, https://jewishcurrents.org/cori-bushs-message-from-the-grassroots.
190 "I don't think that would necessarily happen in another city": Interview with Hannah Rosenthal.
190 "We're not voting on Israel": Leifer, "Cori Bush's Message from the Grassroots."
190 "The core of all the work that I've done": Leifer.

191 **"Organizing was always a big part"**: Interview with Brant Rosen, October 26, 2021.

191 **"always very much on the left edge of Zionism"**: Interview with Rabbi Brant Rosen.

191 **"That was kind of the final straw"**: Interview with Rabbi Brant Rosen.

191 **"Sooner or later, I would have needed to go"**: Interview with Rabbi Brant Rosen.

192 **"'This is who we are'"**: Interview with Rabbi Brant Rosen.

192 **"We're not a local congregation anymore"**: Interview with Rabbi Brant Rosen.

193 **"The Zionist narrative is crumbling"**: Interview with Rabbi Brant Rosen.

193 **"religiously authentic ways to express their solidarity"**: Interview with Rabbi Brant Rosen.

194 **"sanctify standing in solidarity with Palestinians"**: Interview with Rabbi Brant Rosen.

194 **"I think it will always be a dissident movement"**: Interview with Rabbi Brant Rosen.

194 **International Holocaust Remembrance Alliance (IHRA) definition:** "What is Antisemitism?," International Holocaust Remembrance Alliance, n.d., https://www.holocaustremembrance.com/resources/working-definitions -charters/working-definition-antisemitism.

195 **"created primarily so that European data collectors"**: Kenneth Stern, "I Drafted the Definition of Antisemitism. Rightwing Jews Are Weaponizing It," *The Guardian*, December 13, 2019, https://www.theguardian.com /commentisfree/2019/dec/13/antisemitism-executive-order-trump-chilling -effect.

195 **Donald Trump signed an executive order:** Joshua Leifer, "The Real Target of Trump's Executive Order," *Jewish Currents*, December 12, 2019, https:// jewishcurrents.org/the-real-target-of-trumps-executive-order.

195 **as Jared Kushner himself wrote:** Jared Kushner, "Jared Kushner: President Trump Is Defending Jewish Students," *New York Times*, December 11, 2019, https://www.nytimes.com/2019/12/11/opinion/jared-kushner-trump -anti-semitism.html.

196 **"more insidious and perhaps more existentially dangerous"**: Amy Spiro, "Bari Weiss Champions Being Defiantly Jewish," *Jewish Insider*, September 9, 2019, https://jewishinsider.com/2019/09/bari-weiss-champions-being -defiantly-jewish/.

196 **"to commit cultural genocide"**: Jordan Weissmann, "How Not to Fight Anti-Semitism," *Slate*, September 19, 2019, https://slate.com/culture/2019/09 /bari-weiss-how-to-fight-antisemitism-review.html.

196 **the Women's March imploded:** Farah Stockman, "Women's March Roiled by Accusations of Anti-Semitism," *New York Times*, December 23, 2018, https://www.nytimes.com/2018/12/23/us/womens-march-anti -semitism.html.

196 **"All about the Benjamins"**: Cody Nelson, "Minnesota Congresswoman Ignites Debate on Israel and Anti-Semitism," NPR, March 7, 2019, https:// www.npr.org/2019/03/07/700901834/minnesota-congresswoman-ignites -debate-on-israel-and-anti-semitism.

198 **"much more comfortable in the Republican Party"**: Catie Edmondson, "Senate Advances Pro-Israel Bill as G.O.P. Searches for Democratic Divisions," *New York Times*, January 28, 2019, https://www.nytimes.com/2019/01/28/us /politics/senate-israel-boycott-democrats.html#:~:text=%E2%80%9CIt%20is %20a%20message%20to,they'll%20remain%20quiet.%E2%80%9D.

198 **Trump surrogate Jeff Ballabon:** See also Joshua Leifer, "Trump's Orthodox Whisperer," *Jewish Currents*, June 27, 2019.

199 **"You're brutal killers"**: Bess Levin, "Trump Goes Full Anti-Semite in a Room Full of Jewish People," *Vanity Fair*, December 9, 2019, https://www .nytimes.com/2019/01/28/us/politics/senate-israel-boycott-democrats .html#:~:text=%E2%80%9CIt%20is%20a%20message%20to,they'll %20remain%20quiet.%E2%80%9D.

199 **"either a total lack of knowledge or great disloyalty"**: Felicia Sonmez and John Wagner, "Trump Says Any Jewish People Who Vote for Democrats Are Showing 'Great Disloyalty' or 'Lack of Knowledge,'" *Washington Post*, August 21, 2019, https://www.washingtonpost.com/politics/trump -questions-sincerity-of-tlaibs-tears-as-she-talked-about-her-grandmother /2019/08/20/03d7b532-c339-11e9-b72f-b31dfaa77212_story.html.

199 **9 percent of Jewish voters chose Israel:** "2016 Post-Election Jewish Surveys Summary Findings," GBA Strategies, https://jstreet.org/wp-content/uploads /2016/11/J-Street-Election-Night-Survey-Analysis-110916.pdf.

199 **decreased to 4 percent:** "The 2018 Jewish Vote: National Post-Election Survey," GBA Strategies, https://jstreet.org/wp-content/uploads/2018/11 /J-Street-2018-Election-Night-Survey-Presentation-11072018.pdf.

199 **ranked Israel as the lowest of sixteen policy priorities:** Jewish Electorate Institute, "Poll: Domestic Issues Dominate the Priorities of the Jewish Electorate," May 22, 2019, https://www.jewishelectorateinstitute.org /poll-domestic-issues-dominate-the-priorities-of-the-jewish-electorate/.

200 **"between unabashed support for Israel"**: Interview with Rabbi Marc Katz.

200 **"very recklessly shut down honest discourse"**: Interview with Rabbi Sharon Brous, January 11, 2022.

201 **"I saw a celebration on Facebook"**: Interview with Rabbi Sharon Brous.

201 **"Balance has now bequeathed betrayal"**: Daniel Gordis, "When Balance Becomes Betrayal," *Times of Israel*, November 18, 2012, https://blogs .timesofisrael.com/when-balance-becomes-betrayel/.

201 **"I had to put security on my children"**: Interview with Rabbi Sharon Brous.

CHAPTER 6: THE DIASPORIC DOUBLE BIND

203 "Israeli is my skin": A. B. Yehoshua, "Comments at the AJC Centennial Symposium," in *The A. B. Yehoshua Controversy* (New York: American Jewish Committee, 2006), 61.

204 "living in myth about Israel": Yehoshua, "Comments at the AJC Centennial Symposium," 61.

204 forced to apologize: Yehoshua, *The A. B. Yehoshua Controversy*, 6.

205 his follow-up essay: A. B. Yehoshua, "The Meaning of Homeland," in *The A. B. Yehoshua Controversy*.

205 "the negation of the diaspora": See Eliezer Schweid, "The Rejection of the Diaspora in Zionist Thought: Two Approaches," *Studies in Zionism* 5, no. 1 (1984): 43–70.

206 "or we shall remain in exile and rot away": Jacob Klatzkin, "Boundaries," in *The Zionist Idea: A Historical Analysis and Reader*, ed. Arthur Hertzberg (New York: Atheneum, 1959), 319.

206 "the Judaism of the Galut": Klatzkin, *The Zionist Idea*, 322.

206 to negotiate with David Ben-Gurion: Zvi Ganin, *An Uneasy Relationship: American Jewish Leadership and Israel, 1948–1957* (Syracuse, NY: Syracuse University Press, 2005), 92.

206 "Perhaps this is why American Jews think": Hillel Halkin, "More Right Than Wrong," in *The A. B. Yehoshua Controversy*, 41.

210 6 million: Sergio Della Pergola, "World Jewish Population, 2021," in *The American Jewish Year Book 2021* ed. Arnold Dashefsky and Ira M. Sheskin (Cham, Switzerland: Springer), 313–412, https://www.jewishdatabank.org/api/download/?studyId=1185&mediaId=bjdb%5C2021_World_Jewish_Population_AJYB_(DellaPergola)_DB_Public.pdf.

210 By the year 2050, Israel is projected: Pew Research Center, "The Future of World Religions: Population Growth Projects, 2010–2050," April 2, 2015.

211 "as an ellipse with two foci": Simon Rawidowicz, *State of Israel, Diaspora, and Jewish Continuity: Essays on the "Ever-Dying People"* (Hanover, NH: University Press of New England [for] Brandeis University Press, 1998), 151.

214 "Our Homeland, the Text": George Steiner, "Our Homeland, the Text," *Salmagundi*, Winter–Spring 1985, no. 66, pp. 4–25.

215 recovering exile as an ethical ideal: Shaul Magid, *The Necessity of Exile* (New York: Ayin Press, 2023), 19.

215 "an end to political Zionism": Judith Butler, *Parting Ways: Jewishness and the Critique of Zionism* (New York: Columbia University Press, 2013), 18.

215 "less than wretched binationalism": Butler, *Parting Ways*, 215.

215 to "sever Zionism as an ideology": Magid, *The Necessity of Exile*, 18.

215 "not against the State of Israel": Magid, 19.

215 "a critique of nationalism and militarism": Butler, *Parting Ways*, 21.

218 God's hiddenness: For more on *hester panim*, see David Wolpe, "Hester Panim in Modern Jewish Thought," *Modern Judaism* 17, no. 1, February 1997, pp. 25–56.

218 "You shall observe all my laws and regulations": Leviticus 20:22, *The Contemporary Torah* (New York: Jewish Publication Society, 2006), accessed via Sefaria, https://www.sefaria.org/Leviticus.20.22?lang=en& with=all&lang2=en.

219 "Jewish sovereignty will overshadow": Yossi Shain, *The Israeli Century: How the Zionist Revolution Changed History and Reinvented Judaism* (New York: Wicked Son, 2021), 4.

219 Naftali Bennett's desk: Interview with Yossi Shain, July 8, 2022.

220 "the most amazing experiment in Jewish life": Interview with Yossi Shain.

221 "a group of clowns who stab the holy Torah": Ben Sales, "Dogs, Death and 'Clowns': Israeli Orthodox Politicians Are Again Attacking Reform Jews," Jewish Telegraphic Agency, March 4, 2021, https://www.jta.org/2021/03 /04/israel/dogs-death-and-clowns-israeli-orthodox-politicians-are-again -attacking-reform-jews.

221 "his nemesis, not his fellow Jews": Alon Pinkas, "News Flash to American-Jewish Friends: Israel Just Doesn't Care About You Anymore," *Haaretz*, November 25, 2022, https://www.haaretz.com/israel-news/2022-11-25 /ty-article/.highlight/news-flash-to-american-jewish-friends-israel-just-doesnt -care-about-you-anymore/00000184-af14-dd96-ad8c-efbcbd7b0000.

221 "They don't get what's going on here": Interview with Yossi Shain.

222 "In America you could be anything you want": Interview with Yossi Shain.

222 "even if they wanted to": Interview with Yossi Shain.

223 "less and less critical": Interview with Yossi Shain.

223 "to evangelical Christians than to Jews": Sam Sokol, "Israel Should Focus on Evangelicals, Not U.S. Jews Who Are More Critical, Dermer Says," *Haaretz*, May 10, 2021, https://www.haaretz.com/us-news/2021-05-10/ty-article /.premium/israel-should-focus-outreach-on-evangelicals-not-u-s-jews-former -envoy-says/0000017f-e0b9-df7c-a5ff-e2fbcc410000.

223 "Bibi's brain": Ron Kampeas, "'Bibi's Brain' Comes to Washington," *Politico*, December 2, 2013, https://www.politico.com/magazine/story /2013/12/bibis-brain-comes-to-washington-ron-dermer-netanyahu -100561.

223 "You've been replaced": Pinkas, "News Flash to American-Jewish Friends."

224 "the declining stature of the United States in world affairs": Interview with Yossi Shain.

224 "A Clean Break": See Richard Perle et al., "A Clean Break: A New Strategy for Securing the Realm," Institute for Advanced Strategic and Political Studies, https://ia902909.us.archive.org/7/items/acleanbreak/A%20Clean %20Break%3A%20A%20New%20Strategy%20for%20Securing%20the %20Realm.pdf.

224 Aggressive privatizations: See Arie Krampf, *The Israeli Path to Neoliberalism: The State, Continuity and Change* (New York: Routledge, 2018), and Assaf Razin, *Israel and the World Economy* (Cambridge, MA: MIT Press, 2018).

225 vast foreign currency reserves: Adam Tooze, "Chartbook 231 Israel's Nation Security Neoliberalism at Breaking Point?," https://adamtooze.substack .com/p/chartbook-231-national-security-neoliberalism.

225 which ceased in 2008: Congressional Research Service, "U.S. Foreign Aid to Israel," November 16, 2020, https://crsreports.congress.gov/product/pdf/RL /RL33222/40.

225 a discount for Israeli purchases of U.S. arms: Jacob Knutson, "What to Know About U.S. Aid to Israel," *Axios*, November 4, 2023, https://www .axios.com/2023/11/04/us-israel-aid-military-funding-chart.

225 shaking hands with Putin: Raoul Wootliff, "Netanyahu Touts Friendship with Putin in New Billboard," *Times of Israel*, July 28, 2019, https://www .timesofisrael.com/in-another-league-netanyahu-touts-friendship-with-putin -in-new-billboard/.

225 granted the state-owned Shanghai International Port Group: Ricky Ben-David, "Israel Inaugurates Chinese-Run Haifa Port Terminal, in Likely Boost for Economy," September 2, 2021, https://www.timesofisrael .com/israel-inaugurates-new-haifa-port-terminal-in-expected-boost-for-economy/.

226 general James F. Glynn: Tara Copp and Aamer Madhani, "Pentagon Rushes Marine General, Other Advisers to Middle East as Israel's Ground Assault in Gaza Looms," Military.com, October 24, 2023, https://www.military.com /daily-news/2023/10/24/pentagon-rushes-marine-general-other-advisers -middle-east-israels-ground-assault-gaza-looms.html.

226 "Jewsraeli": See Shmuel Rosner and Camil Fuchs, *#IsraeliJudaism: Portrait of a Cultural Revolution* (Jerusalem: The Jewish People Policy Institute, 2019).

227 "If you think Israel is worthy of your effort": Interview with Shmuel Rosner, July 6, 2022.

227 "it should be expected": Interview with Shmuel Rosner.

227 "I'm not deluding myself": Interview with Shmuel Rosner.

228 "this is something I cannot do for you": Interview with Shmuel Rosner.

228 "a self-aggrandizing fantasy": Shmuel Rosner, "Israel's Fair-Weather Fans," *New York Times*, August 7, 2014, https://www.nytimes.com/2014/08/08 /opinion/shmuel-rosner-israels-fair-weather-fans.html.

228 "It's a great challenge": Interview with Shmuel Rosner.

CHAPTER 7: THE TRANSFORMATIONS OF LIBERAL JUDAISM

235 stretches back centuries: Krista Tippett, "Amichai Lau-Lavie: First Aid for Spiritual Seekers," *On Being* (blog), July 13, 2017, updated August 1, 2019,

https://onbeing.org/programs/amichai-lau-lavie-first-aid-for-spiritual
-seekers/.

236 **two important discoveries:** Interview with Rabbi Amichai Lau-Lavie, December 7, 2021.

237 **"able to be the court jester":** Interview with Rabbi Amichai Lau-Lavie.

237 **a 2007 televised interview:** "Hadassah Gross and Amichai Lau-Lavie Meet Yair Lapid," 2007, https://vimeo.com/59147884.

237 **"through a lot of makeup and heels":** "Hadassah Gross and Amichai Lau-Lavie Meet Yair Lapid."

238 **"The adaptation is built in [to the tradition]":** "Hadassah Gross and Amichai Lau-Lavie Meet Yair Lapid."

239 **"to change the text you need to know the text":** "Hadassah Gross and Amichai Lau-Lavie Meet Yair Lapid."

239 **"It was also ego":** "Hadassah Gross and Amichai Lau-Lavie Meet Yair Lapid."

239 **a "pink line":** Mark Gevisser, *The Pink Line: Journeys Across the World's Queer Frontiers* (New York: Farrar, Straus and Giroux, 2020).

241 **Solomon Schechter:** For discussion of his philosophy and the founding of the Jewish Theological Seminary, see Ismar Schorsch, "Schechter's Seminary: Polarities in Balance," *Conservative Judaism 55*, no. 2 (Winter 2003): 3–23.

241 **"ethnic church":** Nathan Glazer, "Conservative Judaism: An American Religious Movement, by Marshall Sklare," *Commentary* (September 1955).

241 **"religiously authentic and amiably inoffensive":** Jonathan Sarna, *American Judaism: A History* (New Haven, CT: Yale University Press, 2004), 284.

241 **the plurality of American Jews:** Jack Wertheimer, *Conservative Synagogues and Their Members: Highlights of the North American Study of 1995–96* (New York: Jewish Theological Seminary, 1996), 7.

241 **8 percent of Jews under age thirty:** "Jewish Americans in 2020," Pew Research Center, May 11, 2021, https://www.pewresearch.org/religion /2021/05/11/jewish-americans-in-2020.

241 **The movement appealed to Jews:** Sarna, *American Judaism*, 284.

242 **In 1972, Hebrew Union College:** Amy Stone, "Out and Ordained," *Lilith* 38, no. 2 (Summer 2011), https://lilith.org/articles/out-and-ordained/.

242 **In 1974, the Reconstructionist Rabbinical College:** Stone, "Out and Ordained."

242 **not ordain a woman rabbi until 1985:** Stone.

242 **Congregation Sha'ar Zahav:** On the significance of this San Francisco congregation, see Gregg Drinkwater, "Creating an Embodied Queer Judaism: Liturgy, Ritual and Sexuality at San Francisco's Congregation Sha'ar Zahav, 1977–1987," *Journal of Modern Jewish Studies* 18, no. 2 (April 2019): 177–93, https://doi.org/10.1080/14725886.2019.1593687.

242 HUC ordained its first openly gay rabbi: Stone, "Out and Ordained."
243 "the justification frameworks, the plausibility structures": Interview with Rabbi Steven Greenberg, July 23, 2021.
243 "not merely an atavistic commitment to literalism": Interview with Rabbi Steven Greenberg.
243 "a lovemaking that doesn't serve life": Interview with Rabbi Steven Greenberg.
244 "members of the *brit*": Interview with Rabbi Steven Greenberg.
244 "responsibility for the broken lives": Interview with Rabbi Steven Greenberg.
245 "the most unpopular person at JTS": Interview with Rabbi Bradley S. Artson, January 4, 2023.
245 "Welcome, but we're not going to do anything": Interview with Rabbi Daniel Nevins, June 25, 2021.
245 "'the best day your position will ever have'": Interview with Rabbi Bradley S. Artson.
245 *Lawrence v. Texas*: "*Lawrence v. Texas*," Oyez, accessed December 7, 2023, www.oyez.org/cases/2002/02-102.
246 "three years of talking about nothing else": Interview with Rabbi Elliot Dorff, July 23, 2021.
246 "A lot of things were happening in America": Interview with Rabbi Elliot Dorff.
247 "it's hard to hate people that you love": Interview with Rabbi Elliot Dorff.
247 "It got ugly": Interview with Rabbi Daniel Nevins.
247 the decision that opened Conservative Judaism's doors: Rabbis Elliot N. Dorff, Daniel S. Nevins, and Avram I. Reisner, *Homosexuality, Human Dignity and Halakhah: A Combined Responsum for the Committee on Jewish Law and Standards*, n.d., approved December 6, 2006, https://web.archive.org/web/20070604193252/http://www.rabbinevins.org/HHH%20Dorff%20Nevins%20Reisner%20Final2.pdf.
248 two-thirds of Conservative Jews: Interview with Rabbi Daniel Nevins.
248 amicus brief in favor of marriage equality: Interview with Rabbi Daniel Nevins.
248 "I actually believe in the halachic system": Interview with Rabbi Rachel Isaacs, July 17, 2021.
249 "real sensitivity to how things need to be changed": Interview with Rabbi Rachel Isaacs.
249 "He was more the activist": Interview with Rabbi Rachel Isaacs.
249 "it wasn't an affirming place": Interview with Rabbi Aaron Weininger, October 13, 2021.
249 "The coming-out process there was quite challenging": Interview with Rabbi Aaron Weininger.

249 **"Change often involves staying in relationship"**: Interview with Rabbi Aaron Weininger.

250 **"that didn't mean leaving the Conservative movement"**: Interview with Rabbi Aaron Weininger.

250 **"unbelievably rapid"**: Interview with Rabbi Rachel Isaacs.

250 **"where there are Jews, there's gay clergy"**: Interview with Rabbi Daniel Nevins.

250 **"There are more and more queer people at the table"**: Interview with Rabbi Aaron Weininger.

250 **"beyond their comprehension"**: Interview with Rabbi Daniel Nevins.

251 **"the shrinking Jewish middle"**: Steven M. Cohen, "The Shrinking Jewish Middle," *American Jewish Year Book 2014*, vol. 114, ed. A. Dashefsky and I. Sheskin (Cham, Switzerland: Springer, 2015), 27–31.

251 **These right-wing critics**: See, for example, Daniel Gordis, "Conservative Judaism: A Requiem," *Jewish Review of Books*, Winter 2014, https://jewishreviewofbooks.com/articles/566/requiem-for-a-movement/.

251 **"where there is a rabbinic will, there is a halakhic way"**: Blu Greenberg, *On Women and Judaism: A View from Tradition* (Philadelphia: Jewish Publication Society, 1994). On the philosophy of Orthodox feminism, see also Tamar Ross, *Expanding the Place of Torah: Judaism and Feminism* (Hanover, NH: University Press of New England for Brandeis University Press, 2004).

251 **began to officiate same-sex marriage ceremonies**: Josefin Dolsten, "Small but Growing Number of US Orthodox Rabbis Officiating Same-Sex Weddings," *Times of Israel*, November 6, 2020, https://www.timesofisrael.com/small-but-growing-number-of-us-orthodox-rabbis-officiating-same-sex-weddings/.

252 **"the Torah does not want human beings to live alone"**: Avram Mlotek, "I'm an Orthodox Rabbi Who Is Going to Start Officiating LGBTQ Weddings. Here's Why," Jewish Telegraphic Agency, April 5, 2019, https://www.jta.org/2019/04/05/ideas/im-an-orthodox-rabbi-who-is-going-to-start-officiating-lgbtq-weddings-heres-why.

253 **"a very real possibility"**: Ari Feldman, "Reform Leader: Merging National Organization with Others 'a Very Real Possibility,'" *Forward*, May 15, 2020, https://forward.com/news/446607/reform-movement-coronavirus-layoffs/.

253 **only fourteen students**: Paula Jacobs, "Wanted: More Rabbis," *Tablet*, March 2023, https://www.tabletmag.com/sections/community/articles/wanted-more-rabbis-seminaries.

253 **first-year rabbinical class had only seven**: Stewart Ain, "Hey Kid, Do You Want to Be a Rabbi?," *Forward*, June 9, 2023, https://forward.com/news/550094/hey-kid-do-you-want-to-be-a-rabbi-facing-a-shortage-conservative-movement-looks-to-teens/.

254 **not returned to its pre-COVID numbers:** See "Religion and Congregations in a Time of Social and Political Upheaval," PRRI (May 16, 2023), https:// www.prri.org/research/religion-and-congregations-in-a-time-of-social-and -political-upheaval/. See also "How the Pandemic Has Affected Attendance at U.S. Religious," Pew Research Center, March 2023, https://www .pewresearch.org/religion/2023/03/28/how-the-pandemic-has-affected -attendance-at-u-s-religious-services/.

254 **"as religion-soaked as ours":** Harold Bloom, *The American Religion: The Emergence of the Post-Christian Nation* (New York: Simon & Schuster, 1992), 30.

254 **"between 6,000 and 10,000 churches close down every year":** Jessica Grose, "Lots of Americans Are Losing Their Religion. Have You?," *New York Times*, April 19, 2023, https://www.nytimes.com/2023/04/19/opinion /religion-america.html.

254 **"rise of the 'nones'":** "'Nones' on the Rise," Pew Research Center, October 9, 2012, https://www.pewresearch.org/religion/2012/10/09/nones-on-the -rise/.

254 **15 percent:** "Jewish Americans in 2020," Pew Research Center.

255 **"being part of a Jewish community":** "Jewish Americans in 2020."

255 **"our creed is a constitution of commandments":** Quoted in Irving Howe, *The End of Jewish Secularism* (New York: Hunter College of the City University of New York, 1995), 3.

255 **"not theological but legalistic":** Quoted in Laura Levitt, "Impossible Assimilation, American Liberalism, and Jewish Difference: Revisiting Jewish Secularism," *American Quarterly* 59, no. 3 (September 2007): 824–25.

256 **"That's the name of the game":** Interview with Rabbi Amichai Lau-Lavie.

257 **operating budget of roughly $1.7 million:** Interview with Rabbi Benay Lappe, January 11, 2022.

257 **"Gettin' Tied Up: A Queer Lens on Tefillin, Liberation, and Bondage":** See Queer Talmud Camp Schedule, July 1–5, 2018, Svara, n.d., https://svara.org /wp-content/uploads/2022/09/QTC-2018-WCR-Participant-Schedule.pdf.

258 **"powering a lot of queer Jews":** Interview with Elaina Marshalek, June 14, 2021.

258 **"That's the dysphoric approach":** Interview with Laynie Soloman, March 3, 2022.

259 **"'What are the profound opportunities for revelation'":** Laynie Soloman, "Towards Halakhic Euphoria," *Svara* (blog), November 20, 2020, https:// svara.org/hot-off-the-shtender-towards-halakhic-euphoria/.

259 **One of Soloman's favorite "euphoric" texts:** Soloman, "Towards Halakhic Euphoria."

259 **"The heart knows the bitterness of its soul":** Soloman.

259 **"I found a witness to my experience":** Soloman.

260 "Inclusion is over": Interview with Rabbi Benay Lappe.

260 "Queer inclusion is not a revolution": Interview with Rabbi Benay Lappe.

260 "they don't question the assumptions, the values, the culture": Interview with Rabbi Benay Lappe.

261 recounted the experience in a remarkable essay: See Benay Lappe, "Saying No in the Name of a Higher Yes," in *Lesbian Rabbis: The First Generation* (New Brunswick, NJ: Rutgers University Press, 2001).

261 "the way soldiers are trained in battle": Lappe, "Saying No in the Name of a Higher Yes."

261 "a form of halachic disobedience": Lappe.

261 a theory of the crisis of American Jewish life: See Benay Lappe, "An Unrecognizable Jewish Future: A Queer Talmudic Take," ELI Talks, May 29, 2014, https://www.youtube.com/watch?v=CBWIEAR_GQY.

261 "build a 'wall' around it": Bet Midrash Reference Guide, Svara, April 1, 2021, https://svara.org/wp-content/uploads/2022/09/BM-Reference -Guide-ed.-2021_4_1-1.pdf.

262 "is in many ways no longer morally plausible": Benay Lappe, "The New Rabbis: A Postscript," in *Torah Queeries: Weekly Commentaries on the Hebrew Bible*, ed. Gregg Drinkwater, Joshua Lesser, and David Shneer (New York: New York University Press, 2009), 311.

263 "the crumble-before-the-crash": Benay Lappe, "And Then They'll Just Call It Judaism," *Svara* (blog), https://svara.org/and-then-theyll-just-call-it -judaism/.

263 "They'll just call it Judaism": Lappe, "And Then They'll Just Call It Judaism."

263 "doing powerful ritual work": Interview with Laynie Soloman.

263 "the last generation did with *tikkun olam*": Interview with Rabbi Benay Lappe.

265 "subverting the status quo": Interview with Elaina Marshalek.

265 "Jews, especially white Jews": Interview with Laynie Soloman.

266 "Rabbis are dealing with just an influx of people": Interview with Rabbi Marc Katz.

267 roughly 78 percent of participants: Interview with Rabbi Julie Zupan, May 25, 2022.

268 largely through key word searches: Interview with Rabbi Julie Zupan.

268 "more about the identity of the individual": Interview with Rabbi Julie Zupan.

268 "as bringing their whole selves": Interview with Rabbi Julie Zupan.

268 "A huge percentage of people": Interview with Rabbi Marc Katz.

269 "a profound and overwhelming interest": Interview with Rabbi Avram Mlotek, April 11, 2022.

269 "does not reflect the multicultural societies that we live in": Adam Mintz, Jonathan Leener, and Avram Mlotek, "Converting to Judaism: Is It Good

for the Jews?," *Jerusalem Post*, July 5, 2023, https://www.jpost.com/opinion
/article-748859.

269 **one of America's three great religions:** See Will Herberg, *Protestant-
Catholic-Jew: An American Religious Sociology* (Chicago: University of
Chicago Press, 1983).

272 **"has moved Judaism into . . . a 'post' state":** Shaul Magid, *American
Post-Judaism: Identity and Renewal in a Postethnic Society* (Bloomington:
Indiana University Press, 2013) 4.

CHAPTER 8: THE ORTHODOX ALTERNATIVE

284 **"even the stones are impure":** Aaron Rothkoff, "The American Sojourns of
Ridbaz: Religious Problems within the Immigrant Community," *American
Jewish Historical Quarterly* 57, no. 4 (June 1986): 560.

285 **"no hope for the continuance of the Jewish religion":** Rothkoff, "The
American Sojourns of Ridbaz," 561.

285 **Simon Rawidowicz's now-famous observation:** See Simon Rawidowicz,
"Israel, the Ever-Dying People," in *State of Israel, Diaspora, and Jewish
Continuity: Essays on the "Ever-Dying People."*

285 **sometimes strikingly lax on issues:** For more on this historical phenomenon,
see Jeffrey S. Gurock, *Orthodox Jews in America* (Bloomington: University
of Indiana Press, 2009), 14.

286 **among the forefathers of ultra-Orthodoxy:** See Moshe Samet, "The
Beginnings of Orthodoxy," *Modern Judaism* 8, no. 3 (October 1998):
249–69.

287 ***chumriusdiker bodem:*** Yitzchok Dershowitz, *The Legacy of Maran Rav
Aharon Kotler* (Jerusalem: Feldheim, 2005), 17.

287 **"a 'reineh vinkeleh'":** Dershowitz, *The Legacy of Maran Rav Aharon
Kotler*, 15.

287 **"without pursuing pleasure":** Dershowitz, 15.

287 **"battered and decrepit":** Dershowitz, 15.

288 **"As long as there is even one Jew":** Dershowitz, 15.

288 **"the raison d'être of Lakewood":** Quoted in William Helmreich, *The World
of the Yeshiva: An Intimate Portrait of Orthodox Judaism* (Hoboken, NJ:
Ktav Publishing, 2000), 43.

289 **"was against the spirit of the country":** Helmreich, *The World of the
Yeshiva*, 44.

289 **"what's the *tachlis*":** Helmreich, 44.

290 **Rachel "Ruchie" Freier:** Sharon Otterman, "Judge Ruchie, the Hasidic
Superwoman of Night Court," *New York Times*, November 17, 2017,
https://www.nytimes.com/2017/11/17/nyregion/judge-ruchie-the-hasidic
-superwoman-of-night-court.html.

290 **Ezras Nashim:** Emma Goldberg, "They Told Her Women Couldn't Join the
Ambulance Corps. So She Started Her Own," *New York Times*, April 19,

2021, https://www.nytimes.com/2021/04/19/us/ezras-nashim-womens-EMT
.html.

291 a video released by Lakewood's BMG: "Ve'at Alis Al Kulana" (feat. Baruch
Levine & The Shir V'Shevach Boys Choir), October 3, 2022, https://www
.youtube.com/watch?v=h1vDG3oI0XU.

291 "a full-fledged rejection of the Torah": Steven Greenberg, *Wrestling with
God and Men: Homosexuality in the Jewish Tradition* (Madison: University
of Wisconsin Press, 2005), 13.

291 "'Do what you will, but dress in black'": Greenberg, *Wrestling with God
and Men*, 4.

292 "something that just isn't done": Interview with Asher Lovy, May 23, 2023.

292 "It's called *mesirah*": Interview with Asher Lovy.

292 "Until there's systemic change at the top": Interview with Asher Lovy.

293 "this itch to become a psychologist": Quoted in "Yeshiva Education," *On
the Nose* (podcast), September 29, 2022, https://jewishcurrents.org/yeshiva
-education.

293 having never heard the word "molecule": Jennifer Miller, "Yiddish Isn't
Enough," *New York Times*, November 21, 2014, https://www.nytimes.com
/2014/11/23/nyregion/a-yeshiva-graduate-fights-for-secular-studies-in
-hasidic-education.html.

294 "a maximum of ninety minutes of secular education": Quoted in "Yeshiva
Education."

294 "the same education as his very own sisters": Quoted in "Yeshiva
Education."

295 "This society has a right to retain its unique way of life": Quoted in
"Yeshiva Education."

296 a Yiddish ode to Trump: "A Yiddish Song of Praise for Trump," *COLlive*,
February 3, 2020, https://collive.com/a-yiddish-song-of-praise-for-trump/.

296 whiskey and cake to celebrate the president's birthday: See https://twitter
.com/AbeRosenberg1/status/1272162463476256769.

296 written for a Trump campaign fundraiser: Sandy Eller, "Shwekey Hopes
Song Composed for Trump Fundraiser Will Spark Wave of Patriotism in
Jewish Community," VIN News, August 13, 2020, https://vinnews.com
/2020/08/13/shwekey-hopes-song-composed-for-trump-fundraiser-will-spark
-wave-of-patriotism-in-jewish-community/.

296 "the first heimish president": Yochonon Donn, "Trump, the First Heimish
President," *Mishpacha*, November 20, 2019, https://mishpacha.com
/trump-the-first-heimish-president/.

297 54 percent of the Orthodox vote: "2017 AJC: Survey of Jewish Public
Opinion," Berman Jewish Databank, n.d., https://www.jewishdatabank.org
/databank/search-results/study/850.

297 "so hyper-partisan, so whipped up": Interview with Eytan Kobre, September
31, 2020.

297 **commuted the sentence of Sholom Rubashkin:** Associated Press, "Trump Commutes Sentence of Kosher Meatpacking Executive," *Politico*, December 20, 2017, https://www.politico.com/story/2017/12/20/trump-commutes-sentence-kosher-meatpacking-business-executive-rubashkin-311389.

298 **issues "impacting the community":** On the meeting, see Ron Kampeas, "Non-Orthodox Movements Left Out of Trump's Meeting with Jewish Leaders," Jewish Telegraphic Agency, April 15, 2019, https://www.jta.org/quick-reads/liberal-streams-adl-not-on-white-house-list-for-pertinent-meeting-with-jewish-leaders.

298 **someone who "gets" Jews:** Donn, "Trump, the First Heimish President."

298 **"That's because he's a *gvir*":** Avital Chizhik-Goldschmidt, "Leading Ultra-Orthodox Rabbi Shmuel Kamenetsky Endorses Trump, in Rare Move," *Forward*, July 30, 2020, https://forward.com/news/breaking-news/451747/leading-ultra-orthodox-rabbi-kaminetsky-endorses-trump/.

298 **"always seen themselves as us versus them":** Interview with Samuel Heilman, September 29, 2020.

298 **"a primary fear propelling support for Trump":** Binyamin Rose, "Many Orthodox Jews Support President Trump. I'm One of Them—Here's Why," Jewish Telegraphic Agency, August 28, 2020, https://www.jta.org/2020/08/28/ideas/many-orthodox-jews-support-president-trump-im-one-of-them-heres-why.

299 **the Orthodox mediasphere:** See Avital Chizhik-Goldschmidt, "Inside the World of Ultra-Orthodox Media: Haredi Journalists Tell It Like It Is," *Haaretz*, August 11, 2015.

299 **"*Mishpacha* has been a little more balanced":** Interview with Eytan Kobre.

299 **A characteristic news analysis for *Yated Ne'eman*:** Avrohom Birnbaum, "The 'Racist' Band-Aid," *Yated Ne'eman*, July 8, 2020, https://yated.com/the-racist-band-aid/.

300 **In *Community Connections*:** Materials handed to author by source.

300 **On the Kol Mevaser Yiddish radio hotline:** Interview translated and transcribed by source, then passed to author.

302 **"By registering as Republicans":** Ezra Friedlander, "Op-Ed By Ezra Friedlander: Our Community Is Powerless: Here's Why," *Yeshiva World News*, June 18, 2020, https://www.theyeshivaworld.com/news/headlines-breaking-stories/1873675/op-ed-by-ezra-friedlander-our-community-is-powerless-heres-why.html.

302 **"we have to work with the local Democratic infrastructure":** Interview with Ezra Friedlander, September 17, 2020.

302 **"falling on deaf ears":** Interview with Ezra Friedlander.

303 **"we're in *galus*":** Interview with Eytan Kobre.

303 **"We dare not do the things that draw the ire":** Interview with Eytan Kobre.

303 **published an open letter:** Avi Shafran, "Open Letter to the Torah Community: Sinai, Not Washington," Rabbi Avi Shafran website/blog,

August 9, 2020, https://www.rabbiavishafran.com/open-letter-to-the-torah
-community-sinai-not-washington/.

303 "Shameless dissembling and personal indecency": Shafran, "Open Letter to
the Torah Community."

304 "The letter was decrying partisanism": Email exchange with Avi Shafran,
September 20, 2020.

304 "Trumpism has twisted the minds": Jacob Kornbluh, "Hasidic Rabbi Assails
Trumpism Rampant Among the Orthodox," *Forward*, November 9, 2022,
https://forward.com/fast-forward/524348/hasidic-rabbi-assails-trumpism
-rampant-among-the-orthodox/.

304 "We are not going to fix America": "'Trumpism Brainwashed Yidden':
Satmar Rebbe Decries Election Fervor," *BoroPark24*, November 10, 2022,
https://www.boropark24.com/news/trumpism-brainwashed-yidden
-satmar-rebbe-decries-election-fervor#:~:text=The%20rebbe%20said
%20he%20worried,ourselves%2C%E2%80%9D%20the%20rebbe%20
proclaimed.

304 those who link greater religious stringency to increasingly right-wing
politics: See, for instance, Samuel C. Heilman, *Sliding to the Right: The
Context for the Future of American Jewish Orthodoxy* (Berkeley: University
of California Press, 2006).

305 German Orthodoxy found common cause with German Catholics: See
Mordechai Breuer, *Modernity Within Tradition: The Social History of
Orthodox Jewry in Imperial Germany* (New York: Columbia University
Press, 1992).

CHAPTER 9: FOUR PATHS FOR THE FUTURE OF AMERICAN JEWISH LIFE

310 when we think of American Jewish identity: For an extended meditation on
this subject, see Stephen J. Whitfield, *In Search of American Jewish Culture*
(Hanover, NH: Brandeis University Press, 1999).

313 "Nobody Wanted to See This Happen": Ellen Braunstein, "Nobody
Wanted to See This Happen," *Jewish Standard*, June 22, 2022, https://
jewishstandard.timesofisrael.com/nobody-wanted-to-see-this-happen/.

313 "Decline is a fact": Jed Esty, *The Future of Decline: Anglo-American
Culture at Its Limits* (Stanford, CA: Stanford University Press, 2022), 1.

314 obsessed with the calculus of reproduction: See Michal Kravel-Tovi, "Wet
Numbers: The Language of Continuity Crisis and the Work of Care Among
the Organized American Jewish Community," in *Taking Stock: Cultures
Enumeration in Contemporary Jewish Life*, ed. Michal Kravel-Tovi and
Deborah Dash Moore (Bloomington: Indiana University Press, 2016),
141–64. See also Lila Corwin Berman, Kate Rosenblatt, and Ronit Y. Stahl,
"Continuity Crisis: The History and Sexual Politics of an American Jewish
Communal Project," *American Jewish History* 104, no. 2/3 (April/July
2020), 167–94.

314 the sole discourse of organized Jewish life: On the history of this phenomenon, see Lila Corwin Berman, *Speaking of Jews: Rabbis, Intellectuals, and the Creation of an American Public Identity* (Berkeley: University of California Press, 2009).

315 "estranged from the future by collective nostalgia": Esty, *The Future of Decline*, 105.

315 "too deterministic about the catastrophic results": Esty, 56.

315 "endangered species": Kravel-Tovi, "Wet Numbers," 148.

317 "to render Jewish identity through the prism of financial perpetuity": Lila Corwin Berman, *The American Jewish Philanthropic Complex* (Princeton, NJ: Princeton University Press, 2020), 10.

318 "as contemporary actual living Jews": The Editors, "The People of the Magazine," *n+1*, Fall 2008, https://www.nplusonemag.com/issue-7/the -intellectual-situation/people-magazine/.

319 "The prophet was an individual who said No to his society": Abraham Joshua Heschel, *The Prophets* (New York: Harper Perennial, 2001), xxix.

319 "a ceaseless shattering of indifference": Heschel, *The Prophets*, xxv.

321 "an attempt to grasp the Infinite one": Conference of Reform Rabbis, "The Pittsburgh Platform (1885)," in *The Jew in the Modern World: A Documentary History*, ed. Paul Mendes-Flohr and Jehuda Reinarz (Oxford: Oxford University Press, 1995), 371.

322 Only a few of the great religious leaders: See Jonathan D. Sarna, *American Judaism: A History* (New Haven, CT: Yale University Press, 2004), 293.

323 And they would make it even better: See Sarna, *American Judaism*, 297–303.

327 "I mean that I am willing to die for it": Quoted in Mark Oppenheimer, "For God, Not Country," *Lingua Franca* 11, no. 6 (September 2001), http:// linguafranca.mirror.theinfo.org/print/0109/feature.html.

328 "un-Jews": Natan Sharansky and Gil Troy, "The Un-Jews," *Tablet*, June 16, 2021.

329 "the text—all text—is dying in America": Harold Bloom, *Agon: Towards a Theory of Revisionism* (Oxford: Oxford University Press, 1983), 321.

329 "the cult of synthesis": Jonathan D. Sarna, "The Cult of Synthesis in American Jewish Culture," *Jewish Social Studies* 5, no. 1/2 (Autumn 1998–Winter 1999): 52.

330 H. Richard Niebuhr: See, for instance, H. Richard Niebuhr's *The Responsible Self: An Essay in Christian Moral Philosophy* (Louisville, KY: Westminster John Knox Press, 1999) and *Radical Monotheism & Western Culture* (New York: Harper, 1960).

330 Will Herberg: See *From Marxism to Judaism: The Collected Essays of Will Herberg*, ed. David G. Dalin (New York: Markus Wiener Publishing, 1989).

330 "The very being of Judaism consists": Yeshayahu Leibowitz, *Judaism, Human Values, and the Jewish State* (Cambridge, MA: Harvard University Press, 1995), 5.

AFTERWORD: ON OCTOBER 7, MOURNING, AND RESPONSIBILITY

337 **"tithing ideologically to the IDF":** Gabriel Winant, "On Mourning and Statehood: A Response to Joshua Leifer," *Dissent*, October 13, 2023, https://www.dissentmagazine.org/online_articles/a-response-to-joshua-leifer/.

339 **That grief is political:** I owe this phrasing to Samuel Moyn.

339 **burials in mass graves:** Adapted from my article "Inhumane Times," *New York Review of Books*, November 23, 2023, https://www.nybooks.com/articles/2023/11/23/inhumane-times-joshua-leifer/.

339 **appears to surface on social media:** For a montage of these videos, see recent CNN coverage: https://www.youtube.com/watch?v=1D3uQbiE8No.

340 **mock opening of a Chabad house:** Reported by journalist Jacob Kornbluh on X, https://twitter.com/jacobkornbluh/status/1732443605824856132.

340 **"total victory":** See, for instance, Ishaan Tharoor, "Netanyahu's Delusional, Deadly Quest for 'Total Victory,'" *Washington Post*, February 9, 2024, https://www.washingtonpost.com/world/2024/02/09/netanyahu-israel-total-victory-hamas-palestine/.

340 **"focusing on maximum damage":** Bethan McKernan and Quique Kierszenbaum, "'We're Focused on Maximum Damage': Ground Offensive into Gaza Seems Imminent," *The Guardian*, October 10, 2023, https://www.theguardian.com/world/2023/oct/10/right-now-it-is-one-day-at-a-time-life-on-israels-frontline-with-gaza.

340 **"We are fighting human animals":** Emanuel Fabian, "Defense Minister Announces 'Complete Siege' of Gaza: No Power, Food or Fuel," *Times of Israel*, October 9, 2023, https://www.timesofisrael.com/liveblog_entry/defense-minister-announces-complete-siege-of-gaza-no-power-food-or-fuel/.

340 **"Burn Gaza":** Rachel Fink, "With ICJ Trial Looming, Israeli Lawmakers Double Down on Calls to 'Burn Gaza,' Relocate Palestinians," *Haaretz*, January 10, 2024, https://www.haaretz.com/israel-news/2024-01-10/ty-article/.premium/with-icj-trial-looming-israeli-minister-doubles-down-on-call-to-burn-gaza/0000018c-f329-d0b4-a7ce-f36b83d40000.

340 **"no innocents in Gaza":** See Avigdor Liberman, "Innocents in Gaza? Don't Be Naïve," *Times of Israel*, December 4, 2023, https://blogs.timesofisrael.com/innocents-in-gaza-dont-be-naive/.

341 **no amount of death:** See, for example, Yehuda Kurtzer, "We Must Continue to Support Israel's War—and Honestly Grapple with Tough Questions from Critics," *Forward*, January 29, 2024, https://forward.com/opinion/577967/israel-just-war-jewish-support/.

INDEX

Jewishness (*cont.*)
diaspora Jew replaced by Israeli Jew, 16–17
essentials of in today's world, 255–256
experimental forms of, 257–265
Holocaust as binding trauma of, 57
library of books, 59–61
liturgy and politics, 183, 233
modern variations of, 255–256
secular Jewishness, 255
unaffiliated, 254–255
Jews
complicit with Israeli government's actions, 213–214
core pillars of American Jewish identity, 8–9, 16, 18, 43, 61, 66, 99, 130–131
demographics in today's world, 210–211, 314
diaspora, 16, 205, 211–212, 219
eastern European Jewry, 10
shtetl life, 23–25, 27
See also American Jews and Jewry; antisemitism; Jewishness; Judaism
Jews for Racial & Economic Justice (JFREJ), 168–170, 181, 182, 184, 319
"Jewsraeli," 226
"Jexodus" initiative, 198
Jones, Mondaire, 300
JTS. See Jewish Theological Seminary
Judaism
anti-institutional, 260, 263
ba'al teshuva movement, 77–78, 87
Chabad-Lubavitch movement, 77, 85–86, 104, 266
conversion to, 267–269, 270
Crash theory, 261–265, 271
disassimilation theology, 264–266
dual threats of assimilation and persecution, 205–206
experimental forms of, 257–265
gay and lesbian clergy, 235, 239–242, 247, 248–249
homosexuality and Jewish law, 242–244
human dignity principle, 247
Israel and Zionism as substitute for, 55–56

Jewish evangelism, 83–85, 266
Kaddish, 149–150, 265, 311–312, 338
kashruth, 54, 321
liturgy and politics, 183, 233
modern synagogue observance, 83–84
mourning ritual, 311–312, 338
mussar tradition, 25, 26, 46, 287
neo-Reform Judaism, 320–322, 325
practice without particularism, 265, 266–267, 271
politics and, 173
polls showing affiliation, 254–256
prophetic protest, 319–320, 321, 325
rabbinic practice and activism, 174–176, 183
return to Orthodoxy in late 20th century, 77–79, 84, 89
Sabbath, 45–46, 54
separation of politics and pulpit, 174
separatist Orthodoxy, 322–323, 329
survival in the diaspora, 205–206, 228
synonymous with Zionism, 3
tikkun olam, 263
"*tikkun olam*" Judaism, 187
Torah reading, 237
Torah study, 280–281, 289
traditional observance, 31, 54, 63, 66, 76, 82, 84, 330–331
yeshivas, 25–26, 46, 292–294
yichus, 25
Zionized liturgy, 89
See also Conservative Judaism; Haredi (ultra-Orthodox); liberal Judaism; Orthodox Judaism; Reform Judaism
JVP. See Jewish Voice for Peace

K
Kaczyński, Jarosław, 225
Kaddish, 149–150, 265, 311–312, 338
Kagan, Yisrael Meir, 284
Kahane, Meir, 72, 104, 152, 179
Kamenetsky, Shmuel, 298
Kaminsky, Tasha, 190
Kaplan, Amy, 119, 120
Kaplan, Mordecai, 266
kashruth, 54, 321

ABOUT THE AUTHOR

Joshua Leifer is a journalist, editor, and translator. His essays and reporting have appeared widely in international publications, including *The New York Times, The New York Review of Books, The Guardian, The New Statesman, Haaretz, The Nation,* and elsewhere. A member of the *Dissent* editorial board, he previously worked as an editor at *Jewish Currents* and at *+972 Magazine*. He is currently pursuing a PhD at Yale University, where he studies the history of modern moral and social thought.